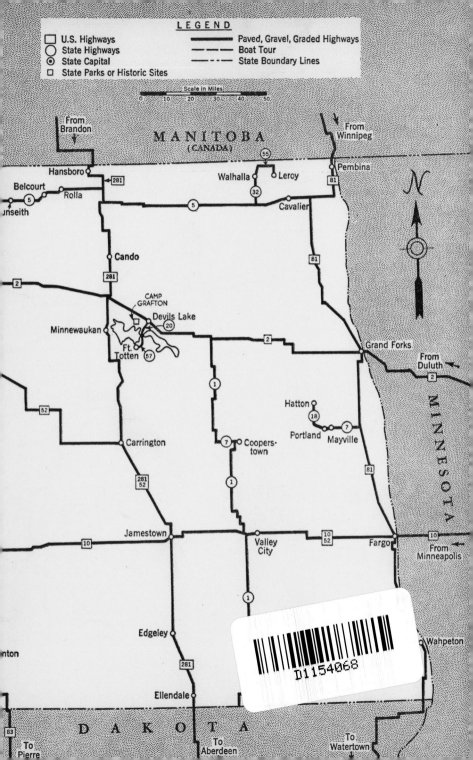

NORTH DAKOTA

A Guide to the Northern Prairie State

NORTH DAKOTA

A GUIDE TO THE NORTHERN PRAIRIE STATE

*Compiled by workers of the Federal Writers' Project of the
Works Progress Administration for the State of North Dakota*

AMERICAN GUIDE SERIES

ILLUSTRATED

Sponsored by the State Historical Society of North Dakota

NEW YORK

Oxford University Press

1950

❖◇❖

Foreword

AS Governor of the State of North Dakota, I am happy to write the foreword to the first comprehensive guidebook that has ever been written for this State. Compiled by North Dakota writers, the publication of this book has been made possible by means of Federal and State funds. The importance of this book lies not only in calling the attention of tourists and other outsiders to the picturesque scenery and the places of historical significance in North Dakota, but in awakening the consciousness of North Dakota people to the historical, sociological, and cultural heritage that is theirs.

(Signed) WILLIAM LANGER
Governor of North Dakota

Foreword

$$\Diamond$$

Preface to the First Edition

NORTH DAKOTA: *A Guide to the Northern Prairie State* is something new in this part of the country. For the first time North Dakotans and their guests have a concise but comprehensive survey of the State, which tells them what should be seen, and why, and how. Our aim has been to produce a book not only to be used in touring the State, but to be enjoyed by fireside travelers and all who would deepen their understanding of North Dakota.

As one of the volumes in the American Guide Series, written by the members of the Federal Writers' Project of the Works Progress Administration, the North Dakota Guide has more than State significance, wide as this is. The national project was designed primarily to give useful employment to needy writers and research workers; it has developed into a more ambitious undertaking. The American Guide Series, covering the forty-eight States, Puerto Rico, Alaska, and numerous cities and towns, is unrolling a unique and inspiring panorama of these United States with their lively background and their vibrant present. The North Dakota Guide adds its contribution to the whole, giving the reader a picture of the State, its land and resources, its history, people, the cities and towns they have built, and the principal points of interest. New chapters in North Dakota's story and other phases of its life and works are still to be told. This volume—a pioneer enterprise in a State where the records of the past and the varied life of today had not heretofore been assembled—may well serve as an incentive and a foundation for further books.

Not ten or fifty or a hundred, but actually hundreds of North Dakotans helped in the making of the Guide, from the many who contributed information about their own communities or fields of work down to the handful of editors and writers who brought that information within the covers of this book. In expressing the Project's appreciation of this friendly and co-operative help, so generously given, I wish particularly to thank Mr. Russell Reid, superintendent of the State Historical Society of North Dakota, and his staff, especially Mrs. Florence H. Davis and Mr. Arnold Goplen; Mr. George Will and Mr.

vii

Robert A. Ritterbush, of Bismarck; Dr. Irvin Lavine, of the University of North Dakota; Mr. E. A. Milligan, of Michigan City; Mr. J. A. Patterson, of Minot; Dr. E. C. Stucke, of Garrison; and Mr. Henry Williams, of Appam.

ETHEL SCHLASINGER
State Director

✧✧✧

The publishers wish to thank the Chambers of Commerce of Grand Forks and Fargo, the Associations of Commerce of Minot and Bismarck, and particularly the State Historical Society of North Dakota for supplying information for the new edition. Whenever possible, the revisions included the latest population figures, changes in highway routes and numbers, and recent statistics on local organizations and industries.

Contents

FOREWORD, *by William Langer*
PREFACE, *by Ethel Schlasinger*
GENERAL INFORMATION

PART I. SURVEY OF THE STATE

Contemporary North Dakota	3
North Dakota: Its Natural Setting	6
Indians and Their Predecessors	18
History	38
Agriculture and Farm Life	64
Industry and Labor	79
Racial Groups and Folkways	85
Schools, Churches, and Social Currents	96
Transportation	104
The Press and Radio	109
Architecture	112
Recreation	116

PART II. CITY NEIGHBORS

Bismarck	121
Fargo	134
Grand Forks	149
Minot	160

PART III. PLAYGROUNDS

Fort Abraham Lincoln State Park	169
Theodore Roosevelt National Memorial Park	174

PART IV. HIGHWAYS AND TRAILS

Tour 1   (Winnipeg, Man., Can.)—Pembina—Grand Forks—Fargo—
              Wahpeton—(Watertown, S. Dak.) [US 81]   183

Tour 1A   Junction US 81—Mayville—Portland—Hatton [ND 7 and
              18]   196

Tour 2   (Brandon, Man., Can.)—Hansboro—Cando—Minnewau-
              kan—Jamestown—Edgeley—Ellendale—(Aberdeen,
              S. Dak.) [US 281]   198

Tour 3   (Virden, Man., Can.)—Westhope—Minot—Washburn—Bis-
              marck—Linton—(Pierre, S. Dak.) [US 83]   202

Tour 3A   Junction US 83—Garrison—Nishu—Elbowoods—Shell Creek
              —Van Hook—Stanley [ND 37 and 8, county and reser-
              vation roads]   206

Tour 3B   Junction US 83—Junction US 10 [County dirt and graveled
              roads]   210

Tour 4   (Moosejaw, Sask., Can.)—Fortuna—Belfield—Amidon—
              Bowman—(Belle Fourche, S. Dak.) [US 85]   213

Tour 4A   Junction US 85—Hanks—Grenora—Sodium Lakes—Writ-
              ing Rock [ND 50 and unnumbered county roads]   218

Tour 4B   Junction US 85—New England—Mott—Carson—Flasher—
              Junction ND 6 [ND 21]   221

Tour 5   Junction US 81—Cavalier—Rolla—Belcourt—Dunseith—
              Bottineau—Mohall—Crosby—(Scobey, Mont.) [ND 5]   225

Tour 5A   Junction ND 5—Walhalla—Leroy [ND 32 and 55 and an
              unimproved road]   235

Tour 6   (Duluth, Minn.)—Grand Forks—Devils Lake—Minot—
              Williston—(Glasgow, Mont.) [US 2]   238

Tour 6A   Devils Lake (city)—Camp Grafton—Devils Lake—Fort
              Totten Indian Agency—Sully's Hill National Game Pre-
              serve—Devils Lake (city) [ND 20 and 57 and Indian
              Service roads]   252

Tour 6B   Junction US 2—Buford—Fort Buford State Park [Un-
              marked graveled road and unimproved road]   257

Tour 7   Carrington—Minot—Bowbells—Portal—(Estevan, Sask.,
              Can.) [US 52]   260

Tour 8   (Minneapolis, Minn.)—Fargo—Valley City—Jamestown—
              Bismarck—Mandan—Dickinson—(Glendive, Mont.) [US
              10]   265

Tour 8A   Valley City—Oakes—South Dakota Line [ND 1]   288

TOUR 8B   Junction US 10—Cooperstown—Junction US 2 [ND 1
           and 7]   292

TOUR 8C   Mandan—Cannonball—Fort Yates—South Dakota Line
           [ND 6, 21, and 24]   296

TOUR 8D   Junction US 10—Center—Beulah—Halliday—Killdeer—
           Junction US 85 [ND 25]   301

TOUR 9   (McIntosh, S. Dak.)—Hettinger—Bowman—Marmarth—
           (Miles City, Mont.) [US 12]   305

TOUR 10   Medora—South Roosevelt National Memorial Park—Bea-
           ver River—North Roosevelt National Memorial Park—
           Cherry Creek—Missouri River—Elbowoods—Stanton—
           Fort Clark—Washburn—Bismarck [Little Missouri and
           Missouri Rivers]   310

PART V. APPENDICES

CHRONOLOGY   321
BIBLIOGRAPHY   327
INDEX   341

List of Illustrations

Between pages 44–5

Nesting colony of ring-billed gulls on an island in Lake Harriet, near Arena
Pasque flowers
Richardson's ground squirrel or 'flickertail'
Little Soldier, Hunkpapa Sioux
Scaffold burial, formerly used by some Indian tribes
Ancient Indian turtle effigy
Sioux sun dance as originally performed
North Dakota in 1879, from an old map of Dakota Territory
Sitting Bull
General George A. Custer
Battle of the Badlands, 1864
A sod shanty of early days
State capitol, Bismarck
Norwegian folk dancing
An early school in Oliver County, 1885
Ole Anderson farm, west of Portland
Threshing
Statue of Sakakawea, Bismarck

Between pages 204–5

A wheatfield near Walhalla
An oat field
Law Building, University of North Dakota, Grand Forks
Statue of Theodore Roosevelt, Minot
Blockhouse of Fort McKeen, Fort Abraham Lincoln State Park
Slant Indian Village lodge, Fort Abraham Lincoln State Park
Marquis de Mores
Clay and sandstone pinnacle in the Badlands
Valley of the Little Missouri, with Rabbit's Ears in the background
Grand Canyon of the Little Missouri
Lignite strip mining, Velva

Arikara woman pounding cherries
Writing Rock, near Grenora
Lake Upsilon, Turtle Mountains
Buffalo, Sully's Hill National Game Preserve
Barnes County Courthouse, Valley City
A John Deere thresher
Sioux hoop dance
Arikara buffalo bull dancer
Magpie Rock, Killdeer Mountains

General Information

Railroads: Chicago & North Western Ry. (Northwestern); Chicago, Milwaukee, St. Paul & Pacific R. R. (Milwaukee); Great Northern Ry. (G.N.); Midland Continental R. R. (Midland); Minneapolis, St. Paul & Sault Ste. Marie Ry. (Soo); Northern Pacific Ry. (N.P.). Main line of N.P. runs almost directly E. to W. across the State. Main line of G.N. runs N., then W., while cut-off runs in northwesterly direction. Soo line runs SE. to NW.

Highways: Eight Federal highways, seven of them transcontinental or with international connections. Inspection at international border. State highway patrol checks violations of State highway laws and enforces regulations. Gasoline tax, 4¢.

Motor Vehicle Laws (*digest*): Nonresidents must have license plates after 30 days' residence; driver's license required after 90 days; speed limits, prima facie, 50 m.p.h., except that some Federal highways marked 60 m.p.h. for daylight only and applying only to passenger vehicles; 25 m.p.h. through municipalities unless lower speed designated; stop required when school bus is loading or unloading passengers; trucks must be spaced 400 ft. on open highway; not more than 2 spotlights permitted; open bottle of liquor in motor vehicle prohibited; accidents involving $50 property damage must be reported to State Highway Department.

Prohibited: Parking on highways; use of stickers, except those required by law, on windshield or windows.

Bus Lines: Carpenter Transport; Central Bus Line; Crown Bus Line; Dakota Bus Line; Great Northern Ry. Co.; Honker Lines; Intermountain Transp. Co.; Intercity Bus Line; Interstate Transp. Co.; Mandan-Bismarck Bus Line; Henry A. Miller; Nodak Bus Lines;

Northern Bus Lines, Inc.; Northern Transit Co.; Northland Greyhound Lines; Stanlet Transfer; Swanson Bus Lines; A. J. Thiessen; Tri-State Bus Lines; Valley Bus Line; Yellowstone Trail Bus Line.

Air Lines: Northwest Airlines: New York to Seattle (stop at Fargo, Jamestown, and Bismarck); Chicago to Winnipeg (stop at Grand Forks and Fargo). Mid-Continent Airlines: Minot, north (stop at Bismarck); Minot to Gulf Coast.

Airports: 148 Airports. Principal fields: Fargo, Grand Forks, Minot, Jamestown, Bismarck, Dickinson, Valley City, and Williston.

Customs Regulations: Persons entering United States must report to U. S. Immigration Office and U. S. Customs Office. Automobiles may be brought into United States for 90 days without formal customs entry, provided proper report is made at port of entry. If cars are to be kept here more than 90 days, bond or deposit must be furnished, together with guarantee of exportation of car within 6 months of importation.

Those entering Canada must report to Canadian immigration and customs officers at point of entry. United States citizens should be prepared to prove citizenship. Persons not citizens should be able to establish that they are legally resident in the United States and that they will be readmitted when returning to this country. Cars may be admitted without charge to Canada for touring purposes and may be operated 60 days under State licenses; on request, period can be extended to 90 days. For period of 90 days to 6 months, bond or cash deposit must be furnished. Cars returning to United States should be checked out by Canadian customs officer at border.

Accommodations: Accommodations outside of cities and towns are limited. Nearly every small town has a tourist camp. A few ranches in the Badlands area accommodate tourists and have horses available for riding trips. Accommodations at lake resorts offered only during the summer months. Quarters at lake resorts crowded Fourth of July week.

Sales and Cigarette Taxes: Two per cent sales tax on all purchases, payable in cash. Tax of 5¢ per package of 20 cigarettes.

Climate and Equipment: Summer travelers should be prepared for extremely warm weather. It is advisable, however, to have topcoats of medium weight, as evenings are generally cool. In spring and fall the days are intermittently cool and warm, and topcoats are a necessity. Persons unfamiliar with the Northwest should heed weather reports and bulletins of the State highway department and dress as warmly as possible during winter travel. What appears as a light flurry of snow may in a few moments become a blizzard, blocking highways and making travel impossible. Towns and farms are far apart; temperatures may suddenly drop far below zero.

Recreational Areas: Turtle Mountain area (*Tour* 5): swimming, fishing, boating, hiking, hunting. Theodore Roosevelt National Memorial Park: riding, motoring, hiking. Sheyenne River Park (*Tour* 1): picnicking, swimming, hiking; suitable in winter for skiing. Killdeer Mountain area (*Tour* 8D): hiking, riding, picnicking. Turtle River State Park (*Tour* 6): swimming, camping, picnicking. Large towns have ski and toboggan slides, skating rinks.

Fish and Game Laws: Game fish are defined as black bass, wall-eyed pike, northern pike, perch, sunfish, crappie, trout, and landlocked salmon.

Open Season for Fishing (*dates inclusive*): Bass, crappie, and sunfish, June 16–Oct. 31; trout and landlocked salmon, May 2–Sept. 30; pike, any species, and perch, May 16–Oct. 31. Governor has power to shorten or close season.

Licenses: Resident, 50¢, nonresident, $3. No license required of persons under age of 12. Issued by game and fish commissioner, State capitol, Bismarck, and county auditors at county courthouses.

Limits: Bass, trout, and landlocked salmon, 5, nor more than 5 of all combined; wall-eyed pike and northern pike, 5; crappie and sunfish, 15, nor more than 15 of both combined; perch, 25. No bass, landlocked salmon, trout, or pike less than 10 in.; no crappie less than 6 in.; no sunfish less than 5 in. These limits daily; no person to have in possession more than 2-day limit.

Prohibited: No use of drugs, lime, fish berries, or explosives. Unlawful to take fish in any manner except by angling with hook and line held in hand or attached to rod. (Commercial fishing allowed in certain sections, under commercial license.)

Open Season for Hunting: Dates of hunting season for deer and game birds vary from year to year, as well as the areas where hunting is allowed. The bag limits and seasons given below represent maximum seasons and bag limits according to State statutes. Regulations may be materially modified by State proclamations each year. Waterfowl seasons and bag limits must conform to current Federal regulations. Copy of hunting laws furnished with hunting license.

Licenses: Big game: resident, $5, nonresident, $50; hunting: resident, $1.50, nonresident, $25. Aliens not permitted to hunt. Licenses issued by game and fish commissioner, deputies, or county auditors.

Limits: Prairie chicken (pinnated grouse), sharp-tailed (white-breasted) grouse, ruffed grouse (partridge), Chinese pheasant, Hungarian partridge: 5 in the aggregate in a day, but the number of each species composing aggregate varies in certain counties; 10 ducks, 4 geese including brant, 12 coots, and 10 jacksnipe a day. Not more than a 2-day bag of migratory game birds may be possessed at one time. Deer may be possessed until 90 days after close of season.

Nonresident licensee may carry with him from State under license tag a 2-day limit of game, if carried openly and labeled with his name, address, and number of license.

Camp Fires: Any person leaving a fire without thoroughly extinguishing it, so that it burns any wood or prairie, is guilty of a misdemeanor punishable by fine, imprisonment, or both.

Poisonous Snakes and Plants: Rattlesnakes are rare, but are sometimes found in the following areas: south of Bismarck in Missouri River vicinity; western Emmons County, along Missouri; in valleys of Heart, Little Missouri, and Cannonball Rivers; and in Badlands.

Anyone bitten by a rattlesnake should cut wound with a sharp knife and suck the blood to remove poison. A tourniquet should be placed above wound, and medical assistance sought at once.

Poison-ivy common in wooded areas. In June it bears loose clusters of dull green-white blossoms, later in season replaced by glossy opaque berries of similar color. Poison-ivy vines often are hidden in long grass and in foliage.

To prevent irritation from contact with poison-ivy, before going into woods bathe hands and face with a 5 per cent solution of ferric chloride in a half-and-half mixture of alcohol and water or glycerine and water. If skin should come in contact with the plant, washing with one of these solutions, or with laundry soap and warm water, is an excellent treatment. Avoid spreading poison through scratching or rubbing. Bathing affected areas in hot water will relieve irritation. If there are open sores do *not* use sugar of lead or zinc oxide.

Tourist Information Service: General information about the State furnished on request by the secretary, Greater North Dakota Association, Fargo, North Dakota; information on State Parks and historic sites may be obtained from the State Historical Society, Bismarck, North Dakota.

PART I

Survey of the State

✧✧

Contemporary North Dakota

NOTHING, probably, arouses the indignation of a loyal North Dakotan or South Dakotan more than hearing his State referred to as 'Dakota.' Just as an earnest Californian would display indignation at being disposed of as merely a 'Westerner,' so the man from North Dakota resents having his identity fogged over by the blanket term 'Dakotan.' And rightfully so; for, while he finds no fault with his neighbors, he is quite different from them, and quite within his rights in insisting on the distinct character of his own State.

The person who asks, 'What sort of place is North Dakota?' may get a variety of answers, all of them true, and still be far from a complete picture of the State. He may be told vaguely, 'It's out West somewhere,' or more specifically, 'North Dakota is a wheat State,' or 'Isn't that where the farmers have this Nonpartisan League?' These answers are only partly correct, for they barely touch on the two major problems, economics and politics, in regard to which North Dakota is now coming of age.

This is a young State. Ruts left by the wagon trains of early explorers, military expeditions, and home seekers have not yet been effaced from the prairies. Red men and white men, who hunted buffalo and fought at the Little Big Horn, who saw the railroads push their gleaming paths across the Plains, who recall a puny young man named Theodore Roosevelt hunting in the Badlands with his short-stocked rifle, still survive to tell their tales. In those fledgling days, the land was rich with promise. Bonanza farms unfolded their ample acres of wheat, thousands of cattle roamed unchecked in the gullies and over the plains of the western counties.

The word spread, and from Europe and the eastern States came men and women to break the new soil. Sod houses and barns and frame homes and windmills set their seal on the prairies. Tons of wheat, thousands of cattle and sheep and horses attested to the fertility of North Dakota.

3

For more than half a century the soil was exploited recklessly. Then suddenly exhaustion and drought drove home the growing realization that this exploitation could not go on. Water conservation, diversified farming, and dams quickly became part of the agricultural scheme, and are repairing the damage of unthinking abuse. Huge mineral resources have been recognized and are being developed commercially, bringing a new aspect to North Dakota's economy.

Marketing of farm products has had reverberations in the economic life of the State and has made its people alert to changing social trends. Characteristically, in the eastern portion of the State, where soil is richer and rainfall more plentiful, the people are more conservative; while to the west, where the climate is more arid and the soil less productive, the 'isms' flourish, providing a stronghold for the leftist elements of the State's tumultuous political parties. Because of antagonism to control of early agrarian activities by out-of-State business interests, the Nonpartisan League, with its socialistic platform, was formed, and many of its enterprises have been established, some successfully, some otherwise. Co-operative economy is prominent in the social consciousness of agricultural North Dakota, and such groups as the Farmers' Union emphasize the trend toward co-operatives, strengthening their position by supplying members with purely social activities, as well as with hard economic problems into which to get their teeth.

Freely admitted is the rural character of the State, and there is seldom an attempt to cover native crudities with a veneer of eastern culture. The few writers in the State recognize and honor the possibilities of their native material; and each year finds a scattered handful of books, usually verse, telling of the North Dakota known to them and to seven hundred thousand other North Dakotans.

What is the North Dakota they know? A State of unbounded plains and hills and Badlands—elbowroom. Superb sunsets. High winds and tumbleweed. Farms and plows and sweeping fields. Gophers flashing across the road. Little towns crowded on Saturday night, and busy cities shipping out the products of North Dakota and supplying the needs of the producers. Sudden blinding, isolating blizzards, and soft, fragrant spring days with tiny sprouts of grain peering greenly through the topsoil. Pasque flower and cactus, flame lily, and fields of yellow mustard. The sad, slow wail of a coyote on the still prairie. People—Norwegians, Germans, Russians, Poles, Czechs, Icelanders, but all Americans. Square dances in barn lofts, and college 'proms' with corsages and grand marches. Teachers building fires with numbed hands in stoves of icy one-room schools. Men in unaccustomed 'best clothes' sitting in majestic legislative halls of a skyscraper statehouse. Political fires, sometimes smouldering, sometimes flaring, always burning.

Endless facets are apparent in the temper and tenor of life, thought, and action of the people of this State, still a new people, pioneers—

> Brave spirits stirred with strange unrest,
> They found broad waters and new lands,
> And carved the empires of the west.

North Dakota: Its Natural Setting

NORTH DAKOTA is a rectangular area of 70,837 square miles, lying in what the United States Geological Survey has designated the center of the North American Continent. It is approximately 1,500 miles from the Atlantic, the Pacific, the Gulf of Mexico, and the Arctic Archipelago of North America. North to south it extends 210 miles, and east to west an average of 335 miles. On the north are the Provinces of Manitoba and Saskatchewan, Canada; on the east, the Red River of the North and the Bois de Sioux form the boundary between this State and Minnesota; on the south is South Dakota and on the west, Montana.

THE SURFACE OF THE LAND

The land surface resembles three broad steps of prairie, rising a half-mile in altitude from the eastern to the western boundary. The first two steps lie in the Central Lowlands of the Interior Plains, the third in the Great Plains area.

The lowest step is the fertile, floorlike Red River Valley, once the bed of glacial Lake Agassiz. Near the Canadian boundary the valley is about 40 miles wide, but it gradually narrows until near the South Dakota line it is only 10 miles in width. With its northward slope of only about one foot to the mile, an even more gradual eastward slope, and few prominent surface features, the land offers no obstacles to a view across miles of level checkerboard fields. Natural woods grow along the Red River and its winding sluggish tributaries, and farmyard groves dot the landscape.

The Pembina Escarpment, a rise of 300 to 400 feet along the western edge of the valley, defines the beginning of the central surface-step, the Drift Prairie, or Drift Plain. At the northern end of the escarpment, which is a continuation of the Manitoba Escarpment in Canada, lie the wooded Pembina Mountains, jutting sharply above the valley floor.

South of these hills the rise is less pronounced, except at the southern end where the hills again become prominent to merge with the Coteau des Prairies, an escarpment lying chiefly in South Dakota.

Glacial deposits, or drift, of finely ground rock, sand, and gravel give the Drift Prairie its name. It is a rolling, fertile plain, varying from 70 to 200 miles in width, and broken by low ridges of hills, shallow coulees, and numerous small lakes. To the northwest lies the Souris River Valley, a small glacial lake bed resembling the Red River Valley. Devils Lake, largest in the State, lies in the northern part of the Drift Prairie, and together with Stump Lake forms the basis of the interior drainage system; near its southern end are the headwaters of the James and Sheyenne Rivers, both flowing southward, the James into the Missouri and the Sheyenne into the Red.

The Missouri Escarpment, rising 300 to 400 feet above the Drift Prairie and cutting across the State diagonally in a northwest-southeast direction, marks the rise of the third surface-step, the Missouri Plateau, which extends west to the Rocky Mountains. Lying along the top of the plateau, in some places not far from the escarpment and at other points 50 miles west of it, is the Altamont Moraine, a belt of rough, stony hills, indicating the farthest advance of the Dakota lobe of the Wisconsin ice sheet. In the north this moraine is a part of the Height of Land forming the watershed between the north- and south-flowing streams of the continent.

Between the escarpment and the Missouri River the plateau is known as the Coteau du Missouri. West of the river it is known locally as the Missouri Slope. The surface of the plateau, typical of the Great Plains, is irregular and rolling, dotted with old lake beds—some of which contain large deposits of sodium sulphate—and underlain with vast lignite beds and valuable clay and bentonite deposits.

In the Missouri Slope is the most unusual area in the State—the Badlands of the Little Missouri. Here erosion has formed, and continues to form, a fantastic array of buttes in which layers of brick-red scoria and gray, blue, and yellow clays are vividly exposed. Abrupt buttes and mesas characterize the landscape, increasing in size and number toward the southwest corner of the State. Among them is Black Butte, 3,468 feet above sea level, the highest point in North Dakota.

CLIMATE

Absence of great variation in physiography gives all portions of the State an almost uniform climate. North Dakota is situated in a temperate region of moderate rainfall, and owing to its position in the center of the North American Interior Plains it has a typically continental climate.

One of the characteristics of such a climate is a wide range of temperature, and to this the State can make good claim. North Dakota has a recorded range from 124° F., registered September 3, 1912, at Medora, to −60° F., recorded February 15, 1936, at Parshall. These temperatures are, of course, unusual, but the mercury often reaches 100° F. during the summer, whereas 30° to 40° F. below zero is not uncommon in winter. The mean temperature for the months of June, July, and August is 65.7° F., and for December, January, and February, 9.7° F. Relatively low humidity, averaging 68 per cent, makes these extremes less uncomfortable, however, than if the atmosphere contained more moisture.

The sections of the State vary more in the matter of precipitation than in any other climatic phase. The average is about 18 inches annually, ranging from about 22 inches in the southeastern corner to about 14 or even 10 inches in the southwestern corner. Most of the precipitation occurs in the late spring and summer.

Long and severe winters are typical of this region. Nevertheless the summers, though comparatively short, are favorable for agriculture, owing to the long hours of sunshine. At the maximum, about June 21, there are as many as 16 hours of sunlight a day; and this, together with cloudless skies, contributes to the rapid growth and early maturity of crops.

HOW THE LAND WAS FORMED

The surface of North Dakota, comparatively unvaried, is no more simple than the geological pattern that lies beneath it. Deposited by the seas of three geologic ages, horizontal layers of rock top each other in methodical and unintricate succession.

In far-off Paleozoic times, when all creatures of the earth were invertebrates, strange shellfish, unlike any existing today, lived among the rich foliage at the bottom of the shallow sea that covered this region. Hundreds of varieties of fossil plants and shells are embedded in the sandstone, limestone, and shale which the sea deposited on the uneven surface of the then-existent crystalline rocks. These Paleozoic rocks have been encountered in deep wells in eastern North Dakota, although nowhere in the State are they found at the surface.

Toward the close of the Paleozoic era, changing climatic conditions caused the death of many forms of life upon the earth, and the development of new and hardier types. With these, in the Mesozoic era, came the new lords of the earth, the reptiles. Must of the globe from the Arctic Ocean to New Mexico was covered by a great sea on whose swampy shores huge dinosaurs, alligators, and crocodiles made their homes. Largest of these grotesque creatures was the brontosaurus, with his long snakelike neck and face and huge body. Struggling with him for supremacy of the swamps was the armored stegosaurus, whose row of vertical plates along his backbone from head to tip of tail made him a formidable enemy. Among the plant and animal life that throve on the sea bottom were shellfish three feet or more in diameter.

The earliest seas of the Mesozoic era deposited the Dakota sandstone that underlies all of the State except the Red River Valley. It is a soft white or gray stone, containing many marine fossils. Although it does not appear at the surface anywhere in the State, it has been studied from specimens obtained from deep wells here or from outcroppings in other States.

Many rivers flowing into the prehistoric seas brought mud and clay to mix with the soils of the sea bottom, forming the shales that today underlie most of the Great Plains, including North Dakota. The lowest of these, Benton shale, is dark gray, almost jet black in places, and contains bits of pyrite (fool's gold) and gypsum. Over it lies the bluish-gray Niobrara shale, in which natural cement is found. In the Pembina Mountains and the Sheyenne Valley, where these rocks appear at the surface, they have yielded shells of lamellibranchs (ancestors of today's clams and oysters) and bones of great sharklike fish. Over these two strata lies the Pierre shale deposit, dark bluish-gray in color. It is frequently seen in the valleys of streams east of the Missouri Plateau, but outcrops in only two places west of the Missouri Escarpment—where the Missouri leaves the State, and in the valley of the Little Beaver Creek in southwestern North Dakota. In it have been found fossils of the chambered nautilus, the oyster, and other marine animals, the crocodile, and the plesiosaur—that ungainly reptile which had 'the body of a turtle strung on a snake.'

Once again the sea covered the State and left the rust-colored Fox

Hills sandstone, which is particularly conspicuous along the Cannonball River where action of underground water has formed it into the rusty-looking spheres which give the river its name. Similarly formed cylinders of this sandstone in concretionary form are also found along the stream, and large cylinders protrude from the top of Cannon Butte in the Badlands like the barrels of cannon from the turret of a huge battleship.

Near the close of the Mesozoic era, the climate of North Dakota became warmer, almost like that of the South Atlantic States. Through the swamps roamed horned carnivorous dinosaurs, especially triceratops, which had 'the largest head with the smallest brain of the reptile race.'

Again and again the sea invaded this swampland, depositing the Lance formation, comprising layers of massive sandstone and shale in which the luxuriant plant life of the area created thin beds of lignite coal. The Lance formation underlies most of the Missouri Plateau, and comes to the surface in two places—in the vicinity of Bismarck, and near Marmarth. Reptilian fossils are found in both the lignite and the intervening layers of rock.

At the dawn of the Cenozoic age, as mammalian life began to develop on the globe, another invasion of the sea left behind it a great plateau interspersed with swamps, marshlands, rivers, and lakes. On the plain grew giant sequoia, cypress, juniper, and other semitropical trees. Over the thick mat of mosses, lichens, and liverwort in the swamps crept turtles, alligators, lizards, and other reptiles, monstrous in size. King of this jungle was the titanothere, with its great body, short stocky neck, and columnar legs. Long-jawed shaggy mastodons and gigantic rhinoceroses challenged its supremacy. As these titans of the forest lumbered through the underbrush, herds of *Merycoidodon culbertsoni* or ruminating hogs, *Leptomeryx evansi*, dainty deerlike creatures no larger than jack rabbits, and little three-toed horses scampered out of their way.

The Fort Union formation, created through successive fresh water deposits of sediment in the swamps, contained vast quantities of rank swamp vegetation. In the intervening millions of years this has been turned into lignite, a very soft coal which has become North Dakota's most valuable mineral resource. The lignite veins in the formation indicate that the sea covered this area at least eleven times during the period when the formation was being deposited. In addition to lignite, the Fort Union clay shales and sandstones contain pure plastic clay beds and some bentonite, a claylike mineral of commercial value.

The recession of the seas left a broad and gently rolling plain cut by sluggish rivers whose wooded valleys were inhabited by the descendants of the great swamp beasts. When the waters again invaded the plain, the bones of these monsters were embedded in the deposits which became the White River formation, youngest bedrock underlying the State. So numerous are the fossil remains in the lower White River beds that these strata are called the titanothere beds. Fossils are found throughout the formation, however, ranging from mammal bones to the remains of fish and turtles. Erosion has worn away much of the White River formation in North Dakota, but it is conspicuously revealed on the summits of White or Chalky Butte, Sentinel Butte, Black Butte, and the Killdeer Mountains, and also in a few other small isolated areas in the Missouri Slope.

Gradually, during the time these formations were being laid down, the winters of this region were becoming more and more severe. Masses of ice moved slowly southward from the Arctic Region, covering much of the land and transforming the near-by forests, meadows, and swamps into a treeless plain of black mucky soil with a permanently frozen subsoil overgrown with moss, lichens, and dwarf shrubs. Fierce wintry storms took their toll of the mammoths, rhinoceros, and reindeer living upon the tundras. As the glaciers moved south, the animals were forced to flee to warmer lands. Soon the ice mass had covered all of North Dakota except a very small region in the southwest corner beyond the Killdeer Mountains. When at length it receded, it left in its wake boulders, gravel, and till—a drift soil composed of clay, sand, gravel, and boulders. Much of this now has been worn away; on the west side of the Missouri only a few scattered areas remain, and on the east side the till, though more continuous, is often merely a veneer a few feet in thickness.

The early glacier was followed by the Wisconsin ice sheet, the Dakota lobe of which covered a large part of this State, pushing back the Missouri River, which had previously flowed north into Hudson Bay, into its present channel.

Eventually this glacier, too, melted and receded, leaving a great lake about 650 feet deep, nearly 700 miles long, and 200 miles wide, with an area of not less than 110,000 square miles, including the region now known as the Red River Valley. This lake has been named Lake Agassiz, in honor of Louis Agassiz, first prominent advocate of the theory that drift was formed by land ice. Lake Agassiz existed some 10,000 years ago, lasted for probably 1000 years, and covered an area greater than the present Great Lakes. Its sole remnants today are Lakes Winnipeg, Winnipegosis, and Manitoba, and Lake of the Woods.

Productive soil and ground water, closely allied resources, are North Dakota's greatest assets. The Wisconsin glacier and Lake Agassiz are largely responsible for the fertile soils that cover three fifths of the State's surface. Through the Red River Valley the lake left a fine claylike silt 20 to 30 feet deep. The successive shore lines of the lake, showing its gradual recession, can be plainly seen in the ridges of sand and gravel that rise 10 to 25 feet along the western edge of the valley. Also on the west border of the valley are three extensive sand plains, the deltas of the Pembina, Sheyenne, and Elk Rivers, formed by glacial debris mingled with river silt. The Souris glacial lake bed, in the loop of the present Souris River, resembles the Red River Valley in geological history, but covers a much smaller area.

Immediately under the silt of the old lake beds and on the surface of the Drift Prairie is glacial drift or till. In much of the southwestern part of the State, particularly along the western tributaries of the Missouri, there are no glacial deposits; the topsoil is composed largely of shale and sandstone, and, though not so fertile as the old lake beds and glacial plains to the east, provides fine range country.

NATURAL RESOURCES

Especially valuable to those who depend on the land for their livelihood are the numerous artesian wells and natural springs that furnish necessary water supplies. The artesian basin on the southern border of the State and extending into South Dakota has been designated by a Federal authority as the most important in America and probably in the world.

People of the State have been awakened in recent years to a consciousness of the need for water conservation. Long abuse of seemingly unlimited artesian supplies resulted in lessening pressure in the wells. Simultaneously, drought, high winds, and the broken unwooded plains conspired to deplete the surface waters left by rains and winter snows. Within 20 years one third of the lakes in North Dakota became extinct.

To counteract these disastrous effects, a program of Federal, State, and private water- and soil-conservation has begun. Trees are being planted to hold the soil and conserve the moisture of rain and snow. A program of dam construction is under way in every county in the State (see pp. 65–6). Dry-land farming and supplemental irrigation have been adopted to conserve the soil and return to it the elements it has lost through constant cultivation.

North Dakota is indebted to the ancient seas and glaciers not only for the fertility of its soil but also for many of its most important mineral resources. Almost inexhaustible is the vast supply of lignite, estimated at 600 billion tons, which underlies the western half of the State. The veins, once the luxuriant plant life of a far distant age, vary from a fraction of an inch to 40 feet in thickness.

The southwestern corner of the State contains excellent beds of clay, deposited by the seas and now used for building materials and pottery. Two beds in the Dickinson vicinity, each containing approximately 29 million cubic yards, yield the finest clays in the State. A layer of yellow sand clay overlies the whitish plastic variety here; the two combine to form a number of colors and have the added advantage of being free from iron. Plastic clay beds of importance, although not so valuable commercially as the Dickinson deposits, are found throughout the southwestern corner of the State. They yield one of the rarest and most valuable types of clay for pottery and other specialized purposes. Shales found near the western clay beds are used in the manufacture of cheaper building materials.

The discovery of two large bentonite fields in southwestern North Dakota in 1930 opened up a new mineral resource. This claylike mineral is used as a binding agent and filler in many commercial processes, such as the manufacture of soaps, paints, and cosmetics. The larger deposit—in the Little Badlands—covers 25 square miles and contains about 100 million tons of the mineral, while the Chalky Butte deposit near Amidon contains about 60 million tons. The beds are easily accessible, being uncovered in many places.

Extensive sodium sulphate deposits have been formed in old lake beds in the northwestern corner of the State, where the mineral-bearing waters have evaporated, leaving a deposit of sodium sulphate crystals. North of the town of Grenora, 1,150 acres are covered with sodium sulphate beds ranging from a few inches to more than 30 feet in depth. Miller, North, and McKone Lakes, near Alkabo, contain more than 20 million tons. Sodium sulphate, also known as Glauber's salt, is commercially valuable, especially in farming. The North Dakota deposits are now being studied and developed by producers throughout the country.

Although oil in commercial quantities has not yet been discovered in North Dakota, from a geological point of view the conditions for its accumulation seem to be present. In recent years there has been renewed interest in searching for oil, and some deep-well drilling has been carried on in the western part of the State, where approximately 6 million acres are now under lease for exploration purposes.

Production of natural gas from 25 wells in Bowman County, in the southwestern part of the State, amounted to 642,687,000 cubic feet in 1948. These wells produce from the Eagle sand of the Pierre shale and are all connected to the distribution system of the Montana-Dakota Utilities Company.

Hidden beneath the earth's surface are other minerals deposited during the geologic formation of the various strata. These include fuller's earth, sandstone, granite, gneiss, and gold; but because of their limited quantity and inaccessibility, they are commercially unimportant. The glacial deposits are important because they include the sand and gravel used extensively for road surfacing. Some of the eastern lake beds contain marl, a clay from which Portland cement is made. The extent and purity of the deposits are not definitely known. (For discussion of industrial development of mineral resources see INDUSTRY AND LABOR.)

PLANT AND ANIMAL LIFE

North Dakota falls into three distinct zones of plant and animal life: the Turtle Mountain region and a few scattered areas in the Canadian, or cold, zone; the Missouri and Little Missouri Valleys in the upper austral, or warmer, zone; and the remainder of the State in the transition zone.

Because of its semi-arid climate, the State has only 600 square miles of wooded area. Native forests are found chiefly along streams and lakes, and in the Turtle and Killdeer Mountains. Despite the limited forested area, a surprising variety of trees is found. Throughout the Red River Valley, Turtle Mountains, and Devils Lake region plant life is similar to the Minnesota type, while such trees as the elm, green ash, box elder, poplar, and cottonwood are also common.

Although the cottonwood's ability to withstand drought makes it one of the most desirable species of trees in North Dakota, efforts are being made in many towns to eradicate the tree because of the ubiquitous soft white 'cotton' which floats from its branches like summer flurries of snow.

During the fall and early winter, the thickets of the northern Red River Valley are aflame with the highbush cranberry, which lent its

THE NORTHERN PACIFIC RAILROAD LINE

THE ONLY FIRST CLASS ROUTE TO THE BLACK HILLS

Big Horn Mountains, Yellowstone National Park, Yellowstone and Upper Missouri Rivers, and all points in NORTHERN

MINNESOTA, DAKOTA AND MONTANA

DIRECT RAIL FROM

ST. PAUL, MINNEAPOLIS
OR DULUTH TO

BRAINERD, DETROIT, GLYNDON, MOORHEAD, FARGO AND BISMARCK

During the Navigable Season Daily Steamers with First Class Accommodations leave

BISMARCK

For FORTS BERTHOLD, BUFORD and BENTON, and all points on the YELLOWSTONE and UPPER MISSOURI RIVERS, BIG HORN CITY, BOZEMAN, HELENA, and the BIG HORN MOUNTAINS. From Bismarck, the Northwestern Express, Stage & Transportation Company run a Daily Line of First Class Four Horse Concord Coaches to

DEADWOOD, CROOK CITY

And other Points in the BLACK HILLS; also, Stages for Standing Rock, Fort Rice, Berthold, Fort Keogh, and other POINTS IN MONTANA.

AT DULUTH Close Connections are made with all the AMERICAN and CANADIAN LINES of STEAMERS to all NORTH and SOUTH SHORE PORTS on the LAKES between DULUTH, BUFFALO and CHICAGO.

AT ST. PAUL AND MINNEAPOLIS The NORTHERN PACIFIC RAILROAD TAKING make Close Connections with trains to and from the EAST and SOUTH.

ELEGANT SLEEPING CARS ON NIGHT TRAINS

THE RAILROAD AND GOVERNMENT LANDS

in Minnesota and Dakota, along the line of the Northern Pacific R. R., offer better inducements to the settler than can be found anywhere else in the United States. These Lands are: CHOICE PRAIRIE, unexcelled in any country for wheat growing; HARD WOOD TIMBERED LANDS, rich soil and excellent for farming; NATURAL MEADOW LANDS, suitable for stock raising. Selections can be made from these Lands near the Road and Stations, having all the advantages of good schools, society, churches, schools, and in a country unsurpassed for healthfulness of climate. Prices Low, Terms Reasonable, Reduced Rates of Fare and Freight to Settlers.

FOR FULL INFORMATION, RATES, ETC. APPLY TO

Indian name to Pembina, first permanent white settlement in the State. Other berries grow profusely along all the eastern streams, and many families assure themselves of a winter supply of jams and jellies by picking the June berries, chokecherries, wild plums, and wild grapes. In the woods along the Missouri and Little Missouri grow trees of the Missouri type—the broadleaf cottonwoods, willows, ash, elm, buffalo berry, and flowering currant. A trace of the Rocky Mountain type of forest is found in the Badlands and on the buttes of the Little Missouri, where the yellow pine and red cedar grow.

Not only trees but other forms of vegetation differ widely from the eastern to the western sections of the State. The long Indian-grass and blue grass typical of the east is replaced on the western ranges by short buffalo grass and grama grass, the two forming a dense mat over the ground. Due to differences in rainfall, the western grasses are much duller and more grayish in color than those of the eastern section.

From early spring to the first frosts of autumn, thousands of wild flowers brighten the prairies. Many species are general throughout the State, while others are typical only of certain sections. Before the last patches of snow are gone, the blue-gray pasque flower, so like the crocus that it is often called by that name, appears on the rolling prairies and the northern slopes of hills. It is soon followed by the wild parsley, Nuttall's or yellow violet, and the vivid plumes of the purple avens. Most of the spring flowers are of soft, delicate hues, such as the white meadow rue, parsley, false-Solomonseal, silverberry, squaw-weeds, meadow parsnip, blue-eyed-grass, and harebell.

With the coming of midsummer, the colors become more brilliant. The fragrant prairie rose, the State flower, blossoms profusely in fields and along roadsides. The showy oxeye or false-sunflower, the flaming prairie mallow, wild blue and yellow flax, the vivid flame lily, the purple coneflower, and the black-eyed Susan emblazon the summer fields. Along the Pembina and Sheyenne Rivers, and in Sully's Hill National Game Preserve, grow the wintergreen and lady's slipper. Water lilies float on pools and shallow streams in the western part of the State. In the Badlands grow the rabbit brush, butte primrose, false-lupine, prickly pear, and the scoria lily, which resembles a thistle during the day and opens its fragile, waxy petals only after the sun has gone down.

Yellow is the color of the prairies in autumn, as amid the fading foliage the goldenrod, sunflower, aster, and blazing star dominate the scene.

Some wild flowers, such as the wild morning-glory, are so common that they are regarded as weeds. These are not so obnoxious to the farmer, however, as the Russian-thistle, pigeon grass, quack grass, pigweed, mustard, burdock, and sow thistle, which often invade the grainfields. The seeds of most of these plants were brought in with seed grain from European countries, and their eradication is a difficult process. Another obnoxious plant, against which a strong campaign has been conducted by farmers, is the common barberry, on which thrive the parasitic fungi that cause wheat rust. Many weeds, however, are considered a valuable asset to the fields and pasture lands where they grow. These include the American vetch or wild sweet pea, which forms an important addition to hay, and the white and violet prairie clovers, which, although too tough to be used for fodder, serve to enrich the soil.

When the first settlers came to this section of the country, they described the land as being covered with innumerable varieties of wild flowers. Since that time, cultivation and drought have changed the picture. Efforts to preserve the native plant life in its natural setting have met with co-operation from Federal and State agencies alike. The reserves that have been established are also sanctuaries for bird and animal life, upon which recent drought and severe winters have had a disastrous effect.

Under the auspices of the State Game and Fish Commission, 11,730 acres of land have been set aside as 9 refuges, while 425,000 acres of privately owned land have been designated as game refuges. The Federal Government has established some 76 sanctuaries on 323,786 acres, of which 68 refuges are privately owned. '

Animal-life zones in the State are more marked than are plant-life zones. The woods of the Turtle Mountains, at the meeting point of the Canadian and transition zones, abound with wild life of both regions. More than 300 varieties of game and song birds live here, including the Dakota song sparrow, the black-billed cuckoo, the oriole, and the blue jay. In the deserted holes of badgers, foxes, and gophers live those queer prairie birds, the burrowing owls. Grebe, ducks, geese, heron, and occasionally swan inhabit the lakes of the region. Deer, red fox, rabbits, red squirrels and northern chipmunks are common; and at night the bright-eyed, mousy Richardson shrew and the silver-haired bat can be seen. Lynx are occasionally reported.

In the Red River Valley and the central prairies of the State, once the scene of buffalo hunts, very little large game is found today. A few buffalo remain in Sully's Hill National Game Preserve, and in the Sheyenne Valley and the Pembina Mountains deer are still found.

Game birds abound in this region, however, and with the restoration of their breeding places they are now being propagated in huge numbers on the many reserves.

Early travelers in the western part of the State were astonished by the prairie-dog villages that dotted the country. Some of these villages still exist, in the extreme western sections. Their inhabitants are typical of the upper austral zone, as are also the coyotes, whose long melancholy wail can be heard across the prairie at twilight or daybreak. Chipmunks, squirrels, gophers, and ferrets also make their homes here. Along the Missouri and in the forested areas of the Bad-lands are both white-tailed and mule deer. The one bird peculiar to the austral zone is the sage-hen; and the American magpie, commonly seen here, is rare in other parts of the State.

Birds such as the robin, sparrow, blackbird, swallow, horned lark, and meadow lark are common to the entire State. The lark is one of the early spring comers, and its clear sweet whistle can be heard when the prairies are just beginning to turn green.

One of the most common animals in the State is Richardson's ground squirrel, otherwise known as the gopher or 'flickertail.' It is from this tiny, agile, yellow creature that North Dakota gets its name of 'the Flickertail State.' Another familiar prairie animal is the jack rabbit.

Fish life, like that of plants and animals, has been adversely affected by past droughts, but efforts are being made to propagate fish and to provide sufficient water for their existence. In the larger lakes and rivers, perch, black and rock bass, pickerel, pike, sunfish, and catfish are found. Some landlocked salmon have been introduced, but they are not adapted to North Dakota lakes and streams. Suckers and carp are common but they are not considered desirable game fish.

Indians and Their Predecessors

PREHISTORIC MAN IN NORTH DAKOTA

JUST when and where in the shadowy, endless past the Indians of North Dakota, or even of the two Americas, began to break away from the parent stem is not known. Weapons and tools shaped from stone and found in strata that settled into place near the end of the Pleistocene, or glacial, period indicate that as long as 15,000 to 20,000 years ago men wandered along the rivers and through the swamps of those areas that later became New Mexico, Nebraska, and Minnesota. Very probably, in long hunts after game, parties of these men penetrated what is now North Dakota. Stone tools and weapons found in the vicinity of Bismarck suggest an early occupation of the area, how long ago no one knows.

A great many years nearer the present day, but still possibly a thousand or more years ago, men were digging busily in the flint quarries 19 miles north of Hebron and 12 miles northwest of Dodge and at other points on the Knife River. With the flint obtained here they fashioned arrowheads and spear points to kill buffalo or to protect their homes against enemy tribesmen. One of these heavily sodded sites on the Knife River contains more than 300 pits, most of which are from 8 to 10 feet across, and from 3 to 5 feet deep.

The extensive mounds and earthworks found in the eastern half of North Dakota have been only imperfectly investigated so far, partly because archeologists have but recently recognized the possibilities of the area. The skeletons and the bone and stone manufactured articles lately discovered, however, as well as the general finds of the region, suggest the probability of outlining tribal movements of importance. There is an increasing suggestion that before the time of the historic tribes the prairies of the eastern half of the State supported large populations. It is thought that, just as the Cheyenne are known to have done in the historic period, in prehistoric time the Assiniboin and the

Blackfeet, and preceding them still other tribes, carried on a settled agricultural life before they became nomadic. Of course the movements of these tribes were not confined entirely to what is now North Dakota.

Perhaps hundreds of years after the construction of the mounds in the eastern half of the State—possibly from one to four hundred years ago— some tribe or tribes, probably the Sioux or certain of the village-building Indians, were putting together the turtle effigies frequently encountered on the hills west of the Missouri and constructing the more widespread and better-known boulder-ring effigies. The purpose of these crude outlines on the prairie is not definitely known. Because the turtle plays a prominent part in medicine ceremonies of the Mandan Indians, some think the turtle effigies were made to win the favor of certain spirits. Others claim they were made to point the weary Indian to good water—a theory which may also apply to a number of the cairns occasionally seen piled on the tops of high hills. Other cairns are ceremonial or commemorative.

Boulder rings, which sometimes appear in large numbers but more often present only one or two specimens in a given location, were once thought to be tipi rings. The fact that many of them appear on the sides and tops of hills has discredited this assumption, however.

Veneration of the so-called sacred stones of the State probably began in the effigy-building period, but the origin of the very interesting writing rocks (*see Tours 3B, 4A, 8A, and 8C*) is undoubtedly far more ancient. The significance of the markings on these rocks has not yet been determined.

THE COMING OF THE NORTH DAKOTA INDIAN TRIBES

About the time the earlier turtle effigies were made—perhaps 200 years ago—in permanent villages of earth lodges in the valley of the Missouri dwelt a most interesting group of people, raising many cultivated plants, building fortified towns, and in general living a rather ordered existence. These were the Mandan, as far as is definitely known the first of the historic tribes to enter the State. Their exact origin is not clear. Certain of their traditions claim that they long ago lived in the East near a great body of water—most authorities suggest the East Coast or Gulf of Mexico.

At any rate, many generations before the coming of the whites, the Mandan—probably crowded by other tribes—began to wander westward. Apparently their long trek finally brought them and their wives and children to the junction of the White River with the Missouri in what is now South Dakota. Grass-grown sites of their old villages along the benchland of the river show how these people, in quest of a new and more satisfactory home, moved northward in successive migrations until in time they arrived at the mouth of the Heart River in the neighborhood of present Mandan and Bismarck. Here they probably remained for generations, carrying on a settled agricultural life. They were visited by the Verendryes in 1738 (*see Tour* 8), at which time they had six large, well-fortified villages. Estimates of their number at this time have ranged from 2,500 to 15,000.

They are one of those four North Dakota Indian groups—Mandan, Hidatsa, Cheyenne, and Arikara—who because of their farming activities are called the agricultural tribes. While the Mandan were building on the Missouri, the Hidatsa were probably living somewhat farther north and east. They have a tradition that they originally came from a large lake to the east, possibly Devils Lake. Later, probably forced on by some other tribe, they moved their families over the prairies to the Missouri in the region of the Heart River and eventually allied themselves with the Mandan. Their history thereafter follows very closely that of the latter tribe.

While the Mandan and Hidatsa were dwelling on the Missouri, the Cheyenne were migrating westward from the headwaters of the Mississippi, by way of Lac Que Parle in present Minnesota, Lake Traverse, and the big bend of the Sheyenne River, to the Missouri, seeking a place where they could till the soil and rear their children in peace, free from the harrying of the Sioux.

At the same time the Arikara, doubtless likewise trying to take their families away from the ravaging Dakota, were ascending the Missouri. The name of this tribe arose from their custom of wearing in their hair two pieces of bone which stood up on each side of the head like horns. They came from the southwest and their language differs only in dialect from the Pawnee. In 1770 French traders encountered them dwelling along the river bank somewhat below the mouth of the Cheyenne River in what is now South Dakota.

The migrations of the Hidatsa, Cheyenne, and Arikara, as those of the Mandan, are traceable by the old village sites, of which there are about 150 known locations on the prairies of the State. Arikara sites predominate lower down the Missouri in South Dakota; the older Mandan—perhaps constructed as early as 1575–1650—in the Heart River region; and the Hidatsa, farther north near the Knife River. There are apparently two types, a newer and an older. The newer, perhaps less carefully laid out than the older, is found at and above the mouth of the Heart River. The older type appears to have had better fortifications than the newer, and the lodges do not seem to have been so crowded. Because of its greater age it is more heavily sodded, and thus manufactured articles left by the village dwellers, such as stone and bone tools and ornaments, are less easily recovered. It seems to center below the Heart River, with the Huff site, just below the village of Huff, as perhaps the best example (*see Tour* 8).

Sometime—perhaps a hundred years—after the Mandan first built about the mouth of the Heart River, the three nomadic North Dakota tribes—the Sioux, Assiniboin, and Chippewa—were ranging the forests near the headwaters of the Mississippi. The Chippewa, however, were not strictly nomadic, as they had more or less permanent camping places, where they built their distinctive bark shelters.

The Chippewa wandered from the Lake region across Minnesota to the Turtle Mountains. They cultivated maize and were apparently more or less at peace with the Sioux until in the early eighteenth century the coming of the whites brought them firearms. With this advantage they overcame the Sioux and drove them south and west.

The Assiniboin were a large tribe, whose language, with only a very slight dialectal difference from that of the Yanktonai tribe of the Sioux, suggests they had not long been separated from the latter when first encountered by the whites near the headwaters of the Mississippi. At the beginning of the eighteenth century they were in the neighborhood of Lake Winnipeg, whence they drifted southward to the territory west of the Turtle Mountain region in present North Dakota.

The Sioux apparently once lived in the Ohio Valley, but prior to the historic period they moved out in several directions. At the coming of the whites in the middle seventeenth century they were found in the woods in northern Minnesota. Pressed by the Chippewa, they extended their range westward over the prairies to the Missouri, and west of that stream, from the Yellowstone River on the north to the Platte on the south, to cover a huge block of territory throughout which the name of this powerful tribe was feared and dreaded by all other Indians.

Of these seven North Dakota peoples—Mandan, Hidatsa, Cheyenne, Arikara, Sioux, Assiniboin, Chippewa—well-authenticated records exist. It will be noted that nearly all except the Arikara seem to have come from the east, particularly from the Lakes region, with the added suggestion of an earlier residence farther east or south. There is also in some cases a definite shift from a settled agricultural life to a nomadic one. They apparently arrived in the State in the following order:

Mandan
Hidatsa, also known as Gros Ventres, Minitari, and Absaroke
Cheyenne
Assiniboin, also called Stone
Sioux, also called Dakota
Arikara
Chippewa, also called Ojibway

Linguistically all the North Dakota tribes are Siouan, except the Arikara, who are Caddoan, and the Chippewa and Cheyenne, who are Algonquian.

EARLY INDIAN LIFE IN NORTH DAKOTA

It is interesting to visualize the prairie scene centuries ago when the Indian ruled the plains. The agricultural tribes usually built their villages of earth lodges so that one or more sides lay along a high cliff or next to a river. This afforded partial protection from the Sioux. In the more ancient types an earthen wall, sometimes built with bastions, protected the exposed sides. A log palisade topped the wall, and around the whole a ditch was dug. The number of lodges in a village varied from 30 or 40 to as high as perhaps 160. Catlin said the lodges had the appearance of huge inverted kettles, above which rose spears and scalp and medicine poles.

The lodges in the older types of villages were arranged with a certain degree of uniformity. In the Mandan villages the lodges faced the center, where stood a large barrel or hogshead, called the Big Canoe. Soon after the Mandan came upon the earth, it is told, a great flood came and would have destroyed them utterly had not a wise Mandan, the First Man, with superlative effort and dexterity, built a great canoe or ark and hurried the surviving people into it. This staunch ark weathered the fury of the waters and finally came to rest on a high hill near the Cannonball River (see Tour 8C). The Big Canoe in the center of the village was a symbol of this ark.

Uniformity was not so evident in the later types of villages. Between the lodges only room enough was left for men and women of the village to pass; consequently, the broad earth roofs served the additional purpose of verandas. Out upon these roofs, especially in the summertime, was much activity—children played, old men watched for enemy tribesmen, sweethearts conversed, neighbors gossiped. Although the tribes were often ruthless and cruel in war, in their prairie homes and villages they were very friendly and companionable people. Both men and women indulged in a great number of games, and spent a good deal of time in visiting, feasting, and dancing. Catlin upon his departure after living with the Mandans for months was loaded with gifts and urged to continue his visit.

Heavy garments were worn in the winter, and at that season the buffalo robe was very much in evidence both for bedcovering and as an article of clothing; but in summertime clothing was rather scanty. Both men and women went down to the grassy shore of the Missouri in the morning to bathe, often with little regard for dress—a fact that greatly shocked some early travelers.

As the morning sun flooded the narrow dirt lanes of one of these villages, braves, clad in breechcloths and moccasins, might have been seen preparing for a hunt, while naked boys played with scores of scampering dogs. If the village was Mandan, some of the hunters were surprisingly Caucasian in appearance—the skin somewhat lighter than that of the average Indian, the nose not so broad, and the cheekbones less prominent. Early travelers noted cases of extraordinarily light complexions, and also instances of brown hair and blue eyes—characteristics suggesting European blood. By certain of the first white visitors the Hidatsa were regarded as being rather superior intellectually, but this was not so apparent in later days.

At their sides the hunters carried knives and bows and arrows in leather sheaths. If they were going out to kill rabbit, ducks, geese, beaver, deer, or elk along the river bottom, they might go afoot. If they sought the wilder bighorn sheep or the buffalo, however, they brought their ponies from the lodges, where they had been quartered overnight, as that was the safest place available. Lariats, bridles, and saddles were of leather. To protect themselves from enemy attack the hunters had spears, tomahawks, shields, and lances, in addition to the ever-present bows and arrows.

As they threaded their way between the lodges, here and there they saw some of their women baking pottery of a mixture of clay and powdered granite or flint—Catlin says they modeled it into a thousand forms, and that some of their pottery held as much as five gallons. Other women, using bone awls and needles, were decorating girdles, fans, moccasins, and dresses with beadwork and embroidery. Clothing, especially headdress, was elaborate and spectacular on ceremonial occasions. Still other women were weaving wickerwork, both flat and in the form of baskets; making bone spoons, ladles, and other household utensils; fashioning implements for the work in their gardens; and working over hides stretched on crude frames, in the process of tanning. In the latter art all the North Dakota tribes were unusually proficient. Hides prepared by them retained their softness and resilience even after being subjected to moisture many times.

Farther on, a group of boys hovered about a hoary old man who sat near the door of a lodge in the soft summer sun and told them the history and traditions of their tribe. They had just come in from the prairie outside the village, where the older warriors had been teaching them the art of war by leading them in a sham battle. The victorious side had danced the scalp dance, just as their elders did after the actual taking of scalps, and now all were gathered about this old man to hear the stories of their people. If the village was Mandan, very possibly the old man was telling them of the great tribal hero, Good Furred Robe, who is supposed to have played so large a part in establishing the Mandan way of living. The narrator would tell them, too, that the Mandan were the first people created in the world, and that originally they lived inside the earth, where they raised many vines. Of course, they were constantly striving and struggling to find a way out of this dark, underground world. Finally one of their vines pushed its way through a hole in the earth overhead, and some of their people climbed up and out into a rich, fine country. A large fat woman, trying to climb out, broke the vine, however, and the remainder of the Mandans live underground to this day.

The storyteller also had another version of the beginning of things. At first the world was entirely water, inhabited by no living creature but a swan, which in some unaccountable way produced a crow, a wolf, and a water hen. Through the unsparing efforts of the crow to improve their situation the water hen was finally sent to the bottom of the waters to fetch some earth. Taking a small quantity of this in her bill, the crow made the earth. Later, persevering in her labor of improving their lot, she assumed the form of an Indian, and made all the beasts, birds, fishes, and insects, and became the first of all Indians.

If the aged narrator had been an Arikara, his story would have been similar to that of the Mandan. The Arikara believed that they together with all other living things existed first in an embryo state deep within the earth. There they gradually developed, and after many generations of patient struggle were at last successful in their attempt to get to the surface. As they emerged, they were directed by a Voice, which remained with them, comforting and guiding them until after many hardships and vicissitudes they came to a fair land. Here there came to them a beautiful woman—the one whose voice had led them. She was Mother Corn, the protective spirit of the agricultural tribes, and the one who gave them their staple food grain.

As the hunters passed along they heard through the village the sound of music—crude flutes, whistles, and drums. All the North Dakota tribes were musical, even though their product was hampered by the limitations of their scale, which had only five notes. Frances Densmore has placed hundreds of their songs in notation, copies of which are published in the bulletins of the Smithsonian Institution.

Now and then, above the sound of the music, voices raised in wailing were heard. These came from the scaffold cemetery on the prairie just outside the village, whither some had withdrawn to lament the death of loved ones. Great mourning followed upon a death—the wailing could often be heard for miles. The Mandan slashed themselves until their bodies were covered with blood and mourned for a year. In the tree or scaffold method of burial, the one usually followed by the North Dakota tribes, the cemetery was ordinarily situated only two or three hundred paces from the village. The body was wrapped in blankets and placed upon the scaffold very soon after death—some say before the sun again sank below the prairies. The Arikara and the Chippewa placed their dead in the ground, the former resting the body in a sitting posture, or on its side, with the knees drawn up, in a shallow stone-lined grave. The latter people believed the spirit followed a wide, beaten path to the west, at the end of which lay everything an Indian could desire.

The Sioux thought the soul must journey after death toward the land from which the west wind comes. They believed that the soul did not leave the body until after nightfall. A horse was killed beneath the tree or scaffold, in order that the spirit of the animal might carry the spirit of the Indian to the Milky Way, which was regarded as the pathway of ghosts. On this pathway the spirit of the dead was met by the Old Woman with the Stick. If he passed the proper tests, she directed him down the left fork of the Milky Way to the Northern Lights, which were regarded as the campfires of the departed heroes and good people of the tribe. If he could not meet the tests, however, she pushed him along the right fork over a precipice; and he and his horse were there changed into beetle bugs forever.

The above-ground type of cemetery undoubtedly contributed to the spread of disease. Of course, the tribes were subject to a variety of maladies, smallpox being the most dreaded. From this scourge the agricultural people suffered disastrously; the Mandan were nearly wiped out by it in the early nineteenth century. In the treatment of disease certain medicinal herbs were used rather intelligently, and the vapor bath was of distinct value; but when it came to the more severe forms of sickness, the primitive sufferers called in the medicine men and trusted to their incantations.

As the hunters, saddened by the wailing of the mourners, went on their way, sounds of an altogether different type might have come to them— sounds of joy—of a wedding in progress. The bridegroom would have delivered the horses with which he paid for his bride, and the guests would be gathered at the lodge for the feast, which usually consummated the relatively simple affairs that courtship and marriage were among the prairie Indians. Perhaps the groom already had several wives—the possession of 6 was common, and the great men of the tribe sometimes had as many as 14. Since the women did much of the work of field and lodge, the acquisition of another wife was not an added burden. Despite the existence of polygamy, however, Indian families were not large.

The babies of the party would be seen strapped to board cradles, where a good part of infancy was spent in those days—a life that must have had its pleasant features. In this point of vantage a child could be set up by the side of the tipi or lodge to enjoy the sunshine, be hung up in a tree to talk to the birds, or be carried at the side of a horse or on the back of its mother to look serenely over the far prairies.

At this point a courier might have detained the hunters and delivered a message requesting the presence of some of them at a council of the leading men of the tribe, called to consider pressing affairs of government. Among the Plains Indians, government varied greatly, being dependent upon a combination of custom and tradition and the personal fitness and character of the chief. Perhaps the latter element played a greater part in the swiftly changing life of the nomadic tribes, while among the more settled agricultural peoples, tradition and the hereditary rights of chieftainship had more authority. Nearly all the tribes were divided into a number of clans or bands.

If the supply of meat was running low, and no buffalo had been near the village for a long time, the big question before the council might have been whether or not the tribe should conduct the buffalo dance. The agricultural tribes did not like to go far from the protection of their villages because of the enemy Sioux and often resorted to the buffalo dance, which never failed to bring the buffalo, because it was danced until buffalo came. The dancers donned buffalo skins, the head of the dancer being placed in the head of the skin so that the eyes looked out as the buffalo's had; the horns projected above the head, and the tail dragged on the ground. Thus garbed, they danced in the center of the village, going through all the antics of the buffalo. During the days of the buffalo dance, the yelping of the people and the beating of drums were continuous and deafening. Each dancer danced until exhausted, and then the other shot him with blunt arrows; whereupon he was dragged to one side and theoretically skinned and cut up. Other dancers replaced those thus removed, and the dance was kept up until buffalo came. Sometimes the Sioux out on the prairie put on buffalo hides and decoyed the villagers forth to be ambushed.

The ceremony of the rain makers was another that was always effective because it was continued until the desired results were achieved. Evidently there were droughts in those days, too, and the fields of Mandan corn withered in the hot summer suns. Catlin tells the story of one rain maker, who, mounting his lodge and vaunting his powers, called upon the clouds to bring rain. Just as he was about to retire in failure and disgrace, out of a clear sky came what seemed to be thunder. The sound, however, turned out to be a salute fired by the steamer *Yellowstone* on her first trip up the Missouri. At first nonplussed, the rain maker finally made capital out of this coincidence when, later in the day, a large cloud jutted up on the horizon, and a heavy rain began and continued far into the night.

The council might have been considering also the conducting of the yearly feast of Okeepa, the most important of all Mandan ceremonies. This centered about the legend of the Ark and the First Man and was regarded as being an essential part of the origin and existence of the tribe. It took place in the summertime, usually lasting about four days.

The feast of Okeepa contained many features common to the sun dance of the other Plains tribes, particularly the element of self-torture. Skewers were thrust through the loose flesh of the dancer's chest, thongs attached, and the dancer thereby hauled up toward the roof of the council lodge until his body was six or eight feet off the ground. Often other skewers were thrust through the skin of the back, and weights attached by thongs and allowed to drag over the floor of the lodge as the dancer swung about the pole. Thus suspended, the warrior boasted of his prowess and bravery until he was released by the breaking of the flesh. This torture was thought necessary to secure the blessings of food, shelter, protection from enemies, and long life.

While the hunters were away, some of the women, engaged in the immemorial food-getting practice of fishing, went out on the river in the tublike bullboat—so-called because it was made from the skin of a single buffalo bull, stretched over a willow frame. Others went along the bluffs and through the valleys, digging tipsin roots, and gathering berries, cherries, and plums.

But probably by far their most important occupation economically was work in the gardens. As far back as their traditions go, the tribes of the Missouri Valley seem to have been agriculturists. Along the river each family kept a field or garden, variously estimated at from one to four or five acres in size. These fields were held by the family with a sort of perpetual lease from the community, dependent only on the condition that good use be made of the land. There was apparently no concept of the white man's practice of fertilizing the soil; when an old field grew impoverished, a new one was selected. A fence of forked sticks protected the crops from horses, while here and there on the outskirts of the fields a sentry brave was on duty to guard the women from the ever-dreaded Sioux. Aiding the women were a few old men, too feeble for the chase. A variety of tobacco, several varieties of sunflowers, squashes, pumpkins, and beans, and a dozen varieties of corn grew in the gardens. Early travelers say the ears of corn were extraordinarily small.

The keepers of the gardens were very faithful in caring for the growing plants and took great pride in keeping the soil free from weeds. They worked among the corn with the willow rake, the antler fork, and, probably most important of all, the shoulder-blade hoe. In each garden stood a platform or watchtower upon which in certain seasons sat one or two Indian women, whose duty it was to frighten away marauding crows and blackbirds. These women also sang watchtower songs to the growing corn, as a mother sings to her babe.

When the hunters and the berry pickers and the gardeners returned home, surplus corn, meat, squashes, and other foods were placed on the drying racks which stood at the doors of the lodges. Corn that was allowed to ripen was usually stored in underground bottle-shaped caches or storage pits, the best ears being placed around the edges of the cache, while in the center were thrown loose corn and strings of dried squash.

As evening came on, within the dome-shaped lodges there was much feasting, especially if it was the time of the new corn. The doorway of a lodge was protected by a kind of porch and hung with a buffalo hide. From behind the windshield just inside the doorway shone the light of the fire, which was built in a stone-lined depression in the center of the lodge, with a hole in the roof to carry off the smoke. This opening also served as a skylight. To the right of the doorway, in a small corral or stall, were the favorite ponies, safely confined for the night. Boxlike beds for the master of the house, his wife or wives, and his children were arranged along the wall on the other side. These were made by covering sturdy wooden frames with hides. In the rear stood an altar—a tall hide-covered structure somewhat resembling a canopied chair—in which were placed all the sacred objects and most prized possessions of the head of the house. Over the fire about which the family or families had gathered—usually two or three families and their relatives lived in one lodge—were kettles of food cooking for the evening meal. Catlin says the Indians ate whenever hungry, or about twice a day. The pot was kept boiling, and each one helped himself. Anyone in the village who was hungry was free to go into any lodge and satisfy his hunger, although the lazy and improvident were scorned.

Overhead, the light from the fire flickered on the huge supporting uprights of the lodge, where hung articles of clothing, tools from the garden, and weapons for war and hunting. Months before, with infinite labor and no little ingenuity, and hampered by the imperfections of the crude tools and equipment at their command, these early Dakota farmers had cut great cottonwood logs from the Missouri bottomlands and dragged them to the top of the bluffs, to form the framework for this earthen home. The lodges varied from 30 to 90 feet in diameter. After a little sod had been removed from a space of the desired size, to form a smooth, firm floor, four heavy posts were fixed upright not far from the center to support the great roof, while at some distance out from these a circle of smaller posts was set to hold up the sides. Rafters of moderate-sized timbers were placed over these supports, after which the whole was overlaid with willows, hay, and earth—a humble covering that guarded with all its passive, effective impenetrability against both the sweltering heat of summer and the intense cold of winter.

Out on the prairies, sometimes along the shores of rivers or lakes, sometimes on the open plain, stood the tipi villages of the enemy—the nomadic Assiniboin and Sioux. Against the evening sky the tipis, which required about 15 buffalo hides each in their construction, rose as much as 25 feet in height. A tipi approximately 15 feet in diameter usually accommodated 2 families.

Not far from the village, and very carefully guarded, grazed the pony herd. The horse was of great importance in the nomadic way of living. He carried the tipi and its contents across the plains and sped the hunters in their pursuit of the buffalo. Every warrior had two, some many more; and Sioux horsemen were probably as daring and expert as any the world has known.

The serviceability of the horse was increased by the use of the travois, a simple implement of transportation consisting of two long poles, often tipi poles, whose forward ends, joined by a short strap, rested on the animal's neck, while the rear ends dragged along the prairie. Camp duffle was strapped to the middle of the poles. A similar but smaller device was placed on dogs.

Gathered about the campfires were the warriors, men of striking physique and strong character, perhaps just in from the chase or war or a pillaging expedition. The clothing of the nomadic tribes was more extensive than that of the agricultural. Moccasins, separate trouser legs, breechcloth, and leather shirt were supplemented in cold weather by buffalo robes. The women wore moccasins, short decorated leggings, and loose-fitting leather dresses falling to the knees. In winter both sexes wore a kind of hood over the head. Clothing was commonly ornamented with bead and quill work.

Here and there about the tipis hung bows with quivers of arrows. As in the case of the agricultural tribes, the bow and arrow was the chief weapon, and the Sioux were expert in its use. Ready to hand, too, were shields, clubs, stone hammers, and spears. It is interesting to note here that as a means of communication in peace and war the tribes made good use of the art of signaling with fires and smoke. By this method messages were transmitted long distances with almost incredible rapidity.

Not far from the fires some of the women were preparing for drying the buffalo meat brought in from the chase. Others were storing dried berries and fruits in caches, in the making and concealing of which the Sioux were very skillful.

About the big fire near the center of the village the old men and chiefs were meeting in council over some weighty matter, perhaps the arrangements for the great annual sun dance. For this a special lodge was prepared on the prairie, around which the whole village pitched its camp in the form of a horseshoe facing the east. The ceremony required several days and involved self-torture similar to that of the Mandan feast of Okeepa.

In one group about the fire an elderly man was relating the history of the tribe to a circle of youthful faces. Some of the tribes kept a chronicle of their history by means of the winter count: the council met in winter and decided on the outstanding event of the year; thereafter the year was designated by this event, which was often pictured symbolically on a buffalo hide.

With the history, of course, as the evening stars came out, were mingled fancy and legend. On this night the boys and girls heard of the great monster who breaks up the ice in the Missouri each spring, of how one of the goose nation was shown in a dream that her people should go south each autumn in order to avoid the harsh winter, and of the Iktomi, the little 'spidermen,' who on moonlight nights, high on hilltops, can be heard with their tiny hammers, shaping arrowheads which they place in piles where Indians can find them.

One of the Iktomi, who was a very excellent singer and dancer, was hungry, continued the storyteller, and went into the woods to catch some birds. Being unsuccessful in his attempts to bag them, he invited them into his house to hear him sing. After they had accepted his invitation, he told them that if they were to hear his sweet voice, they must keep their eyes closed tightly. He warned them that their eyes would turn to a blood red if they opened them. Then he sang and danced. In his dance, however, as he passed each bird, he took it by the head and wrung its neck. This continued until he came to Siyaka, the duck. Siyaka opened his eyes just as the Iktomi seized him, and managed to break away. But where the Iktomi had his hand about his neck there was a red ring which is there to this day, and Siyaka is now the ring-necked duck.

The thunderbirds, so ran another tale of the aged storyteller, live suspended between heaven and earth, their wings supported by lightning. Above are the dark clouds. Below is the earth. When the thunderbirds shake their wings favorably, it rains. There was a time when they tired of living between heaven and earth and asked the Great Mystery if they might become men and live on earth. This the Great Mystery gave them permission to do, but told them that they should become men such as no other men were. Accordingly, they became giants so large that one living on the Big Muddy could reach the Atlantic Ocean in a single step. One of them playfully took up a handful of earth, and the waters flowing into the depression formed Lake Superior, while the handful of earth he tossed aside made a mountain. They dug a ditch to the Gulf of Mexico, and it is now called the Mississippi River. Such antics finally produced all the lakes and rivers. At last the thunderbird men grew old and died and went back to the spaces between heaven and earth. Lightning is the fire from their eyes, and thunder the reverberation from their eggs as they hatch.

While the night settled darker and a breath of cool air stole in from the prairie, the storyteller told of the great giant who lives in the North and whose name is Wasiya. The feathers of his bonnet are icicles, and his clothing is of ice. When he blows his breath, it turns cold and winter comes.

Later, as strange lights began to play far away in the northern sky, the narrator told the story, heard from the Chippewa, of the Northern Lights. A woman in a dream once visited the land where these lights shine and discovered that they are ghosts rising and falling in the steps of a dance. All the women wear gay colors, and the warriors brandish their war clubs.

The boys and girls heard, too, of the beautiful Indian maiden who came from the land of the setting sun and brought the Sioux the pipe of strange red stone, which is the solidified blood of Indians. She told them to use the pipe only when there is peace, or peace to be made, and in times of sickness and distress; and urged them to be kind to the women because they are weak. She is now the morning star, the Indians' sister, and stands in the heavens, wearing a white buffalo robe. The boys and girls were told, too, as the darkness deepened out on the prairies, that the earth is the Indians' Mother, and the sun their Father. Therefore, they should treat kindly and with reverence all things in earth and sky, because they are manifestations of Wakantanka, the Great Mystery, or the Great Spirit, to whom the Indians pray.

DECLINE OF THE INDIAN TRIBES

Shortly after the Verendrye visit the Mandan seem to have declined. When Lewis and Clark came up the Missouri in 1804, the villages about the Heart River were in ruins. Farther up the river, near where it is joined by the Knife, the explorers found the Mandan, diminished by smallpox and by wars with the Assiniboin and the Dakota to two small villages. In 1837 smallpox again broke out, reducing the tribe from 1600 to 150—some travelers give even a lower figure. At the beginning of the twentieth century it numbered about 250.

The other agricultural tribes seem to have suffered fates almost as harsh. The Hidatsa, numbering 2100 at the time of the Lewis and Clark visit, had been reduced at the beginning of the present century to less than 500. In 1804 the Arikara, crowded by the Sioux, had moved up the river nearer to the other agricultural tribes. Lewis and Clark found them in three villages between the Grand and Cannonball Rivers in what is now North and South Dakota. At that time they numbered 2600, but this figure had dropped to 380 by the beginning of the twentieth century. The Cheyenne village on the Missouri, some distance below the site of Bismarck, was in ruins at the time of the expedition. Successive migrations finally brought the Cheyenne to the headwaters of the Cheyenne River in the southwestern part of present South Dakota.

The agricultural tribes on the whole have been very friendly to the whites. In 1870 a large reservation, which has since been much reduced in size, was set apart at the junction of the Missouri and the Little Missouri Rivers for the Mandan, Arikara, and Hidatsa (see Tour 3A). Since the beginning of the century their numbers have increased by large percentages and at the present time they number approximately 1,720. The remnant of those Cheyenne who lived in North Dakota are now on reservations in south-central Montana and in Oklahoma.

The nomadic tribes, especially the Sioux, did not take as kindly to the white invasion as did the agricultural groups. However, of the principal disturbances involving this tribe—the Minnesota Massacre of 1862, which extended to Abercrombie within the limits of present North Dakota; Sibley's campaign to the Missouri in 1863; Sully's expeditions into Dakota in 1863–4; and the battle of the Little Big Horn in 1876, when General George A. Custer and five companies of cavalry were wiped out—none of these major conflicts involved the Sioux as a whole, but rather one or more of the seven Council Fires, as they call their tribal divisions. These seven groups are the Mdewakanton, Wahpekute, Sisseton, and Wahpeton, who inhabited the region about Lake Traverse and the Big Sioux River and east to the Mississippi; the Yankton and Yanktonai, who lived along the course of the James River; and the Teton, who dwelt west of the Missouri. The four Council Fires first named were responsible for the uprising and massacre in Minnesota in 1862, in which about 400 settlers and 100 white soldiers lost their lives. Sibley and Sully were sent into Dakota Territory in 1863–4 to punish the perpetrators of this massacre, but although they punished Sioux, they probably did not punish the offending bands (*see* HISTORY).

While all the Sioux were bitter in their objection to the whites, it was the Teton, or prairie Sioux, whose seven bands constituted more than one half the tribe, who were the most unremitting in their hostility. These bands were the Ogallala, Brulé, Hunkpapa, Blackfeet, Minneconjou, Sans Arcs, and Two Kettle. Of these the Hunkpapa and Ogallala were the most numerous. They were also probably the most inflexible in their determination not to yield to white sovereignty and formed the backbone of the Indian opposition in the disasters at Fort Phil Kearney in Wyoming and at the Little Big Horn in Montana.

The other North Dakota nomadic tribes did not give the newcomers as much trouble as did the Sioux. The Assiniboin were a wandering people, less certain of fixed habitation than the Sioux and Chippewa. In spite of the uncertainty of their lives and their constant warfare with the Sioux, in the early part of the nineteenth century they numbered about 1200 lodges. Not long afterward they were reduced by a plague of smallpox to less than 400 lodges.

The Chippewa made a treaty with the Government in 1815 after the border troubles incident to the War of 1812 and have since remained peaceful, almost all residing on reservations or allotted lands within their original territory in Michigan, Wisconsin, Minnesota, and North Dakota. At the close of the eighteenth century there were perhaps 25,000 Chippewa, while at the beginning of the twentieth there were in the neighborhood of 30,000, approximately 1000 of whom were in North Dakota.

The nomadic tribes now living in North Dakota are on three reservations. Over 1200 Sioux are at Fort Totten (*see Tour 6A*), while Standing Rock (*see Tour 8C*) has about 1,650 on the North Dakota side. On the Turtle Mountain Reservation (*see Tour 5*) there are about 6,450 Chippewas, most of whom are of mixed blood. The members of the Assiniboin tribe now live on reservations in Montana and Canada.

NORTH DAKOTA INDIAN TRIBES TODAY

Present-day North Dakota Indian life offers a vastly different picture from that which the Verendryes saw in 1738, or that which three fourths of a century later presented itself to Lewis and Clark. The lives of the groups on the various reservations bear many points in common. They have all been brought very quickly from the age of stone and thrust precipitately into the bright light of the modern world. They are all survivors of Indian nations whose ranges once extended from the forests of the Great Lakes to the Rockies, and from the prairies of western Canada to the Platte. Now on much restricted areas and amid a complex and alien culture they are endeavoring to build homes and rear children in a manner that will at once accord with the limitations set by the dominant white race, and yet retain what they feel is worthy in their own cultures and traditions.

In spite of these fundamental similarities, the material life of the Indians on the various reserves presents not only a mingling of white and Indian cultures but also somewhat wide differences in economic status. With the exception of that done at Fort Berthold, little farming is carried on, a situation not generally caused by lack of land; while more than 6400 Indians at Turtle Mountain are crowded into 72 square miles, and while the present homes of all of the tribes are rather infinitesimal in comparison with their former wide ranges, most of them do not lack space for farming. However, particularly at Standing Rock, a certain antipathy for the white man's settled mode of life, coupled with semi-arid conditions unfavorable to agriculture, have discouraged efforts along that line.

The land has been allotted in severalty for the most part, and the concept of individual ownership has in general been adopted, although there is a movement in the Standing Rock area to return to the communal form. A small amount of grazing and timber land is held tribally at Fort Berthold and Standing Rock, and the latter reservation has a tribal herd of 1500 cattle. Much Indian land is rented to whites for grazing or farming.

The relatively superior economic situation of the Fort Berthold Indians is doubtless due to the ancient agrarian background of the tribe. Long centuries of farming fitted them for ready adjustment to the agricultural life of the reservation. A general view of the farming section of their area presents an aspect not greatly unlike that of any other farming section in a similar territory. While many of them live in log houses of two to four rooms, others live in better buildings than those of the average rural district. Homes on the other reservations vary from primitive shacks and log cabins to modern dwellings, and are usually clustered about agencies or subagencies. In summertime many of the Indians, showing a longing for the old tipi life, live in tents placed in their yards and cook over open fires. Wikiups, improvised shelters of willows, are also used in fair weather.

Although the primitive food-gathering methods of hunting and fishing have no great economic value at the present time, the Indians still make use of their traditional knowledge of certain native foods and simple ways of preserving them. They dry much of their food, especially meat and vegetables. Among the Fort Berthold Indians one may still be offered pemmican, corn balls, butter from marrow, sausage, and tripe. Mint and balm leaves for tea, chokecherries, berries, red bean and tipsin roots, and wild onions, artichokes, and plums are still added to the larder. Rattlesnake oil, skunk oil, sweet grass, cedar-tree needles, and wild sage are used as medicines. In addition the Sioux at Standing Rock make *wakmiza wasna* by pounding corn meal and raisins into beef tallow, and forming the whole into small cakes. *Wojapi* is made of chokecherries, June berries, and flour, and some women add a little sugar to make a kind of pudding. Wild beans are taken from caches where they have been stored by mice, the supplies thus removed always being replaced with corn. *Kinnikinik* or *killiklik,* a mixture used for smoking, is made of dried and shredded red willow bark, sprinkled with tobacco.

Some basketry is still made, and most of the Indian groups do tanning and very good beadwork. Porcupine quills, horse hair, and feathers are employed in the designs in embroidery, and elk teeth, shells, colored clays, and weasel tails are used for adornments. Objects of Indian art are on display and for sale at the annual fairs on the reservations, and usually can be purchased at the agencies or subagencies.

Complicating the struggle for existence for most of the tribes is the prevalence of tuberculosis, of which one third of the people at Standing Rock are said to be victims. Trachoma also is common. In spite of these facts, however, the tribes are gaining rapidly in numbers, with an average birth rate more than twice as high as the death rate.

The Government has sought to aid the Indian in his transition to the new culture by giving him a part in the realm of political relations. All the reservations have native police, employed by the Government; and Standing Rock has two Indian police judges, who hear all cases and pass sentence on all minor Indian violations of law. At Turtle Mountain there are no Government restrictions in the use of land and stock, and the tribe has complete charge of property. All the Indian groups except that at Fort Totten have tribal councils, which, while their legal powers are not great, have considerable weight in an advisory capacity.

The acceptance by the tribes of the white man's fundamental educational principle of daily formal schooling has had a large part in their assimilation. Mission schools established by the various churches frequently brought the first formal education to the Indians, and most of the groups are still served by such schools. Small and large Government schools have been provided to give the Indian child the same educational opportunity as that afforded the white. Fort Totten and Turtle Mountain both have consolidated Indian schools, and a boarding school offering high-school work is maintained at Wahpeton.

In spite of their work in these schools and the fact that they are fast becoming fluent speakers of English, in most instances the Indians are retaining their native tongues. An exception to this is at Turtle Mountain, where owing to intermarriage of French and Indian the Algonquian mother tongue of the Chippewa is dying out.

While doubtless many ancient habits and customs are retained, such as those pertaining to marriage, formal tribal ceremonies do not appear to be conducted to any great extent at the present time. Marriage assumes the Christian form, and the Christian religion has been generally adopted, with the Catholic, Episcopalian, and Congregational faiths most commonly represented. The ancient tribal religions still exert a powerful influence, however—a fact especially evident at such times as the performance of the annual Arikara ceremonies on the Fort Berthold Reservation and the yearly sun dance of the Chippewa at Turtle Mountain. The large sun dance held at Little Eagle in South Dakota in 1936 by the Sioux of the Standing Rock Agency was the first conducted by that tribe in more than fifty years.

The Indians often participate in the social dances, such as the Omaha grass dance, the rabbit dance, and the hoop dance; and dancing in native costume can be seen occasionally, particularly during Fourth of July celebrations and at the annual fairs. The latter are held on most of the reservations some time in September and October. Music for the strictly Indian dancing consists of singing accompanied by drums—the small Indian hand drums or tom-toms, and the white man's big bass drum. Formerly a large drum of Indian manufacture was used; and rattles, string bells, and flutelike whistles are still made.

A great many group activities center at the schools and churches, where take place the usual athletic, social, and religious events and gatherings found in white communities.

History

THE Atlantic seaboard Colonies still constituted the American frontier on the April day in 1682 when the intrepid Sieur de la Salle, in the presence of a company of uncomprehending red men, took possession of the lands drained by the Mississippi River 'in the name of the Most High, Mighty, Invincible, and Victorious Prince, Louis the Great, by the Grace of God, King of France and Navarre, Fourteenth of that name.'

His words figuratively raised the flag of France over a vast territory which included more than half of what is now North Dakota. Two other European nations were to own parts of this State, and it was to be identified with nine United States Territories before actually becoming a member of the Union in 1889.

La Salle's *Procès Verbal* claimed for France the vast lands in the drainage basins of the Mississippi and its tributaries. All of this territory was ceded to Spain in 1762, to repay her for losses suffered as an ally of France. Adjustments of territorial possessions having been made between Spain and England, however, France 'suggested' that Spain cede back the lands, which she reluctantly did in 1800.

The Louisiana Purchase was negotiated in 1803, and the United States came into possession of the Mississippi basin, including the southwestern half of North Dakota. The northeastern part of the State, drained by the Red and Souris Rivers, was acquired from Great Britain in 1818, when a treaty fixed the Canadian-United States boundary at the Forty-ninth Parallel.

As the growth of the nation extended westward, this State successively became part of the Louisiana, Great Northwest, Missouri, Michigan, Wisconsin, Iowa, Minnesota, Nebraska, and finally Dakota Territories. For the three years from the formation of Minnesota to the creation of Dakota Territory, from 1858–61, almost all of the present State lying east of the Missouri was unorganized territory, without formal government of any kind.

Dakota Territory extended from the Canadian border to the Forty-third Parallel, and from Minnesota and Iowa to the main ridge of the Rockies. When Wyoming Territory was created in 1868 the present western boundary of the Dakotas was fixed, and the southern boundary of the Territory was settled in 1882. In the general election of 1887 residents voted that the Seventh Standard Parallel divide Dakota Territory into two States. President Benjamin Harrison signed the bills admitting North and South Dakota to statehood November 2, 1889: while he signed them, both documents were covered except for the signature space, so that it can never be known which of the twin Dakotas is the elder.

The two States derive their names from the Santee Sioux word *dakota,* which means 'allies.'

THE EARLY WHITE EXPLORERS

Pierre Gaultier de Varennes, Sieur de la Verendrye, was the first white man known to have entered what is now North Dakota. Like so many others of his time, Verendrye, a French-Canadian, was in search of the westward route to India. When the liberal Louis XV came to the throne of France he granted Verendrye permission to explore and claim new lands for France, in return for which Verendrye was to receive exclusive fur-trading privileges. With a fur monopoly to back him Verendrye succeeded in obtaining financial support for his venture, and in 1731 he and his party left Montreal for the explorations that were to occupy the remainder of his life.

It was in 1738 that, having established several forts in what later became Manitoba and Saskatchewan, he decided to visit the Indians called the Mantannes (Mandans), of whom he had heard. Accordingly he journeyed south and west, past the Pembina and Turtle Mountains, and eventually reached a Mandan village located a day's journey from the Missouri. Until 1936 this village was believed by historians to have been near Sanish, but in the light of recent discoveries at a site near Menoken, the latter is now thought by many historians to have been the village visited by the Verendrye party. This theory is substantiated by the journal of Verendrye, in which he states that he sent his sons to visit another village on the Missouri, a day's march distant (*see Tour 8*).

Of this trip to the Mandans, Verendrye wrote that their village consisted of 130 earth lodges and added, 'Their fortification . . . has nothing savage about it.' The people he described as 'of mixed blood, white and black. The women are rather handsome, particularly the light colored ones; some have an abundance of fair hair.' But later he records that he reproved his Assiniboin guides for telling him the Mandans were light-colored and asserted they had lied to him, whereupon they said the fair people of whom they spoke wore metal (armor) and were a summer's journey down the river.

The French party left the Mandan chief a lead tablet claiming the land in the King's name. What became of the tablet is unknown; a similar one, buried by a son of Verendrye on an expedition in 1743, was unearthed in 1913 at Fort Pierre, South Dakota.

This visit of Verendrye to North Dakota was his only trip into the region. Two of his sons passed through North Dakota again in 1742, on which expedition they reached either the Black Hills or the Big Horn Mountains. Unable to make any satisfactory progress toward the ocean, they returned to their friends the Mandans and thence to Fort la Reine in Manitoba.

Fifty years elapsed between the visits of the Verendryes and the next important exploration of North Dakota. In November 1797 David Thompson, an English geographer in the employ of the North West Company, was sent out to survey the boundary and visit the company posts. It was an unusually cold winter, and the party suffered intensely during the 68-day journey. They explored along the Assiniboine and Souris Rivers and the west edge of the Turtle Mountains, then turned southwest to the Missouri, where they visited the Mandans and Hidatsa.

Thompson in his journal has given a thorough account of the homes, manners, food, dress, and agricultural activities of these Indians. He noted that, while their villages were much alike, the Mandans were a more courteous and better-behaved group. Called 'the greatest practical land geographer in history,' Thompson later helped survey the boundary line between Canada and the United States in accordance with the Treaty of 1818. In commemoration of his exploration of this State a monument has been erected to him, in the shape of a large masonry sphere, at Verendrye (see Tour 7).

The same year that Thompson explored central North Dakota, Charles Chaboillez, a fur trader, came to Pembina to establish the first North West Company post within the present boundaries of this State. Both the Hudson's Bay and the XY Companies established posts in the same vicinity in 1801, and with three great companies in deadly competition, life at Pembina was colorful and dangerous. Excusing their own lack of scruples on the grounds of competition, the companies bought furs with liquor, giving rum to the Indians until they agreed to sell or until they were too stupefied to know when the pelts were taken from them.

Three years after the establishment of Chaboillez's post, Alexander Henry, a partner in the North West Fur Company, built a post on the Red River near the mouth of Park River and shortly afterward moved down to the mouth of the Pembina. He made frequent trips to the Grandes Fourches (Grand Forks) and established depots there and in the Hair Hills, or Pembina Mountains. On one occasion he made a trip to the Missouri to visit the Mandans, and his journal says of their farming methods: 'The whole view was agreeable and had more the appearance of a country inhabited by a civilized nation than by a set of savages.'

Liquor flowed freely at the Henry post. Traders found it profitable to deal with Indians who were in a drunken stupor. Henry's journal gives evidence that brawls were an everyday occurrence. One entry reads: 'Feb. 9, 1806. Men and women have been drinking a match for three days and nights, during which it has been drink, fight—drink, fight—drink, and fight again—guns, axes, and knives their weapons—very disagreeable.' Henry left Pembina in 1808 for the Saskatchewan River.

At his post were born North Dakota's first two children of other than Indian parentage. The first, the daughter of Pierre Bonza, Henry's Negro servant, who had formerly been a slave in the West Indies, was born March 12, 1802.

The first white child was born December 29, 1807, to the 'Orkney Lad,' a woman who had worked at the post for several years in the guise of a man, until the birth of the child betrayed her sex. Abandoned by the child's father, John Scart, she remained at the post until a collection was taken up and she and the baby were sent back to her home in the Orkney Islands.

President Jefferson for some time had been eager to have a party explore the Missouri, cross the Rockies, and reach the Pacific. In 1803 the Louisiana Purchase facilitated completion of his plans, and his secretary, Captain Meriwether Lewis, with a friend, Captain William Clark, started out on the journey of exploration.

On October 13, 1804, the expedition came up the Missouri River into what is now North Dakota. Near the present site of Stanton, where the Knife River joins the Missouri, Lewis and Clark discovered villages of the Mandans and Hidatsa. Having been well received, they decided to establish winter quarters. Fort Mandan was built and the flag of the United States of America raised for the first time on North Dakota soil. It was here that the explorers secured the services of Charbonneau, the French interpreter, and his wife Sakakawea, the Shoshone Indian girl who accompanied the expedition to the Pacific and rendered outstanding service (*see* BISMARCK).

After spending the winter with the friendly Indians, the expedition in April 1805 set out along the river again, following its course into Montana. Their journey through the mountains to the Pacific by pack horses and swift-flowing streams is one of the most thrilling adventures in American history.

The party returned in September 1806 to the Hidatsa village on the Missouri, where Lewis and Clark, taking leave of their faithful guide, set out for St. Louis and home. The careful observations recorded in the journals of their party are a valuable contribution to the history of this region.

Lewis and Clark were not the only explorers to visit the Missouri region in the early nineteenth century. A decade before they came, traders were already ascending the river, and in the succeeding year naturalists and military men added their presence to the growing, if transient, white population. Among the many who left interesting records of their explorations and travels were Charles le Raye, who spent three years as a captive of the Brulé Sioux; Manuel Lisa, one of the most important fur traders on the upper Missouri; General William Ashley, Colonel Henry Leavenworth, and General Henry Atkinson, who subdued the Arikara; and Wilson P. Hunt of the Astorian Overland Expedition. Two royal adventurers visited here: Paul Wilhelm, Prince of Wurttemberg, who is said to have taken Sakakawea's son back to Germany with him; and Maximilian, Prince of Wied, who brought with him the Swiss artist Carl Bodmer, whose paintings preserve much of the life and customs of the Mandans. George Catlin, a native artist, was aboard the first steamboat to reach the Yellowstone. He painted and wrote about the Missouri Indians and left hundreds of pictures of their life. John James Audubon, noted naturalist, spent several months in present North Dakota studying the larger types of North American mammals.

ON THE FRONTIER

The earliest attempt at colonization in this State was the Selkirk settlement in 1812 at Pembina in the Red River Valley. The Earl of Selkirk

had arranged for the transportation of a group of evicted Scotch and
Irish peasants to the Hudson Bay region in Canada, and some of the
emigrants had followed the Red River south and settled at Pembina.
The fur traders in that vicinity, however, were not eager to have the
wild country inhabited. They made life miserable for the Selkirk settlers, and finally succeeded in driving most of the newcomers out.

Among the fur companies of that time were two famous competitors,
the Hudson's Bay and the North West Companies. Others were the
Missouri Fur Company, Chouteau and Berthold, Northwestern, Colum-
bia, and Sublette & Campbell, the latter company establishing a post,
Fort William, on the site later occupied by Fort Buford military post.
John Jacob Astor established the American Fur Company, and for years
Fort Union, on North Dakota's western border, was that company's
principal post. (*See Tour 6B.*)

Some of northeastern North Dakota's most noted pioneers came into
this region as fur traders. Joseph Rolette was sent to Pembina by the
American Fur Company in 1842. A member of the Minnesota Territorial Legislature, he was responsible for keeping the capital at St.
Paul. Norman Kittson, who established a fur-trading post at Pembina
in 1843, became the first postmaster, in 1851, in what is now North
Dakota. He, too, was a member of the Minnesota Territorial Legislature.
Charles Cavileer, while not a fur trader, was a contemporary of these
men and acted as collector of customs at Pembina.

The coming of settlers marked the decline of the fur trade, but at
its height it had been colorful. Lewis Crawford, a North Dakota historian, has written:

In this early race for empire none except fur seekers entered. Their
rhythmic paddle blades swished up every stream of the West to its
rivulet head; every mountain height and forbidding gorge knew their
intrepid feet. . . Every nationality had a part. . . These were the
true pathfinders, the true explorers, the heralds of empire. Their fur-
laden vessels floating down the familiar waters of the Missouri and its
tributaries represented the wealth, the adventure, the romance of the
Northwest.

In the time of the fur trader the Missouri River, the 'Smoky Water'
of the Indians, was navigable, though as turbulent and capricious as it
is today. It was the highway of the trader and later of the gold seeker.
The first steamboat to navigate the Missouri through North Dakota was
the *Yellowstone,* which in 1832 ascended the river to Fort Union. To
operate a boat on this river required great skill.

Famous pilots in the heyday of the steamboat who wrestled with the wiles of the Missouri included Joseph LaBarge, Grant Marsh, and C. J. Atkins. In 63 years as a pilot Grant Marsh wrecked but one boat on the Mississippi and never had a wreck on the Missouri or Yellowstone.

The yellow gleam of gold, discovered in Montana in 1863 and 1864, drew a rush of prospectors. The railroads had not yet penetrated this territory, and the Missouri was the pathway to the gold fields. Precious cargoes of yellow dust floated down through Dakota, bound for St. Louis. It is said that one boat, the *Luella,* carried gold dust to the value of $1,250,000 down the river in 1866.

It was not the coming of the railroads to Bismarck in 1873 that marked the decline of the steamboat on the Missouri, but rather the extension of the railroad westward to Montana in 1883.

The Red River of the North was the important channel of traffic for northeastern North Dakota. Steamboats were not as numerous as they were on the Missouri, nor were they operated at such an early date. Fleets of barges and scows were used to transport provisions. The steamer *Selkirk* commanded by Captain Alexander Griggs, best known of Red River pilots, brought passengers down the river to settle at Grand Forks the year after he and his crew had unexpectedly spent the winter there (*see* GRAND FORKS).

In Territorial days United States military posts were numerous but short-lived. Fort Abercrombie on the west bank of the Red River, about 12 miles north of the site of Wahpeton, was established in 1857. Supplies for this post were brought from St. Paul. When the Sioux went on the warpath in 1862, Minnesota settlers sought refuge here during a seven weeks' siege. The fort was abandoned in 1877 (*see Tour* 1).

Fort Rice, on the west bank of the Missouri, came next. General Alfred H. Sully's men cut cottonwood trees to build it in 1864. The fort housed four infantry companies. It was to Fort Rice in 1870 that Linda Slaughter, young, talented, followed her husband, Dr. Frank Slaughter. Her writings, depicting the frontier life, found their way into many eastern papers, and today constitute some of the best material on that era of State history. At Fort Rice she buried her first-born child, her only son, in the bitter cold of January. She heard the arrows of hostile Indians whizzing dangerously near. Her luxuriant hair, which she always wore long over her shoulders, was coveted as a scalp lock, and she came near leaving it with the red men on one of her horseback jaunts from the fort. A woman who could paint, write, or lecture

Nesting colony of ring-billed gulls on an island in Lake Harriet, near Arena, Photo by Russell Reid

asque flowers

Photo by Russell Reid

Richardson's ground squirrel or 'flickertail'
Photo by Russell Reid

Little Soldier, Hunkpapa Siou
Photo by Russell Reid

caffold burial, formerly used by some Indian tribes

Ancient Indian turtle effigy

Photo by Russell Re

North Dakota in 1879, from an old map of Dakota Territory

Sitting Bull

Photo by D. F. Barry

General George A. Custer
From Tenting on the Plains, by E. B. Custer

Battle of the Badlands, 1864; from a drawing by Sergeant F. Brandt, who particpated in the battle

A sod shanty of early days
Photo from the State Historical Society of North Dakota

Norwegian folk dancing

An early school in Oliver County, 1883

Ole Anderson farm, west of Portland

Threshing

Statue of Sakakawea, Bismarck   Photo by Russell Re

at will, she could also cook or nurse as the occasion demanded. In later days she wrote the first telegram that was sent to the world from Edwinton, the village that became Bismarck.

Fort Rice was dismantled in 1878, when Fort Yates, to the south, took its place. Fort Ransom on the Sheyenne was established in 1867. In 1872 Fort Seward, first called Fort Cross, was built at Jamestown. The military reservations of Fort Abercrombie and Fort Seward were opened to homestead entry in 1880.

Fort Totten, near Devils Lake, was constructed in 1867 and served until 1890, when the buildings were turned over to the Indian school. Fort Stevenson on the Missouri at the mouth of Douglas Creek was maintained from 1867–83. Fort Buford was built in 1866 opposite the mouth of the Yellowstone on the north bank of the Missouri. After his surrender in 1877, Chief Joseph was taken through Fort Buford en route to Fort Leavenworth, Kansas, and Chiefs Gall and Sitting Bull went there to surrender after their escape into Canada (*see Tour 6B*). The fort existed officially until 1895, but sometime before its abandonment the garrison had been transferred to Fort Assiniboine in Montana.

Established on the Red River near the site of Pembina, Fort Pembina was maintained from 1870 to 1895. Fort McKeen, established in 1872, became, the same year, part of Fort Abraham Lincoln, garrisoned until 1891. It was from Fort Abraham Lincoln that Custer and his Seventh Cavalry marched to death and disaster on the banks of the Little Big Horn in 1876 (*see* FORT ABRAHAM LINCOLN STATE PARK). After 25 years of occupation, Fort Yates was abandoned in 1903, when the new Fort Lincoln was built near Bismarck with facilities for four companies of infantry and supporting detachments. (*See Tour 8.*)

These early forts were established to protect the settlers along the frontier and to keep the Indians in order. It was after the Sioux outbreak in Minnesota in 1862 that General Henry H. Sibley was sent to punish the Sioux. In June of 1863 he headed his army west from Minnesota toward the Devils Lake region, where he arrived to find the Indians had gone south. He pursued them and on July 24 engaged them in battle at Big Mound about seven miles north of the present town of Tappen. They retreated, and he followed them to Dead Buffalo Lake, northwest of Dawson, where July 26 another engagement was fought. Two days later he met them again at Stony Lake northeast of Driscoll, but the Sioux retreated rapidly and there was no fighting. Moving on toward the Missouri, Sibley encamped on Apple Creek, seven miles east of the present site of Bismarck, and again near its mouth. The Sioux fled across the river.

Sibley, all along the route, had thrown up defensive earthworks at each of his camps. All of these camp sites which were not plowed under have been definitely located under direction of the State historical society.

General Alfred H. Sully was to have met Sibley on the Missouri, but no contact could be made and Sibley set out for Minnesota on August 1, 1863. Sully came up the river from Sioux City, and was near Long Lake when he learned that Sibley had gone home and the Sioux had recrossed the Missouri and departed for the James River. Sully gave chase—he had been sent out to fight Indians, and fight them he would. The Battle of Whitestone Hill, near Ellendale, followed. Whether the Indians Sully fought had taken part in the Minnesota uprising is today regarded as dubious, but the battle is said to have been the fiercest ever fought on North Dakota soil. The field is now marked by a monument of a cavalry trooper (*see Tour 2*).

Sully returned to Sioux City but was sent back the following year to deal out still more punishment to the Sioux. After Fort Rice had been established a scouting detachment was sent after the evasive red men and soon reported Sioux near Killdeer Mountain. Here an engagement was fought July 28, 1864, in which the Indians were severely punished, although afterwards it developed that few of them were Minnesota Sioux.

The troops proceeded up the Little Missouri, where Indians were discovered near Medora. With difficulty Sully traversed 12 miles of Badlands buttes and gullies, continually harassed by the sniping fire of Indians along the route. The fighting of this day is known as the Battle of the Badlands. Following this encounter Sully reached the Yellowstone and returned down the Missouri.

Before he arrived at Fort Rice, he was informed that Captain James L. Fisk, with a party of immigrants, was in danger. Fisk, who had made expeditions through North Dakota in 1862 and 1863, on this trip followed Sully's trail and in the Badlands was attacked September 1 by Indians, with the loss of several men. During the next few days several other attacks were made, although no one was killed. Messengers were sent to Sully for aid, and meanwhile the party threw up what fortifications they could in the form of sod walls and awaited help. After several days the soldiers arrived and brought the immigrants back to Fort Rice, whence most of them returned to their homes. The remains of their impromptu fortification, known as Fort Dilts, can still be seen (*see Tour* 9).

One of the most valuable expeditions made through this State was the Stevens Survey of 1853, sent out to discover the most advantageous routes to the Pacific for future railroads. The party was financed by a Federal appropriation, and the northern route, through present North Dakota, was under the direction of General I. I. Stevens.

The guide on this expedition was Pierre Bottineau, one of the outstanding personalities in the history of North Dakota and Minnesota during this period. Of him it has been written that

It was the guide Bottineau who walked from Winnipeg to St. Paul with James J. Hill, it was the scout Bottineau who headed Jay Cooke's first Northern Pacific survey across the continent, it was the chief Bottineau who gave his name to Bottineau County, and it was the gambler Bottineau who had three queens in his hand, staked Nicollet Island, and lost.

In 1871 the Whistler expedition went up the Little Missouri and into Montana in search of the most practical route for a railway to the Pacific. Two years later the Stanley expedition, accompanied by a large military escort, conducted another western survey. Engagements with Indians cost this expedition a number of men. One Sioux, Rain-in-the-Face, claimed to have had a part in killing two civilian on the Stanley Survey and, as a result, was imprisoned at Fort Lincoln until he escaped. He gained his revenge at the Little Big Horn (*see Tour 8C*).

The Northern Pacific Railway received its charter from the Government in 1864. Magnificent Federal land grants were made: still the road found it difficult to raise the necessary capital to finance the venture, and Jay Cooke & Company undertook the sale of Northern Pacific securities.

On the last day of the year 1871 the line was completed to the Red River at Moorhead, and early in March of the next year it was extended to Fargo. Cooke went into bankruptcy after the financial panic of 1873, but was able to obtain private funds to complete the road to the Missouri that year. Bismarck remained the western terminus of the line until 1879. During the next two years rails were laid to the Montana border, completing the line across the entire State.

In 1870, just before the advent of the railways, the estimated white population of present North Dakota was not more than five hundred. Pembina County, extending the length of the Red River Valley and to the western population limit, was the only organized county in the State.

The Northern Pacific was completed to the Pacific Coast in 1883. Squatters preceded the railroad, settlers followed it, trying to guess future town sites so they could force the company to buy them out at the most profitable price.

The Great Northern was the second important railroad to come into the State. By 1882 James J. Hill, the 'Empire Builder,' had extended a line up the Dakota side of the Red River to Canada. Hill had a vision of a great railroad connecting the Pacific Coast with the Great Lakes, whence produce could be cheaply transported to New York. Construction began in 1880 and the Great Northern was extended westward across northern North Dakota and in 1893 reached the Coast.

The railroads linked Dakota with the East and civilization, but to the west was the frontier. Here Sioux warriors were beginning to resent the encroaching whites and the appropriation of their hunting grounds. It was imperative, therefore, that soldiers be kept at Fort Abraham Lincoln.

To understand the campaign of 1876 against the Sioux, in which General George A. Custer met his tragic end, it is necessary to go back to the Indian treaty of 1868. The Government by this pact promised to abandon and destroy Forts Reno and Phil Kearney in Wyoming and Fort Smith in Montana. This having been done, the Sioux were guaranteed their freedom in the territory between the North Platte and the Missouri and Yellowstone Rivers. But, when gold was discovered in the Black Hills by a Government reconnaissance expedition under Custer in the summer of 1874, white settlers and prospectors begged for admission to the coveted territory. Military guards at first attempted to keep them out, but when the Indians refused in a treaty council in 1875 to sell or lease land to miners, the Government withdrew the guard and settlers poured in by thousands.

Government officials were well aware, when the treaty of 1868 was violated, that an Indian war was inevitable; but although the Government had clearly brought the war down on its own head, it sought the appearance of righteousness.

It was the practice of many Indians to leave their reservations because they wanted to hunt or visit, or because the practices of dishonest agents made life on the reservation unbearable. The Department of the Interior sent out orders for all Indians to be back on their reservations at a certain date, but for many it was impossible to return within the time limit set. The Department designated these people as 'hostiles' and turned them over to the War Department, which now had a pretext for taking punitive action.

The campaign of 1876 was planned to force the Indians onto reservations, in order to obtain the relinquishment of the Black Hills. Generals Crook and Gibbon, with their forces, were to meet Generals Terry and Custer with their troops near the Rosebud River in Montana. All were then to move southward against the Indians who were in the hills along the Rosebud and the Little Big Horn.

On the morning of May 17, 1876, the eastern division of the expedition started out from Fort Abraham Lincoln. The cavalry marched about the parade grounds to the tune of *Garry Owen,* then set out to the strains of *The Girl I Left Behind Me.* Mrs. Custer accompanied her husband on the first day's ride, returning to the fort as the troopers continued west.

The tragic outcome of the Battle of the Little Big Horn is well known. Not a man of Custer's immediate command survived. The reasons for the annihilation have been debated far and wide. General E. S. Godfrey, who participated in the battle as a lieutenant, in *Custer's Last Battle* summarizes the affair as follows: 'The causes of Custer's defeat were first, the overpowering number of the enemy and their unexpected cohesion; second, Reno's panic rout from the valley; third, the defective extraction of empty cartridge shells from the carbines . . . A battle was unavoidable.'

Grant Marsh had pushed his supply steamer, the *Far West,* up the Big Horn to within 15 miles of the battlefield. Reno's wounded were placed aboard and Marsh made the trip of 710 miles down to Bismarck in record time. At midnight July 5 the *Far West* docked. Colonel Lounsberry, editor of the Bismarck *Tribune* and correspondent of the New York *Herald,* gave the story to the world. Mark Kellogg, special correspondent of the *Herald* and the *Tribune,* who had accompanied the expedition, had been killed with Custer. Twenty-six widows wept at Fort Lincoln. With Custer's death the frontier era in Dakota history had ended. Although Sitting Bull's forces were undefeated, they took refuge in Canada and remained there until 1881, when they voluntarily surrendered.

They were returned to the reservations. Wishing to keep them there, the authorities took horses, saddles, and arms from both hostile and peaceable Sioux. This move, while it did not pacify the Indians, put an end to the Indian wars.

TERRITORIAL SOLONS AND STRATEGY

At the time of the Little Big Horn campaign, Dakota's Territorial Government had functioned for 15 years and was destined to continue 13 years longer. The Territory had been organized in 1861 and President Lincoln had appointed his family physician, Dr. William Jayne, first Governor. As first laid out the new Territory included the present States of North Dakota, South Dakota, Montana, and Wyoming, but after a series of changes it was reduced in 1882 to the area of the present Dakotas.

Yankton, in the southern part of the Territory, was the capital city, and there the first legislature met in 1862. It was an assembly representative of every type in the Territory—all with great and varying ideas of how the ship of state was to be kept afloat.

Thirteen members composed the house, while the senate or council had but nine. In attendance at the session for various reasons were Jim Somers, frontiersman, 'armed like an arsenal'; Father Turner of New York; George Kingsbury, newspaperman; Dr. Walter Burleigh, later connected with the Indian Service and the Northern Pacific Railway; and General T. C. Campbell.

Territorial Dakota displayed no small interest in politics. Campaigns were periods of great excitement, with long parades of ardent supporters following the candidates, with cheering and shouting and bragging and fighting by office seekers and votaries alike. It took a brave man to campaign in those days. When Moses Armstrong ran for Congress on the Democratic ticket, his friend General T. C. Campbell invited him into his part of the Territory to speak. During the General's speech his hat was shot off, but his oratory did not falter. When it came Armstrong's turn to speak, he hesitated about addressing such a boisterous crowd, but the General informed him that the time to do his praying was before he crossed the county line, not after.

County-seat removals were a prime source of political interest, and the cities in the Territory fought tooth and nail for the privileges of the county capital. Stuffing ballot boxes was not uncommon, and in many instances where removal was voted the defeated city would refuse to give up the county records, and guards would be posted against nocturnal raids of the courthouse vaults by citizens of the victorious town. When the Emmons County *Record* defeated a plan to move the county seat from Williamsport in 1888, it took full advantage of its success. Beneath the decoration of a crowing cock heading the column, these headlines, typical of the county-seat controversies, appeared in the *Record* November 9 of that year:

ELI

And Billsport Hath The
Appellation Earned,
For Lo! She Doth Get There
With Both Feet.
And She Moppeth the Earth
With the Cohorts of the Wicked.
Yea, Verily, of the Wadites,
of the Bumstedites, and
the Vanbekites,
And They Shall Gnaw a File and
Flee Into the Mountains
of Hepsidam.
FE! FI! FO! FUM!

The entire edition, in celebration of the occasion, was printed in red ink.

Territorial Governors and other high officials were not popular with the people. They were usually from the East and had no interest in the country, their salaries or political advancement being their chief concern. Just after the first legislature had adjourned, an Indian uprising disturbed the settlers. It did not take the Governor and other officials long to quit the Territory. Moses Armstrong, later a Congressman, wrote, 'With such rapidity do they fly, pale and breathless, that a boy could play marbles on their horizontal coat tails.'

Dakota Territory covered about 150,000 square miles and had 36 representatives in the legislature during the 1880's for its population of 300,000. Four judges and three prosecuting attorneys administered matters of Territorial justice.

The second legislative session was no quieter than the first. Because of disputed delegations there were two houses—one met on the levee by the Missouri and the other on the hill above the river. After much time had been lost the differences were compromised and business proceeded.

In 1863 Newton Edmunds of Yankton was appointed Governor of Dakota, the only resident of the Territory ever to hold that office. The next Governor was Faulk of Pennsylvania, then followed Burbank of Indiana, Pennington of Alabama, Howard of Michigan, Ordway of

Vermont, Pierce of New York and Illinois, Church of New York and Indiana, and Mellette of Indiana.

The northern and southern parts of the Territory had little in common, and they kept growing farther apart as time went on. In the session of 1883 removal of the capital from Yankton was the big question. Yankton wanted to keep it, Bismarck, Huron, Mitchell, Pierre, and Chamberlain wanted to acquire it, and Fargo or Jamestown would have taken it if offered. A bill was finally passed providing that the Governor appoint 9 commissioners to choose a capital city; they were to accept an offer of not less than $100,000 and 160 acres of land on which the capitol was to be built. The land remaining after the capitol grounds were provided for was to be sold for the benefit of the building fund.

The commissioners named were Milo Scott of Grand Forks County, Burleigh Spalding of Cass, Alexander McKenzie of Burleigh, Charles Myers of Spink, George Mathews of Brookings, Alexander Hughes of Yankton, Henry de Long of Lincoln, John P. Belding of Lawrence, and M. B. Thompson of Clay.

The commissioners must, according to law, meet and organize at Yankton. Feeling ran high; the city did not intend to part with the capital without a struggle. Yanktonians awaited the commissioners.

But unknown to the citizens of Yankton, the commissioners had chartered a special train, leaving Sioux City April 3, at 3 a.m. The commissioners' coach was dimly lighted as the train pulled into the city limits of Yankton. The meeting was quickly called to order, officers were chosen, and the meeting was adjourned until that afternoon in Canton. The train had still a half mile to go to the city limits when the meeting was over. The commissioners had satisfied the law, having met, organized, and adjourned in Yankton.

The commission thereafter made the rounds of several towns and was royally entertained by prospective capital cities. Bismarck's offer of $100,000 and 320 acres of land was the best bid received. Thus Bismarck became the Territorial capital.

The cornerstone ceremonies took place September 5, 1883. Many high officials and prominent citizens from the East were guests of the Northern Pacific on the Villard 'last spike' excursion and were present as guests of honor at the laying of the cornerstone. Among them were Henry Villard, president of the Northern Pacific Railway; General Grant; General Haupt; Henry M. Teller, Secretary of the Interior; the Hon. Sackville-West, British Minister; members of the Austro-Hungarian, the Danish, and the Norwegian-Swedish Legations; the Imperial German Minister; Territorial Governor Ordway; and numerous United States senators, governors, and mayors.

The next great task was to convince Congress that the Territory was ready for statehood. As early as 1871 the legislature had requested Congress to divide the Territory, and in 1874 Moses Armstrong, while in Congress, had petitioned that the northern part be made into a new Territory named Pembina. Nearly every year a petition was sent to Congress praying for admission as two States. In 1880 it was suggested that the northern part be called North Dakota. The Territorial legislative assembly in 1889 provided that a constitutional convention be held for North Dakota, and February 22, 1889, Congress passed an enabling act for North Dakota, South Dakota, Washington, and Montana.

Delegates to the State convention were elected May 14, 1889, and the convention met in Bismarck July 4 of that year. A parade in which Sitting Bull and other famous Indians participated was part of the entertainment afforded the delegates. Election to approve or disapprove the proposed constitution was held October 1, 1889, and as it was a certainty that the constitution would be accepted, legislators, State officials, and congressmen were elected at the same time. President Harrison on November 2, 1889, declared North Dakota a State, and John Miller at the same moment became first Governor of North Dakota.

Hand in hand with the political development of the Territory had gone social and economic progress. By the time statehood was attained, farmhouses and towns had broken up the barren loneliness of the prairies. Sod shanties, the pioneers' first homes, were being replaced by solid frame structures. Huge bonanza farms were employing hundreds of men and using advanced farming methods that had not yet been introduced on farms in the East (see AGRICULTURE AND FARM LIFE). Schools were being built in every community. Six years before statehood, one private college had been established, and the University of North Dakota had opened its doors and was offering courses in the arts and sciences to ambitious pioneer youth.

POLICIES AND POLITICS SINCE STATEHOOD

When the constitutional convention for North Dakota completed its work on August 17, 1889, the product of its labors was a document six times as long as the Federal Constitution. Based upon a model constitution drawn up by Professor James Bradley Thayer of the Harvard Law School, it contained extremely advanced and enlightened provisions, 217 sections included in 20 articles. To these have since been added 49 amendments.

The civic pattern adopted was very similar to that in force in the older States. The legislative branch in North Dakota consists of a bicameral legislature which meets in January each odd-numbered year. The executive branch is headed by the Governor, who is elected for a term of two years. He has the general veto power and authority to reject any item in an appropriation bill. The judicial department consists of a supreme court of five members, elected for ten-year terms; district courts, county courts, and justices of the peace .The State is divided into six judicial districts, each one under an elective district judge. County courts are courts of record concerned with such matters as probate and guardianship, but in counties having county courts of increased jurisdiction such courts have concurrent jurisdiction with district courts in certain cases.

The State is divided into counties, whose administrative functions are carried out by boards of commissioners elected every two years. Any city or village of 500 population or more may choose either the commission form of government or the mayor and council type.

The framework of government is perhaps not very different from that in many other States. It is the legislation in North Dakota that has been anything but a copy of that in any sister State, and the outcome of some of her political experiments has often been of nationwide interest. The economy of the State is preponderantly rural, and the tendency has therefore been to try anything that seemed likely to help in the solution of the farmer's problems.

The legislature of the State of North Dakota met for the first time November 19, 1889. This session lasted 120 days, but the length of all subsequent sessions was fixed by the constitution at 60 days. The first men this State sent to the United States Senate were Gilbert Pierce of Fargo and Lyman Casey of Jamestown. H. C. Hansbrough of Devils Lake was the first Congressman. The supreme court had for its chief justice Guy C. H. Corliss, and Joseph M. Bartholomew and Alfred Wallin were associate justices.

In this first session the legislature instituted a department of agriculture for 'the promotion of stock-breeding, agriculture, horticulture, manufactures and domestic arts.' A school law enacted at this session was an enlightened and detailed piece of legislation. North Dakota had at the beginning of statehood a well-organized school system of 1,362 public schools with 1,741 teachers; a State university at Grand Forks; Catholic schools at Fargo, Grand Forks, and Bismarck; a Congregational college at Fargo; a Presbyterian college at Jamestown; and at Tower City a Baptist college, which, however, failed to survive.

One of the most exciting battles of the first legislative session was the bill to license the Louisiana Lottery. Rumors circulated to the effect that bribery was being practiced, that the lobbyists for the lottery were making liberal offers for votes. The Governor and his friends had hired detectives from the Pinkerton Agency to mingle with the legislators and lobbyists. When the detectives had all the information they needed, they revealed their identity to the lottery supporters. Fearing exposure, the lottery enthusiasts gave up the fight and the bill was killed.

North Dakota was faced with the drought problem during the administration of Governor Andrew Burke (1891-2), and the people looked to the legislature for some solution to their problems. Their petitions were not at all times considered seriously. One member offered a resolution praying Congress to pass a law establishing a scientific rain bureau and a law offering a reward to anyone discovering a practical system of producing rainfall. The house referred his resolution to the temperance committee.

At the beginning of statehood North Dakota had been subject to a rather autocratic form of government in spite of decidedly democratic constitutional provisions. The State had been economically dependent on the East. The directing powers in the early State government were centered in St. Paul and Minneapolis. Eastern wealth had furnished capital for the railroads, and the railroads had been responsible for the settlement of the State. Likewise, the farmer's crops had also to be sold in the East, and his machinery and supplies must necessarily be purchased there.

At the time North Dakota was admitted to the Union the Republican Party was in control. Democrats at that time in State history and for long afterward were few and far between. These two old-line parties were the only two worthy of note in this early period, although the Populists polled a large vote in the first presidential election and North Dakota divided its first electoral vote, one vote going to the Democratic, one to the Republican, and one to the Populist candidate.

The railroads and financial interests of St. Paul and Minneapolis had very early begun interfering in North Dakota politics. Judson LaMoure and Alexander McKenzie were the lords of this era, both representing railroad interests in State politics, and the favors they were able to bestow were a safeguard against legislation hostile to the companies. In time they came to be the protectors of other interests, including banks, insurance companies, line elevators, and lumber companies.

The first revolt against this system came in 1892. Governor Andrew Burke had vetoed a bill favored by the Farmers' Alliance that would force railroads to lease sites or rights-of-way for grain elevators and warehouses. The Farmers' Alliance, Democrats, and Populists fused, and Eli C. D. Shortridge was elected Governor.

In Governor Shortridge's administration the legislature passed a bill for highway improvement. Money was appropriated to enlarge the State capitol building.

The tendency of legislation during the session of 1893 was definitely toward the principles of the Populist platform. During Shortridge's administration North Dakota attempted its first State ownership venture: $100,000 was appropriated to build a State elevator at Duluth, Superior, or West Superior. The panic of 1893 came on and the plan was not carried out. In 1894 Roger Allin, regular Republican, was elected Governor, and with that election the first brief rebellion against Eastern capitalism was ended.

Governor Allin felt it necessary to veto several appropriations in order to keep within the probable revenue, and State institutions had practically no funds for operation. In the case of the university, salary was provided for the janitor but not for the faculty. President Merrifield and the faculty preferred to serve without any pay rather than close the institution, and necessary expenditures were met by private subscription. Other institutions were kept open in the same way.

During the administration of Governor Frank Briggs (1897–8) the Spanish-American War broke out. The entire National Guard volunteered its services, but many members could not be accepted because of the quota set for North Dakota. North Dakota volunteers took part in 30 engagements and skirmishes during the Philippine insurrection.

Governor Briggs died in July 1898 and his term was completed by the Lieutenant Governor, Joseph M. Devine, who later served several years as commissioner of immigration. Both Briggs and Devine were Republicans, and they were succeeded in 1898 by another member of their party, Frederick B. Fancher, a leader in the Farmers' Alliance. Fancher declined a second term and was succeeded by Major Frank White, who had served in the Philippines. White found the State debt the chief problem of his administration. He served two terms and yielded his office to E. Y. Sarles.

Legislation during Sarles' term tended toward control and regulation of corporations. A board was created to supervise State banks, and the manner of organizing insurance companies in the State was prescribed.

Sarles was defeated for re-election by 'Honest John' Burke, a Democrat, and the first Governor of this State to serve three terms. He then left North Dakota to become United States Treasurer under President Wilson and later served as chief justice of the North Dakota Supreme Court, remaining a member of the court until his death in 1937. Crawford, in his history of North Dakota, has said, 'The legislative history of the Burke administrations is an instructive illustration of the ideals and motives which were so characteristic of the [Theodore] Roosevelt era.' State institutions were liberally provided for, a primary election law was enacted, prohibition laws were enforced, schools were improved, and various regulatory offices and boards were created.

A second revolution in North Dakota political history was ushered in with the election of Burke. The Progressive Republicans, enthusiastic supporters of the so-called 'La Follette reforms,' had formed a coalition with the Democrats to elect this first Democrat Governor of North Dakota. 'It was,' according to Judge Andrew Bruce in his book *The Non-Partisan League*, 'the revolution which laid the foundations for the present Non-Partisan League, for in it the farmers found a new war cry and new objects of anathema. The war cry was "North Dakota for North Dakotans" and the objects of their anathema were "Big Business, McKenzie, and McKenzieism." '

Governor Louis B. Hanna succeeded Burke in 1913. In 1912, a presidential election year, North Dakota's electoral votes went to Woodrow Wilson. New apportionment gave this State three representatives in Congress instead of two. Governor Hanna asserted his belief in businesslike administration of government offices and revised the accounting methods in State departments. Throughout this period tendencies in the State were progressive: social legislation was favored; the State grew rapidly in population; new towns were springing up; the automobile age had arrived.

Through all this ran the thread of the second political revolution, which Burke's election had begun and which was continued through the Hanna administration. It was directed principally against injustices in the grain trade. Farmers were incapable of developing their own marketing facilities. Millions had been invested in the mills and elevators of St. Paul, Minneapolis, and Duluth, and in the 'line' (corporation) elevator companies throughout North Dakota. The farmers complained of unfair methods of grading and docking their grain; they claimed that the Minneapolis Chamber of Commerce was a closed corporation, and that its members were identified with the big milling and elevator interests. Even conservative Senator McCumber of North Dakota protested in 1916 before the United States Senate against abuses in the grain trade.

The Equity Exchange had been organized in 1909 to act as a farmers' general selling agency in St. Paul, but had been denied membership in the Minneapolis Chamber of Commerce. The Society of Equity and the Equity Exchange tried to get a bill through the 1915 legislature for the establishment of a State-owned elevator, but the attempt failed. Indignation at the defeat of the bill resulted in the birth, in February 1915, of a new political party, the Nonpartisan [1] League.

A. C. Townley, a genius in the art of organization, spread the league gospel through the State. Townley had begun life in poverty, had failed in a large-scale flax-growing enterprise, and had for a time been identified with the Socialist Party. A. C. Bowen suggested the formation of the league, and Walter Thomas Mills drafted many of its laws. Charles Edward Russell was the first editor of the newspaper, the *Non-Partisan Leader*. All three of these men were Socialists.

After winning the support of a prominent farmer, Fred Wood, and his two sons, the movement spread rapidly. Before the end of the first year the league had 30,000 members. Its platform embodied five planks:

1. State ownership of terminal elevators, flour mills, packing houses, and cold storage plants.
2. State inspection of grain and grain dockage.
3. Exemption of farm improvements from taxation.
4. State hail insurance on the acreage tax basis.
5. Rural credit banks operated at cost.

'Practical salesmanship, a program of immediate and forceful action and the use of the Ford automobile are the factors principally explaining the rise of the Non-Partisan League,' declares Herbert Gaston in his book *The Non-Partisan League*.

Most of the league membership was Republican; it was therefore an easy step to the use of the machinery of that party. In the primary

[1] The party name was originally spelled 'Non-Partisan' but through usage has been changed to its present form.

election of June 1916 and again in the fall the league was successful. Lynn J. Frazier became the first league-elected Governor, and three league-endorsed candidates, R. H. Grace, James E. Robinson, and L. E. Birdzell, were placed on the supreme court bench.

An appropriation of $300,000 was made by the legislature to carry out the provisions of a Terminal Elevator Commission bill, but Frazier vetoed the act, declaring the amount insufficient. Among the progressive legislation enacted at this session were bills providing for the creation of a State highway department, land-title registration (never enforced, however), increased funds for rural schools, reduction of rate of assessments on farm improvements to 5 per cent of the true value, and guarantee of deposits in State banks.

Entry of the United States into World War I brought new activities to North Dakota in the spring of 1917. National Guard units were sent, a Council of National Defense was created to aid in the work of mobilization, Liberty Bonds were sold, and the State went $200,000 over its quota in the United War Work campaign.

The First World War interrupted, but did not deter, the progress of the league program. Governor Frazier was re-elected in 1918, and seven initiated amendments were added to the State constitution, forming the basis for the league program. The law for initiated petitions was changed to require only 20,000 signers; the $200,000 debt limit of the State was abolished and the State was allowed to issue or guarantee bonds not to exceed $10,000,000.

The league's industrial program was established at the 1919 legislative session. The industrial commission, composed of the Governor, the attorney general, and the commissioner of agriculture and labor, was to manage the industries and enterprises undertaken by the State. Under authority of the new legislation, the North Dakota Mill and Elevator Association was established. A small mill was purchased at Drake and later a mill and elevator were built at Grand Forks with a capacity of 3000 barrels per day and a storage capacity of 1,659,500 bushels (see Tour 1).

In the March primary of 1920 an unusual initiated measure was the center of interest. It was the 'recall,' which provided for the removal of any elective officers, even judges. The measure became Article 33 of the constitution.

The elections of 1920 again saw the league victorious. In the Republican primaries Dr. E. F. Ladd, president of the State agricultural college, defeated Senator Gronna for the nomination as United States

Senator. William Langer, who had been elected attorney general in 1916 with the endorsement of the league, opposed Governor Frazier in the primary and was defeated by a small margin. Frazier and Ladd were elected in November.

Two important initiated measures were passed, one providing for a board of auditors to audit the accounts of the State treasurer, the Bank of North Dakota, and all State industries, the other amending a previous measure so that although State funds and State institution funds must be deposited in the Bank of North Dakota, county, township, municipal, and school district funds need not be deposited there.

In 1920 deflation of the league's boom set in. The United States Supreme Court declared the grain-grading law unconstitutional. The Independent Voters Association, anti-Nonpartisan, argued that the cost of government had greatly increased under the Nonpartisans. In the 1921 session of the legislature committees were appointed to investigate. The minority of the Senate committee reported that the industrial commission had practiced a policy of favoritism in affairs of the Bank of North Dakota in distributing public funds to private banks, so that the bank could not at that time meet its obligations; that the commission had failed to exercise proper control of the North Dakota Home Builders' Association, so that its affairs were hopelessly muddled; that it had approved contracts between the Drake mill and private merchants, especially the Consumers United Stores Company, a subsidiary corporation of the Nonpartisan League, resulting in losses to the State; that it had approved a policy of the Bank of North Dakota by which $2,000,000 of a total $5,200,000 in live claims against solvent banks were against 37 institutions mostly classed as 'league banks' or 'friendly' politically; that it had allowed officers of the bank to deposit public funds in private banks with the result that $1,400,000 of these funds were tied up in insolvent banks.

The recall was exercised for the first time in the United States against the governor of a State. In a special election of 1921, Frazier was defeated by R. A. Nestos, Republican, a member of the Independent Voters Association, or I.V.A.'s, as they were popularly called. The other two members of the industrial commission, Attorney General William Lemke and Commissioner of Agriculture and Labor John Hagan, were also recalled. But measures initiated to curtail the industrial program failed; Governor Nestos had to administer a program to which his party was opposed. Nestos was re-elected in 1922. In the same election former Governor Frazier, running for United States

Senator, defeated J. F. T. O'Connor, Democrat, who later became comptroller of currency under President Franklin D. Roosevelt.

Governor Nestos was defeated by the Nonpartisan candidate, Arthur G. Sorlie, in the primary of 1924 while I.V.A. Republicans won several of the State offices. Senator Ladd died in office and a Nonpartisan newspaperman, Gerald P. Nye, was appointed to fill the vacancy. When Governor Sorlie died, Walter Maddock, Lieutenant Governor, filled out the term.

In 1928 George Shafer, an I.V.A., who had been attorney general under Nestos, was elected Governor, and in 1930 he was re-elected.

The debt limit having been increased at various times, North Dakota's bonded debt in 1930 was estimated to be $36,357,200; $1,000,000 represented in capital stock of the Bank of North Dakota; $4,000,000 in mill and elevator construction and milling bonds; the remainder in various real-estate bond series.

By 1930 North Dakota's population was 680,845, more than double the figure at the opening of the century. Large foreign immigrations accounted for the approximately 88 per cent rise in the 1910 census over that of 1900, and by 1920 the figure had risen to 646,872. Statistics of the U.S. Bureau of Census show North Dakota to have been the only spring wheat State having an increase of population during the period from 1930–35. The growth had been almost entirely rural; from 1920 to 1930 no new urban centers (above 2500) appeared in the State. In 1940 the population fell to 461,935.

The State capitol building was destroyed by fire December 28, 1930, and plans were immediately laid for building a new statehouse. A $2,000,000 building, unique in that it is North Dakota's only skyscraper, today stands on Bismarck's Capitol Hill.

An initiative measure in the election of 1932 repealed the prohibition clause in the State constitution, making North Dakota, dry since it became a Territory, a wet State.

William Langer, who had been elected attorney general on the Nonpartisan ticket with Frazier and later was defeated as I.V.A. candidate for governor by Frazier, was elected Governor in 1932, once more running as a Nonpartisan.

The period following proved a trying one for the rural population of North Dakota. The farmers suffered because of low market prices for farm products, low land values, bank failures, and crop failures. The situation was acute at the beginning of Langer's administration because many farm mortgages had been based on pre-depression valuations. Farmers feared foreclosure and the wastage of their life efforts.

To prevent foreclosure Governor Langer declared various farm-mortgage moratoriums by executive order. For a time an embargo was in effect on agricultural products, forbidding shipment of them from the State in the hope that prices would be forced up. A law enacted to extend the period of redemption on real-estate mortgages was held unconstitutional by the North Dakota Supreme Court as applied to existing mortgages. In 1933 laws were passed outlawing crop mortgages and deficiency judgments.

A stormy period in State history ensued when Governor Langer was removed from office July 18, 1934, having been held disqualified under the State constitution by the supreme court because of his conviction on a Federal charge of conspiracy, arising from solicitation of contributions from State and Federal employes for support of his political newspaper, the *Leader*. (The Federal Courts later reversed the conviction.) Ole Olson, Lieutenant Governor, served the remainder of the term.

Thomas H. Moodie, first Democratic Governor to be elected in 24 years, took office in January 1935, only to be declared ineligible by the supreme court February 2, because of insufficient residence in the State. Walter Welford, Nonpartisan Lieutenant Governor, became acting Governor, the fourth to occupy the gubernatorial chair in little more than six months.

The legislature of 1935 created a State Planning Board to make investigations and surveys relative to the conservation and utilization of the State's natural resources, and a State Welfare Board to act as official agency of the State in any social welfare activity initiated by the Federal Government and to allocate State and Federal funds available for such purpose. The planning board was abolished by the State Legislature in 1939.

Other legislation of the 1935 session provided for a retail sales tax, which resulted in greatly increased revenues for education and public welfare purposes, a drivers license law, and a two-year mortgage foreclosure moratorium. Two radical changes in public policy effected through initiated measures in 1935 were provision for manufacture, sale, and distribution of beer, and for Sunday motion pictures.

Former Governor Langer, defeated by Acting Governor Welford for the Nonpartisan nomination for the governorship in 1936, surprised opponents in both the league and other parties by polling a majority in the election, the first governor of any State elected in the individual column on the ballot. In the same election North Dakota put liquor control in the hands of counties, municipalities, and villages.

Indicative of the increasing responsibilities of State Governments, the social-minded legislature of 1937 made the largest appropriation for public welfare in the history of the State—more than $6,100,000 for the 1937-9 biennium.

John Moses, Democratic Governor from January 1939 to January 1945, was elected by a large majority and served three terms. Governor Moses received active support from many political factions, and his administration may be characterized as outstanding. Upon his retirement he was elected to the United States Senate, but his death occurred a short time after he assumed his duties as Senator.

Governor Fred G. Aandahl, a Republican and the present chief executive, began his first term in January 1945. Governor Aandahl's administration has been similar in character to that of his predecessor. He has actively co-operated with Federal agencies in carrying out a water-development program in North Dakota.

From 1940 to 1949 the State of North Dakota has enjoyed unprecedented prosperity. Generous and timely rains have produced abundant crops and pasture lands. Although the number of individuals engaged in agriculture has been reduced, the income realized per farm has increased tremendously. Having fully recovered from the severe drought of the 'thirties, the State now has the third highest per capita income in the nation.

✿✿

Agriculture and Farm Life

LAND of supersized farms, of spring wheat and winter rye rippling in the wind, of gigantic flower gardens of paradise-blue flax—this is North Dakota, one of the greatest agricultural States of the nation.

Those who have seen the vast fields in the summer know the meaning of this land to the farmer and the stock-raiser; for while the romantically inclined can meditate on the beauties of a bronze wheatfield under the July sun, or the picturesque qualities of fine cattle grazing on a hillside, the agricultural statistician can point out that 87 per cent of the land in the State is devoted to agriculture, and, given sufficient moisture, the richly productive soil will more than repay the efforts of the farmer or stockman who depends upon it for his livelihood.

Here in North Dakota were the original bonanza farms—so-called because of their almost fabulous yields of wheat—some of them two or three townships in extent. They are gone now, but the size of the farms today still startles those familiar with agriculture in other States, for many holdings run as high as 10,000 acres, and the average for the whole State is 463 acres, as against the United States average of 154.8 acres.

North Dakota's precipitation is variable. Ordinarily the rainfall, if properly distributed, is sufficient to bring crops of high value, despite the fact that in the western two thirds of the State it is not abundant. In occasional years the moisture is poorly distributed, resulting in lessened cash values. About twice in a century the dry-land farming area of the United States, of which the western two thirds of this State is a part, is subject to major drought conditions. At such times farming is difficult and in places impossible—without irrigation. In the drought of the 1880's there were few people in North Dakota to suffer. It took the major drought that began in 1929 to impress not only upon North Dakotans but upon the Federal Government as well

64

the necessity for reliance in part upon irrigation, utilizing the waters that flow so abundantly through the State—and out of it.

As a result, the North Dakota Water Conservation Commission was created in 1937 by the State legislature. The commission, in co-operation with the North Dakota Rural Rehabilitation Corporation, established the Lewis and Clark project in McKenzie County and the Sioux irrigation project near Cartwright. Urged by the State Water Commission, the Federal Government authorized the construction of Garrison Dam, which will provide for flood control, for navigation on the Missouri and Mississippi Rivers, for diversion of water to the central and eastern part of the State, and for necessary irrigation. The dam will produce hydroelectric power, in addition to providing facilities for recreation and for wildlife preservation. When completed, the Garrison Dam will be the largest rolled-earth dam in the world. It will be over 2 miles long, 210 feet high from the bottom of the river, and nearly three quarters of a mile wide at the base, tapering up to a 65-foot width at the top to carry a four-lane highway. It will create a reservoir more than 200 miles long, which will impound 23,000,000 acre-feet of water.

Additional aid has been supplied through appropriations by the Federal Government for the Heart River irrigation project in Morton County, the Baldhill Dam and reservoir in Barnes County, and the Homme Dam in Walsh County. Under the Missouri basin development plan, authorized by Congress, it is estimated that construction work in North Dakota will cost $640,000,000, which will be provided largely from Federal Government appropriations, with owners of land benefited by irrigation required to pay a share of the construction and operation costs.

The flood situation in the Red River Valley crop lands has been alleviated by drains constructed by State and local appropriations, and a six-year program of flood-control construction, estimated at a cost of a million dollars annually, has been started. The plan of the Bureau of Reclamation, a subdivision of the State Water Commission, provides for the construction of the Pick-Sloan River basin program, the development of irrigation conservation, control and use of the waters of the Missouri basin, hydroelectric power, conservation of wildlife, flood control, and water for municipal, domestic, and industrial uses. The plan includes the diversion of water from the Missouri River below Fort Peck Dam in Montana into the northwest corner of North Dakota, the diversion of return flows by canal into the proposed Sheyenne

Reservoir, the restoration of Devils Lake, and diversion into the James River to irrigate approximately 55,000 acres of land in the New Rockford unit. Additional projects will include the construction of a reservoir on the James River above Jamestown, the construction of two dams and reservoirs on the Cannonball and Thunderhawk Rivers, the Broncho Dam and reservoir on the Knife River, and several Missouri River pumping projects south of the Garrison Dam.

Because of its strategic location near the headwaters of the Missouri River, North Dakota will ultimately have one of the largest irrigated areas of any State in the basin.

The prosperity enjoyed by agriculture in North Dakota since 1940 has had a marked effect on land sales in the State. Prices have risen sharply and there has been an urgent demand for the purchase of school and other public land. Because of good crops and good prices, the amount of land under cultivation has increased, although the number of farms has decreased.

Naturally, in a State where 87 per cent of the land is devoted to agricultural pursuits, farm conditions are of paramount importance to almost every person. Directly dependent upon the soil are the farm residents, who compose 53.6 per cent of North Dakota's population. Directly dependent upon the wealth of the farmer are the 28.6 per cent who live in small rural towns, and, almost as directly, the 17.9 per cent who compose the urban population. Of the urban group, approximately one third are employed in the processing of agricultural products.

The same general boundaries that divide the State topographically also designate the three agricultural belts. The Red River Valley and Drift Prairie are combined in what is known as the black-earth belt, the Coteau du Missouri constitutes the farming-grazing belt, and the Missouri Slope is the grazing-forage belt.

In the black-earth belt the farms are usually small, averaging less than 400 acres in extent. Here the average annual rainfall varies from 18 to 24 inches, 6 to 8 inches of which falls during the months of May and June, when it is most valuable to small grains.

The black-earth region was the first part of North Dakota to be settled. Furs were the object of the earliest white settlers there, but the value of agricultural pursuits was by no means overlooked even during that early period. Alexander Henry, Jr., the fur trader who foresaw that the Red River Valley would be good agricultural land if the transportation problem could be solved, tells in his diary of planting a garden as early as 1800 at his trading post at the mouth of the Pembina River, where he raised carrots, cabbages, beets, potatoes, and other vegetables. Nor was he free from the evils that beset the modern farmer: his crop was highly satisfactory for several years, but in 1808 everything was eaten by the grasshoppers which swarmed across the land. Henry's agrarian ventures were secondary to his fur trading, however, and it was not until the friends of Charles Cavileer settled at Pembina in 1851 that a permanent agricultural colony was established in the State. An earlier settlement by the Selkirkers of Canada in 1812 had been short-lived. When the Cavileer colony arrived, however, the Selkirk colonists, now established at Fort Douglas, Winnipeg, not only provided Cavileer with a bride but also supplied his people with seed wheat, oats, barley, and field peas.

For almost 20 years the little settlement at Pembina was the only farming community in the State. Dakota Territory had been opened to settlement January 1, 1863, and free lands were offered to anyone over 21 years of age who would cultivate and improve his 160-acre homestead, and live on it 5 years. If he wished, he could also obtain a tree claim of 160 acres.

Ten acres of this quarter-section had to be planted in trees, and proof, substantiated by two reliable witnesses, that the trees had been growing for eight years was necessary before the settler could obtain clear title to the claim. The acquisition of tree claims was sometimes hindered by the perpetration of a cruel hoax on newcomers. One of a group of unprincipled men, interested in money rather than in settlement of the land, and unable or unwilling to file claims, would approach a new settler and offer him a 'deal' on a piece of land, ostensibly planted as a tree claim, with the little green tree shoots already appearing above the ground. The settler would pay a substantial sum for the advantage of having trees already planted, and in good faith would file on the claim, only to find later in the year that instead of a ten-acre grove he had an excellent but over-abundant crop of turnips. Notwithstanding such discouragements, many fine groves were planted which have not only added greatly to the beauty of the Red River Valley and central North Dakota, but have been invaluable as a protection against soil erosion.

A third tract of 160 acres could be secured under the pre-emption laws which permitted the settler to locate on land before or after it was surveyed, file declaration of intent to purchase, and pay for the land within 18 months after filing, at the rate of $2.50 an acre for railroad property or $1.25 for any other land. Additional land could be obtained by buying up grants to soldiers in the United States Army. Military land warrants could be purchased for a nominal price, often as low as 50 cents an acre.

At first, despite the ease of obtaining land, there was no great influx of settlers into the new land. The nation was in the grip of the Civil War, and Indian troubles in the West not only discouraged new settlement but frightened out many who had already made their homes there. Writers who had visited the Territory depicted it as 'a land of blizzards and Indians, drought and grasshoppers.'

Moreover, homesteading in the northern part of the Territory was complicated by the fact that the nearest land office was at Vermilion, 400 miles away, a long and perilous trip in the day of the oxcart and dogsled. The only surveyed land was in the vicinity of Pembina. Here in 1868 Joseph Rolette, pioneer fur trader and settler, filed the first homestead in North Dakota, the only one before 1870. In 1871 a few more claims were filed, but it was not until 1885 that settlement increased to any great extent. During that year so many 'took up' land that Dakota Territory became known as 'the land of the free and the home of the boomer . . . free homesteaders and town site boomers.'

The extension of the Northern Pacific across the Red River into North Dakota was partly responsible for this sudden increase in population. Immigrants found it easier to reach the lands the Government offered them. The Northern Pacific had been given by Government grant alternate sections of land for a distance of 20 miles on each side of its right-of-way. The land between these sections was opened to homesteading; and since the free lands were just as desirable as its own, the railroad could find no market for its property. It was decided, therefore, that the only way to profit on its investment was to encourage settlement, so that there would be an increased need of transportation in and out of the new country. In lieu of its stocks, which had slumped in the panic of 1873, the road sold some of its enterprising stockholders large portions of its land grants for 40 and 50 cents an acre. Among those persuaded to invest were G. W. Cass, B. P. Cheney, and Oliver Dalrymple. The three formed a company and placed their 12,000 acres, in the vicinity of Fargo, under Dalrymple's management. Thus was formed the first bonanza farm, initiating an important era in the agricultural history of North Dakota.

The chief purpose of the early bonanza farms was to demonstrate on a spectacular scale the potential wealth of the Red River Valley. The farms ranged in size from 3000 acres to the 65,000-acre Grandin farm, which covered more than 100 sections of land. Wheat was the sole crop. All operations were conducted on a large scale, with dozens of the most up-to-date farm machines working on the various divisions of the farms simultaneously, and huge crews of a hundred or more employed during the harvest season. Tales of the bumper crops were soon spread by the transient harvest 'hands,' and visitors and home seekers came from far and wide to see whether the stories of the fabulous crops were actually true.

Two new inventions added to the success of the wheat-raising bonanza farms. The first of these was the purifier, which made it possible to produce a superior grade of white flour from spring wheat. The second was a roller simplifying the milling of hard wheat, with the result that this grain was placed at a premium. In a single year, the value of the farms was raised from the original 40 and 50 cents to $5 an acre, and by 1906 the lands were worth from $30 to $40.

Because they raised a single crop, the managers of the bonanza farms found it easy to systematize and mechanize their work. The newest farm machines were common in this newly settled area long before they were introduced in the older States.

Eastern syndicates usually owned the bonanza farms, and resident managers were engaged to supervise the work. As long as only wheat was raised, the system was ideal. With the introduction of other crops, however, difficulties arose, principally because stockholders could not agree on a plan of operation. Almost all the large farms were eventually broken into smaller plots and sold to the immigrants and easterners whom they had attracted to the West. Today, 49,935 of the 69,520 farms in the State are operated by their owners, 19,324 by tenants, and only 261 by managers.

Thousands who were attracted by the success of the bonanza farms and the low railroad rates came west to take up land, and were aided in their preparation by the *Emigrant's Guide,* published by the Commissioner of Immigration for Dakota Territory in 1870. This contained not only such valuable information as data on the land laws, farming methods, and transportation facilities, but also freight rates and a list of prices of staple commodities to indicate supplies that should be brought from the East and those that could be as cheaply purchased in the new land. Tea was one of the most expensive of pioneer commodities, ranging in price from $1.25 and $2 a pound. Sugar was also high—from 12 to 16 cents a pound. For light, the homesteader had a choice of candles at 25 cents a pound or coal oil at 80 cents a gallon. Furniture, too, could be purchased by those who did not wish to carry it across the prairies from their eastern homes. Extension tables sold for $2 a foot, washstands cost from $4.50 to $10. Ox yokes were $3, a double harness $45. So many homesteading necessities could be purchased at the pioneer settlements that after reading Dakota newspapers of this period a North Carolina editor announced that 'the people are fully up to the highest notch of civilization.'

As the lands of the Red River Valley and the Drift Plain were occupied, settlers were forced to go farther west into the farming-grazing belt of the Missouri Coteau. Influenced by the fortunes being made in wheat in the eastern part of the State, they too became wheat farmers. But although the soil of the Missouri Coteau is almost as rich as that farther east, it does not have the same advantageous rainfall during the growing season; and while it produced successfully, it did not have the spectacular production of the bonanza farms in the black-earth area.

Today, the farms in this region are somewhat larger than those of the more easterly belt, being from 450 to 600 acres in size, but the relative production is lower. Although grain farming still predominates, ideally the farming-grazing region is, especially in dry years, a livestock section.

To the west of this central region lies the Missouri Slope, which constitutes the grazing-forage belt. Originally the farms here were much smaller than those in other parts of the State—with the repeal in 1891 of tree claim and pre-emption laws, homesteaders were limited to 160 acres of free land. For a few years the settlers on the Missouri Slope were able to file on desert claims, receiving one section at $1.25 an acre with the understanding that they would improve the land by irrigation; but so many people throughout the arid regions of the United States filed on such claims fraudulently that the act was finally amended to include the requirement that at least $3 an acre must be spent for irrigation.

Despite this land limitation, many new settlers came to western North Dakota during the 'back to the land' movement from 1900 to 1910. Besides the farmers who took up free land, there were many school teachers, laborers, and business and professional persons who followed that method, or took a commuted homestead by filing on land, staying there 14 months, and paying the Government $1.25 an acre. In this region, where it is estimated that 30 per cent of the land is not suitable for cultivation, it was inevitable that many of these inexperienced persons should settle on unsuitable property. Experienced ranchers and farmers realized that only large farms could be operated profitably and purchased homesteads from dissatisfied settlers. In this manner the size of farms increased, until now they run to 800 acres or more.

The most fertile soil of the western region is in the valley of the Missouri. It was here that Verendrye, Lewis and Clark, Catlin, and other early explorers found the Mandan, Hidatsa, and Arikara women carefully cultivating their neat fields of corn, beans, squash, pumpkin, melons, and sunflowers.

Lack of rainfall is the chief drawback to successful agriculture in the grazing-forage belt; but with irrigation, field crops can be raised dependably. The value of irrigation has been demonstrated by the success of the 20,319 acres immediately west of the Yellowstone River in western North Dakota, an area irrigated by the Bureau of Reclamation project of 1906. Similar projects are under construction in the basins of all the large rivers of North Dakota (see pp. 65–6).

The grazing-forage belt as a whole, however, is not well suited to agriculture. Texas cattlemen, driving their herds through western Dakota to furnish beef for frontier military posts, saw its true value as a cattle country. The nutritive grasses and natural shelters make this an ideal cattle-raising section.

Among the earliest ranchers were the Deffenbach brothers, who opened a ranch in the extreme southwestern corner of the present State in 1878. Others soon followed, including soldiers who had finished their period of enlistment in the western Army posts and were eager to settle in the new land. Ranching of cattle and sheep became the industry of the western part of the State. As the natural range showed inroads of the new industry, dry-farming was introduced, the chief crops being forage for winter feed.

The land in the three North Dakota farm belts is still used primarily for the purpose for which it was settled. The leading spring wheat State, North Dakota is second only to Kansas in the total wheat production of an average year. Hard spring wheat, particularly pilot and mida, is an important crop, commanding a premium on the market because of high protein content. Three fourths of the nation's durum, a hardy wheat used in the making of macaroni, is raised here. During the period of 1936–45, North Dakota wheat production averaged 106,-205,000 bushels a year. The State leads in rye and flax and is outranked only by Minnesota in barley production. In production of grain seeds and cereal crops the United States Department of Agriculture ranks North Dakota third and seventh respectively.

Like the gold of the wheat, the blue of the flax flower has been part of the North Dakota picture since pioneer days. First planted for an immediate cash income, flax has proved an ideal secondary crop because it extends the seeding and harvesting periods, and since 1900 it has been an established part of the cropping system of the North-Central States. One half of the flax acreage in the United States is planted in North Dakota. As early as 1890, the State produced 458,117 bushels. In 1948, 10,017,203 bushels of flax were harvested in North Dakota, with an average yield of 8.3 bushels per acre.

Winter rye is extensively planted because of the protection it affords against erosion after a wet autumn. In 1946, 2,156,000 bushels were harvested in North Dakota.

A need for more feed crops for the cattle raised in the State has led to increased production of barley, oats, and emmer—grains used locally for feed. About 85 per cent of the yield of barley is consumed by hogs and lambs. Barley is also useful as a clean-up crop in the control of annual weeds. The average annual production for 1936–45 was 38,-287,000 bushels.

The same desire for an immediate cash crop that was the incentive to raise flax on the pioneer farms was largely responsible for the introduction of potatoes and sugar beets. Potatoes had almost always been raised for local consumption, but no effort was made to produce them in commercial quantities. Then a few enterprising farmers in the Red River Valley planted large acreages and were successful in marketing the crops outside the State. Because of their high flavor, mealiness, and large uniform size, these northern potatoes command a premium on the market. One warehouse specializes in the shipping of hand-picked, wrapped potatoes, packed like apples or oranges, for sale to railways and other markets demanding fancy-grade potatoes. It is, however, for their seed value that North Dakota potatoes are notable. Their low fiber content makes them ideal seed stock, and under Federal and State supervision they are certified for this purpose. In 1947 North Dakota produced 16,885,643 bushels of potatoes, with an average yield of 158.1 bushels per acre.

Experimentation showed that the soil good for northern potatoes was also excellent for sugar beets. The first crop of beets large enough to be listed in statistics for the State was 24,474 tons, harvested in 1924. By 1929 the tonnage had increased to 59,104. This is one crop that showed an increased production even in the dry year of 1934, when production totaled 82,304 tons, and beets were raised on 13,466 acres on 485 farms. In 1947 164,376 tons of sugar beets were harvested. When the industry was first introduced, most of the labor was performed by Mexicans. Under contract to beet farmers, trainloads of these people came north each spring. Not only did they work for very low wages, but they also developed a quality of work rarely equaled by white beet workers. The cultivation and weeding of sugar beets is done almost entirely by hand, a long tedious process in the blazing sun, which the Mexican worker seemed to mind not at all. In the fall, most of them would pack their families into second-hand cars purchased with their summer earnings and return south. Difficulties of these workers in adjusting themselves to northern modes of living discouraged the use of Mexican labor, however, and today, although Mexican labor is still used extensively in the Red River Valley and Williston areas, much of the work is now carried on by local labor, often by school children. In driving through the Red River Valley, one can tell the farms on which sugar beets are a crop of many years' standing, for scarcely one of these is without an old tar-paper shack, a cook car remodeled into a house, or some other crude dwelling which was once the home of a family of Mexicans. In otherwise well-kept farmyards, where the buildings are comparatively modern, these laborers' dwellings are decrepit and out-of-place.

Although not a cash crop like potatoes and beets, corn has become increasingly valuable in North Dakota. This is especially true in the southeastern part of the State, which is the hog-raising area of North Dakota. During 1936–45, the average annual corn production was 21,260,000 bushels. Only in rare instances does North Dakota corn reach the cash markets. It is not husked as in many of the Corn Belt States; instead, the hogs and sometimes the cattle are permitted to feed directly on the stocks in the field. This is known as the 'hogging down' method of harvesting corn. About one half the crop is cut annually for winter fodder.

Other feed crops are also important on the North Dakota farm. Many hay and pasture crops, especially red clover and alfalfa, can be successfully grown in the Red River Valley. In the western sections, alfalfa is raised for seed. Timothy and brome grass are also valuable grass crops in the eastern area.

In 1914 sweet clover was cultivated only on demonstration farms; but each year production of seed increased, reaching a high of 171,600 bushels in 1933. In 1948 148,611 acres were seeded. Sweet clover replaces nitrogen and other essential elements in soil that has been badly depleted by overproduction of wheat. One remarkable feature of this crop is its immunity to disease and insect pests.

Sheep are found generally throughout the State, although the northern part of the Red River Valley and the southwestern corner of the Missouri Slope have proved the best sheep-raising land. The animals were brought into the State when ranching first began here, and in 1947 274,283 lambs were raised and 2,594,130 pounds of wool produced.

Because of the high yields of small grains in recent years, which give a greater return for man hours of labor than can be obtained from dairying, there has been a decrease of 11 per cent in the last eight years in the number of dairy cows on farms. Of the 1,280,858 cattle in North Dakota in 1948, only 350,252 were milk cows, as compared to almost 600,000 even during the drought of the 'thirties.

Although rarely conducted as an independent enterprise, poultry-raising has had perhaps the greatest increase of any farm industry. Some type of fowl is raised on approximately 89 per cent of the farms of the State. In 1947 North Dakota farms had 2,927,401 laying hens and raised 169,596 turkeys.

Poultry organizations are active in the State. The North Dakota State Poultry Association has held annual shows since 1895, and there are numerous regional and county organizations. The North Dakota Farmers Union maintains a poultry co-operative at Williston. North Dakota is second only to Texas in supplying turkeys for the Thanksgiving and Christmas tables of the nation.

The multitudes of wild flowers on the North Dakota prairies are an abundant source of honey; and with this natural incentive to its development, beekeeping has increased rapidly throughout the State. Although it can be successfully conducted in almost every part of the State, the most extensive areas are along the Missouri and in the Red River Valley. The sweet-clover bloom is the chief source of honey and yields abundantly in July and August. It is estimated that the honey and beeswax produced in North Dakota represent a cash income of $250,000 or more annually. Moreover, it is estimated that the pollination service rendered by the bees in gathering the honey is worth 20 times the value of the honey and beeswax produced.

All of North Dakota was affected by the prolonged drought in the Great Plains States that began in 1929 and, except for one year, continued through 1936. High winds, intensive cultivation, and low rainfall combined to create the most destructive period of soil erosion known to the State since its earliest settlement. This combination of conditions brought production in all farm products far below normal levels. Even the Red River Valley, though it fared much better than the western part of the State, had subnormal rainfall and was subjected to frequent dust storms. To counteract the menace of drought to the prosperity of a primarily agricultural region, both State and Federal agencies began promotion of conservation in three forms: water, soil, and vegetation. Through the combined efforts of private groups and State and Federal agencies, many extensive water-conservation projects are under construction, such as the Lewis and Clark, Sioux, Buford-Trenton, Heart River, and Missouri-Souris Irrigation Projects, and the Garrison, Baldhill, and Homme Dams. Planting hedges and forests to hold moisture in the soil and to prevent increased erosion constitutes the soil-conservation program. To conserve vegetation, a program of dry-farming is recommended, including summer fallowing and the planting of drought-resistant crops.

Various agencies are co-operating in a program to educate farmers in these conservation plans. Extension workers, including county agents and their assistants, are employed by the United States Department of Agriculture to assist farmers. The agricultural college at Fargo, the Northern Great Plains Field Station at Mandan, the State School of Forestry at Bottineau, and experimental stations and farms are constantly conducting soil-conservation and moisture-control experiments designed to raise North Dakota agriculture to an even higher rank. These conservation measures, combined with favorable conditions in recent years, are responsible for the agricultural prosperity the State is now enjoying.

FARM LIFE

The fact that eastern and central North Dakota has been settled 25 or 30 years longer than the western part of the State is evident in the appearance of the farms. The average eastern farm home has well-painted and modernized buildings, surrounded by a neat lawn and grove. The Rural Electrical Administration program is providing electricity for a large proportion of North Dakota farms. Telephones, radios, and cars are generally considered necessities. Since the farms are small and close together, and small towns are within a few miles of one another, social contacts are easily maintained. Activities center in the towns, where farm women are members of clubs, lodges, and church societies, and the men of fraternal and civic organizations. Consolidated schools have supplanted many of the one-room buildings, and parent-teacher groups have a prominent social position. Libraries are found in many towns and are patronized by rural as well as city dwellers.

The farms in central North Dakota are as a rule not as modern as those in the east, but on the whole are well kept. A somewhat different picture, however, is presented by the western farms and ranches. The semi-arid climate makes it difficult for even the most ambitious farmer to improve his place with trees, shrubs, grass, and flowers. Moreover, since there were no tree claims in this part of the State, early settlers did not have the incentive to plant groves. Periods of drought have been felt more severely here and have prevented many farmers from making modern improvements on their buildings. On some farms, the shacks erected to establish residence under the homestead act are still in use. There is, however, one modern convenience found more frequently in western rural homes than in those of the east—the furnace. The chief reason for this is the vast and accessible supply of lignite, a fuel that does not burn readily in stoves.

Since farms in western North Dakota are large, homesteads are necessarily far apart and social contacts cannot be made easily. Many homes do not have telephones, because the market is limited to a few patrons and the cost is therefore prohibitive. The longer distances to towns result in lack of interest in urban recreational, social, and church functions.

The one-room school predominates in western North Dakota. Libraries are few, and most of the people fail to take advantage of loaning facilities offered by State libraries.

Farm families in all parts of the State participate in various seasonal activities. During the spring and summer months, school, church, club, and old-settlers picnics are scheduled frequently. When harvest season arrives the farmer is exceptionally busy, but always has time to welcome the visitors from town, who come out to watch the threshers and often stay for a cook-car dinner. Later in the fall, especially in the eastern counties, young people participate in strawstack parties. Dances and card parties are held in community halls and barn lofts during the winter.

Winter activities are limited by heavy snowfalls, which often keep communities and farms snowbound for days. Main-traveled highways are kept open except in unusually bad weather, but side roads are often drifted over for weeks at a time. Then the radio becomes the chief source of entertainment in the farm home; radio reception on the open prairie is exceptionally good. In winter the western farmers have an advantage over those of the east, for they get less snowfall, and chinooks (warm dry winds that descend from the Rocky Mountains) often temper the weather and melt the snow, permitting social life to continue almost uninterrupted.

In every rural community 'fair week' is an important date. Farmers take their best cattle, hogs, sheep, and poultry to compete with their neighbors' entries for the prized blue ribbons. Farm women select their finest handiwork, their choicest jars of jellies, jams, and pickles, to enter in competition. Cookies, cakes, and pies are baked both to exhibit and to fill the picnic baskets, for when the family goes to the fair everyone is prepared to spend the day; one or two hurry home in the evening to do the chores and return in time for the grandstand events at night. Almost every county has its annual fair in June or July, the oldest being the Pembina County Fair, which has been held at Hamilton each year since 1894. Even before this Pembina County Fair, a State fair under State subsidy was being held annually in Grand Forks, where the citizens had donated 80 acres of land for that purpose. When the first State legislature met, it created a department of agriculture, one of the duties of which was to hold an annual agricultural exhibit. Now State help is also received by the fair associations at Fargo and Minot.

Increasingly popular in recent years are the harvest festivals in various towns. These are held in September and October, when the garden products have reached maturity, and therefore often surpass the earlier fairs in the quality of exhibits. The junior chambers of commerce of the State sponsor a Golden Grain Festival which is held the latter part of August, each year in a different city of the State. In October comes the Grand Forks Harvest Festival, and the extension division of the agricultural college sponsors a similar event in Fargo. Bismarck is the scene of the annual North Dakota Conservation Show in September.

Alfalfa Day at Fessenden in March features displays of alfalfa hay and seed and also includes small grains, corn, and potatoes. The mid-winter fair at Park River is sponsored by the Walsh County Agricultural College and consists of exhibits from farmers throughout the Red River

Valley. Other outstanding exhibits include the North Dakota Winter Show held in Valley City the fourth week in September, the Emmons County Breeders Association Stock Show, which takes place in Hazelton each June, and the State Durum Wheat Show held annually at Langdon.

Industry and Labor

O N ANY cold winter night in the early 1800's it was not uncommon to see a fur trader set out from Pembina, with his
dog-sled loaded with valuable pelts, to make the long trek to
St. Paul or Fort Garry. With no roads, few landmarks, and the constant
danger of Indian attack, such a night trip was extremely hazardous.
Daylight, however, presented even more dangers, for the reflection of
the winter sun upon the snowy ground often caused snow-blindness;
daytime temperatures softened the drifts so that the dogs sank deep
into them, while at night they could skim easily over the frozen surface.
Despite the dangers of the fur trade, many men engaged in it, taking
their cargoes to the frontier cities and bringing back sled-loads of
supplies to be exchanged for the furs that Indians brought to the trading posts.

The first stores were at these posts, where the Indians came to barter
for blankets, trinkets, food, and alcohol, using the valuable beaver skin
as the standard of reckoning. To avoid long discussions over the price
of goods, the traders devised a system of marking that could be readily
understood by the natives: a single horizontal line drawn on an article
indicated a value of one beaver skin, two parallel lines placed the
price at two skins, and so on. The size of some English-made blankets
is still designated by a survival of this early system, with lines known
as 'points' woven into the border.

The fur trade prospered until the Indian insurrections of 1863–4.
Then trapping became a perilous occupation, and traders and trappers
returned East. Eastward, too, went most of the settlers who had come to
farm. The only ones to remain were Charles Cavileer and his little
colony at Pembina, who staunchly continued to cultivate their level
farms in the face of Indian dangers. With the exception of a few brave
adventurers, they had the entire area virtually to themselves, until the
extension of the Northern Pacific lines into the Red River Valley in

1871 promoted a period of homesteading. Then, for the first time, agriculture took its place as the leading occupation of this area.

Since agriculture is the chief industry in North Dakota, manufacturing has not been extensively developed. The more important industries are plants that process agricultural products. In 1939 the 350 manufacturing establishments in the State employed 4,125 persons, earning salaries of $1,016,591 and wages amounting to $2,771,468. The value of manufacturing products produced was $43,767,082. The more important industries include: bread and bakery products, 59 establishments; flour and grain mill products, 19 establishments; creamery butter products, 98 establishments; poultry-dressing plants, 17 establishments; meat-packing plants, 3 establishments; and newspaper printing and publishing plants, 80 establishments.

Many of the industries that were important during the development of the State are no longer in existence. Because lumber was an expensive commodity to import, sawmills were established at Grand Forks and Fargo in the 1870's; and because the North Dakota side of the Red River could not furnish a large enough supply for the mills, logs were floated down from the Minnesota woods. Lumberjacking meant cash and wages, and many homesteaders left their families in possession of their claims while they went to Minnesota to earn money for seed and machinery and for building permanent homes on their farms. As traffic on the Red River increased, construction of steamers became an important industry for which North Dakota mills supplied much of the lumber.

On the prairies west of the Red River Valley, the homesteaders could not engage in logging and lumbering to earn money for improving their farms; but, resourcefully, they found another way to get funds. Buffalo bones were scattered abundantly upon the land from Devils Lake westward, and cash prices of $8 to $10 a carload were paid by sugar manufacturers, who used the bones in a refining process. Many homes were built and much machinery was purchased with the income derived from gathering and selling this material. Gradually, however, these pioneer occupations died out. The more efficient railway supplanted the river steamers. The supply of buffalo bones was soon exhausted. New occupations, allied with the expanding agriculture of the region, grew into importance.

The first farmers here found the lack of transportation and marketing facilities a great problem. Fort Garry and St. Paul were the nearest markets for grain until 1851. In that year Father Belcourt, who had established a mission where the town of Walhalla now stands, found that sufficient power could be obtained from the Pembina River there to operate a small flour mill. The mill was built, and farmers came from as far east as Pembina to patronize it. Generally, however, there was a lack of mills throughout the region. Elevators and shipping points were far apart, and many farmers had to drive their wagonloads of grain from 25 to 100 miles to market. When the railroads were extended westward, elevators were built in the towns and at sidings, greatly simplifying the marketing problem. The new freight lines made it possible for mills to import fuel from the East, but unfortunately the cost of shipment was prohibitive. The development of North Dakota lignite mines, beginning in the 1880's, removed an important handicap to mill operation, however, and later the lowering of freight rates allowed importation of other fuel. Although a large proportion of North Dakota grain is still shipped out, there are now in the State 19 flour mills with an annual output valued at $5,303,788. The largest of these is the State-owned mill and elevator opened at Grand Forks in 1922 as part of the Nonpartisan League program of State industries.

One of the important industries that has grown out of the agriculture of North Dakota is seed production. Potatoes, clover, alfalfa, brome-grass, and corn are shipped out in large quantities. A number of nurseries ship trees, plants, and shrubs.

A French nobleman, the Marquis de Mores, was the first person to realize the possibilities of a packing plant in North Dakota. Drawing upon his own and his father-in-law's resources, he established a plant at Medora in 1883. The venture failed, partly because his grass-fed beef, produced at a high cost because of his artless business methods, could not compete with grain-fed meat; but today modern packing plants at Grand Forks and West Fargo prove that the Marquis was not the impractical dreamer his contemporaries thought him.

Since most of North Dakota's industry is concerned with the processing of agricultural products, no large manufacturing centers have been developed; but mills, warehouses, poultry markets, and creameries have been established near the areas they serve—many of the finest creameries are in sparsely settled rural areas.

Difficulties in shipping grain to outside markets provided one of the chief factors in the development of the many co-operatives that are important in the present economic life of the State. Grain farmers early realized that by acting independently they could not trade advantageously with eastern buyers. By 1891 there were ten farmers' elevators in the State, and the co-operative movement grew until the Equity Association, the National Producers Alliance, and the Better Farming Association developed the North Dakota division of the Farmers Educational and Cooperative Union of America. At first exclusively grain-selling organizations, the co-operatives have expanded to include the handling of twine, machinery, petroleum products, tires, electricity, dairy products, and groceries.

The period after the First World War saw the revival of the occupation of the first white settlers—the fur industry. Some trapping is done each winter, but the fur sellers today do not rely upon this nineteenth-century method of getting pelts. Instead they have farms on which they raise the furbearing animals, usually silver-black foxes. The climate is well suited to this industry, for the cold winters produce heavy and valuable furs.

Although agriculture and its allied industries will probably always predominate, recent years have seen the beginning of the development of North Dakota's great mineral resources, which lay neglected or unrecognized for years while farmers attempted to emulate the phenomenal success of the bonanza wheat growers.

Ranchers in the western counties early discovered large deposits of lignite, a black or brownish substance in a stage between peat and bituminous coal, lying at or near the surface of the earth. Lignite has a conspicuously woody appearance, often showing clearly the grain of the wood or the shape of the trunks and branches from which it was formed. It is known to underlie the entire western part of the State, and the U.S. Geological Survey estimates that it constitutes about 64 per cent of the lignite resources of the country. For many years its use was entirely local, chiefly because it contains a large amount of moisture, which evaporates upon exposure to the air, causing the coal to crumble. To overcome this difficulty, shipment is now made in closed boxcars; briquetting of lignite has also proved successful, and the mineral is now common fuel. Lignite is used exclusively by State institutions and by many of the manufacturing concerns in the State. The rapidity with which the industry developed is demonstrated by the fact that there were 67 more mines in operation in 1935 that in 1931. In 1948 lignite production in the State increased to 2,954,363 tons.

The interest of the university school of mines in lignite experimentation did not end with the perfecting of the briquet process. Another achievement of the school is the production from lignite of activated carbon, a substance (hitherto produced largely from animal bones) used in water purification, sugar refining, rubber-tire manufacture, and other commercial processes.

Leonardite, which generally occurs in lignite outcroppings, is formed by the oxidation of lignite coal beds at atmospheric low temperature. The mineral was discovered by Dr. L. P. Dove, while he was assistant state geologist, and was named for Dr. A. G. Leonard, the director of the North Dakota Geological Survey from 1903 to 1932. Seventy-five per cent of the Vandyke brown pigment used in the United States is produced from North Dakota leonardite.

Western North Dakota has, in addition to its lignite beds, large deposits of clay. These, like lignite, engaged the interest of the late Dean E. J. Babcock of the university school of mines, and largely as a result of his efforts the deposits are being developed. Upon his urging, a ceramics department was created at the university in 1910 to determine the commercial value of native clays. From experiments conducted, it was found that certain varieties made excellent brick, tile, and other building materials, while others were especially suitable for pottery. Reproductions of fine European pottery and original pieces of local design turned out at the university have attracted attention at exhibitions throughout the United States. Large-scale commercial development of the State's clay deposits is centered at Wahpeton.

Sodium sulphate and bentonite are two of the more recent mineral discoveries in North Dakota. In the southwestern part of the State are large beds of bentonite which, because close to the surface, are easily accessible for commercial purposes. Bentonite is used in the manufacture of paint, rubber, soap, cosmetics, dynamite, and a variety of other products; it has also been found to give rich gold and brown tones to decorative designs on pottery. The chalky-white crystals of sodium sulphate, sometimes known as Glauber's salt, are found in few places in the United States outside of the old lake beds of northwestern North Dakota. Lewis and Clark were, so far as is known, the earliest discoverers of the mineral in North Dakota. Some 20 million tons of it are easily accessible in the open lake beds where it has been deposited by springs. Because of the increased demand for sodium sulphate in farming, the deposits are being studied by producers and users in various parts of the United States. It is also used in the manufacture of paper.

In 1948 the production of natural gas from wells in Bowman County amounted to 642,687,000 cubic feet. The 25 wells in production during that year were all connected to the distribution system of the Montana-

Dakota Utilities Company. North Dakota also has some undeveloped deposits of fuller's earth and cement rock, some low-grade limestone, and small deposits of manganese and phosphate. In recent years some deep-well drilling has been carried on in the Williston Basin, the largest unexplored potential oil-bearing basin in the United States, but as yet no oil has been discovered in the State. Some 5 or 6 million acres in the western part of the State are now under lease for exploration purposes.

In keeping with the comparative unimportance of the State labor movement at present is the small number of labor unions in North Dakota. The State's first labor organization was the Bismarck Typographical Union, chartered in 1883. In 1906 the American Federation of Labor granted a charter to the Fargo Trades and Labor Assembly, and in 1911 the State Federation was officially organized. Branches of the latter have since been formed in almost all of the larger towns in the State.

State regulation of labor conditions had its beginning in 1907 with the passage of a Workmen's Compensation Act. Many revisions have since been made in this law. A State welfare commission was formed in 1917 to regulate labor conditions; and two years later, partly through the efforts of this commission, a minimum wage law was passed and placed under the administration of the Workmen's Compensation Bureau. At the same time provision was made for regulating the wages and hours of women laborers. In 1936 North Dakota was the only State having an 8½-hour day provision for women in factories, stores, hotels, laundries, cafés, and telephone and telegraph offices.

The first State child-labor act was passed in 1909. Under the present law, employment of children under the age of 14 is prohibited. The proposed child-labor amendment to the Constitution of the United States was ratified by the North Dakota Legislature at the 1931 session.

Racial Groups and Folkways

INTERNATIONAL repute as a farming State brought North Dakota a steady stream of immigration up to the time of World War I. Tales of the rich wheatlands of Dakota drew a continuous procession of settlers with their household goods from the eastern States and from across the sea, to claim a share of the fertile western acres.

Little more than three decades has passed since this influx ceased. The State presents a patchwork of foreign groups, each retaining many Old World customs of speech, dress, and social life, although these are gradually being discarded by the younger generation. Cultural assimilation has slowly veneered the life of the State with an American character that is seeping into and supplanting the ways of the Old World.

The prevalence of foreign speech and customs seemed quite justified by the 1940 census, which showed 74,477 persons, or 11.6 per cent of the total population of 641,935, to be of foreign birth. In addition to this number, a still larger portion of the population is first-generation American, born of foreign parents and therefore in close contact with the speech and customs of its fathers during its formative years.

Forty-two countries, most of them European, have contributed to the foreign-born population of North Dakota. Norway has the largest representation, followed in order of numbers by Russia, Germany, Canada, Sweden, and other countries, including the Netherlands, Denmark, Hungary, Finland, Rumania, and Iceland.

Unfavorable social and economic conditions among the rural population of Norway, coupled with harsh military regulations, prompted most of the Norwegian emigration to the United States. North Dakota was the natural choice of many whose families had, for generations, lived upon the land. Norwegian stock today constitutes 30 per cent of the population of the State, and persons born in Norway make up 29 per cent of its foreign-born population. Their settlements have been made throughout the northern and eastern sections of the State. In contrast with many other national groups, the Norwegians show little tendency to localize, and while predominant in many communities, they manifest no aversion to settling where other groups are already represented.

The hospitality of the Norwegians is their greatest distinction. The coffeepot is always in use, and coffee and pastries made from Old Country recipes are served whenever anyone chances into a Norwegian home, as well as at meals and between meals. The Norwegians have a charming way of bidding each other *Tak for sidst,* meaning 'Thanks for the last time I met you.'

They retain to a marked degree their native tongue in its various dialects or *bygdespraag,* widely mixed with the English language. They are fond of music, and mountain waltz melodies, polkas, and spring dances, played on the accordion or violin, are enjoyed by young and old alike. The Hardanger violin, which has eight strings, it still made and played by the older musicians. The adult Norwegian, being very independent by nature, does not readily fit into an orchestra or large chorus; such organizations are more common among the younger people.

The most fantastic of the Norwegian dances is the Halling Dance, still seen on special occasions. It is reputedly the survival of a 'dance of death' from the days when the knife was the means of avenging jealousies among the young men of Halling Valley in Norway. When a man began the intricate acrobatic steps of the Halling Dance, the other dancers knew he had seen an enemy or rival in the crowd and unobtrusively withdrew to the edge of the dance floor, leaving the enemy, often unsuspecting, in the clear. Then, in a great whirl, the Halling dancer would send his knife spinning through the air with its message of death. The dance today is an acrobatic performance that requires great skill. It includes handsprings, the *Halling-kast*—a whirling and kicking step—and the *krukeng,* a jiglike step done in a half-sitting posture with the dancer moving about the floor.

In many Norwegian towns, *Jule Bokke* or Christmas Fools still make the rounds of the homes between Christmas and New Year. They are young people dressed in costume and masked, who call on the neighbors and are given food and drink at each home visited.

Among the factors that keep alive the Old Country speech and manners are the *lager* or societies, each of which represents a district in Norway. Members are former residents, or descendants of residents, of the district. At their meetings native music, dances, and costumes are revived.

A holiday in all Norwegian communities is the Seventeenth of May, Norway's Independence Day. The festivities usually include speeches, picnicking, and dancing.

Norwegian influence has been felt in every phase of North Dakota life. Among prominent figures in the State have been Paul Fjelde, sculptor; Konrad Elias Birkbough, who discovered a cure for erysipelas; Carl Ben Eielson, pioneer Alaskan aviator; R. A. Nestos, A. G. Sorlie, and Ole Olson, who became governors of the State. In the business world, the Norwegians have influenced the rapid growth of the co-operative movement. Skiing, a Scandinavian sport, is a popular winter recreation. The accordion, favorite of both the Norwegian and the German, is widely used in concert groups and dance bands. Foods that are commonly known, although not widely prepared outside the Norwegian home, include *lutefisk,* which is cod cured in lye; *lefse,* an un-leavened potato bread baked in great flat, rough, gray sheets on top of an iron range; and *fattigmand,* a pastry fried in deep fat.

In the first two decades of the nineteenth century there occurred a German migration into Russia, which was to be felt later in North Dakota. Free lands offered by the Russian Government (desirous of having its people learn German farming methods) drew many Prussians eager to escape the heavy taxation of their homeland. Throughout the Black Sea area German colonies grew up; in later years these con-tributed heavily to the stream of emigration to America. Today Russo-Germans dominate the Russian element, which forms 2.7 per cent of the total population of this State.

Because of this Russo-German constituency, the Russian and Ger-man racial groups in the State often overlap. Native Germans form 1 per cent, and persons of German stock 8 per cent, of the population. The Russo-Germans first came to this State about 1889, settling in the south-central section, in McIntosh and Emmons Counties. Other Rus-sian and Russo-German settlements are in the Missouri Slope and in the central area of the State. German groups are found in the south-eastern part of the State, in Ward County in the northwestern area, and in Morton in the Slope region. Among outstanding Germans who have taken part in the development of the State are two governors, George F. Shafer and William Langer.

In its residence in Russia, the Russo-German group acquired many customs that now distinguish them from their German cousins, but the two groups have much in common. They cling tenaciously to their native tongue in their homes and churches; the Russo-Germans, however, speak a dialect that is a result of their Russian residence. Both groups retain Old Country customs of dress, most noticeable of which is the use of the *tuch* or shawl worn by the women in place of a hat. On Sundays and holidays some of the older women appear in beautiful handworked *tuecher* and full-skirted dresses typical of peasant Europe. White stockings are often worn by the older women on holidays. The occasional appearance of a fez-like astrakhan cap during the winter bespeaks the Russian influence.

Although the dress of the older Russo-Germans is rather somber, their homes are quite the opposite. Floors throughout the house are invariably painted bright orange, this color scheme often extending to the back and front porch and steps. The exteriors of the house and other buildings are likewise sometimes painted in bright colors, with contrasting trimming. A not uncommon decorative scheme consists of two or three brilliant hues alternating in diagonal stripes across the sliding doors of garages, granaries, and barns. The interior of the summer kitchen (which is to be found back of most farmhouses and many town homes) is often painted in contrasting bright colors, one shade being used for a wainscoting effect, another for the top half of the walls and the ceiling, and a third forming a dividing border. Because of American influences, the penchant for these bright colors has become more subdued in recent years.

A popular note in home decoration is the use of bright-colored artificial flowers, which often adorn curtains, picture frames, and the organ or piano in the Russo-German home.

A typically Russian note is the common use of glass tumblers instead of cups for serving hot drinks. Another practice is the use of chicory as a substitute for coffee. A favorite delicacy of the Russo-Germans, also typically Russian, is the sunflower seed, known as the 'Russian peanut.' They eat these much as Americans eat peanuts. The sunflower seed is becoming popular as a confection throughout the State and is now roasted and packaged for sale, in contrast with the old method of drying the ripe sunflower in the sun until the seeds could be brushed from the plant.

One of the most beautiful customs retained by the modern generation of Catholic Germans and Russo-Germans is the visit of the 'Christmas Angels.' Three young girls, trained as a rule by nuns, go dressed as angels from home to home in the community on Christmas Eve. They knock for admission, and when this is granted they enter the home, bless it, and sing one or two Christmas carols. For this service they are given a small amount of money. Another custom is the observance of 'Name Day,' when, on the day of the saint for whom he is named, each person must hold open house for his friends. Callers greet the host or hostess with 'Happy Name Day.' Birthdays, on the other hand, if they occur on a day other than the Name Day, are disregarded almost altogether.

Many German families observe December 31 as 'Sylvester's Day.' On this day the last person arising is 'Sylvester' or the lazy member of the family for the coming year. Of course everyone in an industrious German family tries to avoid this stigma. Another New Year's custom is for all members of the family to leave through a rear door of the home at midnight and re-enter through a front door. The first person to enter the home after midnight is a herald of the coming year: if he is fair, the new year will bring good luck; but if he is dark, he augurs misfortune.

The German people are fond of community music, and numerous bands and choruses have organized almost spontaneously under leaders. They are especially fond of song, and when a group of older people gathers for a social evening their chief pastime is often hymn singing. Much of the social life centers about the church, although in some communities the *verein*, or society, has many members and serves to keep alive the speech and customs of the Old Country, much as does the Norwegian *lag*.

Two interesting German religious sects are the Moravians, represented in the area near Fargo, and the Dunkards or, as they are now known, Dunkers, who have a settlement near Cando. One of the beautiful customs of the Moravians is the 'love feast,' a survival of an early Christian custom of breaking bread as an indication of brotherly love. The feast today generally consists of coffee and doughnuts, but the spirit is unchanged.

The Dunkers, or German Baptist Brethren, follow their early sectarian precepts of plain dress and plain living. While few of the women still wear the 'dropped bonnet'—a small gray or black sunbonnet—the prayer covering or small lace cap is still worn during attendance at church services. Older members of the colony hold to the early rulings of the church in carrying no form of insurance. In early October of each year a harvest festival is held in the form of a religious observance.

From both the Germanic and the Norwegian groups is derived the most prominent foreign contribution to the language of the State: the universal use of *ja* ('yah') for *yes*.

Few group characteristics attach to the Canadians, who constitute 11.7 per cent of North Dakota's foreign-born population and are found in the northeast counties and the Red River Valley. Many of them are descendants of the Selkirk colonists who settled from Fort Garry to Fort Pembina early in the nineteenth century. It is from these colonists that most of the Scottish people in this State trace their descent.

For the French-Canadians the most important festival of the year is St. Ann's Day, July 26. A shrine to St. Ann has been built by French and Indians at Belcourt on the Turtle Mountain Reservation, and here on the saint's day come the lame, the halt, and the blind, to walk or be carried in the processional. Many miracles have been claimed.

In French-Canadian communities in the Red River Valley, the colorful Old Country wedding customs are still observed. As the wedding march is played the bridal pair and their attendants enter, followed by young men dressed in highly padded French costumes, and wearing grotesque masks. They are in both male and female attire and dance and cavort to the delight of the guests.

Like their Norwegian neighbors, the Swedes who have come to America are predominantly a rural people. In North Dakota they constitute .9 per cent of the total population and are found in the eastern part of the State, mainly in Cass County, and in the central section east of the Missouri in Burleigh and McLean Counties.

Smaller racial groups in the State include Hollanders, in Emmons County near the south-central border; Danes, in the east-central counties of Cass, Barnes, and Stutsman; Poles and Icelanders, in the northeast section; Hungarians, in the Slope area; Czechs, in Richland and Walsh Counties in the Red River Valley and in Stark County in the Slope area; and many others, all showing a distinct tendency to localize.

Through their national societies, the Ukrainians in Burleigh, McLean, and Billings Counties in the western half of the State have retained much of the music, dances, and costumes of their native land. These are in evidence at their club meetings and also on holidays. The costumes are colorful and elaborate and testify to the embroidering skill of the girls.

The Bohemians in Richland and Walsh Counties likewise are noted for their musical organizations, but they do not retain their native costumes or dances. The *sokol* or physical-culture group is found in many of the Bohemian communities.

The *sauna* or steam bathhouse is a characteristic feature of the Finnish settlements in the southern and western sections of the State. Water sprinkled on a large brick stove or on heated rocks provides the steam for these baths, which are stifling on first trial but soon become a pleasing habit. The Finns, like the Norwegians, serve coffee to all guests who come to their homes, no matter what the hour. Coffee is drunk from the saucer, through a lump of sugar held in the cheek. Two holidays still celebrated in Old Country style are Midsummer's Day and New Year's. Midsummer's Day, June 24, is an occasion of picnicking, church services, confirmation of scholars, settling arguments or quarrels, and pitching horseshoes. On New Year's Eve, fortunes are told by dropping bits of melted soldering metal into cold water. One piece, melted and hardened before midnight, is a symbol of the old year; and the process is repeated with another piece after the stroke of midnight, to foretell the fortunes of the new year.

Both the Irish and the Icelanders continue to hand down their legends that have been brought from Europe. Icelandic children usually are well posted on the national sagas, including the *alfa sorgur*, which tell of the *huldu* folk or elves; and no Irish child is so poor as to be deprived of the ghosts, the banshees, the leprechauns, and other weird creatures of the Emerald Isle.

At Ross, in northwestern North Dakota, is a small colony of Syrians, most of whom are Ahmadiyya Moslems. They have their own place of worship and conduct services each Friday as well as on other holy days. They retain many food customs of the Near East, one of the most interesting being the use of a meal made by crushing durum wheat that has been boiled and dried in the sun. The meal is then stewed with meats or vegetables or sweet oils.

The sugar-beet industry of the Red River Valley has resulted in the importation of Mexican workers, who provide cheap and skilled labor for cultivation of the beet fields. The Mexican population is not large, however, and has left no permanent imprint of its folklore or customs. The Negro population, never large, is also rapidly decreasing. The 1940 census showed 201 Negroes in the State.

Although not foreign-born, the Indian population constitutes a distinct racial group. Sioux and Rolette Counties, containing the Standing Rock and Turtle Mountain groups, have the greater part of the Indian population and consequently register the highest illiteracy in the State, from 7 to 8 per cent. Other counties usually have an illiteracy rate of less than 1 per cent, and sometimes less than one half of 1 per cent.

The Indians retain many racial customs and legends despite the encroachment of the white man's civilization. The métis, of French and Chippewa blood, were famous as hunters and trappers. Many of them were found in the upper Red River Valley and adjoining territory about 1850. Their descendants now live in small clay-plastered log houses, with much of their household equipment and bedding kept in the yard.

Many of North Dakota's characteristic folkways represent foreign cultures rather than anything intrinsically American. There is no lack, however, of native customs, which are gradually absorbing and supplanting the Old World ways.

Because North Dakota is a farm State, many of its customs hinge on certain matters of rural importance, such as the weather and the crops. Whether or not the farm people are able or inclined to attend is the greatest factor in the success of most social and civic events. Saturday night is the farmer's night in town, a welcome holiday after his week of isolation and work. Shops and garages become social as well as commercial centers, as friends stop to exchange news, gossip, and recipes. In many communities, Saturday night dances are held, and during the summer months a vacant lot will often be the scene of open-air motion pictures, with the spectators seated in their parked cars and blowing the horns in lieu of applause when the pictures meet with approval.

In addition to such general holiday celebrations as Christmas, New Year's, and Memorial Day, in the Norwegian sections of the State, Norwegian Independence Day, May 17, is also marked by festivity. Among the Russo-Germans, Ascension Day is an unusually solemn holiday. At Christmas time, holiday decoration of homes is common, and groups of young people stroll about the streets or ride in sleighs singing carols. New Year's Eve brings about the usual noisy gaiety, and in many towns it is customary to fire guns in a salute as the New Year comes in. Watch parties are held in the churches for the more serious-minded.

The Fourth of July is an important holiday, not so much for its historic meaning as for its local interpretation. For days previously, the skies are anxiously scanned for signs of inclement weather. As the Glorious Fourth dawns a salute is fired, usually by ex-servicemen, and soon in the early morning air the sound of hammers is heard, as booths and 'concessions' rapidly go up to be draped with bunting. Flags appear on the buildings and homes. Cars begin to pour into town, parking near

Main Street, which has been roped off for the races. The square is soon filled with a milling crowd, all in their best clothes, the children clutching their long-hoarded pennies and nickels which they will exchange for soda pop, ice cream, and firecrackers. The program of the day includes patriotic speeches, airplane and parachute exhibits, races, and bowery dances, and in the evening the climax of the exciting day—a fireworks display.

The Russo-Germans know the holiday simply as 'the July,' and in a good year it is an occasion for new clothes for the entire family, commonly designated 'July dresses' and 'July suits.'

Conviviality often joins with practical necessity to provide social occasions for North Dakotans. Butchering, sausage-making, soap-making, quilting, threshing, burials, illness, all furnish opportunity for friends to meet and visit while performing some deed of necessity or kindness. The farmer who is ill during sowing time will often have his crop put in by his neighbors, and he may be called on in the fall to help harvest for the recently bereaved widow of one of his friends. The neighbor who has lost his home by fire or has had some other misfortune will probably be given a 'make-glad' party, at which he will receive gifts in kind and perhaps in money. After harvest, when there is straw to be burned, the young people of the locality will hold strawstack parties, roasting wieners and marshmallows as the burning stacks light the autumn night with their red gleam.

Although today horse-drawn vehicles have been largely replaced by cars, sometimes, with the coming of dusk on winter evenings, bobsleighs slide away from darkened country homes, filled with all the members of the family, from grandparents down to babies. Often the sleigh will pick up additional passengers at a near-by homestead, and sometimes it becomes so crowded that there is scarcely room for the boxes of sandwiches, carefully wrapped cakes, and jars of pickles among the shuffling feet and heated rocks and bricks in the bottom of the sleigh. The singing creak of the sleigh runners accompanies songs that boom out on the night air. Presently a number of sleighs reach an appointed home, but they do not pause long. Across the fields the light of a farmhouse window offers a prelude to their welcome. They become studiously quiet until they reach the door, then burst in with shouts of 'Surprise!' There follows a confusion of greetings. (All North Dakotans like surprise parties and have them on birthdays, wedding anniversaries, and every other plausible occasion.)

The farmhouse is converted into a dual-purpose hall. The accordion is placed near the stove to 'thaw out,' wraps are deposited in corners, on chairs, and on beds, except the one reserved for the babies. Tables, the drophead sewing machine, and everything else that will serve the purpose are arranged for card playing. One room is cleared for dancing. After the first spurt of conversation lags, the musician takes his instrument on his knee, the floor is sprinkled with corn meal or grated paraffin, and soon the house is shaking from studding to rafter. Someone suggests a quadrille, or square dance, and the room resounds with the calls:

> First two gents cross over
> And leave your lady stand,
> Side two gents cross over,
> And take her by the hand.
> Salute your corner lady,
> Salute your partners all,
> Swing the corner lady,
> And promenade round the hall.

> First couple to the right,
> Birdie in the center and three hands round,
> Birdie fly out and hunter step in.
> Three hands round.

At midnight, after three or four hours of dancing and card playing, 'the ladies' serve lunch. The hat is passed for contributions to the musician, but he does not take the money until he is through playing, which is usually about 3 o'clock in the morning. Then, after a general bedlam of looking for mislaid coats, the babies are carefully wrapped, the younger children are wakened and rub their eyes sleepily as they climb into the sleighs, the empty cake plates and pickle jars are collected, farewells are called, and horses, anxious to return to their own stalls, speed the drowsy parties home through the cold night.

The young people of the State usually have ample opportunity for courting at such parties, or at meetings of junior church organizations, church camps, and junior choirs. Matchmaking still exists in isolated Russo-German, German, and Norwegian communities, however. Except in the larger towns—and sometimes even there—the newly married pair is usually honored by a charivari, or 'chivaree,' with the bridal couple seated conspicuously on some slowly moving vehicle and taken through the streets to an accompaniment of blaring automobile horns and clanging tin pans. The bridegroom is expected to climax this procedure by buying drinks or cigars for the crowd.

Cigars are much in evidence at the birth of a first child, and also thereafter at the birth of a son. A child born with a caul is believed by many to have the gift of second sight.

Superstitions attach to many other phases of life, as well as to births. Most of these beliefs are not peculiar to North Dakota, but are rather a part of the folklore of the nation. A dropped spoon means company is coming, and so does the cat's washing its face. Snakes do not die before sundown. A horse-hair put in water will turn into a snake. The number of stars in the ring around the moon shows the number of days before a coming storm. Plants that bear underground should be planted in the dark of the moon, and those that bear above ground in the light of the moon. A window shade rolling up when no one is near it portends a death in the family.

Many of the myriad superstitions are not believed, but nevertheless continue to be passed on. There is some belief in ghosts and occult powers, and scarcely any community is without the story of a strange death and a haunted house—such as the tale of the doctor who was mysteriously killed on a farm near Wilton and whose ghostly galloping team disturbed the farmer so much that he was forced to move. These stories, however, are often not credited but merely passed on for effect. As for fortune tellers, the most popular prophets are those who deal not with tall dark men and long trips but with isobars and isotherms, for the interests of agricultural North Dakotans are inseparable from the weather, which governs their destinies far more surely than any other factor in their lives.

Schools, Churches, and Social Currents

FOR many years education and religion in North Dakota were closely associated, for the earliest schools were organized by priests. The Scottish Highlanders of North Dakota's first white settlement—the Selkirk colony at Pembina—were a highly religious peasant people who keenly felt the absence of churches and schools in the land to which they had migrated. Their sponsor, Lord Selkirk, also felt that a church would add to the harmony and stability of the community and offered to contribute 25 acres for a church and 20 square miles for a school and mission if the Bishop of Quebec would approve a church at Pembina. The bishop acceded, and in 1818 Father Joseph Dumoulin, Father Joseph Provencher, and William Edge, a catechist, arrived to establish churches and schools and study the 'savage languages' in order to 'reduce those languages to regular principles so as to be able to publish a grammar after some years of residence.'

EDUCATION

The first school in North Dakota, at Pembina, had an enrollment of 60 children, white and half-breed, and courses in English were supplemented by lessons in planting small grains, both intended for the enlightenment of the 'savage' Chippewa. The school was conducted until 1823, when, after the determination of the international boundary, many of the Selkirkers moved north to Canada, thus breaking up the colony. The missionaries were withdrawn, and the school and chapel remained closed for a quarter century. When Father George Belcourt came to the region in 1848, he reopened the Pembina Mission and founded another at St. Joseph in the Pembina Mountains. A school conducted at St. Joseph by the Sisters of the Propagation of the Faith received financial aid from the Federal Government, the first Federal support given to education in this State.

In the early settlements of the State, a mother would often gather the children of the neighborhood in her home for instruction, and itinerant teachers occasionally held classes in the tent cities that sprang up in the wake of the railroad. As the communities grew, residents cooperated in hiring teachers and building schools. The railroad companies assisted by shipping lumber free for schools. Between 1853 and the attainment of statehood in 1889, 1,362 schools were opened, many of them in country communities, taught by men or women who had come West to homestead. A teacher's report on one such school, sent to the superintendent of the Griggs County schools in 1886, recorded that he had taught a 62-day term, with 15 pupils enrolled and daily average attendance of $7\frac{7}{31}$; that his salary was $35 a month; and that the school building and grounds were in good condition, the former containing a 'Webster's Unabridged Dictionary, New 8-inch Terrestrial Globe, New Forms and Solids for object Teaching and Two Slate black boards.'

By 1883 two institutions of higher education had been founded in the northern half of Dakota Territory. Jamestown College, the first school in the State to offer a normal course, had been established by the Presbyterian Church, and three months later the Territorial assembly voted to found a University of North Dakota at Grand Forks. Originally a liberal arts college, this institution extended its curriculum until, in 1889, it included a law school, a college of mechanical engineering, and a school of mines. In its first year the university had an enrollment of 79; during 1948, 2,659 attended classes or took correspondence work in its 6 colleges.

Several private colleges were opened prior to 1889, and the Enabling Act of that year provided for the establishment of an agricultural college and normal schools. Like the other private institutions, Jamestown College was forced to close its doors during the financial panic of 1893. Reopened in 1909, it is now the only endowed liberal arts college in the State. The effects of the 1893 depression on the university and normal schools were accentuated by the vetoing of the appropriations for a two-year period. Weathering this crisis, the State colleges and university reached an enrollment of 2000 in 1904, and by 1936 their total registration exceeded 10,000.

Notable in educational history was the affiliation in 1905 of the university and Wesley College, a Methodist school originally located at Wahpeton. Similar affiliations were later made among other colleges, including the North Dakota Agricultural College, where the Wesley

College buildings are now used for an interdenominational school of religion.

To comply with the provision of the Enabling Act requiring establishment and maintenance of a public-school system open to all children and free from sectarian control, the first legislature set up an education department administered by three branches—a State superintendent, county superintendents, and district boards. It also created a tuition fund from the proceeds of school lands, supplemented by poll taxes, school taxes levied by general law, and all fines for violation of State statutes. The money from these sources was made available to all schools in which the English language was taught.

The school lands to which the law referred were received by the State in accordance with the plan of the Federal act of 1785 granting each new State carved from the Ohio Territory section 16 of each township for public school support. For North and South Dakota, under the Enabling Act, this grant was doubled, giving the schools one eighteenth of all land surveyed. Town site boomers and speculators in other States commonly took advantage of school land grants to buy property at prices far below the actual value; but in the Dakotas they were forestalled by the alert Territorial superintendent of schools, W. H. H. Beadle, who incorporated into the constitutions of both States the provision that school lands might not be sold at less than $10 an acre and might be leased as hay or grazing lands but not for cultivation, and that the title of western coal lands included in the grant must always be retained by the State. Similarly guarded were 750,000 acres of land granted to other educational institutions. So successful was Beadle's plan that it has been adopted by almost every other State admitted to the Union since 1889.

At the State School of Science at Wahpeton, opened in 1903 as a trade school and junior college, two methods of industrial education have been originated, the Babcock plan and the North Dakota plan, both of which have attracted the attention of educators throughout the United States. The former provides for the establishment of three departments within the school—a trade school, a junior college, and a business school—each of which, by a plan of interaction, is made to serve the others. The North Dakota plan, evolved to solve the problem of providing industrial education in an agricultural State, concentrates all trades education in one school, with the exception of night courses offered at other points in the State under the supervision of the school of science.

A second junior college was established in 1925 at the school of forestry in Bottineau, and the Bismarck Junior College was established in 1939. Devils Lake also has a junior college now.

Fifty-nine parochial schools, most of them maintained by either the Roman Catholic or the Lutheran Church, offer grade and high-school work and are governed by the State department of public instruction.

Under the supervision of the board of administration, the State supports a school for the deaf at Devils Lake, a school for the blind at Bathgate, and an institution for feeble-minded at Grafton. The board also has jurisdiction over the hospital for the insane at Jamestown, the training school for delinquents at Mandan, the penitentiary at Bismarck, and a sanatorium at San Haven. Several semi-public homes and orphanages are operated by churches and other organizations.

It is compulsory for all children between the ages of 7 and 15 to attend school, and a student who has not completed the eighth grade must continue in school until he is 17 years of age. Agriculture is a compulsory course in public schools. Free textbooks are provided for rural schools, and uniform texts are prescribed for all public schools.

A school census taken in June 1947 showed North Dakota to have a school-age population of 115,070, of whom 112,629 were enrolled in public schools.

Indian children are given grade and high-school education and vocational training in special schools at Fort Totten, Fort Yates, Elbowoods, Belcourt, and Wahpeton. Preservation of tribal arts, including beadwork and pottery, is encouraged.

The North Dakota educational system is greatly influenced by the agrarian character of the State. Because children are needed for farm work, most of the country schools are not opened until October and sometimes operate for a term of only eight months, as against the nine-month term in city schools. A survey made in the winter of 1923–4 showed a sharp decline in attendance records in rural schools, and consequently legislation was enacted providing free transportation for pupils living more than two and a half miles from school. The legislation affected two fifths of the rural school population and resulted in improved attendance in elementary schools. The one-room school is still the most common type of educational institution in the State, although the number of consolidated schools is being increased annually. Sixty high schools, including the Benson and Walsh County Agricultural Schools, receive Federal aid through the Smith-Hughes Act, which provides funds for vocational training and courses in agriculture. This act also enables the North Dakota Agricultural College in Fargo to operate extension service and experimental stations, and to provide a state-wide educational program for farmers.

Reading facilities in public schools were improved by the 1911 legislative appropriation of $25 to each school district for a permanent school library. In many communities these school libraries, supplemented by the loan services offered by the State educational institutions and the traveling libraries of the State library commission, are the only sources of reading material. The first public library in the State was opened in 1897 in Grafton by a group of clubwomen, and many other towns have received similar benefit from the efforts of women's clubs to build up library collections.

RELIGION

Through the influence of three prominent men in the Red River settlement—Joseph Rolette, Norman Kittson, and Anton Gringas—Father Belcourt was able to maintain his Pembina Mission, establish another at St. Joseph, and extend his work west to the Turtle Mountains. He held services for Indians and hunters alike.

Meanwhile, Protestantism was introduced into the State by James Tanner, a half-breed interpreter from the Cass Lake (Minnesota) Reservation who had become a Baptist minister. At his request, Reverend Alonzo Barnard came from the Presbyterian mission at Cass Lake to Pembina and St. Joseph late in 1848. Barnard remained only a short time, being succeeded in 1850 by a young Baptist missionary, Elijah Terry, who was killed by hostile Sioux as he was cutting logs for a chapel. The following summer Barnard returned, accompanied by his wife, David Spencer and his family, and John Smith. Despite severe misfortune, including Mrs. Barnard's death from pneumonia, and the death of Mrs. Spencer, who was pierced by an Indian arrow as she stood in the window of her cabin with her baby in her arms, the mission was kept open until 1858.

Except for occasional visits by priests and ministers from Canada to the Pembina settlement, there was little further religious activity in North Dakota until 1871, when the Presbyterians again sent a minister into the Red River Valley. Oscar H. Elmer, who received the appointment, drove up and down the valley in a homemade cutter and was the first to conduct church services in many of the pioneer towns, including Fargo and Grand Forks.

When the Episcopal Church decided to send a missionary into the newly settled territory, the board, guided by the stories it had heard of Dakota winters, recalled Reverend Robert Wainright from his mission in Labrador, feeling that his experience there should have qualified him to serve in Dakota. Mr. Wainright took over the northern half of Dakota Territory and raised funds to carry on his work by appearing in Labrador costume and giving exhibitions of his skill with a 40-foot whip, with which it is said he could flick water out of a glass.

As settlement increased, other church groups sent missionaries and ministers. At first, services were held in homes, schools, or tents, and often a building used during the week as a saloon or gambling hall would become a place of worship on Sunday. The ministerial duties frequently included janitor work, and since the remuneration usually consisted of donations from the parishioners, many of the ministers supplemented this income by operating small farms. The hardships of pioneer days led to much resourcefulness on the part of early churchgoers. Gopher tails were saved and placed on the collection plate by those who had no cash to give, for the church could then claim the three-cent bounty on gophers offered by the State. As communities grew, new church buildings were erected, until now some of the most notable structures in the State are churches. Religious colonies came to North Dakota to settle, and Mennonite, Dunkard, Moravian, and Mohammedan are among the approximately 25 creeds represented in the State. Most influential are the Lutheran (due to the large number of Scandinavian settlers) and the Roman Catholic.

The actual number of churches is decreasing as parishes are enlarged, and in smaller towns and rural sections the consolidation of churches has been found practical..

SOCIAL CONDITIONS

A movement in 1915 for increased social legislation resulted in the passage of mothers' pension, juvenile court, and old-age pension acts, and in the abolition of capital punishment except in the case of a convict already serving a life sentence for murder.

In contrast to the general trend of prison populations throughout the United States, that of the North Dakota penitentiary has steadily decreased. Today there are 225 at the penitentiary and 30, committed for misdemeanors, on the prison farm.

Impetus was added to the program against juvenile delinquency in

1921 by the publication of the results of a five-year survey that showed that more than 500 children were brought into court annually. Laws regarding juvenile delinquency were made more stringent. The reform school at Mandan was renamed the State Training School, and a corresponding change was effected in the methods of handling delinquents sent there. From a juvenile prison the institution became virtually a boarding school in which boys and girls between the ages of 12 and 21 supplement regular grade and high-school work and vocational training with such extracurricular activities as music, dramatics, athletics, and club work.

Since the survey revealed that, while only 5 per cent of the child population of the State lived in three cities having a population of more than 10,000, these cities reported 45 per cent of the delinquency, social service groups in all the cities were enlisted to deal with the problem. New emphasis was placed on character-building organizations such as Boy and Girl Scouts, Campfire Girls, Y.M.C.A., and Y.W.C.A.; playgrounds were opened, and recreational programs promoted. The American Legion formed a Junior Baseball League for boys under 17 years of age, which was so successful that in many communities boys who graduated from the junior teams are now receiving civic support in the organization of intermediate and senior clubs.

North Dakota's moderate temperature and dry air came in for early prominence in the advertisements of promoters, who assured prospective settlers that this was one of the most healthful States in the Union. It was a fortunate circumstance that they were correct, for lack of transportation facilities and the limited number of doctors often made it impossible for settlers to obtain medical aid. Today the number of doctors is adequate for the population, but their tendency to concentrate in the larger towns leaves many western rural communities, and a few in the east, with no medical aid within many miles. Despite this uneven distribution of doctors, North Dakota has always had a good health record. Since there are no large cities, contagious diseases do not spread rapidly and epidemics are comparatively rare. The death rate in the State is 8.2 per thousand of population, while the figure for the United States as a whole is 10.8. The highest death rate is among the Indians, tuberculosis being the most prevalent cause. Largely through the efforts of Dean H. E. French of the university school of medicine, a State health department was established in 1923, which has set up a health program and secured passage of laws providing for medical inspection in public schools, creation of a board of examiners for nurses, registration of nurses, and employment of county nurses.

The 1935 legislature provided for a Public Welfare Board of North Dakota and also passed an act requiring that the Board of County Commissioners provide for the establishment of a county welfare board for each of the 53 counties. The program of the Public Welfare Board is administered through the Divisions of Child Welfare, Public Assistance, Research and Statistics, Accounts and Audits, and Field Service. A comprehensive program of child welfare reaches approximately 7000 children each year through Child Welfare Services and Crippled Children's Services, and in co-operation with the State Elks Association the Board operates Camp Grassick for physically handicapped and underprivileged children and conducts itinerant crippled children's clinics in various parts of the State. The Division of Public Assistance includes programs for Aid to Dependent Children, Old Age Assistance, and Aid to the Blind, established by the Federal Social Security Act, and the state-county program of General Assistance. In June 1949, 8,793 persons received Old Age Assistance in the average monthly amount of $46.63; 1,740 cases received Aid to Dependent Children in an average monthly amount of $97.71; 117 blind persons received assistance in the average monthly amount of $45.50; and, in April 1949, 1,439 people received General Assistance in the average monthly amount of $45.33. The Director of Field Service is responsible for the effective operation of the Board's programs in the counties and gives assistance to the county agencies.

Stringent pure-food and drug acts were drafted for the State by the late Dr. Edwin F. Ladd, an outstanding figure in the field of public health, who as United States Senator from North Dakota drew up some of the Federal pure food laws. A regulatory department maintains a laboratory where foodstuffs and other products are tested for compliance with State laws. The department of public health also has laboratories throughout the State, and several cities have their own facilities for testing water supplies.

Transportation

W HEN in 1738 the intrepid French-Canadian, Pierre Veren-drye, his three sons, and his nephew set out on foot to trudge weary miles across the prairies to the Mantannes on the Missouri River, they did not dream that some day man-made birds would flash their silver wings against the sky and glide smoothly to rest on the level plains. Less than 200 years were to pass before this miracle of transportation would become so commonplace that a native North Dakotan would think nothing of a trip from Montreal to Bismarck by plane, but would be astonished at the thought of any-one's walking that distance.

Verendrye, the first white man known to have touched North Dakota soil, and other explorers who followed in those early years, came on foot to visit the Indians. They found the Mandans, who lived beside the Missouri, in possession of unusual means of water transportation. The dugout canoe, made of a log, was found on all the rivers of North Dakota, but only in the Missouri Valley did the Indians use the bull-boat, a circular craft of the coracle type which the Indians made by stretching a buffalo hide over a willow frame. Before the introduction of the horse, Indians used the dog train for hauling heavy loads over-land, but North Dakota tribes later acquired horses, descendants of those brought by the Spanish, from Indians to the south and west. Of all tribes the Sioux were the most graceful and daring riders. The horse travois, a rather crude means of hauling baggage devised by the In-dians, soon gave way to the white man's wagon as settlers began to pour in.

The covered wagon served to move the immigrant family to its new home and furnished immediate living quarters. In 1803 at his fur-trading post at Pembina on the Red River, Alexander Henry's traders introduced a two-wheeled cart modeled after those used in France but constructed of wood and rawhide only. These crude vehicles, known as Red River carts, were of great importance in the fur trade and during pioneer days. Long creaking trains of these carts drawn by oxen made their way slowly across the country, carrying settlers and supplies.

Before the coming of modern means of transportation, the Missouri River formed the most important avenue of entry into what is now North Dakota. The ascent of the river by the steamboat *Yellowstone* to Fort Union in 1832 was an event of importance, because the Big Muddy had never before been navigated through this territory.

The Indians who witnessed the coming of this first boat found great significance in it also. According to George Catlin, the artist, who was aboard the steamer, some of them shot their dogs and horses in a sacrifice to appease the Great Spirit, who they thought was offended; some ran frightened to their homes; and some among the Mandans cautiously approached the ship, 'the big medicine canoe with eyes,' which in some mysterious way could see its own way to take the deep water in the middle of the channel.

The frequently changing channel and swift current of the river proved a severe test for the hardy and resourceful pilots who followed in the wake of the *Yellowstone*. As the Sioux City (Iowa) *Register* stated in 1868, 'Of all the variable things in creation the most uncertain are the action of a jury, the state of a woman's mind, and the condition of the Missouri River.'

The humorist George Fitch, as quoted in Edna LaMoore Waldo's *Dakota*, describes the stream in these words:

There is only one river with a personality, a sense of humor, and a woman's caprice; a river that goes traveling sidewise, that interferes in politics, rearranges geography and dabbles in real estate; a river that plays hide-and-seek with you today, and tomorrow follows you around like a pet dog with a dynamite cracker tied to his tail. That river is the Missouri.

A pilot familiar with the river, and able to foresee its vagaries, often received—and was easily worth—$1000 a month, fabulous as that salary may now seem.

The Red River was also a highway of traffic in the heyday of the steamboat. Supplies were carried down it to Grand Forks, Pembina, and Winnipeg (then Fort Garry). The steamboat could be employed only during the summer months, however, when the river was open. During the winters in the 1870's, messages, supplies, and mail were carried by pack horse and dogsled. Regular mail routes were established between Fort Abercrombie and Fort Totten, and from St. Paul to Winnipeg, by way of Pembina.

As news of the vast untouched wealth of the new Territory drifted back to eastern capitalists, they turned their eyes westward. Soon survey parties mapped the projected courses of railroads. By 1871 the Northern Pacific Railway had been completed as far as Moorhead, Minnesota. The next year it crossed the river and in 1873 reached Bismarck, halting at the Missouri. It was no easy task to span this treacherous river; and, with the interruption of the panic of 1873, not until 1879 was there any further westward extension. Construction work to the Montana border was finished in 1881, two years before the Northern Pacific became a transcontinental line. So great was the influence of the railroad in bringing new settlers to Dakota that in the period from 1870 to 1875 the population of the western half of the Red River Valley doubled. General Custer's expedition returned from the Black Hills in 1874 with glowing tales of gold. There was a rush for the Hills, and Bismarck, the nearest railroad terminus, became temporary headquarters for parties leaving by stage for the gold fields. The route that Custer had taken to the Hills from Bismarck was long known as the Territorial Highway.

The first railroad to reach North Dakota was the Northern Pacific, which was built to Moorhead, Minnesota, in 1871, to Jamestown in 1872, and to Bismarck in 1873. Although James J. Hill was one of the first to sponsor steamboat traffic on the Red River, it was not until 1880 that he began building the Great Northern Railway down the Red River Valley to Grand Forks, and thence westward to Minot in 1887. Other lines of the Northern Pacific and Great Northern, main and branch lines of the Minneapolis, St. Paul & Sault Ste. Marie, and branches of other roads soon entered the State. In order to build permanent business for their lines, they brought in new settlers, gave special rates on household and farm equipment, and in every way encouraged settlement. It was because of the railroads that bonanza farming, an important phase of North Dakota history, was introduced. The State is now served by 6 railroads, with more than 5000 miles of trackage.

With the railroads came the telegraph lines, the first of which was established between Winnipeg and Abercrombie, with offices at Fargo and Grand Forks, in 1871. Soon all of the young Territory was in communication with the outside world.

The picturesque era of the steamboat had ended with the coming of the cheaper and speedier transportation by rail, but methods of local transportation remained unaltered. The horse still furnished the power, although fashions in wagons and buggies might change.

It was left for the twentieth century to usher in the age of speed. In the first decade, the wheezing steam automobile chugged with difficulty over sticky gumbo roads in the Red River Valley, and over scoria trails in the west. Automobiles were rare, and possession of one marked the owner as an aristocrat or a public nuisance, according to the point of view of the observer.

When the internal-combustion motor vehicle was improved, road building began in earnest. Bus companies, established to fill a need for north and south transportation facilities not provided by the railroads, opened a campaign for better roads. They were joined by an ever-increasing number of car owners, and as a result road conditions have been steadily improved since the early 1920's.

The first bus line in the State was begun in 1922, between Bismarck and Minot. Although the next two years saw the introduction of many bus and truck lines, these were not regulated by State law until placed under jurisdiction of the board of railway commissioners by legislative act in 1925. Immediately, operating permits were required from all companies, one of the first being granted to the Northland Transportation Company, forerunner of the Northland Greyhound Line. Today a network of bus and truck lines covers the State.

The airplane proved admirably suited to this part of the country. The clear dry atmosphere afforded ideal flying conditions, and almost every part of the State was suitable for landing fields, even without improvement. Municipalities became interested in the new mode of transportation, hangars were built, and runways laid out. Now all of the larger cities and towns have airports, and almost every small town has its landing field. Private planes are found at the airports, and here and there ships are seen on farms, where mechanically minded lads pilot them in leisure hours for their own pleasure. All planes and pilots must be licensed under a State law of 1929, as well as conform to the regulations of the Department of Commerce.

Cheering crowds at Fargo, Grand Forks, and Pembina greeted the pilots of the first air mail between the Twin Cities and Winnipeg in 1928. Hundreds of letters and cards were carried on this flight for collectors who desired copies of the special commemorative cancellation stamp. North Dakotans' air mail letters soon reached Washington, D. C., or Los Angeles 12 hours after mailing. Daily service on the original line is still maintained, and other regular lines have been extended into the

State: Northwest Airlines, between New York and Seattle, stops at Fargo, Grand Forks, Jamestown, and Bismarck; Mid-Continent Airlines between Minot and the Gulf Coast stops at Bismarck.

Transportation has advanced with amazing rapidity since the Territory of Dakota was organized in 1861. Nevertheless, a severe winter such as that of 1948–9 is capable of halting communication almost completely. But even then, with automobile traffic at a standstill because of blocked roads, trains delayed because of mountainous snowdrifts, and planes grounded because snow and ice made landing too hazardous, the radio still kept the State in constant touch with the outside world.

The Press and Radio

WHETHER or not the first printing press in North Dakota, brought to St. Joseph (Walhalla) by Reverend Alonzo Barnard in 1848, was ever used in the State is a matter of conjecture. When Mr. Barnard, a Presbyterian minister, was transferred to Dakota, he took his press—a gift from students at Oberlin College—overland from the Cass Lake (Minnesota) Reservation to Red Lake, by canoe across the lake and down the Red Lake and Red Rivers to Pembina, then by oxcart to St. Joe. Here he may have used it, as he did in Minnesota, to publish news letters and pamphlets for his parishioners, but nothing printed on it in North Dakota has been preserved.

The first North Dakota publication was probably the *Frontier Scout,* a short-lived four-page, three-column sheet that made its appearance at Fort Union in July 1864. In the following year its successor, the *Pioneer Scout,* was issued at Fort Rice and, according to its editors, 'published weekly by the First U.S.V. Infantry for the edification of the people of Dacotah, both civilized and savage; and as "green" spots and "green" backs are so few, we will not mention terms, but bid it, like the grace of God, go free.' The editors further declared that 'every article in this paper is original and sees the light of day for the first time.'

Journalistic activity lapsed subsequent to these military literary efforts and was not revived until the railroad and the resultant influx of settlers in 1872 brought the new Territory to the attention of Minnesota editors. Colonel Clement A. Lounsberry, sent by the Minneapolis *Tribune* to cover colonization in the Fargo area, went on to Bismarck where, on July 11, 1873, the first number of his own paper, the Bismarck *Tribune,* appeared. First a weekly and later a daily, it has been published continuously since that time, missing only one edition, and on that occasion newsboys distributed hastily printed handbills containing formal notice that the *Tribune* plant had been destroyed by fire (*see* BISMARCK).

Early journalism in the Fargo area was stimulated by the offer of the Wells-Fargo Express Company to give a cash bonus for a paper appearing under the name of the Fargo *Express*. First and unsuccessful bidder for the bonus was a sheet bearing the correct name, but printed at Glyndon, Minnesota. The prize was awarded in 1874 to a Fargo-printed publication. Between 1874 and 1891 several other papers were issued, to be merged finally in the Fargo *Forum* in 1891.

In 1874 the Grand Forks *Plaindealer* was founded; five years later the *Herald* was also in the field and eventually absorbed the *Plaindealer* (*see* GRAND FORKS).

With the beginning of settlement newspapers sprang up quickly in the other new towns of Dakota, so that when North Dakota was admitted to the Union in 1889, it had 125 periodicals. Many so-called newspapers were nothing more than a final proofsheet, printed in order that settlers might comply with the homesteading law which required publication of notice of final claim. The cost of establishing such a paper was slight. Official notices, an occasional advertisement, and a few local news items were all it contained. If the editor could win the favor of the United States Land Office registrar, who usually designated the official paper, he might obtain a hundred or more notices an issue; these at $5 each made his income quite substantial. Often the paper was short-lived, but the editor usually remained in the State, setting up his type cases and presses in some promising small town and starting an actual weekly paper. Many villages had two or more rival papers for a time, and the number of publications increased rapidly; in 1904 there were 265 in the State, and in 1919 a high of 336 was reached. The weekly papers were widely read and often had great political influence. Improved transportation facilities, however, led to the retreat of the weeklies before the increasing circulation of the daily papers. North Dakota now has 10 dailies, 2 semi-weeklies, and 125 weeklies.

Always active in the political life of the State, the newspapers have been an especially important factor in the Nonpartisan League fight. With the daily press usually unanimously opposed to its program, the league has purchased weeklies through which it has exercised a great influence on the rural population. Although it does not control as many weeklies now as it formerly did, it still has a strong hand in the editorial policies of many papers in the State.

In May 1922, less than two years after the first radio broadcast in the United States had been put on the air by KDKA in Pittsburgh, WDAY of Fargo presented the first commercial broadcast in North Dakota. By 1938 the State had seven other stations, situated in Bismarck, Grand Forks, Minot, Devils Lake, Mandan, Valley City, and Jamestown. Today Fargo and Grand Forks have 3 stations each, and there are additional stations operating at Dickinson, Wahpeton, and Williston.

KFJM in Grand Forks was one of the first stations in the United States to be owned by a State university. It is leased to private operators with the provision that its facilities be at the disposal of the school for special broadcasts and experimental work (see GRAND FORKS).

The radio has made an important contribution to the State service by broadcasting information on weather conditions whenever necessary. Lives and thousands of dollars in property have been saved by warnings of spring floods. During the winter months frequent weather and highway reports are given, and warnings sent out regarding advisability of sending children to school during storms or extremely cold weather. In November 1930 an unusual service was performed by the Fargo and Bismarck stations. Heavy coatings of sleet had broken down telephone and telegraph wires throughout the State and severed all communication between Fargo and Jamestown, division points on the Northern Pacific. During the first afternoon of the storm, short-wave communication was established between the Fargo transmitter and an amateur set at Jamestown, but after sunset interference forced abandonment of this broadcast. Receiving sets were quickly installed at the studios of the Fargo and Bismarck stations, making possible a two-way conversation. On the one available telephone connection between Jamestown and Bismarck the dispatchers' office in Jamestown was hooked up with the Bismarck studio, in Fargo the dispatcher was linked with WDAY, and for two days all trains on the line were dispatched by radio. Between train orders the facilities of both stations were turned over to the telegraph offices, and Fargo alone sent out more than 200 messages.

Several amateur stations were in operation before any commercial broadcasting had been done in North Dakota. When the convention of the Dakota Division of the American Radio Relay League was held in Fargo in 1936, there were 300 licensed operators in attendance, and each year finds an increased number of people selecting short-wave broadcasting as a hobby.

Architecture

THE buildings of North Dakota cling closely to the low, tranquil landscape of the State, avoiding exposure to the cold northwest winds that sweep across the snowy prairie in winter. Farms and towns huddle in valleys or hug the open plain, and only grain elevators dare to break the comfortable horizontality of the prevailing contours. In the few cities a tendency can be noted toward height in buildings, but the number of skyscrapers in North Dakota can be counted on the fingers of one hand.

Despite this relatively small number, one skyscraper, the State Capitol (designed by Joseph B. DeRemer and William F. Kurke, and Holabird and Root, associates), has aroused more interest and comment than any other building in the history of the State. This interest has not been confined to the borders of North Dakota, for the 'slender shaft of modernity' which dominates the Bismarck skyline represents a trend in the architecture of state capitols that is gaining the attention of the entire nation. Because the basic reasons for the skyscraper— exaggerated land values and proximity to transportation centers—are utterly lacking in this capacious prairie State, much criticism has been directed at the type of statehouse chosen. Nevertheless the point is made that the character and purpose of the building as the seat of State government are well expressed in the impressive height and dignity of its lines, while at the same time the structure is decidedly utilitarian. (*See* Bismarck.)

Utilitarianism characterized the architecture of this region before even the earliest white explorations took place. When Verendrye visited the Mandan Indians along the Missouri in 1738 he found them living in well-built lodges made of earth packed over a framework of logs, comfortably cool in summer and warm in winter. The lodge was constructed of native materials and suited the settled agricultural life of the Mandans. In the same way the easily moved skin tipi of the nomadic

Sioux whom the early explorers found to the east of the Missouri was well suited to their wandering mode of life.

The fur traders were the first white people to build in this region, and, like the Indians, they made use of native materials. Their posts, usually on the rivers where timber was available, were rough affairs of untrimmed logs, roofed with dirt laid over a timber framework, with the earth for a floor. Like the Indians of the Missouri Valley, the traders put up log stockades around their posts to ward off attacks of hostile natives.

The settlers who followed the traders into this country also made use of the trees that grew along the streams, but as settlement began to penetrate the unforested interior of the State the earth itself provided building material for frontier homes. A furrow some three inches deep was plowed into a tough sod containing many grass roots, and the broken sod was cut into lengths the width of the wall, up to two and a half feet. One row of blocks was laid lengthwise of the wall and the next crosswise, with the joints staggered as in laying bricks. The finished wall provided a strong, thick barrier against summer heat and winter cold. The roof, like that of many log houses, was of poles covered with brush, often finished with overlapping strips of sod. Sometimes these sod roofs actually bloomed in the spring as their many roots came to life, and one pioneer told of the small poles that formed the framework of his roof leafing out inside the house in midwinter.

Improved transportation brought lumber into North Dakota, and frame shanties and houses were built. The red barn took a prominent place on the farm, and the silo, for storing fodder, reared its vertical mass, sometimes dwarfing even the windmill with its revolving silvery fins. Except for the more affluent farms, where the homes sometimes boasted as many as 12 rooms and a porch, the farmhouses followed an uninspired cycle of rectangular or L-shaped frame structures, often with a lean-to shed at the back for storing wood or coal. On Russo-German farms in the southern and western parts of the State a European love of color asserted itself as houses were painted sky blue or nile green or pink, and color combinations such as red, white, and blue formed a pattern of diagonal stripes on the barn or granary door.

In each township appeared the one-room country school, usually white or light green in color, with its three windows on each side, coal shed and door in one end, chimney and black board in the other, and possibly a bell tower over the door. The early school was not only a seat of learning, it was also the community center, where a Saturday night basket social might be followed by church services the next morning.

As the stories of rich land and the lure of the frontier brought more people to this region, small towns grew up on the prairie, most of them consisting of one business street and a few residential streets. Along the wooden sidewalks of Main Street the false-front building predominated, its frame façade rising a half story or more above its roof. The motive for constructing the false-front building may have been to provide space for a sign, or it may have been merely to 'put on front' literally as well as figuratively. Often the sole brick building in the young North Dakota town housed the bank, and the hotel could be easily identified by its porches. Near the railroad track was the long gable roof depot of dark red, dark green, or yellow trimmed in red. The school was a box-like white frame structure topped with a bell tower, and every town had at least one rectangular, white, gable-roof church with windows in either side and a steeple and bell on the entrance façade. Residences varied from tar-paper shanties to the ornate, gabled, towered mansion of the 'eighties.

Dominating the silhouette of these little villages were the grain elevators, those bright sentinels which symbolized the reason for the towns' founding, and still remain the most typical buildings in the North Dakota picture today. Like tall men standing head and shoulders above a crowd, they rise 60 to 70 feet above the low prairie. First glimpsed as any town comes into sight is the row of wedge-shaped cupolas, like arrowheads in profile, topping the almost square red, green, or maroon shafts. On the side opposite the railroad track, along which the elevators are lined, each building has its one-story scalehouse, where the trucks and wagons dump their loads of grain. A few feet from the scalehouse is the small rectangular power house and office building.

As towns have prospered, brick buildings have come into use in the business sections, and new homes of bungalow, colonial, old English, Spanish, and other modified styles have been built. Leaving behind the era of metal fronts, towers, and domes, public buildings are emerging in neoclassic, gothic, colonial, and modern architecture. The little white churches have given way in many instances to stone and brick structures varying in design from gothic to modern; the United Lutheran Church in Grand Forks is an example of the latter. The schools have shown perhaps the greatest development of any type of building, and most towns now have well-designed modern schools, which often serve as community centers.

Native building materials are becoming more popular in North

Dakota, and each year an increasing amount of construction utilizes native-made brick and locally quarried sandstone. An interesting development in the use of native materials is the rammed-earth building, the walls of which consist of earth tamped until it is hard as rock. A house and garage of this construction erected on the Scoria Lily ranch near Hettinger (*see Tour* 9), because of their unusually low building cost, have attracted wide attention. The use of native boulders as a building material is well illustrated in the Cairn, home of Mr. and Mrs. Clell G. Gannon in Bismarck.

Even with these attempts there is no native North Dakota architecture. The schools, farms, grain elevators, and false-front business buildings are common to the entire Midwest. Many of these, although old, do not mellow, but have an air of impermanence, as though intended to serve only until something better comes along. A few houses, on the other hand, follow the good, substantial precedent of the older Eastern homes of the country. New buildings represent a variety of forms, a constant flux in ideas.

As evinced by buildings ranging from statehouse to filling stations, North Dakota is architecturally in an irresolute frame of mind, striving, willing to try anything suggested, yet unable, to date, to evolve from these many trials a distinctive architectural contribution of its own.

Recreation

NORTH DAKOTA offers many diverse forms of recreation among scenes varying from the spectacle of the fantastically carved Badlands to the severe beauty of the far-reaching prairies. The Badlands are probably the best-known recreation area of the State. Here the Theodore Roosevelt National Memorial Park has been set aside, and many miles of bridle paths and automobile roads have been built. The strangely colored buttes form one of the most unusual scenic and geologic areas in the United States and contain endless treasures of petrified wood and fossils of prehistoric plant and animal life.

More conventional is the beauty of the wooded Turtle Mountains, where many attractive lakes provide swimming, fishing, and boating. In the woods are countless varieties of wild flowers, and many species of song birds. Of the many lakes in the Turtle Mountains, the largest and best known are Metigoshe in the northwest part of the hills and Upsilon in the east. Here well-equipped resorts have been established for the accommodation of summer visitors.

Lakes are scattered through the region south of the Turtle Mountains and provide the main source of summer recreation in that area. Devils Lake, formerly the principal resort in the State, still attracts many visitors each year; and other lakes, especially Spiritwood near Jamestown, are becoming popular. Some North Dakota lakes offer good fishing, being stocked with pike, crappies, sunfish, black bass, and rock bass. The rivers also yield pike, perch, and sunfish, as well as catfish and pickerel.

For the Indians who once inhabited this region, hunting the buffalo was an activity in which the entire community participated. The buffalo had almost disappeared when a young man named Theodore Roosevelt came to Dakota from the East to regain his health; but big game was still plentiful, for his books tell of hunting not only bison, but also deer, mountain sheep, elk, antelope, wolf, coyote, and grizzly bear. Despite the vanishing of the big game, North Dakota still has excellent hunting.

In the wooded areas of the Missouri and Mouse River valleys and among the Turtle and Pembina Mountains, deer may be hunted during open seasons. Coyotes are present, as the long dreary wail heard on the western prairies on a still night testifies; an interesting sport is shooting them from airplanes. Many such small animals as the prairie dog, gopher, squirrel, and rabbit provide popular sport; and the alert hunter may even bag a red fox, for these crafty animals can still be found in the broken country where there is cover.

Because migratory flocks pass over the State flying south in the fall, and because the many sloughs, swamps, and shallow lakes form ideal breeding and feeding places, North Dakota has an abundance of game birds. Duck hunting is particularly good in the north and central regions; the southeast section of the State is best for pheasant hunting; and prairie chicken and grouse are also plentiful throughout the State. Sportsmen's clubs have taken an active part in the protection of game birds, providing food for them in winter and sponsoring projects to give them more adequate shelter. Through the efforts of these clubs, several artificial lakes have been created: a typical project is Lake Ardoch, where melted winter snows are impounded to form a home for migratory waterfowl.

The climate of North Dakota is conducive to winter sports. Skating, sleighing, and tobogganing have always been popular, and in recent years many fine ski slides have been built and tournaments held annually. Hockey and curling have many followers. Figure skating, formerly regarded as a professional achievement, has also become popular, and many clubs have been formed. The frozen rivers and snow-covered fields are excellent for ski and snowshoe hikes. In the larger cities gala winter-sports carnivals of competitive and exhibition events are held each year, with entries from this State, Minnesota, and Canada; they are particularly interesting because of their international character. Snow modeling is one of the recent items added to the list of contests, and the varicolored snow statues add a festive appearance to the parks in which the carnivals are held.

Hiking is a favorite sport the year round and is the only way many interesting but otherwise inaccessible spots in the Badlands, the Turtle and Killdeer Mountains, and in the many State parks can be reached.

On the Indian reservations, glimpses are afforded of a people who, despite a certain degree of assimilation, remain apart from the white civilization that has surrounded them. Special dances are performed on ceremonial occasions and at fairs. The tribal costumes are retained to some extent, particularly among the older people; many of the ancient methods of cooking, weaving, beadwork, and basketry can be seen, and articles of handicraft purchased.

North Dakota is rich in remains of early Indian life. Mounds and village and camp sites yield arrowheads, stone implements, enigmatic petroglyphs, beads, and pottery. Old trails of early white explorers, soldiers, and home seekers can still be traced in many places, despite the fact that large areas have been plowed up.

Of the numerous fairs and agricultural exhibits held throughout the State, probably the most interesting to the tourist are those in the western counties, where rodeos are usually a part of the program. The rodeo (pronounced ro'deo in North Dakota) customarily is held in a large arena surrounded by a stout fence. The most dangerous sports are riding the 'bucking broncs' and 'bull-dogging'; in the latter, the rider throws himself from his horse to the neck of a running steer, grasps its horns and twists its head in an effort to stop the animal and throw it to the ground, all in the shortest possible length of time. Other events often included are roping running calves; Roman races, in which the contestant stands on the saddles of two horses running double with their bits tied together; and wild-cow milking contests, in which one contestant must draw a half cup of milk from a wild cow while his partner holds the animal. Typical rodeos are held each year in connection with the fairs at Elbowoods and Fort Yates, where interest is increased by the large number of Indians who participate in the contests.

Spectator sports are to be found in almost every town and include baseball, diamond or soft ball, basketball, football, golf, tennis, track events, boxing tournaments, and horseshoe pitching.

PART II
City Neighbors

Bismarck

Railroad Stations: Northern Pacific, Main Ave. bet. 4th and 5th Sts., for N. P. Ry.; Minneapolis, St. Paul & Sault Ste. Marie, 117 7th St., for Soo Line.
Bus Stations: Union Bus & Truck Terminal, 618 Bdwy., for Northland Greyhound Lines and Interstate Transportation Co.; Grand Pacific Hotel, Bdwy. and 4th St., Mandan-Bismarck, for local intercity line, fare 25¢.
Airport: Municipal airport, 2 m. SE. of city on marked and paved road, taxi fare 75¢, time 10 min., for Northwest and Midcontinent Airlines. Day and night service, no public hangars.
Taxis: Fare 35¢ in first zone and to Capitol; 50¢ to outlying districts.
City Bus Line: Busses leave Patterson Hotel, Main Ave. at 5th St. and cor. of 4th St. and Bdwy., through residential district to Capitol, fare 10¢.
Traffic Regulations: No U-turn on through streets, Main Ave. (US 10) and 6th St. (US 83). Turns in either direction at intersections and vehicle to the right has right-of-way. One-way streets border Custer Park in W. end of city. Street signs show hour parking limits in business district.

Accommodations: 7 hotels; tourist camp adjoining Riverside Park at SW. edge of city, reached by turning L. on US 10 just before Liberty Memorial Bridge; 2 tourist camps on entering city from E. on US 10.

Information Service: Association of Commerce, 215 6th St.; Keen Travel Agency, lobby of Grand Pacific Hotel.

Theaters and Motion Picture Houses: Bismarck Auditorium, Bdwy. at 6th St., occasional road shows and local productions; 3 motion picture theaters.
Golf: 18-hole course at Country Club on NW. outskirts of city (*greens fee* 40¢, *Sat. and Sun.* 75¢).
Tennis: Country Club and Hughes Field, 316 Ave. D, W.
Swimming: Outdoor municipal pool, 323 W. Bdwy.
Skating: Floodlighted rinks at 7th St. and Ave. D, 4th St. and Ave. F, Hannafin St. and Ave. A.
Hunting and Fishing: Information can be obtained from State Game and Fish Department in the Capitol.

Annual Events: Slope Poultry Show, World War Memorial Bldg., early January; State high school basketball tournament, World War Memorial Bldg., 215 6th St., March; City Flower show, World War Memorial Bldg., late summer, usually August; North Dakota Conservation Show, World War Memorial Bldg., September; State Art Exhibit, Capitol, November.

BISMARCK (1,670 alt., 15,496 pop.), Burleigh County seat, watched over by its lonely skyscraper statehouse, is the storm center of the State's widely known progressive politics. Ever since it won that honor in Territorial days, its chief claim to fame and most most prized possession has been the capitol, which is an integral part of Bismarck, influencing its development and character more than any other single feature. From the very first the capital city showed signs of enter-prise that has characterized its growth. Its name was selected with a view to flattering Germany's Iron Chancellor in the hope of bringing German capital to the rescue of the financially stricken Northern Pacific Railway.

Bismarck is in the south-central portion of the State where the Northern Pacific Railway and US 10 cross the Missouri River. The natural ford here was long known to Indians and buffalo as one of the narrowest and least dangerous crossings on the Missouri. A 'pay roll' town because of the State and Federal offices, it is a growing city. Modern business buildings constitute the downtown area, and comfort-able, new, bungalow-type homes, clean streets, and well-kept lawns can be seen on the hills, which not long ago were the home of Indian tribes.

The generous western spirit of the residents seems reflected in the structure of the city. Nothing is crowded. On the east bank of the rest-less Missouri River the site of the city is hilly, rising to the north. Gullies and small hills in the residential district have been filled in and smoothed off as the city has grown. Along the Missouri near the city cretaceous rocks are exposed. Strata of shale reaching up almost to the summit of the bank are topped with a thin layer of drift. Butte-like hills can be seen in the distance north and east of the city, their flat tops capped with Fort Union sandstone.

In Bismarck are the headquarters of both of the old-line political parties and the various progressive groups. Hotels are the unofficial headquarters of different parties, especially when the legislature is in session. At such times, although the city is businesslike on the sur-face, there is an air of expectancy as it awaits new developments in the State's changing political creeds.

Pioneers of the city can still remember the first legislative session in 1889, when the lobbyists for the Louisiana Lottery poured their money into legislators' pockets and were shadowed and exposed by private detectives hired by a Governor and his friends. Nor forgotten are the machinations of Alexander McKenzie, who represented the railroad in-terests in all things political, and who in later years exercised his peculiar talents in Alaska to such an extent that Rex Beach accorded him the role of villain in his novel *The Spoilers*. And even the young citizens recall how four governors succeeded one another in the teak-wood gubernatorial office in the course of a little more than six months.

Long before the arrival of the white man, the Mandan Indians found the Bismarck-Mandan area a favorable spot for their homes. Their cul-ture gives this vicinity an interesting archeological background (*see* INDIANS AND THEIR PREDECESSORS). Several village sites of the Man-dans and Hidatsa are in this vicinity, and a full-sized model of an earth lodge is constructed on the Capitol grounds. Artifacts, including implements of warfare and agriculture, pottery, and beads, were re-covered in these sites and are preserved in the museum of the State historical society.

French fur traders, Lewis and Clark, Prince Paul of Wurttemberg, Maximilian, Prince of Wied, and many another early adventurer and explorer passed the site of Bismarck in voyages up the Missouri, but squatters, anticipating the westward path of the Northern Pacific Railway, were the first to settle this vicinity, in the winter of 1871–2. During construction of the railroad a settlement called Burleightown, named for Dr. Walter Burleigh of the Northern Pacific Company, grew up near where Fort Lincoln stands. At the end of the railroad grade on the bank of the Missouri, just opposite Fort McKeen, was a tent-town called Carleton City, later called Point Pleasant, and known to the soldiers of the fort as Whiskey Point.

The site of the city was originally occupied by Camp Greeley, later known as Camp Hancock, a military post established in 1872 for the protection of railroad crews. One of the log buildings of the post is incorporated into the United States Weather Bureau at 101 Main Avenue, the original post site, and is the oldest building in Bismarck.

In 1832 river transportation began on the upper Missouri and was eventually instrumental in opening a vast new region to settlement. In later periods at least 50 cargoes were discharged yearly at Fort Benton in Montana, while it required some 30 or more vessels to transport troops and carry supplies to the various posts, forts, and Indian agencies in the Missouri basin. The 'Crossing on the Missouri' became a stirring steamboat port, attracting many rivermen and wood choppers. The latter served an industry of extensive proportions, since wood supplied all fuel needs for boats on the river and for the military posts and agencies.

The flooding of the flats near Burleightown each spring threatened danger for the railroad grade, however, and this is thought to have been the ostensible reason for changing the route in 1873; actually, the change was probably made to keep land grabbers from obtaining control of the point at which the road would cross the river. A new grade was built about one mile north, running past Camp Greeley. The Lake Superior and Puget Sound Company, a town-site location company auxiliary to the Northern Pacific, was then able to locate another city site which was named Edwinton for Edwin F. Johnson, Northern Pacific chief engineer, but was generally known as 'The Crossing.' When the Burleightown grade was left unused the town was abandoned and the inhabitants moved to Edwinton. In 1873 the name Bismarck was chosen, but the first title of the town persisted. When Mrs. Linda Slaughter became postmistress in 1874 she found it necessary to point out to the Post Office Department in Washington that mail should be addressed to 'Bismarck, D. T.' rather than to 'The Crossing, Northern Pacific Railroad on the Missouri River, D. T.'

Rails were laid into Bismarck on June 4, 1873, and it remained the terminus of the Northern Pacific until 1879. With the coming of the railroad the town became the head of navigation on the Missouri. When river traffic closed in the fall because of low water, no attempt was made to operate the Northern Pacific west of Fargo until the following spring, as the company did not have snow-fighting equipment with which to keep the road open during the winter months. Merchants had to stock up in the fall with enough goods to last until spring. Mail came once a week via a government carrier from Fargo to Fort Abraham Lincoln. Enterprising persons sometimes came from Minnesota with loads of dressed poultry and hogs for Thanksgiving and Christmas. The trip from Fargo to Bismarck took about six days by wagon.

In early days the young town combined the advantages of a river steamboat port and a western railway terminus. A frontier town, the life of its residents was necessarily rugged. A story is told of the young son of a newspaper editor, who questioned a stranger about his family and learned that the father of the visiting gentleman had died. The youngster, familiar with the columns of his own father's paper, said, 'Got shot, did he?' The stranger replied that he had not. 'Drank too much whiskey?' Again the visitor replied in the negative. 'Well, he can't be dead then,' the boy triumphantly exclaimed, ' 'cause that's the only way men die in Bismarck!' There were always the few, however, who made an effort to preserve the social graces. At the first party given in Bismarck, honoring Dr. and Mrs. Slaughter on their fourth wedding anniversary, dancing was part of the entertainment, and the evening ended with refreshments of champagne and buffalo-tongue sandwiches.

The first train arrived in Bismarck June 5, 1873. Part of its cargo consisted of printing presses for the Bismarck *Tribune,* which was first issued July 11, 1873, and continues publication as North Dakota's oldest newspaper. The *Tribune's* greatest scoop was scored in 1876 when it gave the world the story of the Custer massacre at the Little Big Horn in Montana. Mark Kellogg, reporter for the *Tribune* and New York *Herald,* was killed in the battle, but more than a column of notes on the battle was found in a buckskin pouch on his body. When Grant Marsh's steamer *Far West* brought Reno's wounded and the first news of the disaster, Colonel C. A. Lounsberry, founder-editor of the *Tribune,* obtained the story, wiring it to the *Herald* at a reputed cost of $3000 for 24-hours' use of the telegraph wires.

Bismarck felt the loss of Custer's command keenly, for he and his Seventh Cavalry officers from Fort Abraham Lincoln had figured prominently in the social life of the city.

The Bismarck *Sun,* another early newspaper, had a prominent part in the exposure of Indian and military-post corruption that led to the impeachment of Secretary of War William W. Belknap in 1876. James A. Emmons, publisher of the paper, issued a handbill entitled *Pirates of the Missouri,* which alleged that appointments as traders at military and Indian posts were being bought from the Secretary of War. The New York *Herald* sent out a reporter, who obtained a position at Fort Berthold Indian Agency, incognito, and succeeded in exposing the dishonesty prevalent at almost all of the Missouri River posts. The reporter barely escaped with his life when his identity was discovered;

but he returned the next year and succeeded in completing his investigation. Belknap was impeached on a charge of bribery and resigned, but was later acquitted. The episode caused a great furore throughout the country, but particularly in Bismarck.

Gold was discovered in the Black Hills in 1874, and Bismarck experienced its first boom. A regular stagecoach and freight line was maintained to Deadwood, South Dakota. It was more than 200 air line miles cross country, with no towns between. Stations were established every 20 miles and all freight was hauled into the Black Hills by wagon, 10 or 12 yoke of 'wild Montana cattle' being used to pull trains of 2 or 3 wagonloads of freight. Gold seekers flocked to Bismarck, where they outfitted their supply trains before departing for the gold fields. The Bismarck *Tribune* of October 25, 1879, reported:

> There are no rooms available at the hotels in Bismarck tonight as there are many transients in town bound for the Hills. Our freight and passenger business to the gold fields has been very heavy during the past ten days, amounting to 300,000 pounds of freight and seventy passengers. There were also two carloads of horses shipped in for the stage coaches. There are at present two and sometimes three stages a day.

Gold dust and nuggets brought $20 an ounce in trade in Bismarck. Many who came to join in the gold rush stayed to take advantage of the business opportunities.

The year 1881 saw a serious flood of the Missouri River. Most Bismarck residents, with their homes up on the hills out of the river's reach, made light of the occasion, some even to the extent of an excursion. Captain William Braithwaite ran his steamer *Eclipse* to the foot of Third Street, where passengers boarded for a trip to near-by Mandan, the greater part of which, like the five miles of river bottom land between the two towns, was under water. It is reported that everyone on the boat 'danced and had a good time.' Not so pleasant, however, were the experiences of those who lived in the lowlands. The flood came upon them suddenly, drowning their horses and cattle, inundating their homes, and forcing many to climb trees. Perched above the muddy, swirling waters and floating cakes of ice, several of these unfortunates froze their hands and feet or otherwise suffered from exposure. Wildlife also suffered because of the flood, and deer and other game could be seen floating down the river on cakes of ice.

The Northern Pacific railroad bridge across the Missouri was completed in 1882. Previous to this time the trains had crossed the river on barges in the summer and on tracks laid on the ice in winter.

When the Territorial capital was removed from Yankton, South Dakota, to Bismarck in 1883 the city experienced a second boom. Land prices skyrocketed, and blocks of lots often changed hands several times in an incredibly short period, since it was fondly, if erroneously, anticipated that Bismarck would have a phenomenal growth and would soon outrank many well-established and populous cities. The cornerstone of the capitol building was laid that year at an elaborate ceremony attended by members of the Golden Spike Excursion who were on their way west to celebrate the completion of the Northern Pacific Railway. Headed by ex-President Grant and Henry Villard, president of the Northern Pacific, there was present a galaxy of prominent Americans including Sitting Bull and numerous foreign dignitaries and noblemen. These notable guests spent some time in Bismarck and every effort was exerted to make their stay eventful. One young woman went so far as painstakingly to decorate her apple tree with three bushels of apples purchased at a local grocery store. Showing it to her admiring guests the next day she asked, 'What do you think of this for a fruit-growing country?' 'Magnificent, magnificent!' Grant replied. 'I am surprised, wonderfully surprised!' So were townsmen standing near by, but they held their tongues.

Since these early booms the growth of the city has not been remarkable, but it has been steady. A large factor in the prosperity of Bismarck has been the numerous Federal and State institutions and offices.

Bismarck's first church service was held on June 15, 1873, although Mrs. Linda W. Slaughter organized a Sunday school in a Camp Hancock tent as early as August of the previous year. The first church in the city was the Presbyterian, at 303 Second Street. When the Catholic church was built in 1898 the Marquise de Mores gave a large stained-glass window in honor of her late husband. The window, portraying the Immaculate Conception, bears his name and is in the front of the church in the choir loft. Fourteen religious denominations are represented in Bismarck.

Two hospitals and two clinics serve both the urban population and a large rural area. Radio station KFYR, with studios at 202½ Fourth Street, is affiliated with the National Broadcasting Company and operates on 5000-watt power. Four newspapers in addition to the *Tribune* are published in Bismarck: two semi-weeklies, the Bismarck *Capital* and *Der Staats Anzeiger* (German); and two weeklies, the *Leader,* organ of the Nonpartisan League, and the Dakota *Freie Presse* (German). Bismarck and its surrounding territory have a large German and Russo-German population.

The city was the home of James W. Foley, North Dakota poet, during his school days, and later he was a member of the Bismarck *Tribune* staff. His numerous books include *Prairie Breezes* and *Voices of Song.*

Although Bismarck is in the heart of the spring-wheat region, where four times more acres are planted in wheat than any other crop, the city's industrial life is subordinate to its political. Commercially it is a wholesale distributing point for many State or district offices of various lines of merchandise. In addition there are flour mills, creameries, grain elevators, and seedhouses. A pioneer seedhouse and nursery, the Oscar H. Will Company, founded in Bismarck in 1881, is the largest concern of its kind in the State. Specializing in seed corn, in which it followed the example of the agricultural Mandan Indians, the company has propagated many new, and acclimated several established, varieties of plants, grain, and nursery stock that are exceptionally hardy, drought resisting, and quick maturing.

In 1903 several thousand farmers of German extraction migrated from Wisconsin to settle the farm lands in the Bismarck territory. They have made the city a shipping point for a constantly increasing dairy, wool, honey, and corn output. The drought conditions of the 1930's cut into agricultural production, but intensified recognition of the need for diversified farming, which is more widely practiced each year.

One of the most notable events of recent years was the burning of the old capitol in December 1930. The year following there was talk of capital removal, the most serious contender being the city of Jamestown, 100 miles to the east. In the election of 1932, however, popular vote decided in favor of retaining the site at Bismarck, and on October 8 that year Vice-President Charles M. Curtis laid the cornerstone of the new statehouse.

POINTS OF INTEREST

1. The 19 stories of the STATE CAPITOL (*open weekdays 9–5; guide*), N. end of 6th St., high on Capitol Hill, overlook the city and the broad Missouri valley. The white shaft is an impressive sight even to those who quarrel with the idea of a skyscraper capitol for a prairie state. Designed in 1932 by two North Dakota architects, Joseph Bell DeRemer of Grand Forks and William F. Kurke of Fargo, with Holabird and Root of Chicago as associates, its clean hard modern lines are exponent of the fact that, as the architect F. A. Gutheim has said, 'Domed pseudo-Renaissance state capitols are sinking low on the Western horizon.' North Dakota has followed the example of Nebraska and Louisiana in building what may be a forerunner of a new and distinctive style of state capitols.

The possibility of architectural developments from this building does not, however, deter critics who find it difficult to reconcile the skyscraper with the prairies. The customary objection is that those conditions which are the *raison d'être* of the skyscraper—high land values and congestion at transportation centers—are decidedly absent in Bismarck. The justification of the building, therefore, must lie in its expression of the dignity and power of the State government.

Despite criticism, the Capitol has its defenders, who feel the strength and height of the structure to be expressive of its intent. And no matter what the decision may be on the architectural problem, the building at any rate fulfils its utilitarian function: it is one of the most efficiently built government buildings in the country. It provides space for approximately a thousand State and Federal employes. The asymmetrical tower arrangement allows complete separation of the executive and legislative branches of the State, and despite differences of opinion about the exterior of the building, opinion is general that the interior is both remarkable and beautiful.

The building houses State administrative offices in the tower and the State legislature in the circular three-story wing. The two sections of the structure are joined by Memorial Hall. The outer walls of the entire building are faced with Bedford limestone, and the base is trimmed with a broad ribbon of Rosetta black granite (gabbro), a relatively rare stone of volcanic origin.

A sweeping flight of steps leads to the plaza, above which rise the huge bronze-framed windows of Memorial Hall, topped with symbolic bronze figures representing the Indian, Hunter, Trapper, Farmer, Miner, and the Mothers of the State. These figures, as well as others in the interior of the building, are the work of Edgar Miller of Chicago.

The building can be entered from the plaza or on the ground floor through the porte-cochere. The ground floor corridor is wainscoted in rosy-tan Montana travertine. In the lobby is the custodian's desk where visitors register. From this point tours of the building leave hourly. To the right is the elevator lobby, where the sliding bronze elevator doors depict the Indian, the Hunter, the Cowhand, and other figures symbolic of the development of the State. At the end of the elevator lobby is the capitol café.

Steps ascending from the ground floor in a stairwell of highly polished black Belgian marble lead directly into Memorial Hall, which, although 342' long, 25' wide, and 42' high, appears even more spacious with its 10 tall fluted bronze columns lining either side and catching the sunlight which floods through the tall windows of the façade. The walls are of polished Montana travertine and the floors of gray-white Tennessee marble. From the windows in the façade there is a beautiful view of the city, the winding Missouri, and the hazy blue bluffs beyond.

The legislative foyer, a continuation of Memorial Hall into the three-story wing, is paneled in rosewood and curly maple. Inlaid canopies project over upholstered wall seats. Both the House of Representatives (L) and the Senate Chamber (R) are semicircular in design. Paneling of matched chestnut adorns the walls of the House, and the floor and ceiling are blue. An indirect lighting and ventilation system is concealed in the coves of the ceiling. The Senate Chamber, somewhat smaller than the House, has been judged one of the most beautiful rooms in the United States. It is paneled in a rich brown English oak with bronze cross stripes covering the joinings. The ceiling and floor are brown and the chairs are upholstered in cream-colored leather. The House and Senate Chambers are equipped with the most modern electric self-tabulating voting and roll-call systems.

At the end of Memorial Hall opposite the legislative foyer are the offices of the governor, attorney general, and secretary of state. In the governor's suite the reception room is paneled in laurelwood, the private office of the governor in teakwood, the corridor in prima vera, and the conference room in mahogany.

The second floor of the tower is occupied by the supreme court. The dignified courtroom is paneled in rosewood, the judges' conference room is finished in walnut, and Honduras mahogany is used in the office of the chief justice. The supreme court law library of over 50,000 volumes occupies two large rooms. A fine view of Memorial Hall can be obtained from the supreme court elevator lobby, which faces directly on the hall.

Above the second floor of the tower are other State offices. The eighteenth floor is designed as an observation tower, which affords a panoramic view of the entire Bismarck-Mandan vicinity, taking in Fort Abraham Lincoln State Park, Fort Lincoln, the State Penitentiary, the curving river with its wooded lowlands, the gray-blue bluffs beyond, and, all around, the rolling prairie.

2. LIBERTY MEMORIAL BUILDING (*open weekdays* 9–5), SE. of the Capitol, a memorial to World War I dead, designed in 1921 by Keith and Kurke of Fargo, houses the North Dakota State Library Commission, State Historical Society of North Dakota, and its museum and library. A four-story structure of Classic design, with a base of Minnesota granite and walls of Bedford limestone, its Ionic columns rise gracefully above the grass-covered terrace.

The massive bronze doors of the west façade lead into a corridor paneled in Italian travertine with a trim of Kasota stone. The graceful double stairway which rises across the corridor has marble balustrades and travertine newel posts.

Left of the stairway is the historical society superintendent's office, and right is the State library commission which has general supervision of all public libraries in the State.

On the main floor are the offices of the State historical society library. This society was founded in 1887, became a State department in 1905, and in addition to its work in collecting and preserving historical material has been especially active in building up the 49 State parks and historical sites.

The HISTORICAL SOCIETY MUSEUM, on the second and third floors of the Memorial Building, contains excellent collections of North Dakota material. The Indian collection gives a complete picture of the life of the North Dakota Indian, showing examples of clothing, cooking utensils, pottery, knives, drums, saddles, war clubs, bows and arrows, canoe, and bullboat. It also includes many archeological finds made in the State.

In the pioneer rooms are relics of early days of white settlement of the State. A military collection shows many types of guns and cannon in use since settlement. The natural history rooms contain fine displays of flora and fauna, fossils and minerals.

An equestrian statue of Theodore Roosevelt, the plaster model by A. Phimister Proctor for the statue in Roosevelt Park in Minot (*see* MINOT), is on the third floor, and near by is the desk that Roosevelt used for most of his writing at his Badlands ranch. Many models of early forts, Indian villages, and river steamboats are on display.

A bronze STATUE OF SAKAKAWEA stands on the lawn between the statehouse and the Liberty Memorial Building. She was the Shoshone

Bird Woman who accompanied the Lewis and Clark expedition through the unexplored mountainous Northwest to the Pacific Ocean. The statue, by Leonard Crunelle (1910), depicts the Indian woman with her baby strapped to her back, looking westward toward the country she helped to open.

Unsung during her lifetime, Sakakawea in recent years has been recognized as the outstanding woman in the development of the Northwest. Carrying her new-born son, Baptiste, she joined the expedition at the Mandan village near the present site of Stanton, North Dakota. She accompanied the party with her husband, Toussaint Charbonneau, who had been engaged as an interpreter. Soon she proved to be one of the most valuable members of the party. Her services were of particular value in dealing with the Shoshone.

On the return of the exploring party Sakakawea, Baptiste, and Charbonneau were left at the Mandan village where they had joined the expedition more than a year earlier. Mystery and controversy obscure the lives of the Indian woman and her son from this point. Sakakawea is believed by some to have died on the Shoshone Reservation at Wind River, Wyoming, when almost 100 years of age. Others hold that she died at Fort Manuel on the Grand River in South Dakota only a few years after the return of the Lewis and Clark expedition. Painstaking investigation has definitely proved neither theory.

Of Baptiste it is known that he was educated by Captain William Clark at St. Louis. Returning to the Northwest, he became an interpreter like his father, and met Paul Wilhelm, Prince of Wurttemberg, who was exploring North America. With the German nobleman he went to Europe, but sometime after his return his path is lost to the historian.

The PROW OF THE BATTLESHIP *North Dakota,* mounted on a boulder of native granite, stands N. of the Memorial Building, near the statue of Sakakawea.

3. ROOSEVELT CABIN (*open June* 15–*Sept.* 15, *weekdays* 10–5, *Sun.* 2–5), E. of Memorial Building, was the home of Theodore Roosevelt from 1883 to 1885, when he was a rancher in the North Dakota Badlands. Known as the Maltese Cross because of its cattle brand, the ranch was renamed by Roosevelt for near-by Chimney Butte.

The cabin originally had a much steeper, shingle roof, but a later owner replaced this with a sod one, hoping to make the building warmer. The interior furnishings are copies of those used by 'Teddy,' although the cook stove is thought to be the original. Much Rooseveltiana, including books and guns, is preserved in the cabin.

In 1904 the Chimney Butte cabin was purchased by the North Dakota Commission and sent to the St. Louis World's Fair of that year, to Portland, Oregon, for the Lewis and Clark Centennial Exposition in 1905, and then to Bismarck, where it was placed on the grounds in front of the Capitol, and after a few years was moved to its present site. An iron gate, handwrought by Haile Chisholm of the North

Dakota Agricultural College faculty, depicts the initial letters of the various fields of enterprise in which Roosevelt engaged.

4. GOVERNOR'S MANSION (*private*), 320 Ave. B, has been the residence of North Dakota Governors since 1893, when the house was purchased by the State from Asa Fisher, wealthy brewer. Governor Eli C. D. Shortridge was the first chief executive to occupy the mansion. Typical of the architecture of the Territorial day in which it was built, the two-story white frame building, with its spacious, high-ceilinged rooms and four fireplaces, has remained unchanged except for the addition of a front porch. The large elm and box elder trees were planted in 1900. During early statehood many important social functions were held in the mansion.

5. CAIRN (*private*), 912 Mandan St., home of Mr. and Mrs. Clell G. Gannon, is a small house built largely of native boulders, and designed by its owners.

6. HOME OF ALEXANDER McKENZIE (*private*), formerly located at 722 5th St., a large white frame house built in the indeterminate, unpedigreed style typical of North Dakota's architecture of the 'nineties, was the home of Alexander McKenzie (1856–1922), spectacular figure of early Bismarck and State history, master politician, ally of the railroads.

Arriving in Bismarck as a young man in the early 1870's, he soon rose to a position of civic and Territorial importance, becoming an unofficial representative of the Northern Pacific Railway. How much McKenzie had to do with moving the Territorial capital from Yankton to Bismarck will perhaps never be known. However, the fact that a Capital Commission was named and given power to move the capital, and the fact that McKenzie secured for himself a place on the commission, are credited to him as among his most able political maneuvers.

Although he held only one public office—sheriff of Burleigh County for 12 years—his influence and the so-called 'McKenzie ring' survived all attacks by political reformers. He was active in State politics until his death in 1922.

7. BURLEIGH COUNTY COURTHOUSE, Thayer Ave. between 5th and 6th Sts., is a three-story modern-type building designed by Ira Rush of Minot and constructed of North Dakota concrete-brick faced with Bedford limestone, with a base of pearl pink granite. In the main floor vestibule, wainscoted in marble, is a series of murals by Clell G. Gannon, Bismarck artist, depicting early county history. A further native note appears in the balustrading of the stairways, where grilled nickel silver forms a graceful design using the stalk, ear, and slender leaf of the corn as motif.

This is the third Burleigh County courthouse to stand on this block. A marker on the west lawn designates the site of the first, a log building built in 1873. It was replaced in 1880 by a brick structure. The present building was erected in 1930.

8. BISMARCK PUBLIC LIBRARY (*open weekdays* 10:30–9; *Oct.– May Sun.* 2–5), 519 Thayer Ave., a Carnegie institution, is a vine-covered, red brick Georgian Colonial style building. In addition to having a large and varied selection of magazines, newspapers, and fiction and non-fiction books, it maintains a separate children's division with loan service, reading room, and story hour.

9. FEDERAL BUILDING, NE. corner Bdwy. and 3rd St., a tile-roofed Indiana limestone building of Italian design, houses the post office, United States courtroom, and various Federal offices.

10. MARQUIS DE MORES' STORAGE PLANT, 300 Main St., is a plain, somewhat shabby building used as a restaurant, built by the marquis when he envisaged a huge meat-packing industry in the Badlands (*see Tour* 8). The building was formerly situated south of the rail-road. The walls consist of 2-inch planks laid flat on each other. These, together with the brick veneer, form a wall about 14 inches thick.

11. UNITED STATES WEATHER BUREAU (*open*), 101 Main St., was begun as part of the work of Camp Hancock in 1874, and a portion of the structure, the old log building which was Camp Hancock head-quarters, remains. It is the oldest building in Bismarck, but has been sheathed in lumber, and additions have been built. The bureau main-tains the residence of the observer at this site, but the weather station has been moved to the airport SE. of Bismarck.

12. WORLD WAR MEMORIAL BUILDING, 215 6th St., which serves as a community center, is a three-story structure of modern design, built of white Hebron (North Dakota) brick and concrete with limestone trim. It was designed by Liebenberg and Kaplan of Minne-apolis in 1930.

13. BANK OF NORTH DAKOTA (*open weekdays* 8:30–4:30), 700 Main St., was created by a special referendum election of June 26, 1919, passing a law providing that 'For the purpose of encouraging and pro-moting agriculture, commerce and industry, the State of North Dakota shall engage in the business of banking, and for that purpose shall and does establish a system of banking, owned, controlled and operated by it, under the name of the Bank of North Dakota.' It is managed and controlled by the State Industrial Commission. State funds, and funds of State institutions are deposited here. The bank was one of the im-portant features in the program of the Nonpartisan League at the time of its organization, being designed to carry out the fourth plank of the league platform, the establishment of rural credit banks operated at cost. The red brick bank building was originally an automobile ware-house.

STATE REGULATORY DEPARTMENT LABORATORY (*open*), is on the fourth floor of the Bank of North Dakota Building. North Dakota was a pioneer State in pure food legislation. A law passed in 1895 paved the way for the pure food and fertilizer laws of 1903. State inspectors, active at all times throughout the State, send samples for analysis to this laboratory, where trained chemists make the tests. Constant inspection of food and dairy products, feeds, fertilizers, water, oils, and paints is maintained.

14. ST. MARY'S CEMETERY, NE. edge of the city, contains the graves of many of the pioneers who played an important part in the development of the city and State. Among those buried here are Alexander McKenzie and his son, Alexander, Jr.; and General E. A. Williams, first representative from Burleigh County to the Territorial Assembly, and his wife.

POINTS OF INTEREST IN ENVIRONS

State Penitentiary, 2 *m.*; Fort Lincoln, 4.5 *m.*; Sibley Island, 7 *m.*; Liberty Memorial Bridge, 1.5 *m.* (*see Tour* 8). Fort Abraham Lincoln State Park, 9.5 *m.* (*see* FORT ABRAHAM LINCOLN STATE PARK). Pioneer Park, 2 *m.* (*see Tour 3B*).

Fargo

Railroad Stations: Northern Pacific, Bdwy. at Front St.; Great Northern, Bdwy. at 5th Ave. N.; Chicago, Milwaukee, St. Paul and Pacific, 1101 2nd Ave. N.
Bus Stations: Union Station, 502 N. P. Ave., for Northland Greyhound, Dakota, Jack Rabbit, Valley, and Triangle Lines; Webster Hotel, 503 N. P. Ave., for Liederbach and Tri-State Lines.
Airport: Hector Field, NW. outskirts of city, ½ m. W. of US 81, Northwest Airlines, taxi fare 75¢, time 10 min.; day and night service, public hangars.
Taxis: 45¢ within zone, 10¢ for each additional passenger and 10¢ for each additional zone.
City Bus Line: Intra-city, fare 10¢.
Traffic Regulations: Front St. and 1st Ave. N. (US 10), 13th St. (US 81), 10th, and 4th Sts. are through streets. Watch for stop signs and street signals; no U-turn on through streets; turns in either direction at intersections, except at N. P. Ave. and 1st Ave. N. on Broadway. Street signs designate hour parking limits in business district.

Accommodations: 38 hotels; 3 tourist camps.

Tourist Information Service: Greater North Dakota Association, 311 Bdwy.; Chamber of Commerce, 504 1st Ave. N.

Theaters and Motion Picture Houses: Little Country Theater, agricultural college, 13th St. at 12th Ave. N., college productions; Festival Hall, agricultural college, occasional touring artists and stock companies; 7 motion picture houses.
Golf: Municipal 18-hole course, Edgewood Park, 3 m. NE. of city limits.
Tennis: Courts at Oak Grove Park, E. end of 6th and 7th Aves. N.; Island Park, S. end of Bdwy.
Swimming: Outdoor, Municipal swimming pool, Island Park; indoor, Central High School, 3rd Ave. S. bet. 10th and 11th Sts., open during summer; Y.M.C.A., 632 1st Ave. N.
Baseball: Barnett Field, Fairgrounds, 19th Ave. N. and Bdwy., Northern League.
Skating: Island Park; Pershing Park, 14th St. at 8th Ave. N.
Tobogganing: Island Park.
Hockey: Island Park, Commercial League and high school teams.

Annual Events: Jack Frost Winter Carnival, Island Park, February; Bison Brevities, agricultural college, March; Northwest Norwegian Whist Tournament, March; 4-H Club Boys' and Girls' Achievement Institute, agricultural college, March; May Festival, agricultural college, 1st week in May; Lilac Festival, agricultural college, May; State Fair, Fairgrounds, Bdwy. at 17th Ave. N., June; Boys' State, agricultural college, June; Valleyland Music Festival, June; Future Homemakers Institute, agricultural college, June; State Golf Tournament, Fargo Country Club, July; Children's Festival, August; Rural Life Institute, agricultural college, August; Harvest Festival and Homecoming, agricultural college, October.

FARGO (907 alt., 32,580 pop.) is on the Red River of the North at the entrance of two transcontinental railroads into the State. A small,

youthful city, whose varied activities give its business section a somewhat disorderly air, it is the largest town in North Dakota. Over the
flatness of an old lakebed, where 10,000 years ago the water of the
melting glacier stood 200 feet deep, the city now widely spreads its
homes, manufacturing plants, wholesale houses, trees and parks, schools
and hospitals.

The trail that in 1871 led west from the Red River ferry, across the
level floor of prehistoric Lake Agassiz, is now Front Street, which enters
Fargo from the east to be greeted by the city's slum district, where
dilapidated, unpainted frame shacks near the river give way westward
to better buildings in a wholesaling district, until Broadway is reached.
Broadway is the very heart of Fargo, a busy, crowded thoroughfare
whose appearance often causes visitors to believe the city larger than it
actually is. From its wide south end where it intersects Front, Broadway runs north, flanked for six blocks by two- and three-story store and
office buildings. Two of North Dakota's four 'skyscrapers' are on Broadway.

Fargo first appeared on the horizon in the 1870's as an outfitting
point, the last outpost of settlement for those tens of thousands who
pioneered in the State, and through the years of its growth has retained its first excuse for being, for it still serves as chief distributing
point for a large agricultural area. Farm implements, foodstuffs, petroleum products, automobiles, and automotive equipment to the value of
more than $45,000,000 are handled annually.

Although from a North Dakota point of view it is an old city, Fargo
is young enough to have a few of its founders still alive to tell of how
they first advertised their spindly little city by boasting that its volun-
teer fire company, the Yerxa Hose Team, was the world's fastest; or of
how, in later years, Fargo gloried in being the 'Gateway City' to the
'bread basket of the world,' the fertile Red River Valley which real-
estate agents compared to the valley of the Nile. The Valley is no
longer the intensive wheat-raising area it was, but the Fargo Chamber
of Commerce will tell you that this very fertile flat land, through which
meanders one of the few rivers that flow north, is literally a land of
milk and honey, and others no less cognizant of their surroundings
have changed the old slogan to the 'food basket of the world.'

Because it is the distributing point for an agricultural state, changes
in farming methods have been reflected in the business life of the city.
With the introduction of diversified farming to supplement wheat growing, Fargo became an important shipping center for grain, potatoes,
dairy, and poultry products. In 1936 it was the largest primary sweet-
clover market in the world. Seed companies, creameries, a flour mill,
bakeries, and implement distributors are evidence of the relationship
between the city and the large farming area it serves. As late as 1927
Fargo was the world's third largest farm machinery distributing point,
and, although it undoubtedly does not retain this position, as a shipping
point it has become even more significant. A change in freight rates

granted in 1925 by the Interstate Commerce Commission boosted Fargo volume. Two of the three railroads into the city are transcontinental lines which, with their branches, cover almost the entire State of North Dakota. Several 'feeder lines' converge at Fargo and in addition there are a large number of trucking companies. The Minneapolis *Star* said in 1936:

> Fargo stands in exactly the same relationship to the northwest that Minneapolis has always stood. . . The significant point is that it is some 250 miles nearer the western point of consumption. Goods that used to stop at Minneapolis for distribution now flow on to Fargo to be piecemealed out.

The largest single part of the wholesale trade is carried on by agricultural implements and automotive distributors, including the Ford and Chevrolet Motor Companies. Processing accounts for the next largest part of the city's industry, and, although meat packing and creameries are important, there is a constant increase in the manufacture of steel, wood, and glass products. Fargo is likewise a banking and insurance center and has the home offices of two insurance companies.

Its situation, at the point where railroads first entered the State, in what Stuart Chase has characterized as perhaps the richest farming region in the world, has combined with the North Dakota Agricultural College to make Fargo the natural agricultural headquarters for North Dakota. Results of experimental work conducted at the college station and its substations, extension work through 4-H and Homemakers clubs, and judging of farm produce at State and county fairs by college instructors, all contribute to the improvement of agricultural and rural life in the State.

Fargo's percentage of home ownership is far above the national average. Homes clustered around the business district are of early twentieth-century frame vintage, while farther out newer cottages and bungalows, in English and Colonial style, behind small young trees and newly sprouting lawns, are characteristic of the more recent residential additions. Some of Fargo's finest homes are on Eighth Street South.

Fargo's public school system consists of 10 elementary schools, 3 junior high schools, and a senior high school; privately owned are 2 Catholic schools, a Lutheran school, 3 business colleges, 1 music conservatory, and 5 trade schools. The first Protestant church services in the southern Red River Valley in North Dakota were held in Fargo, and now more than 30 denominations have churches in the city. St. Mary's Cathedral is the seat of the diocese of the Roman Catholic Church for the eastern half of North Dakota, and Fargo is likewise the seat of the North Dakota diocese of the Episcopal Church.

The city's best-known musical group, the Amphion Male Chorus, composed of Fargo and Moorhead, Minnesota, singers, has toured near-by cities and eastern United States, giving concerts in New York and Philadelphia. Community singing is popular in Fargo, and during the summer months Island Park is the scene of outdoor concerts and singing contests. In June each year the music-minded of the Red River Valley gather in the city for the Valleyland Music Festival.

The agricultural college, always prominent in the cultural life of the city, has become even more important in late years with the increased number of college lyceum programs and the growth of the community-theater movement. The Little Country Theater, the outstanding players' group in the State, has become a virtual authority on community-theater organization and has received favorable notice nationally.

The city is named for William G. Fargo, a director of the Northern Pacific Railway and founder of the Wells-Fargo Express Company, and its early history is closely linked with that of the railroad. In 1871 the announcement that a railroad would be built 'from Lake Superior to the Pacific Ocean' aroused much speculation about where it would cross the Red River, and the untouched land along the river suddenly became populated. Three settlers, Jacob Lowell, Jr., Henry S. Back, and Andrew McHench, formed a triumvirate and patrolled the Red from the mouth of the Wild Rice to the Elm River from April to June 29 in an effort to discover 'the first indications of the railroad crossing.'

Meanwhile, Thomas H. Canfield of the Lake Superior and Puget Sound Company, a town-site company auxiliary to the Northern Pacific, worked with the railroad engineers in seeking the best point for the line to cross the Red, since he wished to secure title to the land for his company before it was snatched up by some speculator in the hope of selling it to the railroad for a large sum. He and his engineers chose the present crossing because it was the highest point on the river and therefore in the least danger from floods. Andrew Holes, who with his wife had been touring the country in a covered wagon, was sent to Alexandria, Minnesota, to purchase the land on the east side of the river from its homesteader-owner, Joab Smith. In order to locate on the lands west of the Red it was necessary to plow a half acre of each section. Aided by Major G. G. Beardsley, Canfield secured the necessary farm equipment, hid it until Holes returned with the deed to the Minnesota property, and by moonlight secretly made the required improvements.

On June 29, while on his patrol, Lowell found a 'Farmer Brown' squatted with three Scandinavian settlers on what became the Fargo town site. Although Farmer Brown was clothed in well-worn overalls with a brown hat and hickory shirt and 'sat with such ease and unconcern upon the handles of his plow,' Lowell doubted his being a farmer. He hastily summoned Back and McHench, and the three, after a consultation, located near Farmer Brown on July 1 and 2, 1871. Shortly afterwards Farmer Brown's identity as Beardsley became known and a stampede of settlers followed. Since Beardsley and his party were in the employ of the Lake Superior and Puget Sound Company and were not bona-fide settlers, their prior occupancy was disregarded and later, after much litigation, the company withdrew its claim to the Fargo land, retaining only the purchased Moorhead area.

In September 1871 G. J. Keeney was appointed postmaster of Centralia, the little settlement that sprang up at the railroad crossing. Keeney was also a lawyer and real-estate agent and his office was somewhat of a community center, according to one author, who wrote,

> He placed over the door of his 10 x 12 office the sign 'Post Office,' on the door the sign 'Law Office,' and in the window 'Land Office.' He raised lettuce on the earth roof of his log shack, and decorated the inside walls with papers sent by the folks back home. On entering, one was at once impressed with the air of cleanliness and comfort which pervaded the sanctum of this enterprising limb of the law, and it became a popular reading and rest room, but . . . one assumed a risk in becoming interested in a story as some chapter of it was certain to be found on the ceiling.

During the winter following the location of the site, the settlement divided into two communities. 'Fargo on the Prairie,' headquarters of the Northern Pacific engineering department (near the corner of Broadway and Front Streets), was a tent town, home of the railroad engineers and surveyors and their wives and children. Although crude, the tents of 'Fargo on the Prairie' had all the luxuries and conveniences that money could bring into the frontier settlement. In sharp contrast to this was 'Fargo in the Timber,' a town of huts, rough log houses, dugouts, and caves dug in the river banks, which stretched along both sides of the trail leading up from the ferry crossing. The two communities had nothing in common and residents of one would never be mistaken for residents of the other. The Timber used great quantities of whiskey, and popping revolvers made the night dangerous. The postmaster resorted to 'double planking' the sleeping bunk of his tent for safety, and it was well that he did, for in later years he could show a board of the bunk with a bullet embedded in it.

A typical Timber sense of humor was displayed by the resident who, when buying a load of wood from two young Moorhead, Minnesota, men, had them haul it over to Fargo and then drew his revolver and ordered the men back across the river without troubling to pay for the wood.

The difference between Fargo in the Timber and Fargo on the Prairie engendered a rivalry that both sides seldom neglected to intensify. Once when a wagonload of potatoes arrived for General Thomas L. Rosser of the Prairie, residents of the Timber loosened the endgates of the wagon and shot off revolvers to frighten the horses. As the team dashed wildly up the road, the potatoes rolled out of the wagon, to be picked up with relish by residents of the Timber, for many of whom those were the only potatoes obtainable all that winter.

On another occasion, as a sleighload of dressed turkeys and chickens bound for military headquarters drove through the one street of the Timber, with the driver muffled in a heavy buffalo-robe coat, residents of that community gradually lightened his load, audaciously picking off the fowls one by one, until all were taken. The driver did not know his loss until he reached the mess tent.

Whiskey 'in a tin cup' was generally supposed to be more enlivening than if taken otherwise. One Sunday, as the time for church neared, a disappointed minister found only a small group gathered to hear his sermon. One of the men assured the clergyman, however, that there would be more in a few minutes. Taking a bell, he went up and down the street, ringing it and exhorting all Christians to attend an address by Reverend O. H. Elmer of Moorhead, 'whiskey in a tin cup to be served free immediately after the service.' A large crowd heard the sermon.

The law in early Fargo had its amusing moments. H. S. Back, justice of the peace, after performing the first wedding ceremony, invested his $3 fee in drinks for the crowd. The next day he tried his first case, found the prisoner guilty, and fined him $15 and costs. Informed by the prisoner's attorney that there was only $5 in sight, he changed the fine to $5 and no costs.

At this time Fargo was still Indian territory, and the Lake Superior and Puget Sound Company, hoping to regain possession of the town site, informed the Government that residents of the Timber were illegally located on Indian lands and were also selling liquor. On the evening of February 16, 1872, troops passed through the city and camped for the night near General Rosser's headquarters on the Prairie. The troops, it was said, were on their way west to fight Indians, but a commotion before daylight the next morning awakened the Timber to find soldiers stationed before the door of each dwelling. All residents of the community were arrested and taken to the tent that served as a temporary jail, and those for whom the soldiers had warrants for selling liquor were removed to Pembina for trial. The others were ordered to leave the city lest their property be confiscated and burned and they be removed by force. They were not so easily defeated, however, and appealed to the Government for their land rights. A treaty was made with the Indians whereby the land was opened to settlement and those residents of the Timber who were guilty of no other offense were allowed to hold their land according to their original claims.

From a virgin prairie land where the Sioux battled the Chippewa, the terrain around Fargo became a rich farming country, well peopled and with acres of land sown to wheat. As late as 1868 the Red River Valley was generally believed to be a barren country, and in the early 'seventies Cass County was still a Sioux reservation. The first wheat sown by the acre was harvested in 1872, and there was barely enough grain to make bread for the few people in the vicinity. James Holes, whose farm was one mile north of the Northern Pacific depot in what is now Holes' addition to the city of Fargo, complained to the railroad that the exorbitant freight rate of 30 cents a bushel from Fargo to Duluth made wheat raising unprofitable for anything but local consumption. Freight rates were reduced in 1873, and Holes' 175-acre crop brought him nearly $5000 in 1876 and by 1893 he was harvesting a 1600-acre tract.

Bonanza farms, demonstrating the profit in large-scale wheat raising, were largely responsible for the enormous increase in acreage and the equally large gain in population through immigration.

The influx of new settlers who came on the first train of the Northern Pacific across the Red River June 8, 1872, brought law and order to the city. Even the saloons felt the difference—one of them closed every Sunday, and an admonition printed on its curtains read, 'Remember the Sabbath and keep it holy.'

The Father Genin Mission House on the Red River above Fargo, established in 1866, was the only place of regular Christian worship until the Episcopal church was built in 1872. The first school was a private one, presided over by Miss Mercy Nelson, aged 15.

As the Yuletide season of 1873 approached, Fargo residents laid plans for a community Christmas celebration. A tree purchased for the occasion was stolen, however, and at a mass meeting of protest the suspected culprits, Moorhead, Minnesota, residents, were hanged in effigy from the railroad bridge. Next morning a mock funeral was held; a locomotive and boxcar draped in mourning proceeded slowly to the bridge, the effigies were cut down and buried in a snowdrift. That night the tree was returned. It was set up at 27 Front Street and decorated with silver half dollars, one for each child under 14. A locomotive headlight was used to illumine the tree. Most of the children had never seen a half dollar, as the coins, intended as souvenirs of the occasion, were new at the time.

Although there was traffic on the Red River as early as 1857, not until the railroad crossed the Red, and Fargo became the southern terminus of river transportation, did steamboating boom. In the season of 1872 three steamers of 100-ton capacity reported carrying 1000 passengers and 4000 tons of goods on trips north. Bonanza farming brought greater need for transportation of grain and merchandise and by 1879 river traffic was at its height. There were several shipyards at Fargo, and Government engineers were employed in clearing and improving the channel of the river. The Kittson Line, owned by the Hudson's Bay Company, was the largest line on the river. It successfully outlived all competitors and enjoyed a monopoly a large part of the time. The income from a single eight-day trip of the steamer *Sheyenne* from Fargo to Fort Garry (Winnipeg, Manitoba) is said to have resulted in a profit large enough to cover the entire cost of building the steamer and the three barges it towed. Construction of the Great Northern Railway northward through the Red River Valley in 1880, however, inaugurated the decline of river transportation at Fargo.

By 1880 the city had a population of 2,693. An interesting cross-section view of the community is given by Finlay Dun, a British agricultural expert who toured the Red River Valley in 1879:

In Fargo, built of stone and brick, there are already three good hotels, and another in contemplation; rather too many drinking saloons; a concert and ball room, where recently a grand subscription ball was given for which gentlemen's tickets were stated to be $25. There is a courthouse and two portly courteous judges, and a provost marshal or commandant of police, all those important officers holding their appointments from year to year; a successful daily newspaper, two corn-merchants, a thriving school, while preparations are being made for building churches. An Opera-Comique is in successful operation . . . (and) from an area of many miles the dark-visaged farm-fellows with slouch hats, many with blue guernseys, some lumberers in red flannel jackets, and occasional Indians, and many half-breeds, congregated in large numbers to this opera-house in Fargo. . . The immense and varied collections of agricultural implements are strikingly indicative of the breaking in of new lands. The light wagons are drawn by horses, mules, and oxen, but the ox teams are rather the most numerous.

Even as he wrote, Fargo was rapidly changing from a frontier village to a city, for he says, 'But Fargo is a metropolis compared with the "primordial cells" of towns budding at roadside stations. . .' While almost everyone in the city owned a buffalo-robe coat, and one of the duties of locomotive engineers was to use their steam whistles for fire alarms, a horse-car line was in operation during the winter of 1879–80; unfortunately the track layers failed to prepare a firm bed for the rails and when spring came the track disappeared into the mud.

Early in the city's life William G. Fargo offered a premium of $500 for the establishment of a newspaper to be called the Fargo *Express*. In order to secure the bonus A. H. Moore and Seth Boney started a paper under that name in June 1873, but payment was withheld for the reason that it was printed on the press of the Glyndon, Minnesota, *Gazette*. On January 1, 1874, the Fargo *Express*, the first paper actually printed in Fargo, was published and received the promised bonus. From a combination of the *Express* and seven later papers has emerged the Fargo *Forum*, today leading the newspaper field in Fargo and the State. The *Normanden*, a Norwegian weekly, successor to the Red River *Posten* established in 1886, is the only foreign-language paper published in the city.

Fargo had a private college as early as 1887, but when North Dakota was preparing for statehood in the late 1880's, and each of the various cities in the State was trying to annex at least one State-maintained institution, progressive Fargo citizens succeeded in getting the promise of an agricultural college. There was one close call, when only a veto by the governor averted transfer of the school to Valley City, but in the fall of 1889 Fargo saw the opening of the North Dakota Agricultural College. The prairieland that had been designated as a campus boasted not one building, so rooms were rented from Fargo College until 1891, when the administration building was erected.

On a hot windy day in June 1893 the most severe fire in the city's history broke out on Front Street. Burning almost the entire business section and northeast part of the city, it left many homeless. Although the four to five million dollar loss was a serious setback, the fire marked the end of the wooden era, and rebuilding with brick began at once. For many years a fire festival was held on June 7 to celebrate the anniversary of the event which resulted in so many civic improvements.

Four years later, March 31, 1897, the Red River, dammed by an ice jam north of Fargo, began rising and continued until April 7. Conditions became appalling. Residents who had moved from the first floor of their homes were forced to leave for still higher spots via second story windows. Merchants carried their stocks up to top floors and attics, and groceries and the necessities of life were delivered by boat. When the Great Northern and Northern Pacific railroad bridges were in danger of being swept away, locomotives and threshing machines were run out on them to hold them down. The Fargo *Forum* wrote:

> A. N. Hathaway's family left Island Park by crawling out of the second story windows. Colonel Morton decided that discretion was the better part of valor and retreated . . . from his Oak Grove residence Saturday night. Passengers from the east this morning saw three horses and four cows on the roof of one barn.

Later the paper complained editorially when Congress appropriated only $200,000 for flood sufferers in the Mississippi and Red River Valleys, saying, 'Fargo before the world begging for a handout. . . It wouldn't buy a good dose of quinine for each resident of the inundated district to stave off the chill he's sure to have.' When the waters had subsided it was found that 18 blocks of sidewalk and 20 blocks of wooden street paving had floated away. During the flood and the six weeks while the debris was being cleared away and the damage repaired, the *Forum* was published without interruption. A temporary office was set up with a threshing-machine engine furnishing power to operate the presses, and deliveries were made by boat.

The attractions of open farm lands and expanding industries brought thousands of settlers to North Dakota, and by the turn of the century Fargo had a population of 9,589. Important among the industries listed in a 1901 paper were two harness and horse-collar factories, one of which issued a 300-page catalogue of its merchandise. One of the larger wholesale houses was Brown's Bicycle House on Broadway at N. P. Avenue.

The city was taking on a metropolitan air. An opera house, seating 1000, was built in 1893 and belonged to the 'Bread Basket Circuit,' which included Winnipeg, Grand Forks, Crookston, and Brainerd, with headquarters at Fargo. Fargo was a favorite 'stopover' for theater companies, and among the celebrities who thrilled those early audiences were Mrs. Fiske in *Becky Sharpe,* and Blanche Walsh and Chauncey Olcott in *A Run Away Girl.* In 1899 an item in the *Record,* a magazine published in Fargo, remarked, 'It is considered quite the thing to drop in at the Coffee House on Broadway . . . between one and five p.m. and spend a few moments drinking coffee and chatting, etc.' This fad may have been due to the divorce colony that flourished in Fargo then. A 90-day divorce law was in effect, and the city became the temporary abode of many wealthy people who came to establish residence and obtain a separation from their mates. Lawyers, hotels, cafés, and bars did a rushing business.

In the 30 years between 1900 and 1930 Fargo tripled its population.

Almost half of its residents are of Norwegian descent. Feeling the effects of an economic depression in their own country in the late nineteenth century, thousands of Norwegians, exhorted by transportation companies and influenced by the glowing tales of their countrymen in the United States, emigrated to North Dakota. Taking advantage of the free lands opened to homesteading, they became some of the first farmers in the upper Red River Valley and helped settle Fargo. Those who made their homes here are today well mingled with the rest of the population and few of their Old World customs are kept alive with the exception of the preparation of Norwegian foods such as *lefse, lutefisk, fattigmand,* and *flad broed.* (*See* RACIAL GROUPS AND FOLKWAYS.) Not forgotten, however, are important national holidays such as May 17, Norwegian Independence Day, which is celebrated with parades and appropriate ceremonies. The Norse influence is further seen in the statues and sculpture of and by noted Norsemen found throughout the city.

POINTS OF INTEREST

1. THE NORTH DAKOTA AGRICULTURAL COLLEGE, 13th St. at 12th Ave. N., occupies a level, 100-acre campus in the northwest outskirts of the city. The large tree-enclosed square is cut by graveled driveways curving between rows of hedges, trees, and clumps of shrubbery connecting the irregularly placed, architecturally heterogeneous buildings.

Under the Enabling Act of 1889 North Dakota, upon entering statehood, became possessed of a Federal grant of 40,000 acres for an agricultural college. A year later the first State legislature took advantage of the earlier Morrill Land Grant Act and acquired an additional 90,000 acres of Federal lands. Proceeds from these lands, together with Congressional appropriations, have created an endowment fund that enables the school to offer courses at a minimum tuition fee and to conduct extensive agricultural experiments.

A group of only five students under the supervision of eight instructors gathered October 15, 1890, for the opening classes, held in quarters rented from Fargo College, but before the end of the term the enrollment was 122. Elaborate dedication services for the college were planned in connection with the laying of the cornerstone of the administration building the following spring. After the program had begun it was discovered, to the consternation of the participants, that there was no flag available for the ceremony. A quick-witted student saved the day by contriving a make-shift pennant from a pair of overalls.

From the entrance at 12th Ave. N. and 13th St., a graveled road makes a loop through the campus. Past the TENNIS COURTS (R) is a TABLET (L) of Norwegian granite, in which is set a medallion of Bjornstjerne Bjornson, Norwegian poet and patriot. Best known as author of the Norwegian national anthem *Ja vi elsker dette landet* (Yes, I love this land), Bjornson was also a prominent exponent of scientific agriculture. The medallion is the work of Sigvold Asbjornson, Norwegian sculptor.

ADMINISTRATION BUILDING (R), a two-story red brick and sandstone structure, shows architectural influence of the Medieval and Romanesque periods. On the second floor is the LITTLE COUNTRY THEATER, founded in 1914 as a country-life laboratory by Professor A. G. Arvold, head of the department of public discussion and social life. With facilities available in the average rural community, students are taught to present entertainments that will provide recreation and education for the communities in which they expect to live.

The LIBRARY (L), of Classic design, contains over 84,000 volumes, and is a depository for United States Government documents. The ENGINEERING BUILDING (R), including the engineering and architectural departments, is a neoclassic structure of pressed brick with sandstone trim. As the road turns R., SCIENCE HALL, a rambling brick structure, is L. It houses the schools of science, literature, and education, and the laboratories of the experimental station where research is conducted in botany and plant pathology. A three-section GREEN-HOUSE (L) is maintained in connection with this department.

The AGRICULTURE BUILDING (L), a three-story tile-roofed structure showing influences of Roman and Spanish architecture, houses the school of agriculture, offices of the experimental station, and the extension division.

Right is the CHEMISTRY BUILDING. FRANCES HALL (L) houses the farm management division and the school of pharmacy. The DAIRY BUILDING and the old BARRACKS are R.

At the next curve of the road are the FARM BUILDINGS of the agriculture division (L and R). Just before reaching 13th St. the road passes the PHYSICAL EDUCATION BUILDING (L), erected in 1930. It has an indoor track, swimming pool, and auditorium with seating capacity of 3600. Athletic events featured today at the college with its modern gymnasium and floodlighted football field were impossible during early days at the school, for even if enough students had been enrolled to allow football and basketball teams, there was no athletic coach, and lack of transportation facilities prohibited games with other colleges. In those days one of the chief pastimes of the students was bronco busting, facilities for which were readily available.

Right on 13th St. is the MEN'S DORMITORY (R) and the home economics PRACTICE HOUSE (R). The SCHOOL OF RELIGION (L), of modern design in white stucco, originally conducted as a branch of Wesley College, has been turned over to the agricultural college under a 99-year rent-free lease of its buildings and equipment, together with a charter for conferring degrees in religion.

Right on a campus road is CERES HALL (R), named for the goddess of grain, and housing the women's dormitory, gymnasium, and the home economics department. FESTIVAL HALL (R) is used for R.O.T.C.

drill, college entertainments, proms, and informal dances. The FOOTBALL FIELD is R. of Festival Hall.

An outstanding organization on the campus is the NDAC Gold Star Band, which was organized in 1902. Directed by William Euren, it participates in special military events, appears at athletic contests, and has made several tours through North Dakota and Minnesota.

With its campus on the plains of the Red River Valley where great herds of buffalo once roamed, it is appropriate that the school should have the bison as its insignia. The college emblem is a green and yellow shield (the college colors) bearing the letters 'N D' surmounted by a bison. The traditional Homecoming banquet held each fall features a bison barbecue.

The college maintains an extension division and experimental stations. The extension service includes the formation of agricultural clubs in rural communities and at the college and administers Federal funds allotted the State for agricultural education. A primary function of the experimental department is the study of plant diseases and the development of disease-resistant grains. H. L. Bolley, a member of the faculty, discovered the formaldehyde treatment of seed for the prevention of smut on wheat and other grains and perfected a wilt-resistant flax while using these experimental facilities.

2. UNITED STATES VETERANS ADMINISTRATION FACILITY (*visiting hours: 2–4 and 7–9 p.m.*), 19th Ave. at the NE. edge of the city, is generally referred to as the Veterans' Hospital. Erected in 1929, the three-story brick veneer hospital now contains 400 beds. The grounds cover 50 acres; they are beautifully landscaped, with sunken gardens, ivy arbor, sundial, and Japanese gates. A rock garden was partially financed by the '40-and-8,' a veterans' organization.

3. BLACK BUILDING, 114–118 Bdwy., is one of the few buildings in North Dakota of skyscraper proportions. Designed by Lang, Raugland, and Lewis of Minneapolis, with Brasseth and Houkom of Fargo as associates, it is constructed of concrete, steel, and white brick faced with blocks of Indiana limestone with contrasting black spandrels between the windows. Consisting of 8 floors and basement, it rises 122 feet above the ground.

RADIO STATION WDAY has its studios on the top floor. The oldest commercial station in North Dakota, it began to function in May 1922, operating on 100 watts. In March 1931 it became an associate member of the National Broadcasting Company, and a number of chain programs, including several from the agricultural college, have originated in its studios.

4. FIRST LUTHERAN CHURCH, 619 Bdwy., is of English Gothic architecture, a modern adaptation of the cathedrals erected in northern Europe in the sixteenth century. It was designed by Magney and Tussler of Minneapolis. The interior appointments are simple and severe, following the traditional arrangement for formal Lutheran services. In an arched sanctuary is the altar of golden Siena marble. The congregation

represents a consolidation of two church groups, the Norwegian Evangelical Lutheran Church founded in Moorhead in 1874 and moved to Fargo four years later, and St. Paul's Evangelical Lutheran, organized in Fargo in 1903.

5. FIRST PRESBYTERIAN CHURCH, cor. 8th St. and 2nd Ave. N., in modified English Gothic style, is of Faribault gray sandstone with slate roof, in cruciform construction. It was designed by Lang, Raugland, and Lewis of Minneapolis, with William F. Kurke of Fargo as associate. The altar was hand-carved by a cousin of Anton Lang, the *Christus* of the Passion Play at Oberammergau.

The three-manual pipe organ is a gift of Mr. and Mrs. Norman B. Black of Fargo. A stained-glass window, designed by Homer L. Huntoon and presented by him in 1932 in memory of his wife and infant son, contains three panels, the central one of which depicts the sacrifice of motherhood, showing a young mother with her baby kneeling before an angel who holds the chalice and host, symbols of redemption. Art and music are represented in the two side panels.

6. UNITED STATES POST OFFICE AND COURTHOUSE, 705 1st Ave. N., erected in 1929–30 at a cost of $600,000, is in Italian Renaissance style, built of reinforced concrete faced with limestone. Ninety tons of steel were used in the first floor, making it strong enough to support 10 stories in addition to its present three.

7. FARGO'S FIRST HOUSE (*private*), 119 4th St. S., is the home of Mr. and Mrs. Henry Hector. It was built in 1871 of oak logs cut in what is now Island Park, and, although used for two years as a hotel, it was originally intended as the home of A. H. Moore, United States marshal.

8. CASS COUNTY'S FIRST COURTHOUSE, 708 1st Ave. S., has been remodeled into the DeVolne Flats. This two-story gray frame building has had a varied existence. Built in 1874, it served for 11 years as the seat of the county government. It was then moved to the corner of Seventh and Front Streets and used for a Government land office until October 4, 1886, when the construction of a new Northern Pacific depot made it necessary that the building be again moved, this time to Eighth Street. It remained there for a few months, then was sold for $500 and moved to its present location where it became the first club rooms for the Fargo Y.M.C.A.

9. MASONIC GRAND LODGE MUSEUM (*open weekdays 9–12, 1:30–5; Saturdays 9–12*), 501 1st Ave. N., houses the Masonic Library, the only lodge library in the State. The museum includes exhibits ranging from Indian artifacts and historical relics to religious articles. Fargo's first sewing machine was donated to the lodge because its owner found it so 'noisy to run.'

The library specializes in genealogical research for Masonic families. Originally it was part of the museum and contained only copies of rare books. The lodge members became interested in a State-wide program of adult education, and began a lending library of non-fiction books. A collection of 800 rare volumes, a gift to the library of T. S. Parvin, secretary of the Iowa grand lodge, was destroyed in the Fargo fire; the library later bought Mr. Parvin's entire private collection. Important items include *Orationes Philelphi* printed in 1491; a collection of Bibles dating from the time of King Christian III of Denmark (1503–59); a copy of the first printed constitution of Freemasonry, dated 1723; and histories of some of the early guides.

10. MONUMENT TO GANGE ROLF, Bdwy. at 5th Ave. N., stands in the Great Northern depot park. Rollo, as Gange Rolf was also known, entered France in 909 with a band of Northmen and founded Rouen. Two years later he installed himself Duke of Normandy. His line through William the Conqueror became the royal house of England in 1066, and the reigning family of Norway in 1905. The statue, a gift of the Society of Normandy to the Norse people of America, was unveiled in 1912 on the 1001st anniversary of the founding of Normandy.

11. ISLAND PARK, Bdwy. at Red River, Fargo's first park, was donated for a recreational center in 1877 by the Northern Pacific Railway. It was undeveloped until the early 1880's when the city council undertook the task of landscaping. In the attractive grounds are various athletic facilities and a building that serves as a community center.

A granite MONUMENT in a fenced plot near the south driveway was intended for a sundial but was never completed. The oddly phrased religious sentiments on the sides are by O. W. Lien of Breckenridge, Minnesota, donor of the shaft, who said they were dictated to him by a voice.

Near the west drive is a bronze MONUMENT TO HENRIK WERGELAND, a Norwegian poet noted for his efforts in opening the doors of Norway to the Jews and the naming of May 17 as Norwegian Independence Day. The monument is a gift of the Norwegian people to North Dakota and was presented during the Wergeland centenary in 1908.

12. OAK GROVE PARK (*tennis courts, horseshoe courts, playground apparatus, soft-ball diamonds, wading pool, picnic facilities*), on the Red River, has entrances at the E. end of 6th and 7th Aves. N., known as South and North Terrace. So sharp are the curves of the river that at one point one can look from North Dakota west into Minnesota. Oak Grove covers 39 acres.

13. EL ZAGAL PARK (*private*), 1411 Bdwy., is the property of the El Zagal Shrine Club. On the nine-hole golf course is the El Zagal Bowl, a natural amphitheater, used during the summer months for concerts and dramatic presentations. Programs each year include recitals by the Amphion Male Chorus of Fargo and Moorhead. North from the park are North Drive, which follows the Red River, and Memorial Drive, leading to Edgewood Park.

14. GOOD SAMARITAN SCHOOL FOR CRIPPLED CHILDREN, 716 7th St. S., stands on the site of a log cabin, the birthplace on August 27, 1871, of Anna Thoresen, later Mrs. Anna Roe, first white girl born in Fargo and Cass County. The school is housed in the build-

ings once occupied by the first college in the city, Fargo College, founded in 1887 as a Congregational school. The campus and main building had a beautiful setting overlooking Island Park. A shrinking income closed the school in 1919. In 1933, sponsored by the Good Samaritan Society, it became a school for crippled children, a private organization dependent upon donations from churches, fraternal societies, and other sources. It operates as a boarding school, with vocational training and academic courses from the first grade through high school.

15. On the SITE OF THE HEADQUARTERS HOTEL, between Bdwy. and 7th St. S., N. of the Northern Pacific Railway, stood a large two-story frame building which was the railroad station, hotel, and social center of Fargo during its early days. Built by the Northern Pacific in 1872, the hotel was formally opened April 1 the following year. After a disastrous fire in 1874 it was rebuilt by Fargo business men at a cost of $45,000. The new three-story combined hotel and depot was a prominent landmark, visible for many miles on the flat prairie. Around it flowed the life and business of the little frontier settlement and through it filed the men and women who helped make the history of the West. Its register carried the names of such notables as President U. S. Grant and General William T. Sherman. Generals George A. Custer and Nelson A. Miles often stayed there on their way to and from the frontier. A menu preserved from the hotel's Christmas dinner in 1887 lists the following game dishes: 'wild turkey, stuffed chestnut dressing; possum with browned sweet potatoes; partridge with English bread sauce; baked squirrel; saddle of venison, currant jelly; young black bear; antelope, game sauce; buffalo steak; reed birds *à la provençale;* broiled quail on toast'—and any of these for 50 cents. One of the few buildings to escape the fire of 1893, the hotel burned in 1899.

16. ST. MARY'S CATHEDRAL, Bdwy. at 6th Ave. N., seat of the diocese of Fargo since 1891, is a red brick structure showing influences of Classic and Gothic style. A prominent feature is a 190-foot bell tower and steeple topped with a bronze cross. On the northeast corner of the building a small tower forms a niche and canopy for a heroic-size statue of the Virgin Mary. In bas-relief on either side of the east window over the entrance portals are figures of SS. Peter and Paul. The cathedral, completed in 1899, was dedicated by Bishop John Shanley, first Roman Catholic Bishop of North Dakota.

POINTS OF INTEREST IN ENVIRONS

Armour Packing Plant and Union Stockyards, West Fargo, 5 *m.* (*see Tour* 8). Wild Rice River, 7 *m.;* Holy Cross Cemetery, 8 *m.* (*see Tour* 1).

❊❊

Grand Forks

Railroad Stations: Great Northern, DeMers Ave. bet. 6th and 7th Sts. N., for G. N. Ry.; Northern Pacific, 202 N. 3rd St., for N. P. Ry.
Bus Stations: Northern Hotel, 425 Kittson Ave., for Triangle Transportation Company, Northland Greyhound, and Liederbach Lines.
Airport: Municipal airport, 1 m. W. of city, ½ m. S. of US 2, for Northwest Airlines; taxi fare $1, time 10 min.
Taxis: Fare 50¢ first m., 25¢ additional each ½ m., 75¢ to university.
City Bus: Throughout city, to university, and East Grand Forks, Minn., fare 10¢, 2 for 15¢.
Traffic Regulations: Left and inside turns permitted at all intersections except 3rd and DeMers. N. 5th St. and Belmont Rd. (US 81) and University Ave. are through streets. W. from N. 5th St., 60 min. parking limit from noon to 6 P.M. No U-turn in business district. Traffic signals on DeMers Ave. at 3rd, 4th, and 5th Sts., on 5th St. at 2nd Ave. N.

Accommodations: 5 hotels; municipal tourist camp, Riverside Park, NE. outskirts of city; 2 cabin courts.

Tourist Information Service: Chamber of Commerce in Ryon Hotel, 25 N. 3rd St.; Travelers' Aid Bureau, Chamber of Commerce.

Theaters and Motion Picture Houses: City auditorium, 5th Ave. N. at 5th St., local and university productions, concerts; Masonic Temple, Central High School Auditorium, local and university plays, concerts; 3 motion picture houses.
Golf: Municipal 18-hole course, Lincoln Park, SE. outskirts of city on Belmont Rd.
Tennis: Courts at Riverside and Lincoln Parks, university campus.
Swimming: Outdoor pool, Riverside Park, open June to September, charge for adults; indoor, Y.M.C.A., 15 N. 5th St.
Hockey: Winter Sports Bldg., university; Riverside Park; 1st Ave. N. at Washington St.; and Central Park.
Tobogganing: Central Park, S. end of 3rd St., toboggans (*small hourly charge*).
Skating: Winter Sports Bldg., university; lighted outdoor rinks at Central and Riverside Parks; 1st Ave. at Washington; neighborhood rinks throughout city.
Trap Shooting: Grand Forks Sportsmen's Association, range just outside city limits on University Ave.

Annual Events: Winter Sports Carnival, city parks and Winter Sports Bldg., February; Carney Song Contest, university armory, February 21; Flickertail Follies, March; Engineers' Day, university, 4th Friday in April; Norwegian Independence Day, May 17; Interfraternity Sing, Bankside Theater, university, 4th week in May; High School Week, university, May; State Fair, fairgrounds, NW. outskirts of city on US 2, June; State Peony Show, June; Water Carnival, Riverside Park, July; Homecoming, university, October.

GRAND FORKS (830 alt., 20,228 pop.), seat of Grand Forks County, is named for its situation at the confluence of the Red River of the North and Red Lake River. The broad low profile of the city, dominated by the State Mill and Elevator and the radio station towers, is visible long before it is reached. Even the many trees do not obstruct the view, for they grow chiefly along the river, roughly paralleling the highway.

Like other small Midwest cities, Grand Forks is a heterogeneous mixture of nineteenth-century and modern architecture. The south part of town, along US 81 and its neighboring streets, is the finest residential district. University Avenue, lined with rooming houses and quiet homes, culminates in an architectural spectacle along Fraternity Row, an impressive group of houses vying for prominence and grandeur.

Meat packing, milling sugar beets and potato flour, and processing of other agricultural products constitute the city's chief industries. The largest railroad terminal between St. Paul and Seattle, Grand Forks is headquarters of the Dakota Division of the Great Northern Railway, the largest division in the world, containing more than 1800 miles of main-line track. The Northern Pacific Railway and several truck lines add to the shipping facilities.

The State university is not only a material asset of the city, but is a vital part of its intellectual and social life. University musical and dramatic performances are popular with townsfolk, college parties and proms are leading society events, and athletic contests draw a large attendance, not only from the city but from the entire northeast section of the State.

It is thought that the early French-Canadian explorers of North Dakota may have given this site the name of Grandes Fourches; by this name it was commonly known to the French fur traders of the late eighteenth century. In 1801, under direction of Alexander Henry, Jr., John Cameron established a North West Company depot here. Where Henry's men traded furs with the Indians, Grand Forks stands, the second largest city in the State, and hub of a rich agricultural region in the Red River Valley.

Nothing is known of the occupants of the first house in Grand Forks, a tumble-down shack discovered by travelers near the shores of the Red River in the early 1850's. The site is now occupied by the warming house of the Central Park skating rink.

In 1868 Nicholas Hoffman and August Loon, carrying mail from Fort Abercrombie to Fort Pembina, built a log cabin at the present corner of Eighth Avenue South and Almonte. They used it as an overnight shelter on the long trip across the prairies.

Following his expedition by dog-sled through Dakota in 1860, James J. Hill, who later built the Great Northern Railway, sent Captain Alexander Griggs to explore the Red River. By the fall of 1870 Griggs had built up a good freighting business, using flatboats to carry his cargoes. George Winship, later publisher of the Grand Forks *Herald,* also went into the flatboat freight business and a friendly rivalry developed between the two commanders and their crews.

On one occasion Winship loaded two flatboats with merchandise at

McCauleyville, scheduled for Pembina. At the same time Captain Griggs was loading a fleet of flatboats destined for Fort Garry (Winnipeg). Winship set out a half day before Griggs finished loading, but Griggs' crew boasted they could overtake the rival fleet. At the Goose Rapids Winship was forced by low water and the rocky channel to reload his entire cargo to a 'lighter,' a two-day task. Toward evening of the second day, shouts up the river announced Griggs' arrival at the head of the rapids. Confident of keeping their lead, Winship and his crew tied up for the night. Before morning a violent storm washed overboard several kegs of beer that were part of their cargo. All were retrieved but one, which floated unnoticed downstream, to be salvaged by the Griggs crew. As a result of the ensuing party most of Griggs' men were incapacitated, and he was forced to tie up his fleet at Grandes Fourches to await recovery.

Winship reached Pembina safely, but before Griggs could proceed the river froze, and he was forced to unload his cargo and store it in improvised sheds. His crew, with no alternative but to spend the winter here, were the first white people known to have domiciled on the site of Grand Forks.

Captain Griggs built a squatter cabin at the mouth of the Red Lake River, and after a trip to St. Paul in 1871 built the first frame house in the settlement on the bank of the Red River, at the foot of what is now Kittson Avenue, and brought his family to the new community.

In its early years Grand Forks was a typical river town, developing into an important station for the heavy river and oxcart traffic on the St. Paul-Fort Garry trail. Dwellings began to dot the prairie beside the river, log huts and crude frame structures built from the product of Captain Griggs' sawmill. A post office was established in 1871, and mail arrived once or twice a week by dog team. In the same year a telegraph station was established, on the first line in the State, running between Fort Abercrombie and Winnipeg. It was about this time that the English pronunciation of the community's name came into general use.

In the winter of 1872 there was much unemployment and saloons were filled with idle men. During this winter 'Catfish Joe,' a half-witted Frenchman, murdered a local character known as Old Man Stevens, who, while intoxicated, called him uncomplimentary names. The saloon crowd decided on a lynching, and all through the night plans were discussed, but with so many rounds of drinks that action was impossible. Catfish Joe was tried for murder at Yankton, spent two years in prison, and returned to terrify Grand Forks by strutting about the streets decorated with a bowie knife and a Winchester. One courageous towns-man, Bert Haney, seized the gun and struck Joe a terrific blow on the head, breaking the rifle barrel from the stock, but with no damage to Joe's head. Catfish Joe later went to Montana where he murdered his partner for refusing to get up in the night and prepare breakfast.

By the spring of 1872 Captain Griggs' sawmill was doing a flourishing business, turning out lumber for building and repairing river boats and barges. Logs were cut and floated down the river to Winnipeg. When Frank Viets opened the first flour mill in the Red River Valley at Grand Forks in 1877, he added another industry to the growing settlement. The Hudson's Bay Company operated a store, managed by Viets, who purchased it when the company moved to Winnipeg in 1877.

Since five families in the city had children of school age in 1873, it became necessary to establish a school. As some of the families lived on North Third Street and others in the Lincoln Park area, they could not agree on a suitable location, and each faction held a school of its own. Claim shanties served as school buildings, and a drayman, one of Captain Griggs' hired men, taught the north-end school.

There was no dentist in the community in the early days of Grand Forks. Alex Walstrom, a blacksmith, used a pair of homemade tongs about two feet long to pull aching teeth.

On October 26, 1875, Captain Griggs filed a plat of the original town site of Grand Forks, covering 90 acres of his claim. The following spring Viets filed the plat of his first addition. In 1879 the village of Grand Forks was organized and three years later was incorporated as a city.

Although life at the little river post lacked many refinements, the social aspect was not entirely neglected. Weddings were carried out with pomp and ceremony, and anniversaries appropriately celebrated. A popular social custom, New Year calling, was introduced on January 1, 1876. Groups of men rode together in sleighs to call on their friends, and then drove to the Hudson's Bay Company store, purchased flour, sugar, tea, and other necessities, which they took to the homes of the destitute.

Until 1879 traffic moved by steamboat or stage, but the coming of the Great Northern Railway in that year brought the rapid decline of both these early modes of transportation. Their end was hastened by the extension of the Northern Pacific Railway from Crookston, Minnesota, to Grand Forks two years later.

George Walsh founded the *Plaindealer*, the first newspaper northwest of Fargo, in 1874, and published it without competition for five years until George Winship started the *Herald*. There began a continuous quarrel between the two editors, which was at times decidedly heated, although when the plant of the *Plaindealer* burned in 1884 Winship shared his equipment with Walsh. While acknowledging the courtesy, the *Plaindealer* continued to attack the editorial policies of its benefactor. Winship eventually purchased his rival's paper and merged it with the *Herald*, which since 1881 has been published as a daily. The late J. D. Bacon, when publisher of the *Herald*, established the Lilac Hedge Farm northwest of Grand Forks to demonstrate the practicability of diversified agriculture and the value of using purebred stock.

Colonel Viets' mill on South Third Street was one of the first industries established in the city and was the only flour mill until 1882, when John McDonald founded a mill at the present corner of Fifth Street and Kittson Avenue. This was operated later by the Diamond Milling Company and then sold to the Russell-Miller Milling Company.

Cream of Wheat was first processed in Grand Forks and was manufactured locally for a number of years about the turn of the century, before the manufacturer moved to Minneapolis.

In Grand Forks politics and the weather were of great importance. Elections were always exciting. When D. M. Holmes ran for mayor in 1886 his friend James J. Hill ordered all Great Northern trains of the north, south, and west lines to run into Grand Forks so that the train crews could vote for Holmes. Against such odds Holmes' opponent withdrew.

A tornado that struck Grand Forks in June 1887 killed two women and wrecked many buildings. Ten years later the city experienced one of the worst floods in its history. The Red River made an all-time record by flowing four miles an hour. Houses along the river flats were floating or completely submerged. The piers of the west approach of the Minnesota Avenue bridge were swept by ice, and the Northern Pacific tracks were under water. When water filled the basement of the *Herald* building, the staff was forced to resort to hand composition to continue publication. Many families lived in second stories, and on near-by farms platforms were built on the roofs of barns and fenced in for the livestock, which was fed from boats.

In 1890 a brick plant was established in Grand Forks, and another in 1900. Other industries that sprang up during this period were bottling works, breweries, and foundries. Besides the Grand Forks *Herald,* two weeklies were established, the *Red River Valley Citizen* and the *Normanden,* the latter in the Norwegian language.

In 1919 a group of farmers and businessmen from Grand Forks and the surrounding territory opened the Northern Packing Company, designed to handle 500 hogs and 150 cattle and sheep daily, with a plant one and one half miles north of the city (*see Tour* 1). The State Mill and Elevator began operation in 1922 (*see Tour* 1). A candy company that uses locally produced beet sugar has an annual output of about a million pounds. A large potato warehouse with laboratory and experimental department was constructed in 1935 at the corner of North Third Street and Lewis Boulevard.

The population of Grand Forks has increased from 200 in 1873 to 20,228 in 1940, and is composed of many nationalities, mainly Norwegian and Canadian. Much political activity of an earlier period centered about the community known as 'Little Norway,' since it generally voted as a bloc. Politicians of that day believed that the candidate who was most liberal with ale would receive the community's vote, and on the eve of election torchlight parades marched through the streets of this district and candidates for office generously dispensed both oratory and beer.

POINTS OF INTEREST

1. FEDERAL BUILDING, 1st Ave. N. at N. 4th St., houses the post office, United States courtroom, a branch of the United States Immigration Service, and the Federal Reemployment office. The superstructure is of white Bedford stone and pressed brick, with a base of solid granite. It has a 12-foot cornice of stone with carved and blocked ornaments. The lobby has marble floors and high wainscoting of marble, contrasting shades being used for borders. Fixtures are of quarter-sawed oak.

2. CENTRAL HIGH SCHOOL, 1st and 2nd Aves. N. between 4th and 5th Sts., has an auditorium unit constructed entirely without windows. It was the first public building in North Dakota to utilize indirect lighting throughout. It was erected in 1936-7 with WPA assistance at a cost of $275,000 and includes a pipe organ, the gift of the Grand Forks Music Association.

3. SORLIE MEMORIAL BRIDGE across the Red River connects Grand Forks, North Dakota, and East Grand Forks, Minnesota, on US 2. It is dedicated to the late A. G. Sorlie, former Governor of the State, and was built in 1929.

4. RADIO STATION KFJM (*open daily* 2:30-5 *p.m.*), top floor of the First National Bank Bldg., cor. DeMers Ave. and N. 4th St., is one of the few State-owned university radio stations in the United States. It is leased to a local company. A studio is maintained at the university.

5. TRIANGLE APARTMENTS, 5th and Chestnut Sts. and 5th Ave. S., mark the site of two of the most important buildings in early Grand Forks history. The city's first school building stood across the street from this triangle, on the courthouse site. In 1883 the old building was moved into the triangle and converted into the Park Hotel. The Arlington House, a hotel built by the Hudson's Bay Company in 1873, was also moved to this lot and in 1906 Colonel Andrew Knutson purchased both buildings and operated them as the Arlington-Park Hotel. This hotel was torn down and the lumber used in the construction of the apartment building that now occupies the site.

6. GRAND FORKS COUNTY COURTHOUSE, 4th and 5th Sts. S. between Kittson and Bruce Aves., was erected in 1913 and designed by Buechner and Orth of St. Paul. It is a three-story Indiana limestone building of modified Classic design, with a figure of Justice surmounting its dome. The halls are finished in white marble with mural decorations. Embellishing the upper part of the rotunda are four painted lunettes showing typical North Dakota scenes.

7. SOLDIER'S MONUMENT, 6th St. S. and Belmont Rd., was donated by George B. Winship, early newspaper publisher, as a memorial to 168 local Civil War veterans, whose names are engraved on a bronze tablet. Mounted on a square base of Vermont granite, the monument represents a Union soldier 'at rest.'

8. CENTRAL PARK (*picnicking not allowed*), Red River bank, S. end of 3rd St., is a beauty spot and playground. The flower gardens, a mass of brilliant bloom, are lighted at night. At the bandstand in the center of the park concerts are presented, usually each week, during the summer months. In front of the bandstand are millstones from the first flour mill in the Red River Valley, which was built on the site of the city waterworks plant in 1877. An outdoor skating rink is lighted for winter skating. The warming house is on the site of the first building erected within the present boundaries of the city. Across the drive from the ball diamond are the toboggan slides, partially hidden from view by evergreen trees and shrubs.

9. UNIVERSITY PARK (*playground equipment and supervised play*), University Ave. between 24th and 25th Sts., has a children's library at the clubhouse.

10. LINCOLN PARK (*municipal golf links, tennis courts, picnic and play equipment*), Belmont Rd. at S. edge of city, contains the old Red River Oxcart Trail (*see Tour* 1), which crossed the little hill on which the clubhouse stands. Later, when the settlement became a stage station on the St. Paul-Fort Garry Trail, the Stewart House was built here and housed Grand Forks' first post office. This old log building is now the kitchen of the clubhouse.

11. UNIVERSITY OF NORTH DAKOTA is at the W. end of University Ave. 2 miles from the principal business section of Grand Forks. (*University bus at 3rd St. and DeMers Ave., fare* 10¢.)

The campus facing the avenue is bordered by a low hedge, and the two main entrances are marked by large brick pylons. Tree-shaded roads wind past the buildings and along the banks of English Coulee. In the spring and summer the wide expanses of green lawn are broken by plots of flowers and clumps of lilacs, spirea, and flowering almond. All of the buildings erected since 1910 are in modern collegiate Gothic style, a modification of true English Gothic architecture adapted especially for educational institutions.

The University of North Dakota was established by the Territorial Legislature before North Dakota became a State. The cornerstone for 'Old Main' was laid October 12, 1883, on the prairie beside the banks of the winding English Coulee, and September 8, 1884, the university opened classes with 79 students and a staff of 4 instructors. Enrollment now numbers over 2500 students and the school has more than 150 instructors.

Selection of a site two miles from the city was opposed by many of the townspeople, who thought the university should be located at the south end of Third Street, on the present site of Central Park. During the tornado of 1887 the roof of Old Main, then the only building on the campus, was blown almost to the south end of Third Street. Agitation was begun to bring the remainder of the building to join the roof, but State officials refused to consider the plan, chiefly because the property originally used was school land. Old Main was remodeled and a women's dormitory erected near it. That settled the controversy.

For students who were unable to live on the campus, transportation was a troublesome problem. Only a country road of sticky Red River Valley gumbo connected the campus with the city, and, except for the fortunate few who caught rides on horse-drawn vehicles, city students walked to classes. During severe weather it was often necessary to flag a freight or passenger train of the Great Northern to make the trip to town. About 1900 a trolley line was established to the university, and despite its erratic service, it greatly facilitated attendance of non-resident students.

Although given an endowment of 86,080 acres of public lands in 1889 when it became the University of North Dakota, there were many years when the school derived no revenue from this source, but had to depend entirely upon legislative appropriation. In 1895 Governor Allin vetoed most of the appropriation, leaving money for the janitor's salary but none for the faculty. The institution was kept open through private contributions, and President Webster Merrifield and other professors served without salary during a trying two-year period. Despite financial difficulties, attendance at the university in its first 15 years increased more than 40 per cent and in 1898 President Merrifield reported to the legislature that the facilities of the institution were inadequate. Continued expansion added law, pre-medical, and commerce schools, and mechanical, electrical, and mining engineering departments at the university by the end of the 1901 term.

During the first six years of university history there were only two buildings on the campus. The main building, later known as Merrifield Hall, contained classrooms, book store, post office, and men's dormitory. The other building, later named Davis Hall for Hannah E. Davis, one of its early matrons, housed the girls' dormitory, and, in the basement, the university dining hall. Alumni of those days relate that the dining hall was a very popular place. When meals were ready to be served a napkin was hung out the basement window, and the first student in the main building who spied the sign, regardless of whether he happened to be in a class or not, yelled, 'Rag's out!' The shout was taken up and a stampede to the dining-room followed. This custom prevailed for several years. One day President Merrifield was showing some of his Eastern friends through the institution when suddenly 'Rag's out' reverberated through the halls. The visitors wondered if there was a riot, and the mortified president realized for the first time how the dinner call sounded to outsiders. He suppressed it with difficulty, after many student debates on the sacredness of college traditions.

With the advent of football teams, 'Odz, odz, dzi,' an imitation of a Sioux war cry, became the college yell and has continued to the present.

When a delegation from the first North Dakota legislature visited the campus on a tour of inspection in 1889, residents of the girls' dormitory held a tea in their honor. In order to improve upon the barrenness of the sparsely furnished parlor, pieces were borrowed from the girls' rooms and from friends. The expedient was more successful than the girls had anticipated, for the legislators considered the furnishings more than adequate and thereupon decreased the amount allowed in the budget for dormitory equipment.

Although the University of North Dakota has been in existence only 66 years (1949), it has had its share of distinguished alumni, among whom is Maxwell Anderson (class of 1911), playwright, author of *What Price Glory, Mary of Scotland, Winterset,* and other dramas. In 1933 his play *Both Your Houses* was awarded the Pulitzer Prize.

Vilhjalmur Stefansson, explorer, attended the university from 1899 to 1902 and left at the request of the faculty. His escapades, though doubtless improved upon with the years, are quite typical of him. It is said he attended classes as seldom as possible, yet always received the highest grades. The story goes that he went to his calculus class only on the first day of the term, then returned for the final examination, which the professor allowed him to write, with gloomy prophecies of his ruin. Stefansson's mark was 98. The professor could not help remarking that he had done well considering that he had attended only one class. 'And,' retorted Stefansson, 'if I hadn't come here the first day I'd have got one hundred.'

The Arctic explorer has been credited with pranks such as releasing a small pig on the speaker's platform at convocation, and rolling a keg of beer across the campus to win a bet when North Dakota was a very dry State. There was then no trolley from Grand Forks to the Campus, and President Merrifield was driven the two miles to and from town in his private carriage. One day Stefansson saw the carriage parked downtown. The driver was old in service, and when Stefansson stepped into the carriage and said 'Home, Peter' in a good imitation of the president's voice, Peter suspected nothing. Stefansson rode in comfort to the campus, while President Merrifield, it is said, walked. Expelled in 1902, Stefansson was called back to his Alma Mater in 1930 to have the LL.D. degree conferred on him in recognition of his contributions to science.

The east campus road passes the LAW BUILDING, WOODWORTH HALL, CHEMISTRY BUILDING, and BABCOCK HALL. In Woodworth, the school of education, is the campus broadcasting studio. The University of North Dakota was the second university in the United States to offer courses in radio administration, and engineering students use the KFJM transmitter, adjacent to the campus, for practical class work in technical radio instruction. Just S. of the Chemistry Building are the university tennis courts, and a nine-hole golf course is E. of MEMORIAL STADIUM (L), erected in 1927. The university athletic department is a member of the North Central Conference and books games with schools from coast to coast. The UNIVERSITY MUSEUM on the top floor of Babcock Hall (*open* 9–5 *daily*) contains a large collection of Indian artifacts and geological and historical items.

The road curves back of Babcock and the COMMONS past CAMP DE-
PRESSION (L), established in 1933, where railroad cabooses are fitted
up for enterprising students to provide co-operative accommodations
at a minimum cost. Left of Camp Depression is the shiny arched steel
WINTER SPORTS BUILDING. Around the curve is the ARMORY (L) where
athletic and social events and weekly convocations are held. The road
to the R. passes BUDGE HALL (R), men's dormitory, built in 1889; OLD
MERRIFIELD HALL (L), generally known as 'Old Main,' the first building on the campus and now occupied by administrative offices, post
office, book store, and offices of the extension division; NEW MERRI-
FIELD HALL (L), the liberal arts college building, completed in 1929;
SCIENCE HALL (R), housing the medical school and State Public Health
Laboratories; and the LIBRARY (L), containing over 77,000 catalogued
books and periodicals and about 17,500 uncatalogued Government
documents.

Curving L., the road passes the PRESIDENT'S HOUSE (R), a spacious
Georgian Colonial brick residence. Next is MACNIE HALL, a co-operative men's residence hall, named for John Macnie, for 20 years a member of the faculty, and composer of the university *Alma Mater*. Vine-
covered CHANDLER HALL (R), named for Elwin Chandler, dean emeritus of the school of engineering, is headquarters during Engineers'
Day held the last Friday in April each year. DAVIS HALL (R), women's
dormitory, is the second oldest building on the campus, erected in 1887.
It houses the home economics department.

ENGLISH COULEE (R), so-called because an Englishman is said to
have drowned in it, borders the campus on the W. Between Davis Hall
and the WOMEN'S GYMNASIUM the stream curves, creating the impression that the opposite bank is a wooded island. This far bank is the stage
of the BANKSIDE THEATER, and the concave bank facing it is used to
seat the audience. The theater is the scene of an Interfraternity Sing
held the last week in May.

The original Bankside Theater, about one block N. of the present
site, was dedicated in 1914 and is said to have been the first open-air
theater to make use of the natural curve of a stream to separate the
stage from the auditorium. The initial performance given here, *A
Pageant of the Northwest*, was written by students of the Sock and
Buskin Society (now the Dakota Playmakers) under the direction of
Professor Frederick Koch, distinguished for his work in American folk
drama.

The banks of English Coulee have fostered both drama and romance.
College sweethearts spend their evenings by this stream, admiring the
reflection of the moon in the water. The custom is known locally as
'coulee-banking.'

Eleven national fraternities and 7 sororities are represented at the
university. The houses along Fraternity Row on University Avenue and
the other streets near the campus present the architecture of many
nations and periods. A French chateau shouldering a stucco cottage, a

graceful Georgian Colonial residence standing between an English country house and an Italian mansion, and houses of Spanish and English design form a quaint architectural democracy that is, perhaps, a fitting background for the social life of a student body representing various nations.

12. WESLEY COLLEGE, N. of University Ave. opposite the University of North Dakota, is the first of the Methodist schools in the United States designated by that name and the first church school to affiliate with a State university. Its residence halls are open to students of all church affiliations, as are the classes in religion, music, and expression. Work in any department of Wesley College is credited toward university degrees.

The campus contains four buildings, Corwin, Larimore, Sayre, and Robertson Halls, constructed of white brick with trimmings of white glazed terra cotta in Grecian style. Robertson Hall, the newest building, contains the administrative offices, school of religion, and expression department. This building, costing $40,000, was made possible by the contribution of an alumnus, John M. Hancock, and his family of Hartsdale, New York, and was completely furnished by Mrs. Hancock. Corwin Hall houses the well-equipped music department. Larimore Hall, the women's dormitory, is immediately behind Corwin, while the men's dormitory, Sayre Hall, adjoins Robertson Hall.

POINTS OF INTEREST IN ENVIRONS

North Dakota State Mill and Elevator, 1 *m.*; Red River Oxcart Trail, 1.5 *m.*; Northern Packing Plant, 1.5 *m.*; Grand Forks Silver Fox Farm, 4 *m.* (*see Tour* 1). American Sugar Refining Co. plant, 2 *m.* (*see Minnesota Guide Tour* 7).

Minot

Railroad Stations: Great Northern Station, W. end of Central Ave. across viaduct, for G. N. Ry.; Minneapolis, St. Paul & Sault Ste. Marie Station, 17 N. Main St., for Soo Ry.

Bus Stations: Union Bus Depot, 123 W. Cent. Ave., for Greyhound, Interstate, and Manitoba Border bus lines.

Airport: Municipal airport, 1¼ m. N. of business district on outskirts of city, E. of US 83, taxi fare 50¢, time 5 min.; scheduled air service by Mid-Continent Airlines, public hangars.

Taxis: 35¢ to any point in city, 25¢ for each passenger to same destination.

City Bus Line: Throughout city, to State Teachers College, fare 10¢.

Traffic Regulations: Valley St. (US 52), 4th Ave. SE. and SW. (US 2), 2nd St. SW. and NW. (US 83), are through streets. No U-turn on through streets and no left turns out of alleys. Turns may be made in either direction at intersections.

Accommodations: 11 hotels; 5 tourist camps (4 on US 2 E., 1 on US 2 and 52 W.)

Tourist Information Service: Association of Commerce, 11 E. Cent. Ave.

Theaters and Motion Picture Houses: McFarland Auditorium, State Teachers College, 9th Ave. NW., college productions and concert series; Minot high school auditorium, 2nd Ave. SE. between 1st and 2nd Sts.; Parker's Auditorium, 117 1st Ave. SE.; 3 motion picture houses.

Athletics: Ice-skating, roller-skating, and hockey rinks.

Golf: Municipal 9-hole course SW. edge of city on US 2 (*greens fee 25¢*); Country Club (*private*).

Tennis: Courts at Oak Park, W. end 3rd Ave. NW.; and Roosevelt Park.

Swimming: Municipal outdoor pool. Roosevelt Park.

Curling: Rink near 701 4th Ave. SE.

Annual Events: North Dakota State Class B Basketball Tourney, March; North Dakota State Fair, fairgrounds E. end of 4th Ave. SE., July; Homecoming, State Teachers College, October; Nat'l Col. Sheep Show and Sale, October; *The Messiah,* State Teachers College, December.

MINOT (1,557 alt., 16,577 pop.) is still young and growing, although past its sixtieth birthday. Its name (pronounced MY-not) was given it to honor Henry D. Minot, young Eastern capitalist and college friend of Theodore Roosevelt. Situated in the deep valley of the Souris (Mouse) River, the town overflows the level mile-wide flood plain to thrust itself up the south slope of the valley onto the open prairie. Rough, well-worn block pavement in the business section evolves into smooth, tree-bowered asphalt avenues lined with fine homes in the residential districts. The twisting, sluggish river winds through the center of the city, in some sections its banks scarred with piles of refuse, in others rimmed by trim lawns.

The hills that rim the Souris at Minot are evidences of the mighty force of the raging waters that during the glacial period poured from the melting edge of the great Dakota ice sheet to plow deep valleys and lay the basis for the town's future prosperity. The products of the geological past yield valuable returns. One, the rich, fertile bed of glacial Lake Souris, provides good crops. The other is lignite, the soft brown peatlike coal that underlies much of the northwestern portion of the State, and for which Minot is an important shipping point.

James J. Hill's Great Northern Railway was pushing west through Dakota Territory in 1887 when it was found necessary to stop near here and build a bridge across a coulee. Where construction halted there immediately sprang up a large tent town, which was generally assumed to be the start of a permanent settlement. The railroad company, however, had selected a town site to the east, on the Souris River, and when this became known the exodus was sudden and complete; almost overnight the tent town was transplanted to the new location. This mushroom-like appearance, coupled with an almost phenomenal growth to 5000 population during its first year, earned the new frontier settlement the title of the Magic City.

The first white man to settle on the ground now incorporated into the city of Minot was Erik Ramstad, who in May 1885 had come from Grafton, North Dakota, and settled by squatter's right on a quarter section bisected by the Souris. Late in the summer of 1886 he relinquished 40 acres south of the river to the town-site people, and this land together with another 40 acres to the south became the original site of Minot. On July 16, 1887, less than a year after settlement, Minot was an incorporated city. A few weeks later an entire slate of city officers was selected in a campaign that set a high standard for many heated city elections of later years. Principal interest centered about the candidates for mayor, and with typical frontier camaraderie the defeated man was the first to sign the bond of office for his victorious opponent. At its initial meeting the newly elected city council selected as the city's first police chief William Flumerfelt, a saloon-keeper.

When Minot's first Christmas arrived, in 1887, not a church graced the town. To observe the season a Christmas tree was set up in Jack Doyle's saloon, which stood on the site of the present Woolworth store at the corner of Central Avenue and Main Street. Most of the town turned out for the celebration, gifts were hung on the tree, and everyone was given candy.

Many early residents were buried in a cemetery in southwest Minot, although no markers remain. This burial place on one occasion almost saw the interment of a person who, by virtue of being very much alive, was quite undeserving of inclusion here. It happened that a local character known as Spider had gone to his reward, and 'the boys' had taken over his obsequies, stopping on the way to the cemetery to fortify themselves at a saloon. Reaching the grave, they attempted to lower the coffin, but one end dropped down and the other caught on the side of the grave. John J. Powers, a well-known rancher, was selected to straighten the coffin, but in getting down he was caught between it and the wall of the grave. Disregarding his protests, the high-spirited pallbearers proceeded to shovel in dirt, and he was covered except for his head and shoulders when passers-by, hearing his cries, arrived on the scene and effected a rescue.

It was events like this that earned Minot the name of a wild town; and, considering the type of people who flocked into the new city—transient railroad workers and hangers-on, horse and cattle thieves who at that time infested the west and northwest sections of the State, gamblers who saw opportunity in the new settlement, and criminals who had escaped across the boundary from Canada—it is hardly remarkable that the town soon had a reputation for lawlessness and iniquity. Many pioneer residents of Minot still remember a certain railway passenger conductor who would call the name of the station, 'MINOT, this is M-I-N-O-T, end of the line. Prepare to meet your God!'

In spite of the disreputable element, many dependable citizens selected the boom town for their permanent homes, and to them the development of the city has been due. As early as 1887 Marshall McClure was publishing the first newspaper, the weekly Minot *Rustler-Tribune*. The city had its first wooden sidewalk in 1888, and the same year Main Street was lighted with kerosene lamps. The city council passed an ordinance against speeding with horses, the limit being set at 8 miles per hour. Apparently the council of that day believed that actions speak louder than words, for on one occasion it adjourned to go out in a body to grub stumps and fix a road that needed repair. In 1889 this same progressive body voted that the city pay 50 cents per barrel for the first 10 barrels of water delivered at any fire in the city. The first fire wagon was John Strommen's dray, which was used to haul water every time an alarm was turned in.

Burlington (*see Tour 7*), the first community in the Souris region, had confidently expected that the Great Northern would be routed past its door, but instead the road chose the Minot site. The Magic City thereupon set out to deprive its rival of the county seat as well. Arrangements were made for the railroad company to sidetrack an old freight car at Lonetree 28 miles west of Minot. Telegraph wires were strung into it, and the roadmaster presented an affidavit to the county commissioners stating that a station had been opened. Burlington protested: Lonetree belonged in the Burlington precinct, it claimed, and there were not enough residents to open the polls. The railroad installed two operators, a station agent and a helper; Lonetree was declared a precinct, and it is said that railroad crews as far west as Glasgow, Montana, voted. Minot became the county seat.

Settlers rushed into 'Imperial Ward' County when it was surveyed and opened to homesteading in 1896. The origin of the county's nickname is apparent from the following description in Colonel Lounsberry's *Record:* '. . . a small sized empire of 5000 square miles rich in soil, clays, coal, and the energy of its people, immigration unequaled, steady and firm like the flow of a river.' Land entries at Minot during the first nine months of 1905 were said to be greater than at any other U.S. land office in the country. Homesteaders slept on the floor of the office to avoid losing their turn in filing for land.

Imperial Ward remained intact until 1910, when its ample acres were carved into Renville, Burke, Mountrail, and present Ward Counties.

Deer, antelope, prairie and timber wolves, foxes, mink, otter, beaver, ducks, and geese provided early settlers of the Minot area with food, furs, and sport. In the winter, when water holes were opened in the frozen river for stock, fish would come up to the openings in such numbers that they could easily be speared with pitchforks, and it was not uncommon at these watering places to see fish frozen and stacked up like cordwood.

Since the Souris winds through Minot for a distance of eight miles, its overflow can cause great damage, and several times there have been severe floods. The worst occurred in 1882, 1904, 1916, 1923, and 1927. The 1904 flood took the town by surprise, as there were no telephones in the territory upstream from Minot by which the alarm could be given, and small houses were torn from their foundations as the crest of the flood hit the city. Railroad tracks were under water and traffic on the Great Northern and Soo was at a standstill. The flood continued for about three weeks, and children rejoiced as school was discontinued. People went about their business in boats, using their front porches for piers. Many north-side residents moved in with friends living on the higher south side.

Now there are dikes to keep the Souris within bounds, and Federal works on the river above the city, the subsistence homestead project at Burlington, and the Upper Souris migratory waterfowl project (*see Tour 7*) constructed dams that enable engineers to control the flow of water.

While the Great Northern was responsible for Minot's origin and early growth, several factors have shared in the city's later development. Extension of the railroad westward added to the trade territory, all of which is agricultural, and the city became the logical wholesale distribution point for northwest North Dakota. The arrival of the Soo in 1893 tapped untouched areas southeast and northwest, again enlarging the trade region. The first bus line in the State began operation between Minot and Bismarck in 1922. Truck and bus lines now radiate from Minot to serve the many outlying communities not on the transcontinental railroads. The city is a center for an area of 22,500 square miles, extending north to the Canadian line and west into Montana.

Its location in an extensive agricultural area has established Minot as a farm market. During both prewar and postwar periods of heavy crop yields and high prices, Minot boomed as a grain-shipping point. Two flour mills have been a factor in maintaining cash grain prices at higher levels than in other communities. Processing of dairy and poultry products has become an important industry, and a cash livestock market has brought additional returns and marketing facilities. A plant of the poultry co-operative maintained by the North Dakota Farmers Union is situated in Minot. The droughts lessened grain marketing, but pushed forward in another direction the production and stability of diversified farm products, as indicated by the expansion of one and the erection of another creamery and processing plant.

Its rail facilities have helped to make Minot a natural shipping point for the great quantities of lignite mined in this vicinity. The Truax-Traer Company, with headquarters here, is one of the largest lignite strip-mining companies in the United States, and operates the three largest strip mines in the State.

Out of the *Rustler-Tribune,* which reported Minot's earliest events, there grew the Minot *Optic Reporter,* which is now the Minot *Daily News.* The *Democrat,* a political publication, has grown into the *Dakota State Journal,* and the weekly Ward County *Independent* is also published in Minot. A radio station, KLPM, maintains studios in the Fair Block on South Main Street.

With improved transportation facilities and good roads, Minot has become a medical center for the northwest section of the State. Two large hospitals and three clinics are maintained, and a large veterans' hospital is operated by the Federal Government.

POINTS OF INTEREST

1. MINOT STATE TEACHERS COLLEGE, 9th Ave. NW. between 2nd and 8th Sts., with an average quarterly enrollment of 715, is the largest normal school in the State. It is an accredited four-year college with a teachers training school in connection.

Its 70-acre campus, 60 acres of which were donated by Erik Ramstod, Minot's first settler, lies at the foot of the hills bordering the Souris valley on the N. and contains seven brick buildings of modern construction, including a main educational building with auditorium and gymnasium, two dormitories, two training-school buildings, a Student Union building, a powerhouse, and a floodlighted athletic field.

The college offers a two-year standard teachers course as prescribed by State law, a two-year junior college course, and a four-year curriculum leading to an A.B. degree in education. In the training school a model primary, grade, and high school is maintained, enabling prospective teachers to secure actual experience in their profession. Many children in the northwest section of the city attend the college school.

2. WARD COUNTY COURTHOUSE, 3rd St. SE. between 3rd and 4th Aves., was dedicated May 31, 1930. It is said to be the first North Dakota public building of modern design. A motto inscribed upon the front elevation reads: 'Let Us Develop the Resources of Our Land, Call Forth Its Power, Build Upon Its Institutions and Promote All Its Great Interests.'

This austere spacious structure, designed by Tolz, King, and Day of Minneapolis, and erected at a cost of $450,000, succeeded an old-fashioned brick courthouse built in 1891 and razed in 1928. The old courthouse, built after Minot had won the county seat from Burlington, was by no means adequate, but the commissioners feared to submit the question of a new courthouse to a vote, since the county as a whole was not reconciled to Minot's county seat victory. As the law allowed repairs without popular approval, the commissioners 'repaired' the $8000 courthouse to the extent of a new $25,000 addition.

3. PUBLIC LIBRARY (*open* 12–9, *except July and Aug.*, 9–6), 101–107 2nd Ave. SE., is a buff brick Carnegie institution containing 20,000 volumes.

4. ROOSEVELT PARK (*swimming pool, playgrounds, picnic grounds, athletic field, tennis courts*), E. end of 4th Ave. SE., on the S. bank of the Souris River, is an 85-acre tract beautified by rustic bridges, lagoons, flower beds, and sunken gardens. A Zoo containing many species of foreign and domestic animals attracts thousands of visitors annually.

In the park is a bronze EQUESTRIAN STATUE OF THEODORE ROOSEVELT, depicting him as a Rough Rider. The base of the statue is a reproduction of the Badlands formations along the Little Missouri River where Roosevelt once lived. This memorial, designed by A. Phimister Proctor of New York and presented to the city in 1924 by Dr. Henry Waldo Coe, pioneer North Dakota physician and life-long friend of Roosevelt, is dedicated to the school children who contributed the cost of the base.

COE DRIVE, a scenic two-mile route through the woods bordering a loop of the Souris River, connects with a mile drive through Roosevelt Park. It is reached by driving one block into the park from the entrance and turning right.

5. OAK PARK, W. end of 3rd Ave. NW., has more than 50 acres of wooded land. Provided with tennis courts, wading pool, and picnic tables, it is a favorite spot for Sunday picnickers from the surrounding country.

6. ROSEHILL CEMETERY, 3rd St. SE. at 11th Ave., contains the nine-foot marble WORLD WAR MEMORIAL SHAFT and the DAUGHTERS OF UNION VETERANS OF THE CIVIL WAR MEMORIAL.

POINTS OF INTEREST IN ENVIRONS

Burlington underground lignite mines, 8 *m.*; Burlington Subsistence Homestead Project, 8 *m.*; Velva lignite strip mine, 32 *m.* (*see Tour* 7).

PART III

Playgrounds

❉❉

Fort Abraham Lincoln State Park

Entrance: 4.5 *m.* S. of Mandan on graveled road (*see Tour* 8).
Points of interest in park: Fort McKeen, Slant Indian Village, site of old Fort Abraham Lincoln.
Regulations: Park open during daylight hours only; parking cars on highway prohibited.

The 750 acres of Fort Abraham Lincoln State Park lie on the west bluffs of the Missouri River, encompassing three sites of historical and archeological interest—a Mandan Indian village and two old military posts. The park was developed by the State Historical Society of North Dakota in co-operation with the National Park Service and the Civilian Conservation Corps.

As the roadway enters the park, the bluffs rise steeply to the right, while below on the left is spread a beautiful view of the Missouri winding away to the distant hills, tracing the outlines of Sibley Island, the Heart River below, flowing into the Missouri, and Bismarck and the capitol set against the background of the valley rising on the other side of the river.

Fort McKeen is on the river bluffs, and the Indian village is below on the river bank, slightly higher than Fort Abraham Lincoln, the cavalry post, on the broad ancient plain near the mouth of the Heart.

Left as the highway enters the park is a crude log palisade that guards the old SLANT VILLAGE. Before these prairies saw the invasion of the white man, perhaps two centuries ago, a group of Mandan Indians, seeking a new location in their advance up the Missouri Valley, selected this narrow point of land which had such excellent natural protection. On the east was the Heart River and on the south a deep coulee. Along the exposed sides the Indians built a palisade and dug a moat to secure their little town.

Depressions in the earth show that the settlement contained 68 lodges. Five have been restored by the park administration, four of them homes and the other the large ceremonial lodge. All have been placed as nearly as possible on their original sites, and in some cases the locations made by park workers were so accurate that remains of the old lodges were found in excavating for the restoration work. The five lodges have been carefully reproduced in every detail. (A general description of the construction and equipment of the typical Indian earth lodge will be found under INDIANS AND THEIR PREDECESSORS.)

Crude tools such as the inhabitants of this town used in domestic and agricultural work are on display in one lodge. Hoes and shovels were flat bones fastened to wooden handles, and brooms were bunches of brush bound together. A short post with a hollowed center served as a mortar, a club about the size of a baseball bat as a pestle, and with this apparatus corn was ground for meal.

Furnishings in the lodge include the horse corrals, beds, and altars which were part of the domestic scene. There are specimens of dog and horse travois, and an Indian bullboat, made by stretching a green buffalo hide over a wooden frame and drying it. The result resembled nothing so much as an ungainly washtub, but the awkward-looking craft would carry two or three persons quite safely across the treacherous currents of the Missouri.

The women of the Indian tribes built the lodges in the river villages, although the men gave them assistance in placing the heavy timbers that supported the thick earth walls. A Mandan legend relates that when the first Mandan village was built under the leadership of the tribal hero, Good Furred Robe, the First Man told them how to build the earth lodges.

The ceremonial lodge, with a diameter of 84 feet, has been restored in its original position in the center of the village court, and the interior of this surprisingly large building furnishes an index of the architectural advancement of these supposedly savage people. In this lodge tribal ceremonies were held, and the site doubtless witnessed many enactments of the most holy Mandan religious service, in which the young men of the tribe were inducted into manhood with bloody and gruesome torture rites.

Right of the highway, almost opposite the entrance to the village, the restored and graveled military road branches steeply upward to where FORT McKEEN commands a far view of the plains and the twisting Missouri. Although Bismarck, the two bridges across the river, and many other marks of settlement are now part of the scene, the entire view from this point was one wild, untouched, verdant picture when Army engineers came from Fort Rice in 1872 in search of a location for an infantry post to protect the surveyors, engineers, and workmen who prepared the way for the gleaming intrusion of the Northern Pacific rails. This site was selected, as the Mandan 200 years before had selected the one below, for its natural protection. The fort was built in 1872 and was named for Colonel Henry Boyd McKeen of the Eighty-first Pennsylvania Volunteers, but on November 19, 1872, the name was officially changed to Fort Abraham Lincoln in honor of the martyred President. A triangular area was fortified, with a blockhouse at each corner and palisade walls connecting them on two sides. The steep face of the bluff protected the remaining side. Within the stockade were officers' quarters, barracks, kitchens, hospital, and laundry. The scouts' headquarters and the laundry were built of cottonwood logs cut along the river, while most of the other buildings were of lumber.

The soldiers stationed at the fort led a varied life, the monotony of frontier existence being tempered by fighting the Sioux, maintaining order among the lawless element that followed the progress of the railroad, and even building smudges to protect the workers from the tormenting swarms of bloodthirsty mosquitoes.

The three blockhouses and the palisade have been restored, so that the fort looks much as it must have looked more than 50 years ago when it crowned this bluff, guarding its prominent position on the river. None of the buildings within the enclosure is left, but the sites of all are marked.

To avoid confusion, the restored fort is commonly referred to as Fort McKeen, distinguishing it from the later Fort Abraham Lincoln, although the latter included both posts. The FORT ABRAHAM LINCOLN SITE is right of the park road just south of the Indian village. Markers indicate the sites of the various structures, and holes partly filled with debris also show where the buildings of the Northwest's strongest fortress once stood. A row of cottonwoods, which grew along Officers' Row, stands in lonesome splendor.

When General George A. Custer and his spirited Seventh Cavalry came to Fort Abraham Lincoln in 1873 it became a nine-company cavalry and infantry post, with the cavalry established on the level plain below, where a good drill and parade ground was available. Custer, with his long sandy-colored hair and restless vivacity, was one of the most personable and interesting military men of his time. He and his wife, a young and talented woman, soon drew about themselves a social circle that was widely known and aspired to. Balls, musicales, and other entertainments drew people from the surrounding territory, including the new town of Bismarck across the river. The social life at Fort Abraham Lincoln would have been a credit to any city, as, beneath crystal chandeliers, to the music of the Seventh's band, stately couples moved in the graceful figures of the dance.

For the soldiers, life consisted chiefly of maintaining order among the Indians and the incoming white population. At one time the guardhouse at the fort had a distinguished occupant, Rain-in-the-Face, the Sioux warrior. He had been heard boasting of 'counting coup' on the bodies of two white men killed on the Stanley expedition in 1873, and Tom Custer, brother of General Custer, was sent to take him into custody at Standing Rock Agency (*see Tour 8C*). Rain-in-the-Face was arrested and imprisoned at Fort Abraham Lincoln, but escaped in a jailbreak engineered by friends of some of the other prisoners, and joined Sitting Bull.

Life at the post often grew monotonous for the troopers, who in winter found their activities hampered by the severe cold and in the summer suffered from the torments of the heat and the mosquitoes.

When the routine of military life palled too greatly on the soldiers, they took refuge in the activities of the Point, a little settlement of dance halls, saloons, and similar places of entertainment that flourished on the opposite bank of the river directly across from the fort. Since there was no bridge across the Missouri the Point could be reached only by ferry or on the ice. At the time of the spring break-up, however, even the ferry could not be used, and many of the soldiers missed the customary recreational and liquid facilities afforded by the Point. One spring, as the ice was going out, a young man, whose fine physique was equaled only by his foolhardy daring, offered to cross the river for some liquor. Crossing a river on breaking ice has been known as a daring feat since even before the days of Eliza and the bloodhounds, but crossing the Missouri is a particularly hazardous exploit, for this river, always maliciously menacing, is even more so in the spring, with great ice blocks eddying and whirling, crunching violently together, then flung apart by the swift current. The slightest misstep or miscalculation meant death to the young, thirsty soldier, but with the greatest nonchalance he made the crossing and the return, bringing his precious burden back with him, and great and twofold was the rejoicing when he safely reached the home shore.

Three years of existence left Fort Abraham Lincoln in comparative quiet, with only an occasional Indian skirmish. Then events on the frontier conspired to bring the Indian troubles to an end. The campaign of the Little Big Horn was planned (*see* HISTORY). One day in 1876 the Seventh, with bands playing and colors flying, marched away along the Heart in pursuit of the Sioux. On a stifling night early in July the residents of Bismarck were awakened from their sleep by loud sounds of shouting, of wagons and horses moving, at the river. Captain Grant Marsh had arrived from the Little Big Horn with his steamer, the *Far West,* loaded with the wounded of Major Reno's command, survivors of the Battle of the Little Big Horn. But more than the wounded, he bore news—news of the death of 267 men, of the annihilation of Custer and his immediate command. Twenty-six of the waiting wives at Fort Abraham Lincoln were widows.

The only living thing left of Custer's command was Comanche, Captain Myles Keogh's horse. Through the rough country filled with hostile, victorious Sioux, Reno's wounded men had been carried to the *Far West,* and Captain Marsh had made his epic 54-hour run to Bismarck and the fort 700 miles away.

Captain Marsh's story of how he learned of the Custer tragedy is strange and almost unreal. He related later that, as he waited on the river for word from the military commanders, a Crow Indian peered from the brush along the shore and signed that he wished to board the boat. On deck the Indian, unable to speak a word of English, squatted and began to make signs. He drew a group of dots, designated them with the Crow word for 'white men.' Then he showed a circle of dots around the white men and for them spoke the word for 'Sioux.' And then, with a sweep of his hand, he wiped out the inner group of dots. In this simple, abrupt manner, Marsh related, the tragedy was first told to the world.

The story of Custer's annihilation was put on the telegraph wires by Colonel C. A. Lounsberry. James W. Foley, North Dakota poet laureate, has commented: 'It was, for stark tragedy, horror and surprise, perhaps the greatest news story ever flashed over a telegraph wire to a stunned and stricken country, in the history of the United States.'

The Little Big Horn disaster was the beginning of the end of the era of Indian fighting in this region, and troops were withdrawn from Fort Abraham Lincoln in 1891, after which the buildings were carried off piecemeal by the settlers in the vicinity. A new infantry post, known as Fort Lincoln, was later established across the river (*see Tour* 8).

Fort Abraham Lincoln State Park has been developed for recreational and historical purposes by the Federal Government in co-operation with the State historical society. The grounds are landscaped, foot trails laid out, and picnic shelters built. The Fort Lincoln Museum (*open April–November*) is built of cut native granite with flagstone floors and interior trim of natural cottonwood paneling. The museum collection tells the story of the Mandan Indian, Fort McKeen, and Fort Lincoln.

Theodore Roosevelt
National Memorial Park

Season: Open year round. June to September most favorable period.

Tourist Information: Superintendent, Park Headquarters, Medora, North Dakota; State Historical Society of North Dakota, Liberty Memorial Building, Bismarck, North Dakota.

Admission: Free.

Transportation:
NORTH SECTION. E. entrance, US 85 (*see Tour* 4). Branch of Great Northern Ry., Fairview, Montana, to Watford City; Carpenter Bus Line from Williston.
Roads: 14 *m.* gravel and scoria highway; 10 *m.* horse or hike trail. No guide service.
SOUTH SECTION. Entrances: E. entrance, W. entrance, US 10 (*see Tour* 8). Main line Northern Pacific Ry. and Northland Greyhound Bus Line to Medora (*see Tour* 8).
Roads: 10 *m.* gravel and scoria highway; 10 *m.* graveled truck trail; 5 *m.* horse or hike trail.
Guide service: Buddy Ranch, 1.5 *m.* E. of Medora on US 10.

Accommodations:
NORTH SECTION. Hotel accommodations at Watford City (*see Tour* 4); camping and trailer facilities at Squaw Creek Picnic Area (*see Theodore Roosevelt National Memorial Park, North Tour, below*).
SOUTH SECTION. Hotel accommodations at Medora (*see Tour* 8).
Camping and trailer facilities at camping area in park (*see Theodore Roosevelt National Memorial Park, South Tour, below*).
Meals, cabins, and horses at Buddy Ranch, 1.5 *m.* E. of Medora.

Climate, clothing, and equipment: Summer tourists should prepare for hot days and cool evenings and for sudden rain or dust storms. Those who expect to tramp in the Badlands should dress for walking through brush and soft, clayey soil. Breeches and high-top boots are in order, the latter serving the additional purpose of protection against snake bite.

Medical service: Watford City (*see Tour* 4); Belfield (*see Tour* 8).

Special regulations: No hunting allowed. Camping permitted at points where facilities are provided. Fires allowed only at points designated.

Warnings: Avoid low places during heavy rainstorms. Horse trails should not be attempted after rains until trail makers have had an opportunity to repair. Use only native horses. Rattlesnakes are encountered only infrequently (*see* GENERAL INFORMATION).

Summary of attractions: Badlands views, petrified forests, horseback riding, camping.

Theodore Roosevelt's biographer, Herman Hagedorn, writes:

Between the prairie lands of North Dakota and the prairie lands of Montana there is a narrow strip of broken country so wild and fantastic in its beauty that it seems as though some unholy demon had carved it to mock the loveliness of God. On both sides of a sinuous river rise ten thousand buttes cut into bizarre shapes by the waters of countless centuries. The hand of man never dared to paint anything as those hills are painted. Olive and lavender, buff, brown, and dazzling white mingle with emerald and flaming scarlet to make a piece of savage splendor that is not without an element of the terrible. The buttes are stark and bare. Only in the clefts are ancient cedars, starved and deformed. In spring there are patches of green grass, an acre here, a hundred acres there, reaching up the slopes from the level bottom-land; but there are regions where for miles and miles no green thing grows, and all creation seems a witch's caldron of gray bubbles tongued with flame, held by some bit of black art forever in suspension.

Here in this broken country, known as the Badlands of the Little Missouri, the Theodore Roosevelt National Memorial Park is being developed by the National Park Service to preserve parts of the strange area as scenic and recreational centers and, at the same time, to establish a memorial to the former President, who as a young man spent part of each year from 1883 to 1886 ranching here. (*See Tours* 8 *and* 10.) To view the freakish, tumbled, unearthly valley is to appreciate and at the same time be amused by General Alfred Sully's oft-quoted characterization of the region as 'hell with the fires out.' It must be remembered that the general received his impressions as he jolted along in a wagon, sick, while his troops fought Sioux through the confused, uncertain terrain all one hot day in August 1864. Others visiting it under more favorable circumstances, especially during the freshness of spring, concede the unparalleled fantasy of the landscape and agree on its strange, wild, potent beauty. Twenty years after Sully fought the Sioux here Roosevelt wrote, 'I grow very fond of this place . . . it . . . has a desolate, grim beauty, that has a curious fascination for me.' Since then many noted travelers and writers have marveled at its beauties and deplored the fact that its attractions have not been made more widely known.

The traveler approaching the Badlands from the rolling prairies on either side suddenly finds himself overlooking a valley cut abruptly into the heart of the plain, a valley filled with a strange welter of bare ridges and hillocks, buttes and domes, pyramids and cones, forming one of the most extraordinary topographies on the surface of the earth. In broad horizontal stripes across the varied shapes of the buttes are the browns, reds, grays, and yellows of the sand and clay laid down centuries ago when during successive ages arms of the sea covered large parts of the North American Continent. Where today the visitor stands and looks out over the naked buttes once lay a mighty sea in which swam monsters whose fossilized skeletons are imbedded in the strata laid down by the primordial waters.

Here and there, standing out against the lighter coloring of the sands and clays, are black veins of lignite. Ages ago dense forests, rivaling those of the tropics of today, rose over the swamps of the receding seas. The motorcar speeds through a region where the giant hog, the three-toed horse, and the saber-toothed tiger roamed among lofty trees. The cast-off growth of the forest fell into the swamps below, where, shut away from the air by water and mud, it turned into peat. Centuries later the seas returned to crush it with heavy layers of shale and clay, until pressure and heat drove out most of the volatile oils of the wood, leaving carbon or coal. It is not surprising to find that lignite coal has the came cellular formation as wood, and that it at times bears the imprint of leaves or of whole trunks of trees. The forms of stumps 15 feet in diameter have been found in the coal beds of the State.

Lighting up the dull strata of the buttes are the ever-present pinks and reds of scoria—clay burnt into a brick-like shale by the centuries-old fires of burning coal veins. Some of these burning veins still exist in the Badlands, being more easily discoverable in the wintertime, when the heat from combustion causes steam to rise. This burning has been one of the major factors in the production of the present Badlands topography, for as the fires have eaten into the coal veins in the cliffs, the earth has crumbled and been carried away by the rains and streams. These fires were an awesome sight to the Indians, who believed the hills were on fire.

The chief agent, however, in the formation of the Badlands has been the Little Missouri River, which centuries ago began to carve its way down through the soft shales and sandstones with which the early seas had covered the area. Aided by the eroding action of wind, frost, and rain, by huge landslides, and by burning coal veins, the once swift, always silt-laden river and its tributaries have floated away all the age-old clays of the region except these buttes and domes piled in indescribable confusion along the valley floor. The Indians called the valley 'The-place-where-the-hills-look-at-each-other,' and the first white explorers, impeded in their travel, named it 'bad lands to travel through,' a phrase inevitably shortened to Badlands.

Adding to the bizarre coloring of this unusual valley are the blue-gray and silver of the sage, so often remarked by Roosevelt, the light green of the sparse grasses of butte top and valley, and the darker green of the cedars which cling to the shady sides of buttes. Cottonwood, ash, box elder, elm, bull pine, dogwood, and flowering currant grow along the Little Missouri, while gooseberries, buffalo berries, and chokecherries ripen in the gullies. In June the large, white, open flowers of the low-growing gumbo lily, also known as the cowboy lily and the butte prim-rose, appear in the otherwise barren soil at the foot of the buttes, to be followed shortly by the purple-centered white and lavender Mariposa and creamy white yucca lilies. In midsummer the small, wine-colored flowers of the ball cactus and the large, waxy, lemon-yellow and brown blossoms of the prickly pear cactus show on the drier soil of the buttes, and the scoria lily, with its thistle-like foliage, opens its large, white flower only after sundown. In addition to these striking, gaudy blooms, a great variety of more common North Dakota flowers also appear in the valley of the Little Missouri, especially in the springtime.

When white men first visited the region, it was rich in wild life. Beaver and otter swam the streams, flocks of game birds hid in the breaks, droves of elk, deer, and antelope fed along the Little Missouri, and huge herds of buffalo often darkened the prairie above the valley. In Roosevelt's ranching days game was still abundant, and grizzlies and mountain lions were encountered occasionally. Rocky Mountain, or bighorn, sheep were killed as late as 1906. Bobcats and coyotes are found occasionally even today. The valley harbors more than 300 species of birds, including many game birds and the golden eagle.

On patches of dry grassland here and there, down in the bottoms or up on the buttes, there are prairie-dog towns—areas sometimes as much as a hundred acres in extent, thickly dotted with the small mounds of their cunning inhabitants. Prairie dogs, somewhat larger than good-sized rats, are burrowing rodents allied to the marmot. In digging their burrows they throw the earth up into little mounds, upon which, whenever anything has aroused their curiosity or fear, they sit to chatter, barking like very small dogs, or perhaps more like gray squirrels.

Interesting in connection with any description of the origin of the Badlands is the Sioux legend of their formation. Unknown centuries ago, it is said, the Badlands were a fertile plain, covered with rich grasses and abounding with game. Every autumn the plains tribes came here to get meat for winter and to hold friendly councils beneath the trees which grew along the rivers. Tribes, hostile at other times and in other places, while here greeted each other in peace.

This happy arrangement continued for many years, but one season a fierce tribe came from the mountains to the west and drove the plains tribes from their hunting grounds. Being unsuccessful in their attempts to dislodge the invaders, the plains people finally called a great council and fasted and prayed. Many days passed, however, and no answer came from the Great Spirit, and they began to despair.

Then suddenly a great shudder convulsed the earth, the sky grew black as midnight, and lightning burned jagged through the gloom. Fires hissed from the earth and the once pleasant land rolled and tossed like the waves of the sea, while into its flaming, pitching surface sank the invading tribe, the streams, the trees, and all living things. Then just as suddenly as it had begun, the upheaval and the conflagration ceased, leaving the plain fixed in grotesque waves.

In this way the Great Spirit destroyed the prize that had stirred up strife among his children, and the Badlands were created.

THEODORE ROOSEVELT NATIONAL MEMORIAL PARK, NORTH TOUR

East entrance (*see Tour* 4)—Sperati Point (*see Tour* 10), 14 *m.*

The north section of the Park, which has an area of approximately 40 square miles, presents many of the best Badlands features, including a petrified forest and the remarkable views of the Grand Canyon of the Little Missouri River from Sperati Point.

From the eastern entrance the winding graveled and scoria park highway proceeds in a general westerly direction along the northern side of the LITTLE MISSOURI.

At 1.5 *m.* is the CHALONER CREEK HORSE TRAIL.

> Right on this trail which affords an opportunity for a ride of 5 *m.* among the buttes and along the edge of the higher land above the brush-filled gullies or breaks. Some parts of the trail are cut through groves of aspen, ash, elm, and cedar on the north side of buttes, while other parts move over the face of the cliffs or on high and narrow ridges with precipitous canyon walls 300 ft. or more in depth dropping on either side. Petrified stumps are along the trail.

The highway, continuing W. more directly than the river, which here makes a deep bend to the S., skirts patches of woodland along the bottoms to reach SQUAW CREEK PICNIC AREA, 5 *m.,* the best-developed camping center in the two parks. This picnic area on the banks of the Little Missouri has excellent grass and shade. Its one-way road leads among aspen, aromatic sumac, oak, poplar, and cottonwood to a number of individual camp sites. In addition to a stone and log shelter and numerous fireplaces, the area has 4 wells and 45 tables. At the east edge of the area a rustic footbridge leads over a little ravine, to clean, grassy picnic grounds.

Northwest of Squaw Creek Picnic Area the road passes along the edge of the breaks overlooking the river to a junction with CEDAR CANYON HORSE TRAIL at 5.8 *m.*

> Left on this 5-mile trail, which is very similar in character to the Chaloner Creek Horse Trail, are lookout points affording excellent views. In spring portions of the trail show a profusion of wild flowers.

At 7 *m.* is CEDAR CANYON LOOKOUT, which commands an exceptionally good view to the S. across the Little Missouri River and beyond, where as far as the eye can reach stretch the tumbled outlines of the buttes.

Northwest of Cedar Canyon the road moves out upon the plateau above the Badlands and then turns W. and SW. in a large arc along the edge of the breaks to SPERATI POINT, 14 *m.* (*see Tour* 10), a high shoulder of the plateau, overlooking the spectacular GRAND CANYON OF THE LITTLE MISSOURI. Lying just W. of the bend of the Little Missouri where it turns E. toward the Missouri, the point affords views up and down the canyon, which in places is 600 ft. deep.

From Sperati Point an unmarked and indefinite trail, which should not be tried without a guide, leads SW.

Left on this trail to a PETRIFIED FOREST, 2 *m.*, one of those Badlands areas, often many acres in extent, which abound with petrified logs and stumps. Petrified stumps are a common sight throughout the valley of the Little Missouri, suggesting that at one time it must have been heavily forested. When the originals of these stone trees died, their trunks, either standing or fallen, soaked up soil water holding mineral matter in solution. As the water evaporated, the mineral matter was left behind, filling the pores of the wood and the tiny cavities produced by decomposition. In time decay removed all the wood and the trees became stone, or, popularly, petrified wood. Some of the logs—for, of course, the trees are not now standing—are as much as 35 ft. in length and 2 ft. in diameter. In some places the soil has been washed and blown away from beneath the stumps, leaving odd formations shaped like toadstools.

THEODORE ROOSEVELT NATIONAL MEMORIAL PARK, SOUTH TOUR

East entrance (*see Tour* 8)—Hell's Hole—West entrance (*see Tour* 8), 10 *m.*

The south section of the Park comprises an area of approximately 70 square miles, lying along the Little Missouri just N. of US 10. In addition to the fantastic beauty of the Badlands buttes, it contains a petrified forest, and one of the largest burning coal mines in the Badlands.

From the eastern entrance the route leads NW. over the broad, pale-pink ribbon of the graveled and scoria park highway.

HELL'S HOLE (L), 4 *m.*, was named for a burning coal mine once situated in this valley. The mine burned out, causing the earth to crumble and destroy a tiny lake which lay under the cliff.

At 7 *m.* three trails form a triangle on a level area adjacent to the LITTLE MISSOURI RIVER. Here it is proposed to develop a recreational center with full tourist accommodations, including cabins, store, lodge, and stables. At the north end of the proposed area is the old PEACEFUL VALLEY RANCH, which served tourists many years. It has been acquired by the park, and the ranch house and corrals are to be preserved as a recreational center. At Peaceful Valley Ranch are the junctions with an unimproved trail, a graveled truck trail, and an unmarked and indefinite horse trail.

1. Right from the ranch on the unimproved trail to PADDOCK CREEK, 0.4 *m.*, which like all the creeks here is dry except in rainy seasons. Up the creek, one on the L. bank at 1 *m.* and the other on the R. at 1.5 *m.* are the mounds of two PRAIRIE-DOG TOWNS.

2. Right from the ranch on the truck trail that crosses JONES CREEK, 0.8 *m.*, and turns E. just before reaching CATHEDRAL BUTTE, 2 *m.*, an old landmark on the trail.

Left from Cathedral Butte 0.5 *m.* on an unimproved trail to WIND CANYON, a narrow, deep valley leading down to a broad elbow of the Little Missouri. Its name was suggested by the striking examples of erosion by winds, which, whipping at the buttes for centuries, have worn them into odd shapes. From Wind

Canyon the trail passes NW. along the river to SHELL BUTTE, 0.8 *m.*, a high butte into which the river has cut deeply, revealing large deposits of marine shells.

East of Cathedral Butte on the main side route, following the truck trail for about a mile and then NE. across JUEL CREEK, 3.3 *m.*, to GOD'S GARDENS (R), 4.5 *m.*, an unusually attractive stretch of butte and lowland, from which the road leads NW. across GOVERNMENT CREEK, 5.3 *m.*, where to the R., one on either side of the creek, are two PRAIRIE-DOG TOWNS. At the crossing of Government Creek is the junction with an unimproved trail (*do not follow without guide*).

Right on this trail 3 *m.* to a BURNING COAL MINE, which is one of the largest in the Badlands. The burning of the coal causes cracks to form in the earth above the vein; one guide says he has brought water to a boil in 15 minutes by placing it above one of these cracks. As the vein is consumed, the earth crumbles and falls, and the rains carry it away to the streams.

Amid some of the finest Badlands scenery the truck trail continues in a general northwesterly direction to the north boundary of the park, 10 *m.*

3. Left from the ranch on the unmarked and indefinite horse trail to a PETRIFIED FOREST, 5.5 *m.*, considered one of the best examples of a petrified forest (*see Theodore Roosevelt National Memorial Park, North Tour, above*) in the Badlands. The trip to this forest, which makes a nice day's outing, requires a guide.

Southwest of Peaceful Valley Ranch, the route runs along the east bank of the winding, shallow Little Missouri to a CAMPING AREA (R), 8 *m.*, sheltered by trees along the stream. It is furnished with tables, fireplaces, and wells, and several individual camping spaces have been developed along the road that circles through it.

At 8.5 *m.* the route fords the river—a passage that in times of high water cannot be effected by motorcars—and, turning SW. along the western bank, reaches a level piece of bottom land overshadowed by lofty buttes.

At 9.5 *m.* is a junction with a graveled road leading uphill away from the river.

Right on this trail is a PICNIC SHELTER, 0.5 *m.*, built over a spring and provided with a fireplace.

Right from this shelter 5 *m.* on a marked HORSE TRAIL, which winds among the buttes in a figure 8. At some points on the trail the tops of Square (Flat Top) and Sentinel Buttes (*see Tour* 8) are visible far away to the SW. At the center of the figure 8, forming a pleasant place for lunch, is a clump of trees with a spring flowing down over little sandstone terraces.

At 9.8 *m.* is the sandstone portal of the west entrance, beyond which is the junction with US 10 (*see Tour* 8), 10 *m.*

PART IV

Highways and Trails

Tour 1

(Winnipeg, Man., Can.)—Pembina—Grand Forks—Fargo—Wahpeton—(Watertown, S. Dak.); US 81.
Canadian boundary to South Dakota Line, 251 *m.*

N. P. Ry. parallels route between Canadian border and Joliette; G. N. Ry. between Hamilton and Fargo; Milwaukee R. R. between Fargo and South Dakota Line. Winnipeg-Fargo route of Northwest Airlines parallels route between Canadian border and Fargo.
Graveled roadbed 81 *m.*, bituminous surface 170 *m.*
Accommodations of all types in principal towns.

US 81 crosses North Dakota along its eastern boundary from the Canadian to the South Dakota border, and passes through the rich low valley of the Red River of the North, a wide level plain that was once the bed of the great prehistoric Lake Agassiz. The route parallels the Red River to Wahpeton, and the Bois de Sioux River between that city and the South Dakota Line. Constantly in sight to the left of the road are the heavily wooded river banks, but except for crossing several timbered tributaries the route runs through almost unbelievably flat green fields, broken here and there by an occasional farmstead.

During the early settlement of this region the Red River provided transportation into the newly opened Northwest, and beside its course slow-moving trains of creaking oxcarts preceded the steamboat into the new land. It was in the Red River Valley that the first white settlements in the State were made. Here in the last quarter of the nineteenth century flourished the bonanza farms—those huge land tracts entirely devoted to the growing of wheat that earned for this valley the title of 'the bread basket of the world.' Today the Red River Valley produces many other crops—potatoes, sugar beets, alfalfa—in addition to wheat. Its natural endowments of rich soil and good rainfall combine with the man-made facilities of transportation to constitute the most prosperous section of North Dakota.

US 81 crosses the Canadian border 68 *m.* S. of Winnipeg, Canada.

PEMBINA (Chippewa, *highbush cranberry*), 2 *m.* (792 alt., 703 pop.), named for the berries that lend their flaming color to the near-by woods in autumn, is the cradle of North Dakota white settlement. Here, at the confluence of the Red and Pembina Rivers, the earliest trading posts and the first white colony in the State were established. Charles Chaboillez, representing the North West Company, built the first fur post on North Dakota soil on the south bank of the Pembina River within the present site of Pembina in 1797–8. Rudely constructed and of short duration, it had already disappeared when Alexander Henry, Jr., also of the North West Company, came up the Red River in 1800. The following year he built a post on the north side of the Pembina, and in the same year both the XY and the Hudson's Bay Company opened posts at the mouth of the river. The three competing companies, with their free rum and unscrupulous trading, brought about a lawless social condition in the new settlement. Drinking bouts and brawls were continuous as the Indians were plied with liquor by the conscienceless traders, who excused their conduct on grounds of competition.

It was during this time that the first child of other than Indian blood was born on North Dakota soil. The child was not white, but Negro, the daughter of Pierre Bonza, Henry's personal servant. The first white child in the State was born at Henry's post in 1807, the illegitimate son of the 'Orkney Lad,' a woman who had worked at the post for several years in the guise of a man. Her imposture was not generally known until the birth of her child, after which a collection was taken up and she and the child were sent back to her home in the Orkney Islands.

During the middle of the nineteenth century Pembina was the rendezvous for white and metis hunters, and the town was the starting point for the great Pembina buffalo hunts (*see Tour 5A*).

The fur trade brought some white settlers to this area, but it was not until 1812 that systematic colonization was attempted. In that year William Douglas, Earl of Selkirk, brought a group of dispossessed Scottish peasants to the Red River Valley to farm under an agreement with the Hudson's Bay Company. Untrained for the rigors of frontier life, and persecuted by the fur traders of the rival North West Company who did not want settlers in their lucrative area, many of the Selkirk colonists moved to Canada in 1818 after establishment of the international boundary defined Pembina as United States soil. The next 30 years saw a slow influx of settlers into the Red River Valley and by 1851 Pembina had become a fairly important river port. In that year Norman Kittson, a fur trader, was named postmaster, the first in North Dakota; and Charles Cavileer, for whom the town and county of Cavalier were later named (*see Tour 5*), was appointed collector of customs at Pembina. Cavileer became postmaster in 1852, and, as under his influence newcomers arrived to farm, the fur trade declined and there developed the first permanent agricultural community in the State.

Pembina appears from a distance more like a grove of trees than a town. Most of its buildings are old, reflecting the rococo architecture of an earlier day.

On the Red River at the eastern end of Rolette St. is MASONIC PARK, where a marker commemorates the site of the first Masonic lodge in the State, organized at Pembina in 1863. Each year, both on July 1, which is Dominion Day (the Canadian holiday similar to the U.S. Independence Day) and on July 4, the flag of the United States and the

Canadian Union Jack fly together from the park flagpole, a practice illustrating the neighborliness of the border States and Provinces. The Canadian flag is a gift of the Masonic Grand Lodge of Manitoba.

The highway crosses the Pembina River, which in dry seasons is likely to appear more like mud than water. Left on the highway is PEMBINA STATE PARK (*good water, firewood, kitchens, and tables*), which includes the site of the Chaboillez trading post.

A bridge over the Red River connects Pembina with St. Vincent, Minnesota, situated on US 59 (*see Minnesota Guide Tour 17*).

At 3 *m.* is the PEMBINA AIRPORT (R), airport of entry operated by the Northwest Airlines. It is on part of the former military reservation of Fort Pembina, established in 1870. The reservation was turned over to the U.S. Department of the Interior in 1895 and sold at public auction. The fort was situated a mile and a half S. of the city of Pembina on the Red River.

JOLIETTE, 14 *m.* (796 alt., 150 pop.), is a French-Canadian community named for Joliette, Quebec.

At 15 *m.* is the junction with ND 44, a graveled highway and an alternate route of shorter distance between Joliette and Manvel (*see below*).

Left on ND 44 is BOWESMONT, 8 *m.* (794 alt., 131 pop.), named for William Bowes, the first storekeeper. It lies on the level land just W. of the Red River, its treeless streets more like a western North Dakota prairie town than the usual Red River Valley village. The story is told that Bowes won the opportunity to name the town in a game of cards. Bowesmont was first built on the banks of the river, but settlers experienced great hardships when the stream overflowed its banks each spring, and the buildings were moved.

Near Bowesmont in the spring of 1860 occurred an event illustrative of the hardships suffered by the missionaries to this region. The Reverend Joseph Goiffon, assistant at the Pembina Catholic Mission, returning from a trip to St. Paul, left his party behind in an effort to reach the mission in time to conduct a certain Mass. A driving rain had been falling and this suddenly turned to a swirling snowstorm. In a short time the ground was covered with six or seven inches of snow, and the driving wind made it impossible for him to continue. The blizzard did not abate, and in two days his horse had died from exposure and his own legs had frozen so that he was unable to walk. For five days he remained on the prairie, living on the flesh of his horse, until the storm subsided and a passer-by heard his feeble cries for help. It was found necessary to amputate parts of both legs, but in spite of this he returned to the Pembina mission and was later transferred to St. Paul and Mendota, where he served until his death in 1910.

DRAYTON, 17 *m.* (800 alt., 688 pop.), first known as Hastings Landing, was given its present name by settlers who came west from Drayton, Ontario, Canada. In contrast with its neighbor Bowesmont, Drayton is situated directly in the timber on the banks of the Red. Its 42-acre city park is unusual in that it lies in another State, across the river in Minnesota. The bridge leading to the park is also unusual; it is a drawbridge, built in 1911, when the high stage of the Red aroused hope of reviving steamboating. After the bridge had been completed the river stage fell and has never risen, so that the draw has not been lifted since it was built.

Drayton is an active sports town, especially interested in curling, and 10 teams compete in the large enclosed rink each winter.

Left on ND 44 to ACTON HALL, 28 *m.*, a community building.

On ND 44 to the junction (R) with a graveled road, 34 *m.* In a triangle formed by the junction is a CRUCIFIX. On a base of natural boulders, in summer the clear, marble-like whiteness of the cross and canopied figure stands out in contrast with the green of the surrounding countryside.

At 50 *m.* is the junction with US 81 (*see below*).

HAMILTON, 25 *m.* (830 alt., 255 pop.), also a Canadian settlement, is named for Hamilton, Ontario. The oldest State bank in North Dakota, organized in 1886, is operated here. The Pembina County Fair, established in 1894, is held here (*June or July*) each year. In Hamilton is the junction with ND 5 (*see Tour 5*).

In GLASSTON, 32 *m.* (843 alt., 75 pop.), named for Archibald Glass, first postmaster, and ST. THOMAS, 38 *m.* (846 alt., 503 pop.), named for St. Thomas, Ontario, are the homes of many retired farmers. The latter is also a potato and sugar-beet shipping center.

AUBURN, 46 *m.* (848 alt., 20 pop.), was larger than its neighbor GRAFTON, 53 *m.* (833 alt., 4,070 pop.), until the latter became a railroad junction. Named by early settlers for Grafton County, New Hampshire, Grafton is on the Park River in the center of a rich farming area. It was the first city in this part of the Northwest to maintain a municipal light plant and had the first public library in North Dakota, established by a women's club in 1897. A SPANISH-AMERICAN WAR MEMORIAL, one of the few in the State, is on the Walsh County Courthouse grounds. On a hill W. of the town is the GRAFTON STATE SCHOOL for the feeble-minded. Opened in 1904, the institution in 1937 had 778 inmates and a faculty and staff of 110. The grounds, including the school farm, cover 20 acres.

Right from Grafton on ND 17, a graveled highway, to the junction with ND 18, 10 *m.*

Right on this highway 8 *m.* is HOOPLE (901 alt., 346 pop.), one of the largest primary potato-shipping points in the State. More than a thousand carloads of Red River Valley potatoes are loaded here each year. The town is named for Allen Hoople, an early settler. Lynn J. Frazier, former Governor of the State 1917–21) and U.S. Senator (1922–40), lived on a farm NE. of here.

On ND 17 is PARK RIVER, 17 *m.* (1000 alt., 1,408 pop.), on the PARK RIVER, probably named by early explorers for the buffalo parks along the stream. The Indians had no weapons which were effective on buffalo at long range, so they constructed corrals of brush into which the animals could be herded for killing. Whenever possible these corrals, which the first white explorers called buffalo parks, were built near the bank of a river or edge of a hill so that the buffalo would charge over the edge and be killed or badly injured in the crushing fall. The WALSH COUNTY AGRICULTURAL AND TRAINING SCHOOL, secondary vocational institution, is located in the town. In Park River are offices of the SOUTH BRANCH PARK RIVER PROJECT of the Soil Conservation Service, which has a demonstration area of 51,000 acres in central Walsh County on which contour farming and wind strip cropping are practiced. Sinclair Lewis, the novelist, owns a farm 1 *m.* S. of Park River, which he has never seen.

William Avery Rockefeller, father of John D. Rockefeller, the late oil magnate, lived on a Park River farm for some time. In 1881 an elderly man who gave his name as Dr. William Levingston homesteaded on a quarter section of land just E. of the town, where he lived each summer for 15 years. He later purchased an adjoining quarter, but the deed to this land was in the name of Pierson W. Briggs, a son-in-law of William Rockefeller and then purchasing agent for the Standard Oil Company. In 1895 George W. Towle, former Park River banker, who transacted much of Dr. Levingston's business, saw a picture of the senior Rockefeller in a copy of *McClure's Magazine* and recognized it as that of his former client, Levingston. William A. Rockefeller was not a doctor, but sold patent medicines and acted as a cancer specialist.

A large earth-filled dam has been constructed on the Park River W. of Park River City. In addition to flood control (the primary purpose), recreational areas will be provided.

MINTO, 63 *m.* (826 alt., 630 pop.), originally settled by Canadians and named for an Ontario town, is now a Czech and Polish settlement. The Feast of St. Wenceslaus, September 28, and Czechoslovakian Independence Day, October 28, are occasions of festivity. Minto is situated on the FOREST RIVER. There is a park by the stream S. of the town (*swimming pool, recreational area, and campgrounds*).

ARDOCH, 70 *m.* (830 alt., 119 pop.), also named for an Ontario town, is now predominantly Polish. LAKE ARDOCH, a large artificial lake constructed as a water conservation and migratory waterfowl project, adjoins the town on the E.

At 82 *m.* is the second junction with ND 44 (*see above*).

MANVEL, 82 *m.* (826 alt., 209 pop.), is named for General A. A. Manvel of the G. N. Ry. Originally known as the Turtle River station, it was one of six stops on the Fort Abercrombie-Fort Garry trail in the 1860's. The stage station was a crude log hut, roofed first with prairie sod and later with a thatch of weeds when the rain washed the sod away. The hut had one window and one door. Cooking was done on a fireplace made of clay dobes or handmade bricks. For meals, served on an improvised table, the traveler paid 50 cents, and for the same price he had the privilege of sleeping on the dirt floor. These stations were comfortable, however, in the coldest weather, with great fires roaring in the fireplaces to warm and cheer the traveler.

At 93 *m.* is the junction with a graveled road.

Left on this road to the GRAND FORKS SILVER FOX FARM, 2 *m.* (*visitors allowed Jan. 1–June 1; arrange with manager*). About 200 pair of foxes are kept at the farm each winter.

Left at 93.5 *m.* is a stone memorial marking a point on the old RED RIVER OXCART TRAIL between St. Paul, Minnesota, and Fort Garry (Winnipeg), Canada. During the late summer and fall most of the traffic through the region was on this trail. It was first used by traders at Fort Garry to transport furs to St. Paul. The exact route is not known today, but it is believed to have run through Grand Forks on 3rd St., turned S. at the present corner of S. 3rd St. and Minnesota Ave., whence it followed approximately the route of US 81 to the Lincoln Park golf course. Here it is believed to have turned E. toward the river, which it followed to Frog Point (*Belmont, see below*), and thence up the valley. Mr. and Mrs. Charles Cavileer, pioneer settlers at Pembina, made a romantic honeymoon journey to St. Paul on this trail in 1840.

At 93.5 *m.* is the junction with a graveled road.

Left on this road to the ARMOUR AND COMPANY PLANT, 0.3 *m.*, which is a meat-packing and processing plant.

At 94 *m.* (R) is the NORTH DAKOTA STATE MILL AND ELEVATOR (*open weekdays* 9–5; *conducted tours*), a State-owned plant. A product of the Nonpartisan League's industrial program, this institution has played an important role in State politics since its opening in 1922. As early as 1915 the Society of Equity and the Equity Exchange had attempted to establish a State-owned elevator, but had failed, and this failure hastened the formation of the Nonpartisan League. By 1919 the league was strong enough in the legislature to establish its industrial program, part of which was a State mill and elevator. The State Industrial Commission governs the mill and elevator.

A State law requires all official State documents to be stamped 'Buy "Dakota Maid" Flour.'

The mill and elevator consists of 6 steel-and-concrete fireproof buildings. The mill proper has 3 storage wings and contains 3 mills, each with a daily capacity of 1000 bbl. The elevator, equal in height to the average 12-story skyscraper, has a capacity of 1,659,600 bu. Thirty-two storage tanks each have a capacity of 50,000 bu. The elevator is operated independently of the mill, which buys in the open market and pays a rental to the elevator for storage space. In addition to Dakota Maid Flour the mill manufactures cereals, oatmeals, and poultry feeds.

GRAND FORKS, 95 *m.* (834 alt., 20,228 pop.) (*see* GRAND FORKS).

At N. 16th St. and Skidmore Ave. N. is the junction with US 2 (*see Tour* 6).

At 105 *m.* is the junction with ND 15, a graveled highway.

Right on this road is THOMPSON, 3 *m.* (972 alt., 276 pop.), the center of a large potato-farming area.

At 116 *m.* is the junction with a graveled road.

Right on this road is REYNOLDS, 2 *m.* (915 alt., 315 pop.), named for Dr. Henry Reynolds, an early settler and temperance apostle. The town is on the Grand Forks-Traill County line and many of the residents have their business places in one county and their homes in the other.

At 121 *m.* is the junction with a graveled spur.

Right on this spur is BUXTON, 1 *m.* (935 alt., 404 pop.), a Scandinavian town named for Thomas Buxton, a business associate of Bud Reeves, the townsite owner. Reeves, active in State politics, was one of the leaders in the drive to obtain funds for maintenance of State colleges after veto of the appropriation bill in 1895 (*see Tour* 1A). When Reeves campaigned for election to Congress on the Democratic ticket in 1894 he traveled over the State in what was probably the first house trailer ever used here, and one of the first used in the region. He had a log cabin built on wheels, and in this he visited every part of the State, a large cowbell attached to the cabin announcing his arrival in each town. No mean patriot, during his speeches he had with him on the platform the American flag and a live eagle.

Several important personages have been residents of Buxton, including two

Governors of the State, R. A. Nestos (1877–1942) and A. G. Sorlie (1874–1928); U.S. Senator A. J. Gronna (1858–1922), one of the six members of the Senate who opposed entrance of the United States into the First World War.

At 123 *m.* is the junction with a dirt road.

Right on this road is BELMONT, 11.5 *m.*, a ghost town which in the 1870's was a booming river port known as Frog Point. It was named by Captain Sam Painter, one of the first Red River pilots, on an early trip down the river, probably in 1860. Finding the shores almost covered with frogs, he is said to have erected a rude sign reading 'Frog Point,' and through the rise and fall of the town that grew up there the name remained. In 1871 the Hudson's Bay Company established a trading post on the point. A year later, because of the fall of the river, Frog Point became head of navigation and in short order was a rendezvous for boatmen, trappers, hunters, teamsters, and drifters, all living in tents or hastily constructed buildings. Teamsters hauling freight overland from the S. in their heavy, eight-horse, high-wheeled 'jumpers,' and trappers and Indians with their catches, here boarded the Hudson's Bay Company steamer *International,* and James J. Hill's *Selkirk.* The town, cut from the woods on the bank of the Red, and towered over by tall oaks, became a wilderness metropolis, and its reputation spread to Europe. In England it was believed by many to be a city of broad avenues and tall spires, second in size only to Liverpool, and filled with the hum of industry. Foreign visitors, traveling to Fort Garry, looked eagerly for this Red River capital, and even their disillusionment on seeing the little backwoods city could not dim its reputation. In its streets rough, rugged, heavy-booted woodsmen, rivermen, and trappers thundered up and down the wooden walks, and many a citizen was hastily despatched by their 44's. Heavy-jowled saloonkeepers, slim-fingered sleek gamblers, and gay dance-hall girls were all a part of the mushroom town.

Nature brought downfall to the Point as quickly as she had elevated it to importance. The river fell lower still, and Frog Point lost its position as head of navigation. Many of its inhabitants departed as swiftly as they had come. Fire wiped out a number of buildings which were never rebuilt. Trade dwindled and storekeepers shut up shop. Some 20 years later, with the river level again up, the town revived as a grain-shipping center, but the flood of 1897 ruined grain elevators and their contents, and within a short time the bustle of the town again faded into the past.

CUMMINGS, 124 *m.* (935 alt., 85 pop.), named for Henry Cumings, an early G.N. employe who helped build the railroad, is principally a Scandinavian community. Originally spelled with one 'm,' its name was misspelled so consistently that the Post Office Department legitimized the misspelling by inserting the second 'm.'

At 125 *m.* is the junction with ND 7, a bituminous highway, which unites with US 81 to 136 *m.* (*see Tour 1A*).

HILLSBORO, 132 *m.* (907 alt., 1,338 pop.), named for James J. Hill, the 'Empire Builder' of the G. N. Ry., was platted in 1880 on the attractive GOOSE RIVER. A bitter fight for the Traill County seat was prominent in the early history of the town. Neighboring Caledonia, on the Red River, had been the county seat since organization of Traill County in 1875, but the routing of the G. N. Ry. through Hillsboro gave that young city aspirations, and in 1890 it came forward as a contender for the county seat. The campaign grew heated, and Caledonia citizens carried arms and posted guards around their village. To lead their defense they organized a committee, whom Hillsboro residents dubbed Tigers of the Jungle and Irreconcilables. The Tigers imported Colonel W. C. Plummer, a widely known professional standard bearer who had served as campaign speaker in many parts of the country, and whom James G. Blaine once called 'one of the three best political speakers in the United States.' The colonel became the leading figure in the county-seat fight. He was an impressive speaker, and the floods of oratory he loosed in behalf of Caledonia were greatly enjoyed by his listeners. The majority of them, however, apparently remained impervious to his arguments—when the votes were counted Hillsboro enjoyed a 1,291 to 218 majority.

WOODLAND PARK, a 25-acre recreational and tourist camp area in the northern part of town, contains a log cabin, originally built at Belmont, in which are an old-fashioned loom once used in weaving the homespun clothing of a pioneer family, and other relics of pioneer days.

Right from Hillsboro on a graveled highway to STONY POINT, 1.5 m., site of a camp used by pioneers freighting their supplies overland from Fargo during early settlement of the region. The camp site, situated on a sandy ridge left by the recession of glacial Lake Agassiz, is marked by a large, pointed boulder 20 ft. in diameter, which once served as a landmark. In early days it was believed, from the manner in which the rock was situated in the earth, that it might have dropped from the sky.

South of Hillsboro are many well-built farmsteads—some of which were once part of bonanza farms—and four peaceful villages which in bonanza days were busy wheat centers, but now lie quietly basking in their memories.

GRANDIN, 145 m. (898 alt., 158 pop.), is the largest of these towns. It was named for J. L. Grandin, one of the two Tidioute, Pennsylvania, brothers who bought 99 sections of Red River Valley land and farmed them under the bonanza system. Dividing their land into 1500-acre farms, each with a superintendent and a foreman, they harvested their first crop in 1878. They had 14,000 acres under cultivation near Grandin, and 6000 at Mayville. Before the advent of the railroad the wheat raised on their land was hauled on barges towed by the steamers *Grandin* and *Alsop* to Fargo, a distance of 90 miles—overland Grandin is 35 miles from Fargo. The Grandin farm was one of the earliest practical users of the telephone, although whether the first in the State was installed on this or the Dalrymple farm (*see Tour* 8) is in dispute.

GARDNER, 152 m. (891 alt., 103 pop.), named for the town site owner, was founded in 1880 when the surrounding territory was being developed as wheat country, but was not incorporated as a village until 1929.

ARGUSVILLE, 159 m. (889 alt., 145 pop.), is believed to have received its name from the *Daily Argus*, Fargo newspaper published at the time of the town's founding in 1880.

HARWOOD, 165 m. (892 alt., 100 pop.), was named for A. J. Harwood, a prominent Fargo real-estate dealer who bought all the town sites between Fargo and Grand Forks when the G. N. Ry. was built.

At 175.3 *m.* is the junction with a graveled road.

Right on this road to HECTOR AIRPORT, 0.5 *m.*, a U.S. Department of Commerce A-1 field, land for which was donated by Martin Hector, pioneer Fargo banker, in 1931. The buildings include a city hangar of laminated truss-arch construction, completed in 1936 under the Works Progress Administration.

FARGO, 173 *m.* (907 alt., 32,580 pop.) (*see* FARGO).

At Front and 13th Sts. is the junction with US 10 (*see Tour* 8).

The WILD RICE RIVER, which the route crosses at 180 *m.*, was named for plants resembling the wild grain which formerly grew on its banks. Near here, in a battle between the Sioux and Chippewa in 1807, Tabashaw, a Chippewa chief, was slain while avenging the death of his eldest son, who had been killed a short time before by the Sioux.

At 181 *m.* is the junction with a dirt road.

Right on this road is HOLY CROSS CEMETERY, 0.3 *m.*, one of the first cemeteries in the State, established in 1862. The first burial here is said to have been that of a priest who had been beheaded by an Indian. Another victim of frontier tragedy whose body rests here was Archibald Montrose, a young English nobleman who came to America to establish a home. He was found frozen within a few rods of his own door during a blizzard in 1871. His devoted young wife ordered a covered shelf built on the outside wall of their cabin beneath her bedroom window and had his coffin placed there. In the spring, when the ground had thawed sufficiently to permit the digging of a grave, she unwillingly consented to the burial of her husband's body. Soon afterward their baby daughter, born after the father's death, died also, and the mother, her mind affected by the grief of her bereavements, joined them in the near-by burial ground. For many years a large wooden cross marked the spot where Montrose died.

WILD RICE, 182 *m.* (909 alt., 21 pop.), is the center of a French-Canadian farming community.

HICKSON, 188 *m.* (915 alt., 27 pop.), is named for the Ole Hicks family who were early farmers in the vicinity.

At 191 *m.* is the junction with ND 46, a graveled highway.

Right on this highway to a bridge crossing the SHEYENNE RIVER, 9 *m.* On the bridge a tablet has been placed reading: 'Sibley Trail 1863. Sibley's Indian Expedition crossed the Sheyenne at this point Aug. 20, returning from the Missouri to Fort Abercrombie.'
At 9.5 *m.* is the junction with a graveled spur.
Right on this road to KINDRED, 1 *m.* (948 alt., 450 pop.), a tree-shaded town named for F. E. and W. A. Kindred, surveyors who platted the town site and later were large landholders in the vicinity. The community is principally Scandinavian. An interesting COLLECTION (*open by arrangement*) of European museum pieces and Indian artifacts is owned by Hjalmer Rustad of Kindred and is kept at his home.
ND 46 traverses a low range of sandy hills, the western rim of glacial Lake Agassiz. At 19 *m.* is the junction with a dry-weather dirt road. Left on this road at 26.5 *m.*, just across the river to the SHEYENNE RIVER PARK (*central building of native logs, spring-fed swimming pool, picnic areas, cabins, and camp sites*), has been developed as a recreational center by a Federal land-utilization project and is under the direction of neighboring county agents. The park includes an area of unusual scenic attraction. A road winds along the heavily wooded river bottom, and side roads and graveled trails lead out of the valley

to the sand dunes which stretch away to the S. The great plain here was deposited in glacial days, when the rushing Sheyenne, then a large stream carrying the sediment-laden waters of the melting ice sheet, flowed into Lake Agassiz. As the lake retreated the sand was left to the winds, which pushed and whipped it into dunes that dip away toward the horizon. Hummocks of trees and shrubs appear like green islands in this wide sea of dull brown. In some places, to combat the moving sand, elm and oak bark has been laid lengthwise in the road to preserve the trail. The park is extensively used for 4-H clubs and similar camps.

CHRISTINE, 196 m. (926 alt., 200 pop.), has a population 95 per cent Scandinavian. When Christine Nilsson, the noted Swedish operatic soprano, appeared in the United States in 1873, she was honored by American Scandinavians, who named this town for her. A COLLECTION (*open by arrangement*) of pioneer implements, including spinning wheels, brass kitchen utensils, and relics from Fort Abercrombie, is owned by Dr. M. U. Ivers.

ABERCROMBIE, 207 m. (935 alt., 215 pop.), is a typical peaceful small town on the banks of the Red River. The air of serenity which lies over its tree-lined streets and substantial homes is in decided contrast with the bustling activity of the settlement which surrounded the pioneer post of Fort Abercrombie, first Federal fort in North Dakota, built in 1858. It was named for Lieutenant Colonel John J. Abercrombie, officer in charge of its erection. The most westerly outpost of the settlers' advance during the 1860's, Fort Abercrombie became the gateway to the Dakotas. From here expeditions set out to the unexplored plains of the Northwest, and trains of settlers left by oxcart and covered wagons to seek homes on the prairie beyond.

It was between Fort Abercrombie and Fort Garry that the first steamboat to ply the waters of the Red River of the North carried passengers and freight. Built in Georgetown in 1859, the *Anson Northrup,* named for its owner, who hauled the machinery overland from the Mississippi River, made its maiden trip to the Canadian post the same summer.

Because of its position on the outskirts of the white settlement, Fort Abercrombie was particularly vulnerable to Indian attacks, and during the Minnesota uprising of 1862 was besieged for five weeks by the hostile Sioux. The first attack, September 3, was repulsed with the loss of one man. At the close of this encounter the defenders discovered that only 350 rounds of rifle ammunition remained—a supply had been ordered in the spring but had not arrived. The ingenuity of the garrison was exercised; canister shells for the 12-pound howitzers contained balls which fitted the rifles, so the women in the fort were put to work opening the canisters. The makeshift ammunition served its purpose well.

The fort had no stockade; consequently, after the first attack, the defenders threw up around the entire fort a cordwood breastwork 8 feet high. In the meantime messengers had slipped through the Indian lines to summon aid from Fort Snelling at Minneapolis. On September 6 a force estimated at 400 warriors again attacked the fort, but was driven back after a long fight in which two soldiers were killed and many wounded. The Indians made no more determined attacks on the fort, but continually harassed the beleaguered settlers with desultory sniping until the arrival of a detachment of 350 infantrymen from Fort Snelling relieved the garrison September 23.

In November of the same year 10 acres of the fort reserve were enclosed by a heavy oak-log stockade with blockhouses at three corners, and about the same time a larger garrison was stationed at Abercrombie. It was from this enlarged post that the Sibley expedition set forth to punish the Sioux the following summer (*see* HISTORY). The enlarged garrison was maintained until the abandonment of the fort in 1877. During the 1870's Fort Abercrombie was the point from which trails led W. to Forts Totten, Ransom, Wadsworth, and Garry, and many a train of home seekers or gold seekers spent a few days there before embarking on the hazardous trip through Dakota.

Fort Abercrombie in 1870 was the scene of a treaty between the Chippewa and Sioux, concluded through the influence of Father J. B. Genin, a Roman Catholic priest. After this treaty the eastern part of the Territory was comparatively free from fear of Indian attacks.

FORT ABERCROMBIE STATE PARK, on the eastern edge of the town, preserves 22 acres of the original 7 square miles of military reservation. The park lies along the river, and its natural beauty makes it a pleasant recreation center. An old cabin in the park houses a collection of early-day relics. Near by stands a Red River oxcart whose wooden wheels once creaked over the old river trail before the days of railroads and highways.

DWIGHT, 218 *m.* (959 alt., 168 pop.), was named for Jeremiah W. Dwight, head of a large bonanza farm company organized here in 1879, and was the home of John Miller, first Governor of North Dakota. Miller was superintendent of the Dwight Farm and Land Company, which operated 27,000 acres, and was established with a cash capital of $150,000. The MILLER RESIDENCE (*private*), former home of the family, is R. of US 81 in the southeastern corner of the village.

At 221 *m.* is the junction with ND 13, a graveled highway.

Right on this road is MOORETON, 6 *m.* (966 alt., 146 pop.). Here is the headquarters farm of F. A. Bagg, one of the largest landowners in the Red River Valley. He maintains three airplanes in a hangar on his farm and supervises his holdings by air.

WAHPETON (Sioux, *village of the leaves*), 227 *m.* (969 alt., 3,747 pop.), is at the confluence of the Bois de Sioux (Fr., *forest of the Sioux*) and Ottertail Rivers, where the two streams meet to form the Red River of the North. From 1871 to 1893 the town was known as Chahinkapa (Sioux, *top of the trees*), an old Indian name given this area by the Sioux who, coming from the W. to fight the Chippewa, would here see the tops of the trees appear over the level prairie.

Alexander Faribault, for whom Faribault, Minnesota, was named, has told of visiting the present site of Wahpeton in 1810 when 3000 Indians were encamped and engaged in hunting buffalo and drying the meats for food. At that time the grasslands along the Red River were black with bison, who summered on the grazing lands here, and wintered on the uplands of the Missouri Slope W. of the Missouri River.

That politics was a momentous vocation when Wahpeton was a young county seat is indicated in this political advertisement in an 1880 issue of the Richland County *Gazette:*

Republicans of Richland County please remember and vote for me on election day. Come old and young, father and son, one and all and vote for me. Do not look on money or on the rich man but on an honest man. I have come to this lovely country and have made my happy home and I will be a good citizen of Richland County. You know I am a candidate for County Treasurer of Richland County. Come and spend the whole day on election day and vote for me. We are all brothers and sisters. It makes no difference whether a man is rich or poor, if he is honest; then he is a good man. Come all and see me on election day, in our nice town of Wahpeton.

The RICHLAND COUNTY COURTHOUSE here, built in a modified Classic style with a cupola, is considered a good example of the official buildings in this State. The first floor exterior is of Kettle River sandstone, with upper stories and dome of Bedford limestone. Across the street from the courthouse is the LEACH PUBLIC LIBRARY, a light-colored brick and sandstone building presented to the city in 1923 by Mr. and Mrs. O. A. Leach, Wahpeton residents since 1896. The library contains over 14,000 volumes.

In the northern part of Wahpeton are the STATE SCHOOL OF SCIENCE and the U.S. INDIAN SCHOOL. The science school is a vocational institution and junior college with a trades educational program that has received recognition outside the State. Near the entrance to the landscaped campus is a cast bronze life-size bust of the Norwegian poet-dramatist Henrik Ibsen, the work of Jacob Fjelde, distinguished Norwegian sculptor who made his home in Minneapolis from 1877 until his death in 1896. Another portrait of Ibsen in Como Park in St. Paul, Minnesota, is also the work of Fjelde; these are said to be the only statues of Ibsen in the U.S. The bust at Wahpeton was a gift to the city and Richland County from the Norwegian people of the county and was unveiled at ceremonies held on Norwegian Independence Day, May 17, 1912. The figure stands on a tapering rough-hewn 8-foot granite pedestal.

The Indian school consists of 40 red-brick buildings housing 282 students, mainly Sioux and Chippewa from reservations in North and South Dakota and Minnesota. In addition to academic work through the ninth grade, vocational training in farm methods is taught the boys, while the girls receive instruction in home economics and sanitation.

CHAHINKAPA PARK, in the northeastern part of Wahpeton, lies between the high banks of the old bed of the Red River and the present channel, its inviting woods cut off from the mainland by meandering lagoons. Improvements and recreational facilities (*swimming pool, playgrounds, athletic field*) by Federal agencies were completed under the Works Progress Administration (1937).

Wahpeton was the home of the late U.S. Senator Porter J. McCumber, who gained national recognition for his work on the Fordney-McCumber Tariff Bill.

The route leaves Wahpeton by way of 2nd St., and for 5 *m.* follows a winding course parallel to the Bois de Sioux. This portion of the highway runs over a trail used in 1823 by the military expedition of Major Stephen H. Long sent to establish the Canadian boundary, and still later as a freight route between St. Cloud, Minnesota, Fort Abercrombie, and Pembina in the 1860's and 1870's.

FAIRMOUNT, 242 *m.* (985 alt., 705 pop.), named for Fairmount Park in Philadelphia, Pennsylvania, was platted in 1887 until which time it was known as Michigan Settlement because many of its settlers came from that State. Of interest in the town is the widely known SERMON IN STONE, an obelisk erected in St. Anthony's Roman Catholic churchyard by Reverend G. C. Bierens. Stones and ores, some semi-precious, have come from all parts of the world to be patterned into this bright-colored shrine. The Ten Commandments, Faith, Hope, and Charity, the Trinity, the Sacraments, and many other abstractions are symbolized in stone.

Father Bierens, an authority on bird life in the Red River Valley, operated a U.S. Fish and Wildlife Service BIRD BANDING STATION (1937), one of the few in the State. In April 1935 he banded the first European starling caught in North Dakota.

At the F. P. Nelson store in Fairmount is a COLLECTION (*open by arrangement*) of Indian artifacts and of firearms, including a Chinese gun made in 1526.

Right from Fairmount on ND 11, a graveled road, is HANKINSON, 15 *m.* (1,068 alt., 1,420 pop.), named for R. H. Hankinson, town-site owner. Here are the CONVENT AND ACADEMY OF THE SISTERS OF ST. FRANCIS, the mother house of the Order in the United States. This Order was established in Germany in 1241. The convent and academy, founded in 1927-9, are housed in a three-story Renaissance-style building of tapestry brick trimmed in Indiana limestone. In a niche over the entrance is a statue of St. Francis, carved in Danube limestone by the Joseph Mueller Art Institute of Munich, Germany, and donated to the Order.

South of Fairmount the distant Coteau des Prairies is visible (R). Back in these hills, which form part of the watershed between the Gulf of Mexico and Hudson Bay, live the Sioux Indians of the Sisseton Reservation, a triangular section of which juts into the State from South Dakota.

At 251 *m.* US 81 crosses the North Dakota Line, 106 *m.* N. of Watertown, South Dakota (*see South Dakota Guide Tour* 10).

Tour 1A

Junction US 81—Mayville—Portland—Hatton. ND 7 and 18.
Junction with US 81 to Hatton, 28 m.

G. N. Ry. branch line parallels route between Mayville and Hatton.
Bituminous roadbed entire route.
Accommodations in principal towns.

This short route traversing a fertile farming area twice crosses the
Goose River, which the French Canadians who first explored it called
Rivière Aux Outardes (*River of the Geese*), because of the great number
of wild geese that nested on its banks. The route proceeds along the
western edge of glacial Lake Agassiz. The rich, black soil—a sandless,
clayey silt, peculiar to western States and locally known as gumbo—becomes a muggy, sticky mass when wet. Before the era of graveled highways, travel was virtually impossible after even the lightest rainfall,
as wagon or automobile wheels became clogged with the heavy, gummy
earth; even today this is true on unimproved roads.

ND 7 branches W. from US 81 (*see Tour 1*) 1 m. S. of Cummings.

MAYVILLE, 12 m. (891 alt., 1,351 pop.), was named for May
Arnold, first white child born in the Hudson's Bay Company trading
post established near the present town site in the early 1870's. It is a
small, tree-shaded, staid college town on the banks of the GOOSE RIVER.
First settled in 1881, it was moved to the railroad which was built
through here in 1883. In that year Mayville and Portland conspired
to win the county seat for a new town, Traill Center, platted midway
between the two older towns, planning that if their candidate won the
election the three towns would merge into one city. So brisk was the
campaign that the ballots cast outnumbered the legal voters, and Traill
Center won 2,011 to 450. The election was contested, however, and
while the case was in litigation the Territorial legislature transferred
the two western tiers of townships in Traill County to Steele County.
This lost Traill Center its strategic position and with it the county
seat.

MAYVILLE STATE TEACHERS COLLEGE, in the northern part of the
town, founded in 1889, held its first classes in 1893. When Governor
Roger Allin in 1895 vetoed funds for operating the colleges in North
Dakota, enterprising citizens kept the schools open by popular sub-
scription. Bud Reeves, wealthy Minneapolis man who pioneered at
Buxton and later became a political figure in the State (*see Tour 1*),

was one of the leaders in the drive for funds to support the schools. In one day he collected $2000 from heads of large Minneapolis grain firms.

On the college campus is a log cabin built in 1879 and used as the first schoolhouse in the Mayville area.

ALM'S PARK, on the eastern edge of the city, is a tourist park and camp; ISLAND PARK, in the western part, is a recreational center. RAILROAD PARK, E. of the Great Northern depot, contains a tall marble pillar on which is a bronze plaque bearing a relief of Bjornstjerne Bjornson, famed Norwegian author. The plaque is the work of Paul Fjelde, who once attended the Valley City Teachers College (*see Tour* 8).

In Mayville is the home of Reverend and Mrs. A. M. West, parents of the etcher Levon West (1900–   ), who has also won recognition for photography under the pseudonym of Ivan Dmitri.

At the western end of the long business street of PORTLAND, 14 *m.* (987 alt., 551 pop.), is the gravel ridge of CAMPBELL'S BEACH, second hump of sand laid down in prehistoric times by the retreating waters of Lake Agassiz. Portland has four producers and consumers co-operatives—an oil company, elevator, creamery, and store. Across the street from a large Lutheran church in the western part of the town stand the now unused buildings of BRUFLAT ACADEMY, one of the first private educational institutions in the State, established by the local Lutheran Church in 1889. Portland and vicinity were first settled in 1871, and the place became a boom town when the railroad arrived in 1881.

At 20 *m.* is the junction (R) with ND 18, a graveled highway on which the route proceeds N.

At 25 *m.* is the junction with a county dirt road.

Left on this road to the THORVAL STAVENS FARM, 1 *m.*, where the success story of an outstanding but nevertheless typical Norwegian immigrant family is told by the buildings ranging from the lowly sod house of Hans Anderson Stavensbraaten, who homesteaded here in 1870, to the 15-room home and the airplane hangar of his grandson, Thorval Stavens. The original family home and its contents are preserved as a MUSEUM. Across the road is the first school in the district, built in 1879.

HATTON, 28 *m.* (1,085 alt., 933 pop.), named for Frank Hatton, Third Assistant Postmaster General when the town was founded in 1882, is at the southern end of the Elk River Delta, a rich, fertile deposit laid down in ancient times as the waters of the melting glacier flowed into Lake Agassiz.

Hatton was the birthplace and boyhood home of Colonel Carl Ben Eielson (1897–1929), pioneer Alaskan aviator. Eielson left the University of Wisconsin to enlist in the Army Air Service in 1916. Following the First World War he barnstormed in North Dakota and neighboring States in a plane purchased for him by friends in the vicinity of Hatton. In 1922 he went to Alaska where he pioneered in aviation and flew the first air mail in the Territory. His experience as an Arctic flyer drew the attention of the English explorer Sir Hubert Wilkins, and in 1928 the pair made their flight across the top of the world from Point Barrow to Spitzbergen. When Wilkins gave his attention to the Antarctic, Eielson piloted him on several flights over that continent. He returned to Alaska in 1929 and late that year was killed while attempting to save the passengers and cargo of the ice-bound ship *Nanuk* off North Cape, Siberia. He had already made one trip to the ship, bringing back six passengers and part of the fur cargo, when a fierce storm took its toll. Eielson and his mechanic, Earl Borland, crashed, and it was more than a month before their bodies were found in the wreckage of their plane. Eielson's body was returned with honors to Hatton, where it was interred in the family plot, marked with an unpretentious stone. The Alaskan, a Fokker high-wing monoplane used by Eielson and Wilkins when exploring the Arctic in 1926, and a large collection of Eielson medals and mementoes are displayed in the museum of the State historical society (*see* BISMARCK).

✿✿

Tour 2

(Brandon, Man., Can.)—Hansboro—Cando—Minnewaukan—Jamestown—Edgeley—Ellendale—(Aberdeen, S. Dak.); US 281.
Canadian boundary to South Dakota Line, 234 *m.*

Branch of G. N. Ry. parallels route between Cando and Churchs Ferry, branch of N. P. Ry. between Brinsmade and Jamestown, Midland R.R. between Jamestown and Edgeley.
Graveled roadbed 65 *m.*, bituminous surface 169 *m.*
Accommodations in principal towns.

South of the international boundary the route traverses an uneven terrain formed by mighty glaciers as they retreated across the region during the ice age. It passes Devils and Arrowood Lakes and crosses the pleasant wooded valleys of the Sheyenne and James Rivers. Between the groves and farmhouses along the way are thousands of acres of open fields and grasslands. Brown and black in spring, these soon turn green with the crops of wheat, oats, barley, corn, and cultivated grasses grown in this diversified farming area. The southern part of the route passes through some of the best pheasant-hunting country in the State, while grouse and duck are also plentiful.

US 281 crosses the Canadian boundary, 0.0 *m.*, 8 *m.* S. of Cartwright, Manitoba, Canada.

HANSBORO, 3 *m.* (1,595 alt., 196 pop.), is named for Henry Clay Hansbrough, the first Representative (1889–91) sent to Congress from North Dakota, and later U.S. Senator (1891–1909). The town is a port of entry, and the U.S. customhouse is here.

At 15 *m.* is the junction with ND 5 (*see Tour 5*), a graveled highway, which between this point and 20 *m.* is identical with US 281.

ROCK LAKE, 21 *m.* (1,548 alt., 348 pop.), is on the southern end of the long, narrow, fresh-water lake of the same name. The U.S. Fish and Wildlife Service has created a migratory waterfowl sanctuary by constructing a large, earthfill dam on the lake just NE. of town. Overflow from the water impounded will be sufficient to raise the levels of a number of smaller lakes in the area. At Rock Lake is a junction (L) with ND 5 (*see Tour 5*).

At 35 *m.* is a junction with a county road.

Left on this road to SNYDER LAKE, 3 *m.*, a recreational center (*swimming and picnicking facilities*).

CANDO, 44.5 *m.* (1,486 alt., 1,282 pop.), received its name at a county commissioners' meeting in 1884, when, during the heat of an argument over the selection of the Towner County seat, P. P. Parker, chairman of the board, called out above the confusion, 'There has been much talk about our not having power to locate this county seat where we see fit. But we'll show you that we can do it. And furthermore, just to show you what we can do, we'll name this county seat "Cando." '

Left from Cando on ND 17, a graveled highway, to a DUNKER (Dunkard) COLONY, 8 *m.*, the first settlement of this religious organization in the State. The sect, known officially as the German Baptist Brethren, originated in Germany in 1708. Shortly thereafter its members began to come to Pennsylvania, whence they spread westward. The group at Cando was brought in by the G. N. Ry. in 1894 to aid in colonizing the land along their route. The practices and tenets of the Dunkers (Ger., *those who dip or immerse*) are similar to those of the Baptists. Older members still retain many of the early customs of plain dress, no jewelry or other adornment, simple living, and no form of insurance; the women wear the small lace prayer cap for church attendance. A harvest festival in early October has become an outstanding holiday of the church life.

MAZA, 53.5 *m.* (1,463 alt., 66 pop.), is the center of a wheat-producing and stock-raising community. The derivation of the name of the town is not definitely known, but is believed to have been from *maize*, the Indian word for corn.

At 54 *m.* is the junction with a graveled county road.

Left on this road is LAC AUX MORTES (Fr., *lake of the dead*), 4.5 *m.*, named by French trappers who visited the region in the early 1860's. Indian tradition says that one winter during a severe smallpox epidemic the dead were so numerous that the trees were filled with bodies. Fire destroyed the woods a few years later. Although in 1938 the lake was nearly dry, it has now returned to normal level. It is also known as Lake Alice and is a Federal migratory bird refuge.

At 59 *m*. is the junction with US 2.

At 66 *m*. a road goes R. to BRINSMADE (1,560 alt., 206 pop.), named for a noted Congregational minister, the Reverend S. Brinsmade, of Beloit, Wisconsin.

MINNEWAUKAN (Sioux, *spirit water*), 74 *m*. (1,458 alt., 521 pop.), the Benson County seat, during its early years stood on the western shore of Devils Lake, and there was a steamboat landing on the eastern edge of town, where the Benson County fairgrounds now stand. The shore line of the lake has receded, however, and for many years the water has not reached within several miles of this point.

South of Minnewaukan the road skirts land that was the bed of Devils Lake when that body of water was truly an inland sea, and crosses drift prairie, from which the chain of high morainic hills bordering Devils Lake is visible (L) in the distance, and reaches the pretty valley of the SHEYENNE RIVER, named for the Cheyenne (Sioux, *people of alien speech*) Indians. Early explorers misspelled the name, changing C to S—an error that aids in distinguishing this river from the Cheyenne of South Dakota. In crossing the stream here the route descends into the valley over terraces cut by glacial waters thousands of years ago.

SHEYENNE, 95 *m*. (1,476 alt., 431 pop.), on the river, originally was a mile and a half from its present site and was moved when the survey for the N. P. Ry. was made.

NEW ROCKFORD, 106 *m*. (1,533 alt., 2,017 pop.), on the James River approximately 25 miles from its source, was first called Garrison, later Rockford, and still later, with the coming of the N. P. Ry., New Rockford. It is the Eddy County seat and the home of Ole H. Olson, a Governor of the State (1934).

BARLOW, 114 *m*. (1,537 alt., 42 pop.), was named for its founder, F. G. Barlow, who as a member of the first North Dakota Legislature (1889) fought the Louisiana Lottery bill (*see* HISTORY).

CARRINGTON, 122 *m*. (1,579 alt., 1,850 pop.), is named for M. D. Carrington, who platted the city in 1882, and gave sites for the school, churches, and Foster County Courthouse. It has a 10,000-volume MUNICIPAL LIBRARY in the City Hall on Central Ave. and 1st St. N. On the western side of town is a landscaped and well-equipped tourist camp. Here is a junction with US 52 (*see Tour 7*), which unites with US 281 between this point and Jamestown.

MELVILLE, 131 *m*. (1,597 alt., 40 pop.), was originally laid out as New Port, but because of a disagreement over the price of the site the railway company moved the town one-half mile W. and called it Melville.

At EDMUNDS, 138 *m*. (1,594 alt., 60 pop.), is the junction with a graveled county road.

Left on this road to ARROWOOD LAKE, 6 *m*., the largest of the chain of three lakes through which the James River flows. Before white settlement the

Indians came here from great distances to obtain Juneberry shoots for their arrow shafts. On the western shore is the ARROWOOD MIGRATORY REFUGE. This reserve is highly valued by the Fish and Wildlife Service as a summer breeding ground and is an important feeding place for pelicans.

PINGREE, 144 *m.* (1,547 alt., 167 pop.), was named for Hazen Senter Pingree, who, with a rack and wagon and a team of oxen, came to Dakota Territory in 1880 to start a potato plantation. His venture was a failure, so he went to Michigan, where he became an important shoe manufacturer, was made mayor of Detroit, and twice served as Governor of the State (1897–1900).

BUCHANAN, 152 *m.* (1,546 alt., 125 pop.), was named for its founder, James A. Buchanan, a prominent early settler.

South of Buchanan the route continues over rolling terrain toward the valley of the James River, a steep-sided, flat-bottomed trough, approximately a mile wide.

JAMESTOWN, 165 *m.* (1,405 alt., 8,790 pop.) (*see Tour 8*).

At 5th Ave. and 3rd St. is the junction with US 10 (*see Tour 8*).

The area L. of the route here was once the scene of one of those devastating prairie fires that terrorized and impoverished the early farmers of the Plains States. This blaze, which began Sept. 25, 1888, swept the entire region from near Jamestown to LaMoure.

'A heavy and smoke laden atmosphere and a sky streaked with a dull red reflection of burning grass proclaimed the fierce raging of prairie fires north, south and west of the city last night,' reported the Jamestown *Daily Alert* . . . 'For at least 40 miles in width the fire burned off every vestige of grass unprotected by breaks. One could hardly recognize the charred land the next day. Thousands of bushels of grain were burned and many men lost all they had, grain, buildings and stock.'

EDGELEY, 203 *m.* (1,565 alt., 803 pop.), was named by Richard Sykes, once owner of the site, for his former home in England. It is the meeting point of an N. P. Ry. branch line, a branch of the Milwaukee R.R., and the Midland main line.

From Edgeley to the South Dakota Line, the hills of the Missouri Plateau loom (R) in the distance.

At 217 *m.* is a junction with a graveled county road.

Left on this road to WHITESTONE HILL BATTLEFIELD STATE PARK, 16 *m.*, where General Alfred Sully and his command met a band of Sioux Indians on the evening of Sept. 3, 1863, in the most severe engagement fought on North Dakota soil since the coming of the white man. A granite monument 25 ft. in height, bearing the figure of a mounted cavalryman, has been erected about three fourths of a mile NW. of the site of the battle. Reinterred about the base of the monument, each with an appropriate marker, are the remains of the soldiers who died here. A museum covering the history of the area is open from June till October. Generals Sully and Sibley had been sent out from Minnesota to punish the Indians who had taken part in the Minnesota Massacre of 1862. Sully was to move up the Missouri, while Sibley marched W. across the country. When Sully, delayed by low water, arrived in the neighborhood of present Bismarck, where he was to meet Sibley, he found the latter had given up the idea of the proposed meeting and started on the return journey to Minnesota. He also discovered that the Sioux, who had fled over the Missouri upon Sibley's approach, had now recrossed to their old hunting grounds on the James River. He immediately set out in pursuit and overtook them in a three-day march. The Indians retreated while the soldiers, on higher ground, poured in a murderous fire. Sully's casualties were 34 men wounded and 19 killed, while the Indian loss was estimated at 150. It is now believed that the Sioux encountered here did not take part in the Minnesota Massacre. The perpetrators of the massacre were known to have fled W., however, and it was natural for the soldiers to regard any Indians they met as enemies.

ELLENDALE, 229 *m.* (1,448 alt., 1,517 pop.), named for Ellen Dale Merrill, wife of a Milwaukee R.R. official, is the Dickey County seat. At the end of Main St. on the eastern edge of the trim little town, attractively arranged on a well-kept campus, are the six brick buildings of the STATE NORMAL AND INDUSTRIAL SCHOOL, a teachers college and vocational institution. When it opened its doors in 1889 it offered the first free course in manual training in the United States.

At 234 *m.* US 281 crosses the South Dakota Line, 35 *m.* N. of Aberdeen, South Dakota (*see South Dakota Guide Tour* 11).

✧✧✧

Tour 3

(Virden, Man., Can.)—Westhope—Minot—Washburn—Bismarck—Linton—(Pierre, S. Dak.); US 83.
Canadian boundary to South Dakota Line, 272 *m.*

Soo Ry. branch parallels route between Max and Bismarck, N. P. Ry. main line between Bismarck and Sterling. N.P. branch roughly parallels between Sterling and Linton, Milwaukee R.R. branch between Linton and Strasburg.
Bituminous surface except for 29 *m.* of graveled roadbed.
Accommodations in principal towns.

South of the Canadian boundary US 83 follows a southwesterly course across the flat fertile bed of glacial Lake Souris, over the central Drift Prairie and the hilly upland of the Coteau du Plateau du Missouri, crossing the South Dakota Line near the center of the boundary.

Most of the area is diversified dry-farming country, where the emerald blades of young grain in summer blend with the green and blue of flax and the verdant stalks of growing corn. As the crops mature the chief tones of the landscape gradually change to amber and gold, until after harvest the fields are covered with tawny, violet-shadowed stubble, dotted with the dull taupe of Russian thistle. Along the Mouse River and the Missouri, the timberland is a vivid green in summer, and in autumn becomes a fantasy of fall color in which yellows, ochers, scarlets, and copper all strive for dominance.

US 83 crosses the Canadian border 8 *m*. S. of Coulter, Manitoba, Canada. Here is a customhouse.

WESTHOPE, 6 *m*. (1,508 alt., 460 pop.), is a port of entry to Canada. It was named by an official of a G. N. Ry. town-site company, who expected exceptional agricultural prosperity for the town. Far to the L., beyond the level prairie that is the bed of the great prehistoric lake, are the blue shadows outlining the Turtle Mountains (*see Tour 5*).

At 12.5 *m*. is the junction with ND 5 (*see Tour 5*), which unites with US 83 to 29.5 *m*.

MINOT, 66.5 *m*. (1,560 alt., 16,577 pop.) (*see* MINOT).

At 2nd St. and 4th Ave. SW. is the junction with US 2 (*see Tour 6*) and US 52 (*see Tour 7*).

South of Minot the route is over level drift prairie, gradually rising to a ridge of hills at 85 *m*. This is the HEIGHT OF LAND, the northern rim of the Plateau du Missouri, which is the watershed between the Gulf of Mexico and Hudson Bay, and also marks the farthest advance of the last glacier. In addition to its geologic interest. the elevation commands a view northward almost to the Canadian border.

MAX, 94.5 *m*. (2100 alt., 423 pop.), a Russo-German community, was named for the eldest son of an early settler.

At 106.5 *m*. is the junction with ND 37 (*see Tour 3A*).

COLEHARBOR, 114.5 *m*. (1900 alt., 150 pop.), derives its name from the unsuccessful attempt to make this a river shipping point for lignite coal, which is mined in this vicinity.

UNDERWOOD, 122.5 *m*. (2,020 alt., 613 pop.), is the center of a large diversified farming area. The railway conductor for whom it was named, in appreciation of the honor, donated a bell to the school. The town has a circulating library, begun by a 72-year-old man, Edward Erickson, who bound newspaper and magazine stories into books. With these he began his collection, and by the time of his death in 1932 his work, together with donations, had resulted in a library of 8000 volumes, most of them now available to the public at the office of the Underwood *News*.

WASHBURN, 139.5 *m*. (1,731 alt., 901 pop.), McLean County seat, on the eastern bank of the Missouri River, is named for General W. D. Washburn of Minneapolis, who was instrumental in its development. One of the earliest Missouri boat landings was established at Washburn, and the town was an important trading post in pioneer days. Where the waterworks stand NW. of the city is the SITE OF A SIOUX-ARIKARA BATTLE fought on May 22, 1869; it resulted in the death of Swift Runner, young Ree chieftain. On E. Main St. stands the LOG CABIN OF JOSEPH HENRY TAYLOR (*open by arrangement; inquire at Leader office*), trapper, hunter, and author, who built the house near

Painted Woods (*see Tour 3B*) in the early 1870's. He established a woodyard there and also became the first postmaster of the settlement; the postoffice was a hole cut in the trunk of an oak tree. Taylor printed his books in his own shop, writing the stories as he set the type by hand. His books include *Frontier and Indian Lives* and *Kaleidoscopic Lives*, both reflecting the somewhat florid literary style of the time, but nevertheless giving a colorful and engrossing picture of the frontier of his day.

Right from W. Main St. in Washburn on a well-marked country road to FORT MANDAN STATE PARK, 14 *m.*, site of Fort Mandan on the north bank of the big bend in the Missouri. Here the Lewis and Clark expedition spent the winter of 1804–5 with the friendly Mandan Indians. It was here that Sakakawea, or Bird Woman, a young Shoshone Indian girl, joined the expedition which she helped to guide to the Pacific (*see* BISMARCK). Warring Sioux destroyed the buildings of the fort in 1805, and the ever-changing river channel has altered the landscape so that it is impossible to identify the exact site (*see Tour 10*). Near the markers that have been erected are the trenches of unidentified expeditions.

At 147 *m.* is the junction with a county dirt road (*see Tour 3B*).

WILTON, 156.5 *m.* (2,152 alt., 851 pop.), named for Wilton, Maine, is on the McLean-Burleigh County line and is the center of a Ukrainian settlement. These people came from Galicia, a province of the former Austro-Hungarian Empire, and found work in the lignite mines which at that time were just opening here. One group arrived in 1897 and a second two years later. Many old customs are preserved, including folk dances performed in picturesque, brightly colored costumes by both old and young people. The Ukrainians are fond of flowers and their homes usually have beautiful gardens, in which they can be seen working in the early hours of summer days.

On opposite sides of the highway at the northern end of town are two unusual churches, both focal points of the Ukrainian settlement. SS. PETER AND PAUL GREEK CATHOLIC CHURCH (R) has two steeples topped with fourchée crosses. It is of the Greco-Slavonic branch of the Greek Church. The RUSSIAN ORTHODOX GREEK CATHOLIC CHURCH (L) belongs to the Russo-Greek branch; a cruciform building, it has three steeples, each bearing the Greek schismatic cross of papal design, symbolizing the Trinity, with the lowest member set obliquely to denote that the church does not recognize the authority of the Pope. Both churches use the Julian calendar and have similar services and holidays.

A bird-banding station established in Wilton in 1931 by Mrs. W. H. Gray under the U.S. Fish and Wildlife Service banded 5,805 birds of 86 species in its first five years.

BISMARCK, 181 *m.* (1,672 alt., 15,496 pop.) (*see* BISMARCK).

POINTS OF INTEREST

State Capitol, Liberty Memorial Building, State Historical Society Museum, Roosevelt Cabin.

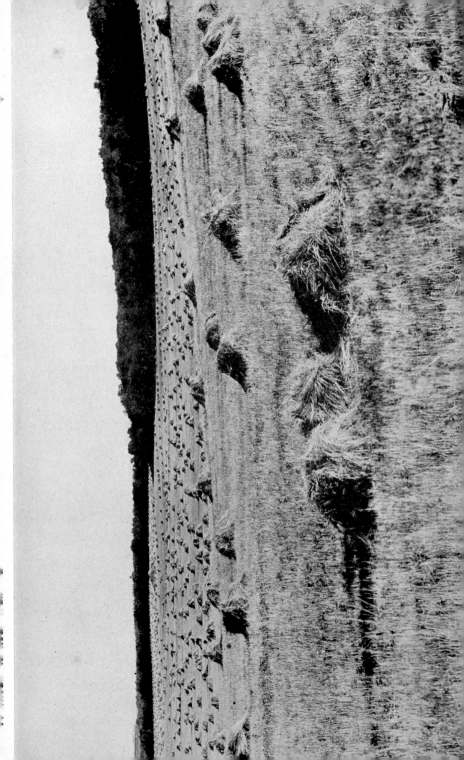

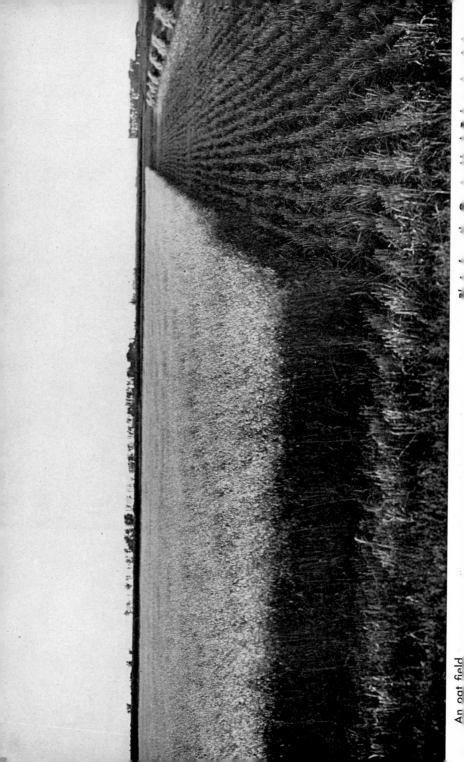

An oat field

Law Building, University of North Dakota, Grand Forks

Photo by Melvin Kobe

Statue of Theodore Roosevelt, Minot

Blockhouse of Fort McKeen, Fort Abraham Lincoln State Park
Photo by Russell Reid

Slant Indian Village lodge, Fort Abraham Lincoln State Park
Photo by Russell Reid

Marquis de Mores, from an etching by Edward Chinot

Clay and sandstone pinnacle in the Badlands
Photo by Russell Reid

Photo by Russell Reid

Valley of the Little Missouri, with Rabbit's Ears in the background

Grand Canyon of the Little Missouri

Photo by Hugh W. Hempel

ignite strip mining, Velva

Arikara woman pounding cherries

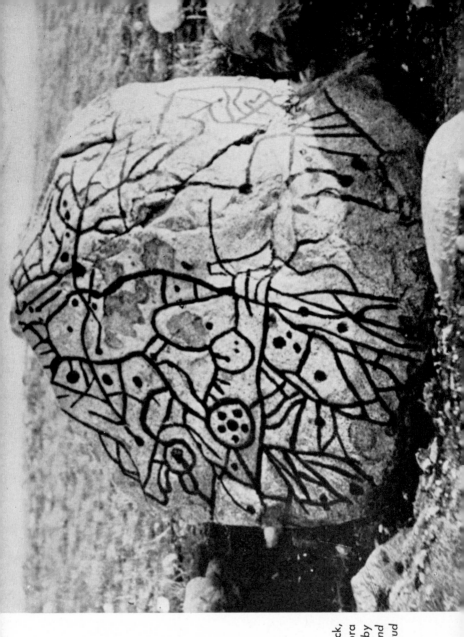

Writing Rock, near Grenora
Photo by Edgard and Henry Syverud

ake Upsilon, Turtle Mountains   *Photo by Russell Reid*

Barnes County
Courthouse,
Valley City
Photo by
R. Kenneth
McFarland

A late Deere thresher.

oux hoop dance

Photo by Russell Reid

rikara buffalo bull dancer

Photo by Russell Reid

Magpie Rock, Killdeer Mountains

At 6th St. and Main Ave. is the junction with US 10 (*see Tour* 8), which unites with US 83 between this point and STERLING, 209.5 *m*. (1,807 alt., 100 pop.).

MOFFIT, 215 *m*. (1,738 alt., 184 pop.), is near the southwest shore of LONG LAKE, a large section of which has been developed by the U.S. Fish and Wildlife Service as a migratory waterfowl refuge. The town is named for the Moffit family, who were the first settlers.

As HAZELTON, 229 *m*. (1,975 alt., 500 pop.), is neared it has the appearance of an oil town, owing to its numerous windmills, which a forerunner of the modern high-pressure salesman succeeded in selling in the community. The town is named for Hazel Roop, the daughter of the town-site owner.

South of Hazelton the route enters a Russo-German farming area. The odd, brilliant colors of some of the houses and farm buildings are characteristic of the taste of these people. Diagonal stripes of alternating bright colors form a favorite decorative scheme for barn and granary doors. Since the American influence has made itself felt, however, many gaily painted buildings have been dimmed by coats of conservative white or buff paint.

LINTON, 245 *m*. (1,706 alt., 1,602 pop.), was named for George W. Lynn, an early settler. Protected by high, flat-topped hills, the town is in a valley at the confluence of Beaver and Spring Creeks. The most prominent building in town is the EMMONS COUNTY COURTHOUSE, of modern design, constructed of North Dakota brick. Hand carving on the spandrels above the first floor windows depicts the story of progress in Emmons County. Several of the public buildings in Linton, including the hospital and the Episcopal church, are constructed of native sandstone quarried a short distance from the town. SEEMAN'S PARK (*picnicking, swimming, camping*) on Beaver Creek, named for L. D. Seeman, its donor, is a recreation and tourist camp.

Right from Linton on an improved county dirt road to the junction with an unimproved road, 0.5 *m*.; L. on this prairie road, unsuitable for trailers, to what appears to be an almost perfect specimen of an INDIAN TURTLE EFFIGY MOUND, 1.5 *m*. The road passes directly over the turtle's back, and from the top of the mound the outlines of the head to the E. and the tail to the W. are clearly visible.

STRASBURG, 255 *m*. (1800 alt., 994 pop.), gets its typically German name from a German settlement in Russia whence many of its settlers came. It marks the dividing line between the Russo-German and Dutch settlements of this vicinity. Both racial groups make up the population of the town, which is the center of a large grain and dairy area. Rising from the compact little village is the double spire of the Roman Catholic church, which is attended by the largest rural Catholic congregation in the State. The feast day of SS. Peter and Paul (*June* 29) is an annual occasion for celebration.

South of Strasburg the route passes through territory settled by Hollanders, and the landscape is dotted with their neat, well-kept farms. Although many of them are American-born, the native tongue is retained in their homes. The Dutch Reformed Church forms the focal point in their communities; many of their children attend college at Holland, Michigan, and members of the settlement annually go to Michigan for the Holland Tulip Festival.

HULL, 264 *m.* (1800 alt., 28 pop.), is one of the Dutch communities, named for Hull, Iowa.

At 266 *m.* is the junction with ND 11, a graveled highway.

Left on this highway is HAGUE, 4 *m.* (1,899 alt., 442 pop.), named for The Hague in the Netherlands. In a level farming area, it is one of the market towns for the Dutch settlements, although its population is principally Russo-German. The Roman Catholic church is the outstanding building of the community.

US 83 crosses the North Dakota-South Dakota boundary at 272 *m.*, 141 *m.* N. of Pierre, South Dakota (*see South Dakota Guide Tour 12*).

✿✿

Tour 3A

Junction US 83—Garrison—Nishu—Elbowoods—Shell Creek—Van Hook—Stanley; ND 37 and 8, county and reservation roads. Junction with US 83 to US 2, 117 *m.*

All state highways and important reservation roads graveled. The principal points of interest on this tour will be inundated when the Garrison Dam is completed.

ND 37, which runs through the Fort Berthold Indian Reservation, branches W. from US 83 (*see Tour 3*) midway between Max and Coleharbor.

GARRISON, 6 *m.* (1,920 alt., 1,117 pop.), named for near-by Garrison Creek, was formerly the center of a large wheat area and is now a primary turkey market. Lignite is mined in the surrounding country, and just S. of Garrison, where the Missouri makes the Big Bend, is the site of the Garrison Dam, now under construction.

At 18 *m.* is the junction with ND 28 and a county graveled highway. Straight ahead on the county highway to a small store and filling station, where is the junction with an unimproved dirt road, 29 *m.*; L. to enter the FORT BERTHOLD INDIAN RESERVATION at 33 *m.* Established in 1870 with an area of more than 2,000,000 acres, it has now been reduced to 625,000. The region is principally rugged and broken—typical Badlands, best suited for grazing, although the eastern portion of the reservation contains some good farming land. The population figures for 1947 list approximately 1,720 Indians, including Arikara, Hidatsa, and Mandans (although few of the latter are of pure blood), remnants of the three agricultural Indian tribes that once occupied the Missouri River Valley.

At 38 *m.* is the junction with a dirt road, not suitable for trailers.

Left on this road to the junction with another dirt road, 3 *m.*; R. on this road to another junction at 4 *m.*; L. to another junction at 5 *m.*; R. to a fence gate, 5.8 *m.*; R. through the gate, pass a small farmhouse to the SITE OF FORT BERTHOLD, 6 *m.* Above the river bottoms, overlooking a bend in the Missouri's course, are the ruins of a trading post built in 1845 by Bartholomew Berthold, a Tyrolese. He had traded in the river country for many years, and his success at this new fort named for him made it one of the most important Missouri River posts. Harassed by the warlike Sioux, the Hidatsa Indians left their village at the mouth of the Knife River and came to live at Fort Berthold, where, because of the bend in the river, they named their new home Like-a-fish-hook Village. The Mandan Indians later joined the Hidatsa at this site. From the first the history of Fort Berthold is a tale of many assaults by wandering parties of Sioux. In 1864 a portion of the second Sully expedition was sent to protect the outpost, and the following year Fort Berthold became a military post. It was garrisoned until 1867, when Fort Stevenson, 12 *m.* E., replaced it. The rough-hewn log buildings which Berthold and his men erected were later replaced by frame buildings, the dismantled remains and cellars of which are all that mark the site today.

The GRAVES OF SON-OF-THE-STAR AND WHITE SHIELD, famed Arikara chiefs, are marked by a cement monument about 250 yards NW. of the fort site. Both chiefs were friendly to the white men and helped them in their conquest of the region. Son-of-the-Star was head of the Arikara tribe during the trying times with the Sioux in 1876, and through his reputation for gentleness and a lofty sense of justice stood high in the estimation of both red and white leaders. The two graves are sacred to the Arikara Indians.

A few yards SW. of the monument are the graves of more than 100 Indians of the reservation who served as scouts or enlisted as soldiers with the U.S. Army since the founding of the reservation in 1870. The white marble slabs marking the individual graves stand in precise rows as an army quietly at salute. Each Memorial Day the American Legion posts of Elbowoods (Indian) and Garrison (white) hold joint services here.

At 39 *m.* is the junction with a dirt road, rutted and winding; not suitable for trailers.

Left on this road to the MISSOURI RIVER, 2 *m.*, known to the Mandans as Mata (*division between two parts of land*), and to the Hidatsa as Anati (*navigable water filled with earth*). Here in the area adjacent to the route live the Mandan Indians. Left to BEAVER CREEK STORE, 6 *m.*, a tiny trading post known locally as Ree. Right to the JAMES HOLDING EAGLE FARM, 12 *m.*, typical of the modern Mandan home, and far removed from the earth lodges used by the Indians a century ago.

About 200 ft. L. of the farm is a circular depression believed by the Mandans to be the SITE OF GRANDMOTHER'S LODGE. Grandmother, according to legend, is The-Woman-Who-Never-Dies. She built her home on the first bench of the river, and on the bottom land below planted her vast cornfield, which the deer and blackbirds helped her cultivate. She now lives in the moon, where prayers for favorable weather for crops are addressed to her.

Within the hollow of the lodge site is what appears to be an ordinary granite boulder. Beneath its edges are often found coins of large and small denominations, given as offerings for good crops. The Mandans say that many offerings are left by members of the Crow tribe of Montana, distantly related to the

Hidatsa. It is told that an earth girl married the Man-From-the-Sky and went to live with him, but became homesick for the earth, and attempted to leave the sky on a cord of buffalo hide. Her husband discovered her hanging by the cord, and, angered by her infidelity, threw a boulder at her. The rock crushed her to earth, and today lies where it fell, in the circle of Grandmother's Lodge.

At 39.8 *m.* is NISHU (Arikara, *arrow*), community center of the Arikara (Ree) tribe. The few buildings of the community are scattered across the level land between the river lowlands and the hills to the N. Of particular interest is the circular log dance hall or MEDICINE LODGE. At the appropriate seasons of the year are held the ancient tribal ceremonies pertaining to the successful conduct of agricultural and personal pursuits. In front of the medicine lodge is the boulder that plays a prominent part in the annual cedar-tree ceremonial, a New Year ritual usually held sometime in August. The cedar and the boulder represent the Grandfather and Grandmother of the tribe, and the tree is left standing beside the boulder until spring, when it is decorated with children's moccasins and placed on the ice of the Missouri. When the ice goes out the tree is borne downstream, to carry greetings from the Arikara to their old village sites down the river. Other ceremonials of religious significance include the Mother Corn ritual, the sage dance of thanksgiving, and medicine ceremonies. Since they are seasonal, no set date can be given for these occasions (*usually open to public*). Arikara beadwork and other articles of handicraft are sometimes available at the store in Nishu.

At 40 *m.* the route turns R. and follows the only telephone line on the reservation. The steep rolling country is occupied mainly by the Arikara. Their farm homes are usually white frame buildings, although occasionally there is a poorer log house. There are few barns on these farms; the Indians seldom have milk cows, and they let their horses run on the range throughout the entire year.

At 54 *m.* is the junction with ND 8, a graded dirt road; straight ahead on this is SACRED HEART MISSION, 54.5 *m.,* a Roman Catholic church and mission school established in 1889.

Left from the mission on a road lined with towering cottonwoods is ELBO-WOODS, 0.5 *m.* (1,770 alt., 175 pop.), agency headquarters for the reservation. Its name is derived from the elbow bend of the timber belt along the Missouri at that point. The town centers about the square of agency lawn. Most of the population is white. The town was settled in 1891 when the agency was established. In addition to its regular governmental functions, the agency operates a non-profit flour mill and conducts an experimental farm to educate the Indians in modern agricultural methods. Despite this, many Indians lease their farming lands to white people. What is now the GOVERNMENT SCHOOL was built in 1876 as the Congregational mission, the first on the reservation.

Just SW. of the town are the Indian FAIRGROUNDS where three-day celebrations, with rodeos and tribal dances, are held each year (*July or Aug.*).

ND 8 at 55 *m.* passes SCATTER VILLAGE, a little group of filling stations and garages that grew up around the approach to the highway bridge across the Missouri.

At 56.5 *m.* is the junction (R) with a dirt reservation road, on which the route continues.

Left on ND 8 to FOUR BEARS BRIDGE, 1 *m.*, the bridge with 19 names. When it was built, the Mandans wished it named for their chief Four Bears, subject of many paintings by the artist Catlin who visited this section more than a century ago. The Hidatsa wished it named for their chief Four Bears, who died a few years before the bridge was built. Because of these tribal jealousies it was decided to name the southern end of the bridge for the Mandan chief, and the northern end for the Hidatsa chief. At each end of the span is a plaque bearing the names of chiefs of both tribes given as associate titles to the bridge: for the Mandans there are Charging Eagle, Red Buffalo Cow, Flying Eagle, Black Eagle, and Waterchief; for the Hidatsa, Poor Wolf, Porcupine, Crow Paunch, Big Brave, Crow-Flies-High, Big Hawk, and Old Dog. This arrangement proved unsatisfactory to the Arikara, and a partial compromise was effected by adding the names of five of their chiefs, Bear Chief, Son-of-the-Star, White Shield, Peter Beauchamp, Sr., and Bobtail Bull, as associates.

The dirt reservation road proceeds NW. along the river lowlands, enters a reservation timber reserve at 60.5 *m.*, and skirts the eastern wooded shore of the Missouri before rising again to the benchland. At 68 *m.* is a store and filling station. The route now passes through the area occupied by the Hidatsa, also known as the Minitari or Gros Ventres (Fr., *big bellies*). Their homes are much like those of the other two tribes. The Hidatsa and the Crow Indians of Montana at one time were a single tribe. During a period of want one winter in the eighteenth century, a buffalo was killed by the tribe, and the animal satisfactorily divided until they came to the stomach. The division of this organ led to a quarrel which split the group, and one faction moved W. and became the Crow tribe.

SHELL CREEK, 79 *m.*, is the Hidatsa community center. A few stores, a dance hall, a handful of dwellings, and the central agency experimental farm make up the town.

At 82 *m.*, N. of Shell Creek, is the reservation boundary.

North of the boundary is VAN HOOK, 89 *m.* (1,843 alt., 329 pop.), named for a teamster who served the railroad surveyors. It is one of the trade points adjacent to the reservation and has the only creamery in the vicinity, a $20,000 co-operative plant. Here is a junction with ND 8.

North of Van Hook on ND 8 is BELDEN, 104 *m.* (2,250 alt.), the center of a settlement of Finnish people who homesteaded here in 1903-4. The Finnish tongue is used in most of their homes, and they also have the *sauna* or steam bath without which no Finnish community is complete. The peculiar European three-cornered head scarf is still worn by many of the women. Most of the people have been naturalized and are greatly interested in political trends. About one third of them are members of the United Farmers and Workers League of America, an organization professing communistic doctrines. The radical views and intensive political activity of these members of the community have earned it a reputation as the communistic center of North Dakota.

At 117 *m.* is the junction with US 2 at STANLEY (*see Tour 6*).

Tour 3B

Junction US 83—Junction US 10. County dirt and graveled roads, 'The River Road.'
Junction with US 83 to junction with US 10, 35 *m.*

Dry-weather dirt road except for 6 miles gravel between 29 *m.* and US 10.
Drive carefully as route is hilly with many curves. Route parallels Missouri River.

The River Road between Washburn and Bismarck approximates the overland freighter trail established in the early 1870's between the end of the Northern Pacific Railway at Bismarck and Fort Buford near the mouth of the Yellowstone.

Lewis and Clark, when they came up the Missouri River on their history-making expedition in 1804–5, sent outriders along this side of the river. Along much the same route the freighter trail was established in 1873 when the Northern Pacific brought to Bismarck goods destined for Forts Stevenson, Berthold, and Buford, and this soon became the main-traveled highway for soldiers, traders, and later for ranchers and settlers. Today ruts cut into the prairie by heavily laden wagons, plodding ox teams, and flying hoofs of couriers' horses are still visible in many places along the road.

The route is one of the most attractive in the State as it follows the winding, wooded course of the Missouri where the high hills and buttes along the river's edge contrast with the green meadows and wooded lowlands of the river bottom. This region was once the home of three Missouri Valley Indian tribes—Mandan, Hidatsa, and Arikara—and the route passes three Mandan village sites.

The route branches W. from US 83 (*see Tour 3*) 10 *m.* N. of Wilton on a county dirt road.

At 2 *m.* is the junction with a dirt road.

Right on this road to WILDWOOD LAKE, 1 *m.*, in an old channel of the Missouri. The permanent summer camp of the Missouri Valley Area Council, Boy Scouts of America, is on the eastern shore of the lake.

At 13 *m.* a large farmhouse and a decrepit log hut with a sod roof (L) mark the site of Painted Woods Post Office, one of the early Missouri River settlements. Between the old post office and the river are the PAINTED WOODS, so named by the Indians. According to legend, the woods were a neutral ground between hostile tribes until a Mandan girl fell in love with a Yanktonai Sioux warrior. She planned to leave her people and go with him, but her kinsmen slew him in her embrace; as she knelt by his bier, avenging Yanktonai arrows pierced her. The two tribes began a bitter warfare. The bodies of the lovers were placed in the branches of a tree in the woods, and the tree soon withered and became white and bleached, like the bones in its branches. Yanktonai warriors, coming to the woods to paint their faces and prepare for battle, boastfully portrayed their victories on the tree, and in retaliation the Mandans painted the surrounding trees with war paint to mock their enemy.

At 19 *m.* is the junction with a dirt road.

Right on this road to HALF MOON MANDAN INDIAN VILLAGE SITE (also known as the Larson site), 1 *m.*, unusual in that a ditch, still visible, apparently divided the site in two parts and yet offered no means of defense. A sunken area in the site may have been the village square, and the circular hollows of the earth lodges are still visible in some places despite cultivation of the vicinity.

SQUARE BUTTES, early landmarks, raise their flat-topped heights across the river near the Larson site, and dominate the landscape for the next 10 miles. Their odd beauty, contrasting with the graceful slopes of surrounding hills, has appealed to both red men and white. George Catlin, the artist and explorer who spent eight years in this region more than a century ago, painted a good oil of the Square Buttes.

At 22 *m.* is the junction with a trail (L).

Up the steep bluffs here to DOUBLE DITCH INDIAN VILLAGE STATE PARK. Archeologically designated as the Burgois site, it is also known to the Indians as the ancient Village of Yellow Clay. The inner ditch of the two from which the site receives its name is still traceable in its entire course. The journals of the early French explorer, Verendrye, tell that the village was surrounded by a rampart and protected by an 18-foot palisade and a ditch 18 ft. wide and 15 ft. deep. The cup-shaped depressions of the earth lodges, still visible, are as large as 40 ft. in diameter. Excavations made here by the Peabody Museum, Harvard University, disclosed fine specimens of agricultural implements, religious pieces, and artifacts of warfare. Positions of human skeletons found in the excavations indicate that shallow burial was the custom of the Mandans occupying the site.

At 33 *m.* the River Road passes through PIONEER PARK. On the flood plain of the Missouri, between BURNT CREEK and the road, a picnic and camp ground (*rustic shelters, tables, benches, chairs*) has been built among the towering cottonwood trees.

At 33 *m.* is a junction with a winding gravel road.

Left on this road to the top of the sheer bluffs to LOOKING VILLAGE, 0.5 *m.*, Mandan site named for Chief Looking. Now part of Pioneer Park, the village is known as the Ward site, and several of the earth lodges were reconstructed under a CCC project. The natural defenses of this village were exceptional. On a level, circular summit almost completely cut off from the surrounding benchland, its eastern side was well protected by a ditch, still visible, and a wall. To the N., where the hill is less steep, a ditch and wall were also means of protection.

Built-in log steps and a graded path lead up a round knoll overlooking the river. On the western slope of this formation is a large granite boulder believed to be a petroglyph, or picture rock, of some religious significance. Close observation of the rock will reveal many small, round impressions that may be a form of rock-writing known as cup sculpture. From this point, and from the parking spaces near the Indian village site, is a beautiful view up and down the Missouri.

At 34 *m.*, almost in the long shadows of the railroad bridge, Burnt Creek drains into the Missouri. A story related by Joseph Henry Taylor in his writings tells that, in the summer of 1863, 24 white people, including a woman, a small girl, and a baby, were killed here by the Sioux, and nearly $90,000 in gold dust strewn on the banks of the river. The white people had spent the winter mining at Bannock, Montana, and were returning east with their gold carried in belts and hidden in holes drilled in their flat-bottomed mackinaw boat. Stopping at Fort Berthold on their journey down the Missouri, they were warned by the trader, F. F. Gerard, that it was unsafe to continue until a large group was ready to make the trip through the territory occupied by the hostile Sioux. Thinking Gerard only wished to sell them supplies at high prices, the party disregarded his advice. This was shortly after General Sibley had pursued the Sioux across the Missouri. The Indians, however, following the departure of the military forces, had returned to the east side of the river, as game was more plentiful there, and a party was camped on Burnt Creek. The ever-changing Missouri had cut a long sand bar near the creek mouth, forming a narrow, shallow channel between the shore and midriver. On this bar an old Sisseton was fishing as the white men's boat floated into sight. In a gesture of friendliness the old man waved the boat away from the shallow channel, but his motion was mistaken for a signal, and the white men shot him. Indian women bathing at the river's edge ran screaming to their camp, bringing the warriors. The party of whites had a small cannon on board, and with it killed many of the Indians. The recoil of the cannon fire, however, sank the boat in the shallow water, and after the leader of the white party had been shot the Sioux swarmed on board and disposed of the others. They found the gold dust, but, thinking it only yellow clay, scattered it on the sands. It was several days later that Gerard heard of the massacre and sent a party of 10 Mandans, headed by his brother-in-law Whistling Bear, to recover the gold. They scooped up approximately $70,000 worth in a coffeepot found in the boat, for which Gerard gave a fine horse and a few small presents to Whistling Bear, and a feast to his helpers. The gold thought to be hidden in the hull of the boat was never recovered, although several attempts were made by fortune hunters in later years.

At 35 *m.* is the junction with US 10 (*see Tour* 8) just L. of Liberty Memorial Bridge, 1 *m.* W. of Bismarck (*see* BISMARCK).

✿✿

Tour 4

(Moosejaw, Sask., Can.)—Fortuna—Belfield—Amidon—Bowman—
(Belle Fourche, S. Dak.); US 85.
Canadian boundary to South Dakota Line, 264.5 *m.*

G. N. Ry. branch line roughly parallels route between Alexander and Watford City.
Graveled roadbed 139.5 *m.*, bituminous surface 125 *m.*
Accommodations in principal towns.

US 85, a direct route through western North Dakota between Saskatchewan and the South Dakota Line, traverses the Coteau du Plateau
du Missouri, crosses the Missouri River, and enters the severe, majesti-
cally beautiful region of the Missouri Slope with its expansive range
country and scenic Badlands. Between the Canadian border and the
Missouri, boulder-strewn, smoothly rounded hills are evidence of gla-
ciation. In the rough country along the Missouri and Little Missouri
Rivers, the high, mesa-like buttes, flat-topped and capped with thick
layers of rock, mark the level of the land before it was worn by ages
of erosion.

It has been said that men have been equal at only three times since
creation—once in the Garden of Eden, once in the Declaration of Independence, and once in the 'cow country' before the fence. When white
settlers were just beginning to invade these wide plains and rough
Badlands, cattle were being driven here from the Texas Panhandle.
The famous Chisholm Trail that ran north from Texas to Abilene,
Kansas, had many branching trails, one of which ran through the area
now traversed by US 85. In 1934, when P. P. Ackley of Elk City, Oklahoma, an old southwestern cattleman, marked the Chisholm Trail he
included this northern branch.

US 85 crosses the Canadian boundary 50 *m.* S. of Weyburn, Saskatchewan, Canada.

At 0.0 *m.* are clustered the small buildings of the customs office and
the border patrol.

At 7 *m.* is a junction with ND 5, a graveled highway (*see Tour* 5),
which unites with US 85 between this point and 11 *m.*, where US 85
branches R.

FORTUNA, 8 *m.* (2,190 alt., 214 pop.), a Scandinavian community,
named for the Roman goddess of fortune, was established in the summer of 1913 when the branch line of the Soo Ry. was extended from
Ambrose, North Dakota, to Whitetail, Montana. The day lots were

sold, temporary business houses, which had been squatting a mile from the present site at a post office called Norge, were put on wheels and rolled away to the new town by night. Here are the American customs offices.

> Right from Fortuna on a country road to the DEWITT SPRING, 1 *m.*, whose flow fills a two-inch pipe of water the year round. It has furnished water for Fortuna since the founding of the village.

In the vicinity of ZAHL, 34 *m.* (2,000 alt., 150 pop.), are many small underground lignite mines that supply local markets and truckers. The town is named for F. R. Zahl, who came to this region in the early 1870's and became an outstanding buffalo hunter. The first post office here was at his ranch, E. of the present town. ND 50, a graveled highway (*see Tour 4A*), unites with US 85 between Zahl and 38 *m.*, where US 85 branches R.

South of Zahl the route parallels the wide, flat-bottomed trough formed by LITTLE MUDDY CREEK. At 58 *m.* is the junction with US 2 (*see Tour 6*), and the two highways are one route to 73 *m.*, where US 85 branches L.

At 75 *m.* the route crosses the MISSOURI RIVER on the LEWIS AND CLARK BRIDGE, built in 1927, the second bridge in the State to span the Big Muddy. Natural gas from the Baker, Montana, field is piped into the Williston territory through lines that cross the bridge.

South of the bridge the highway winds through the draws and ravines of the Little Badlands, a small area showing the results of severe erosion. At 92 *m.* is the junction with ND 23, a State graveled road.

> Right on ND 23 is CARTWRIGHT, 13.5 *m.* (1,896 alt., 50 pop.), named for Samuel George Cartwright, the hunter-trapper who was its first settler. At 17 *m.* is the YELLOWSTONE RIVER, the largest tributary of the Missouri, and an important factor in the history of exploration, settlement, and development of trade in Montana. Here, where the river joins the Missouri just within the North Dakota border, the valley once was a hunting paradise for the upper Missouri Indians, but fur traders, trappers, hunters, and settlers gave little thought to conservation, and the big game is now extinct. The three-million-dollar irrigation project completed in 1909 by the Federal Bureau of Reclamation has brought the region the title of Prosperous Valley. Sugar beets form the principal crop, although grains, vegetables, and forage crops are raised successfully, and there is some small-scale fruit farming. Center of the sugar industry is the refining plant at Sidney, Montana (*see Montana Guide Tour 9*). The entire irrigated area contains 58,561 acres, of which 19,500 are in North Dakota. Sugar-beet acreage in the Yellowstone Valley in this State is approximately 1800. Mexican labor is used in the beet fields; most of the Mexicans make their homes in the Sidney and Fairview, Montana (*see below*), areas.
>
> The Yellowstone can be crossed here on the G. N. Ry. bridge, on which timber planking has been placed over the ties to permit automobile traffic. In one span of the bridge is a vertical lift to allow passage of river boats, although these are much more scarce than they were when the bridge was built in 1913.
>
> Just E. of the bridge is the only railroad tunnel in the State, a 1,456-foot timber-supported excavation piercing the soft earth hills bordering the Yellowstone. It serves a single track on a curved alignment of 3°.
>
> At 21.5 *m.* the road crosses the Montana Line at the city limits of Fairview, Montana (*see Montana Guide Tour 9*).

ALEXANDER, 96 *m*. (2,146 alt., 415 pop.), was platted in 1905 shortly after organization of McKenzie County by special legislative act and was designated temporary county seat by proclamation of Governor Sarles. Alexander McKenzie, political dictator of the early Dakota scene, was one of the town-site incorporators, and both the town and county are named for him. Still standing is the old log building that served as the first county courthouse.

ARNEGARD, 108 *m*. (2,237 alt., 222 pop.), was named for Evan Arnegard, an early settler. The community is predominantly Scandinavian. Certified potatoes, both for southern markets and foundation stock for growers in the eastern part of the State, form one of the leading products of the surrounding agricultural area. Turkeys are also raised here.

Left from Arnegard on a graded road 2 *m*.; L. here to LAKE PESHECK, 3 *m*., formed by impounded creek waters. It is surrounded by fine trees and is fast becoming a summer recreation point. The lake was recently stocked with 1500 trout.

WATFORD CITY, 116 *m*. (2,082 alt., 1,073 pop.), was named for a town in Canada. It is the county seat, and Federal agencies have offices in the city.

The town is the terminus of a G. N. Ry. branch line, and the trade center of the 'Island Empire' county, so called because the Missouri on the N. and E., the Yellowstone on the W., and the Little Missouri on the S. almost surround it with water. A tourist camp is one half mile E. on ND 23, a graveled highway.

Left from Watford City on ND 23 is SCHAFER, 5 *m*. (1,950 alt., 75 pop.), in the little Cherry Creek valley (*see Tour* 10). Its white frame buildings and dingy log huts cluster about the frame courthouse which is an object of long-standing contention with Watford City. The town is named for Charles Shafer (1850–1930), an early rancher of the region, whose son George Shafer (1888–1948) served as Governor of the State from 1929–32. On the Shafer homestead S. of the town along the creek are the Schafer Springs, near which are excellent camping grounds. The springs have a flow of nearly 6000 gal. per hour, a flow which has not diminished during recent years of subnormal rainfall.

A slight curve at 128 *m*. reveals a spectacular view. The grassy plateau ends abruptly, and below, as though a huge, careless knife had slashed into the prairie, lies a confusion of endless gray-, ocher-, slate-, and red-layered buttes, through which winds a maze of ragged ravines and coulees. In the distance the meandering LITTLE MISSOURI RIVER looks hardly capable of producing the strange BADLANDS which it and its tributaries have carved out of the earth. The red of the scoria-topped buttes, the myriad hues of the strata laid down ages ago by successive prehistoric seas, and the brilliant green of the juniper or cedar trees clinging to the steep hillsides form a startling, almost weird, picture.

Like a miniature at the bottom of the valley is the silvery steel of the ROOSEVELT BRIDGE. In 3 miles the tortuous, twisting highway drops 600 ft. (*drive carefully*) to reach the north entrance to the Theodore Roosevelt National Memorial Park at 131.5 *m.* (*see* THEODORE ROOSEVELT NATIONAL MEMORIAL PARK, NORTH TOUR).

After crossing the river and its wide flood plain the highway climbs through the Badlands to emerge upon the prairie at 135 *m.* In the distance (L) at 141 *m.* are the Killdeer Mountains (*see Tour 8D*).

At 149 *m.* the highway rounds a grass-covered prominence to enter GRASSY BUTTE (2,300 alt., 40 pop.), a little town founded in 1913 and named for the neighboring butte, which has long been a landmark in the region. Although there are many similarly shaped elevations in the vicinity, Grassy Butte is the only one not bare of vegetation. Ten Russian laborers first homesteaded in the Grassy Butte region, forming the nucleus of the present-day farming population. The old post office building still stands, a typical frontier log structure. In the early days of the town, when there were buildings on only one side of the main street, it was a local jest that Grassy Butte had the widest main street in the country, 'from McKenzie County to the Atlantic seaboard.'

The people who inhabit the area surrounding Grassy Butte are Little Russians or Ukrainians. They preserve many of their Old Country customs and retain their Greek Catholic religious allegiance, though a difference of opinion has resulted in a schism.

A wedding custom of these people requires that the bride and bridegroom return to their respective homes after the marriage ceremony. At midnight a delegation representing the bridegroom abducts the bride and brings her to her husband's home. Wedding celebrations often last two or three days.

At 155 *m.* is the junction with ND 25 (*see Tour 8D*).

At BELFIELD, 187 *m.*, is the junction with US 10 (*see Tour 8*).

At 213 *m.* is the junction with ND 21 (*see Tour 4B*).

At 222 *m.* is the junction with a graded dirt road, not suitable for trailers.

Left on this road to CHALKY BUTTE, also known as White Butte, 6 *m.*, a long high butte topped with one of the few White River limestone formations in the State. On its steep talus-covered slopes fossilized teeth and bones of prehistoric animals have been found. Outcroppings of large bones are plainly visible in the limestone cliff. The complete skull and other bones of an oreodon (small prehistoric hoofed animal) have been taken from this fossil bed.

In early days of white settlement it was believed that a treasure was buried somewhere on Chalky Butte because an Indian chief often went there and returned with gold. Although he was followed, he always managed to elude his pursuers; his cache, if it existed, has never been found. According to another story, a small party of soldiers once left Fort Meade, in the Black Hills, to take the pay roll to Fort Keogh, Montana. The pay roll never reached Fort Keogh, and no trace was found of the men, unless the three revolvers marked 'U.S.' and several U.S. Army wagon irons with charred pieces of wood clinging to them, found about 1900 near Sunset Butte S. of here were the remains of their luckless expedition. Whether or not there is any connection between these two stories is a matter of conjecture.

AMIDON, 222 *m.* (2800 alt., 102 pop.), named for a U.S. district judge, Charles F. Amidon (1856–1937), was organized in 1915 and shortly thereafter was selected Slope County seat. In an enclosure near one of the filling stations in the town is an 8-ton petrified stump almost 6 feet in diameter, which was uncovered on the county fairgrounds N. of Amidon. The town commands a good view of the surrounding country, with Chalky Butte to the SE., the angular outlines of the Badlands to the N. and W., and Black Butte (*see below*), highest point in the State, to the SW.

At 224 *m.* is the junction with a graded dirt road with sharp curves and abrupt hills (*unsuited for trailers*).

Right on this road 2 *m.*; then L. across rolling range land, gradually descending into the Badlands to the junction with a little-used trail, 11 *m.*

Right on this trail 1 *m.* at the end of a small valley are the BURNING COAL MINE and the COLUMNAR CEDARS. Across the ravine on a hillside sloping to the W. is the burning mine, which at dusk casts a carmine glow over the hill, and a heavy odor of coal gas hangs in the little valley. How long the lignite bed has been burning underground is not known. The Indians have legends telling of the burning ground, and old settlers in the region say that the burned area has not advanced more than a few hundred feet in the 50 years since the region was first settled by white men. The cause of the combustion is not known. As the coal burns underneath, the earth overburden crumbles and falls, taking with it all rocks, trees, and vegetation on the surface, leaving in its wake red scoria and other less brightly colored clays. The burned area succumbs easily to weathering and erosion. From large crevices in the earth intense heat pours, but with care one can peer into the flaming underground pits. (*Approach from the downhill side where there is no danger of the earth crumbling underfoot.*)

In the bottom of the tiny valley, and on its western slope, grow the columnar cedars, bright green conical trees averaging 15 feet in height. These trees, found in North Dakota only in this small area adjacent to the burning mine, taper from a large base to a narrow tip. Their brilliant green forms a decided contrast with the dull grays and tans of the hills surrounding them.

On the main side road beyond the junction with the trail, the dirt graded road winds down to the Little Missouri and upstream to the SITE OF A LOGGING CAMP, 15 *m.* When the N. P. Ry. was being built W. of the Missouri a wood cutters' camp was maintained here. The camp bunkhouse is said to have been equipped with loopholes to shoot through in event of Indian attack. The cedar ties and pilings cut at the camp were floated down the Little Missouri, but many became snagged in sand bars or scattered over the river flood plain, and few reached their destination. Across the river from the site are the two peaks known as the RABBIT'S EARS.

US 85 at 228 *m.* passes directly between Chalky Butte (L) and Black Butte (R).

At 229 *m.* is a junction with a dirt road.

Right on this road 1 *m.* to an advantageous point from which to hike to the top of BLACK BUTTE (3,468 alt.), highest elevation in the State. The butte is some 8 miles in circumference, and near the top solid rock cliffs rise perpendicularly 50 to 100 feet above its grassy slopes. At its base lie huge boulders, broken from the sides by the action of weather. Springs form numerous creeks on the northern side, and their tree- and brush-lined banks are a favorite ground for berry-picking parties. At the northern corner of the butte is a hole about 3 feet wide, from which a slight draught of air can be felt. When a pebble is dropped into this opening a dull thud can be heard, as though the stone had not struck solid bottom. On the S. side of the butte is SNOW CAVE, where the deep winter snows often remain until August. There is a fine view from the top of the butte.

At the western edge of the mesa are two rock-lined EAGLE PITS, about 4 feet wide and 3 feet deep, from which hidden Indians caught eagles and plucked out their tail feathers for their war bonnets. These quills were very valuable, often worth a pony in trade.

Black Butte is also known as H.T. Butte, since it was part of the H.T. ranch, which in the 1880's and 1890's was the largest horse ranch in the State. The surrounding country in those days was given over to the ranging of cattle, sheep, and horses, and it was not until the coming of the 'honyocks,' as the stockmen called the homesteaders, and the cultivation of former range lands, that the ranching of this section was curtailed.

Concerning H.T. Butte old-timers of this section tell a story of a cowhand named Bob Pierce, who because of his merciless riding was known to his fellow workers as 'Crazy Loon' as well as by numerous other uncomplimentary titles. He rode his mount at any speed anywhere, and it was hard to 'keep him in horses.' It chanced that at one time Bob was paired, on the circuit, with talkative old Colonel Sullers. Thinking to harry the colonel, Bob began to spur his horse to breakneck speed. Sullers kept beside him, holding up both ends of a political conversation and trying to pretend not to notice the speed. His horse, unfortunately, stepped into a hole, and the rider went sprawling. Stopping at a near-by creek to wash the dirt and blood from his head and face, he reviled his tormentor, declaring, 'When you're dead your ghost will ride the tops of the hills and howl like a gray wolf.' In the course of time Bob Pierce died, or he may have been killed on one of his wild rides. Since then, it is said, a horseman is seen, on dark nights, riding at breakneck speed up the steep, inaccessible sides of H.T. Butte, and sometimes the howl of a gray wolf is heard.

BOWMAN, 246 *m.* (2,958 alt., 967 pop.), seat of Bowman County, lies at the base of flat-topped, sandstone-capped TWIN BUTTES. Known successively as Lowden Post Office and Twin Buttes, the town won the county seat election in a bitter fight with Atkinson (later Griffin) in 1907, and in January 1908 was given its present name. Both town and county are named for E. W. Bowman, a prominent Territorial legislator.

The junction with US 12 (*see Tour* 9) is in Bowman, and US 85 turns L. and reaches the South Dakota Line at 262 *m.*, 103 *m.* N. of Belle Fourche, South Dakota (*see South Dakota Guide Tour* 13).

✿✿

Tour 4A

Junction US 85—Hanks—Grenora—Sodium Lakes—Writing Rock; ND 50 and unnumbered county roads.
Junction with US 85 to Writing Rock, 30.3 *m.*

G. N. Ry. parallels route between junction with US 85 and Grenora.
Graveled roadbed 12 *m.*, graded dirt roads and prairie trail remainder of route.
Accommodations in principal towns.

This short route passes through a region of boulder-strewn, smoothly rounded hills left by glacial action and leads to extensive but undeveloped sodium sulphate beds and the archeologically important Writing Rock State Park. The populations of both towns on the route are chiefly Scandinavian; they were settled by immigrants who arrived with or shortly after the railroad.

ND 50 branches W. from US 85 (*see Tour 4*) at Zahl.

HANKS, 5 *m.* (2,114 alt., 192 pop.), named for W. F. Hanks, a Powers Lake rancher and banker who was connected with the townsite company, begins its history with the arrival of the G.N. branch line in 1916. In the 1890's the N-N (N Bar N) Cattle Co. of St. Louis, which ran herds of livestock S. of the Missouri River in central Montana, refused to ship their stock over the G.N. because of a disagreement with that line. As a result they had to trail their large herds many weary miles to the nearest Soo Line points, which were at Bowbells and Kenmare, North Dakota (*see Tour 7*). As many as 30,000 of these Chicago-bound cattle passed through Hanks in a single season on their way to the railroad, herded by dust-caked cowboys of the authentic, original, Wild West variety.

Ranching was the chief industry of this section when it was first settled, and there is still some small-scale ranching in the vicinity.

GRENORA, 11 *m.* (2,105 alt., 425 pop.), has a name derived from the first three letters of the words Great Northern and as terminus of that railroad enjoyed a brief boom in 1916.

West of Grenora ND 50 is a graded dirt road. At 14 *m.* is the junction with a county dirt road (R) which is now the route.

At 17 *m.* is the junction with a prairie trail.

Left on this trail to FERTILE VALLEY LAKE NO. 2, 1 *m.*, largest of the several shallow lakes in this vicinity that contain millions of tons of sodium sulphate, a valuable mineral resource. These lakes and sloughs, with no drainage outlets, are part of a linear series lying NW. to SE. along a preglacial stream course. The beds range from a few inches to as much as 80 feet in depth. Because of the low rainfall in recent years many of the lakes glisten white in the sunlight.

Literally, a wild goose chase led to the discovery of these sodium sulphate deposits. A Grenora hunter waded into a shallow lake to recover a goose that had fallen into the water, and found the lake bottom covered with a hard crystal formation resembling salt deposits he had seen in Canada, which he knew to be commercially valuable. He directed attention to the lake, and as a result an FERA survey was undertaken in 1934, and a large amount of the mineral was found here. Fertile Valley Lake No. 2 was estimated to contain 11,000,000 tons, and two other lakes in the vicinity 5,000,000 and 1,750,000 tons each.

Sodium sulphate is also known as Glauber's salt. Commercially it has a value of about $20 a ton and is used medicinally, in paper manufacture, as salt for cattle, and in manufacturing soap and munitions. In 1937 the University of North Dakota, in co-operation with the State Highway Department, was conducting experiments to determine the value of sodium sulphate in highway construction. At present there is little demand for North Dakota sodium sulphate because of the accessibility of sources nearer the points of consumption.

At 21 *m.* is the junction with another county dirt road; R. on this road to the junction with a county highway, the Grenora-Alkabo route, at 23 *m.*; R. on this road; at 30 *m.* the route turns L. and proceeds up a hill to WRITING ROCK STATE PARK, 30.3 *m.* Of gray granite, Writing Rock stands in a slight hollow on the crest of a hill, commanding a wide view of the surrounding country. The top and two sides of the rock are covered with hieroglyphs, consisting of lines, dots, circles containing dots, and, near the top, a flying bird. Many attempts have been made to decipher the writing, which apparently was carved into the rock at several different periods. Whatever the meaning of the inscriptions, the rock is regarded as sacred by Indians, who, even after the settlement of the State, made pilgrimages here from the Fort Peck (Montana) Reservation and other distant points. The site, because of its elevation, served advantageously for smoke signals.

Several graves have been found in the vicinity, and excavations have revealed hammers, hatchets, arrowheads, sea shells, elk teeth, and beads of many shapes and colors. One grave is said to have yielded beads that measured 52 feet when strung.

The Indians have many legends associated with the rock. The one most often heard is that told by Joe Lagweise and Tawiyaka, two old Sioux Indians of the Qu'Appelle Agency in Saskatchewan, Canada, who as young men visited Writing Rock and heard the story from an old man camped there. Many years ago a party of eight warriors stopped for the night near this rock, and just as they were falling asleep they heard a voice calling in the distance. Fearful of an enemy attack, they investigated but found nothing. The next morning they heard a woman's voice calling, but still they found no one. In their search, however, they saw this large rock with a picture on it, showing eight Indians—themselves—with their packs lying on the ground. Unable to understand this mystery, the warriors went on their way. On their return they again passed the rock and noticed that the inscription had changed, and appeared to hold a picture of the future. When they reached home they told their people of the mysterious rock, and the entire village moved near it, only to find that the picture had again changed, this time showing the village with its tipis. From that time on the rock was believed to foretell the future until white men moved it; whereupon it lost its power. An old Indian chief once pointed out that the three lines on the rock indicated three graves near the stone, one of which he said was that of a white child. It has been suggested that the inscriptions may be the work of some race that lived in this region before the Indians known to history.

Writing Rock is approximately 5 feet high and 4 feet thick, and weighs an estimated 10 tons. A smaller rock, weighing about a ton, which stood near a spring about a mile below Writing Rock, also contains inscriptions and has been moved to New Merrifield Hall at the University of North Dakota for study.

Ten acres of land surrounding Writing Rock were acquired in 1936 by the State Historical Society of North Dakota in order to preserve the Rock as a historic site.

✿✿

Tour 4B

Junction US 85—New England—Mott—Carson—Flasher—Junction
ND 6.
ND 21. Junction with US 85 to junction ND 6, 126 m.

N. P. Ry. branch line roughly parallels route from Mott to Flasher; Milwaukee
R.R. branch between New England and Elgin.
Graveled roadbed except for 45 m. bituminous surface.
Hotel and tourist camp facilities limited in most towns; many natural camping
places along the Cannonball River.

Traversing the northern part of the Missouri Slope, this route passes
through what was ranch land, now used for diversified farming. Most of
the land adjacent to the route is underlain with deposits of lignite,
and on many farms the winter's fuel is easily obtained by a little digging.
Dominating the general rolling terrain are jagged, mesa-like hills capped
with brown sandstone formations. Gentle, grass-covered slopes, whose
rich spring green turns to amber in the fall, rise to steeper hillsides,
above which jumbled, broken, weathered rocks lead to the steep cliffs
crowning the flat mesas.

Trees are few along this route, except for the tiny groves on occasional
farms, and the woods and bushes that edge the Cannonball River and
its tributary creeks.

ND 21 branches E. from US 85 (see Tour 4), 26 m. S. of Belfield
(see Tour 8). Dominating the landscape immediately E. of the junction
are the two high, flat-topped, coffin-shaped RAINY BUTTES (R). At
6 m. the highway passes 2 miles N. of West Rainy Butte, and at 8 m.
passes East Rainy Butte, which appears to be only a short distance from
the route, but actually is 6 miles S. The tops of these twin heights are
sometimes clouded in a faint gray mist, and according to Indian lore
they get rain at least once a day, despite the weather. Although this is an
exaggeration, it is nearly true, for at times when warm currents of air
strike the cold surface of the sides of the buttes the moisture in the air
is condensed, resulting in fogs or mists that usually veil the heights.
This phenomenon is also common to other buttes in this area. There are
evidences of Indian burials on the Rainy Buttes.

NEW ENGLAND, 16 m. (2,593 alt., 895 pop.), its seven grain
elevators standing like sentinels overlooking its level site N. of the
Cannonball River, was founded in 1887. It was named and first settled
by the New England Colony Association, an organization from the New
England States headed by Thomas W. Bicknell (1834–1925), who was

the author of several histories dealing with Rhode Island. Streets of the new town were laid out by plowing furrows in the prairie. Before the end of the first summer 50 families had arrived, but from 1888 to 1911, when the Milwaukee R.R. came in, New England was little more than a trading post. Although originally founded by New Englanders, today it is predominantly Scandinavian.

ND 22 forms the main street, at the southern end of which, in St. Mary's Catholic schoolyard, is a SHRINE TO THE VIRGIN MARY, made of huge slabs of petrified woods, scoria, odd rock formations from the Badlands, and 'cannonballs' (*see Tour 8C*) from the river. The shrine was built by school children. Midway between the two schools on Main St. is a modern, stuccoed MEMORIAL BUILDING, a community center completed under the Works Progress Administration in 1936.

Between New England and 24 *m*. ND 21 unites with ND 22.

At 19 *m*. is the junction with a graveled county road.

> Left on this road along the north bank of the Cannonball River is HAVE-LOCK, 6 *m*. (2,566 alt., 30 pop.), named for an English stockholder in the Milwaukee R.R. In 1915 a small group of Moravians settled here and erected a church, but by 1924 the colony had dwindled, and the church was sold to the Congregationalists. The Moravians held their immersion baptismal ceremonies in the Cannonball. Right from Havelock (*inquire directions at post office*), 1 *m*., to a BURNING COAL MINE, operated until 1934, when it was discovered to be afire. At times smoke, accompanied by an unpleasant odor of sulphur, is emitted from the mine.

At 24 *m*. is the eastern junction of ND 21 and ND 22; L. here on ND 21. Rising ahead (R) is a series of conical hills, the TEPEE BUTTES, resembling a giant Indian encampment. The highway parallels them their entire length between 25 *m*. and 28 *m*.

At 38 *m*. is the junction with a graveled county road.

> Left on this road is REGENT, 0.8 *m*. (2,461 alt., 261 pop.), named by the railroad company when it was believed that its situation in the center of the county would make it the county seat. The town is on the south bank of the Cannonball. Richard Tooker, one of the State's successful fiction writers, attended high school in Regent.
> North of Regent at 1.3 *m*. is the junction with a county road; R. on this road to REGENT LAKE, 2.8 *m*. (*camping, picnicking, swimming*).

East of Regent on ND 21 the route proceeds for a few miles over a level plain lying S. of the almost treeless Cannonball River valley.

MOTT, 54 *m*. (2,399 alt., 1,220 pop.), is in the valley of the Cannonball. On an elevation to the NW. the strikingly modern HETTINGER COUNTY COURTHOUSE overlooks the river valley. The town is the terminal of an N. P. Ry. branch, and is also on the Milwaukee. CENTRAL PARK (*tourist camp, tennis courts*) is between 3rd and 4th Sts. Its recreation facilities were built as an FERA project.

BURT, 62 *m*. (2,358 alt., 50 pop.), originally known as Alton Post Office, was named by the N. P. Ry. to honor A. M. Burt, superintendent of the Dakota division. More than 500 poplars and Chinese elms are planted in the town schoolyard.

At 67 *m.* the highway crosses THIRTY MILE CREEK, one of the larger tributaries of the north fork of the Cannonball.

At 70 *m.* is the junction with a side road.

Left on this 0.1 *m.* to a LIGNITE STRIP MINE, the largest of several in this vicinity. It produces 8000 tons annually, and rough hummocks of earth are thrown up in the stripping process.

NEW LEIPZIG, 71 *m.* (2,311 alt., 366 pop.), is a Russo-German community, named for Leipzig, Germany, and is on both the Milwaukee and N.P. branch lines where the two roads run parallel only 200 feet apart.

Several years before the establishment of New Leipzig the territory to the S. was settled by a large group of Finns, of whom about a dozen families now remain. Because the settlement has dwindled in recent years, many native customs have disappeared, although a few of the older people retain a superstitious belief in witchcraft, and there are five or six *saunas,* or steam baths, in which water is poured on hot stones in a tightly closed shelter. At butchering time each autumn, rye and wheat flour are hulled, ground oats are mixed with the blood of beeves, and baked in round, thin rings similar to doughnuts. These rings are placed on long sticks, 30 or 40 at a time, thoroughly hardened near a fire, then stored in barrels, with lime as a preservative, for use through-out the winter and coming summer.

ELGIN, 78 *m.* (2,330 alt., 583 pop.), with its many trees, is a pleasant Russo-German town. Its first name, Shanley, was discarded when the N.P. came through because of its similarity to Stanley. A new name was being discussed by a group waiting for a train one day when a member of the group, having looked at his watch, suggested the trade name, Elgin, as a good town-site name. His suggestion met with the approval of the railroad company.

Right from Elgin on an unimproved county road to the north fork of the Cannonball River, 2 *m.,* where are several suitable camping places under the trees of the narrow river valley.

The road continues S. of the river. Sloping up from the stream, MEDICINE BUTTE (L), 3 *m.,* is a high hill topped with a large, almost cubical block of sandstone used for many years as a PRAYER ROCK by Indian tribes, and carved with picture symbols of human hands, buffalo heads, bear paws, and other fig-ures. It was the practice of the Indians to leave offerings at the rock and return the following day, when, the older Indians still relate, the pictures on the rock would tell them whether their prayers were to be answered. Beads, pieces of pot-tery, and other traces of votive offerings are still found near the stone. At the foot of the hill to the W. is a circular area, approximately 80 yards in diameter, where it is believed that native worshipers danced while encamped near the sacred hill. Little vegetation grows on the plot, indicating that years of dancing packed the earth firmly.

At Elgin is the junction with ND 49, a graveled highway.

Left on this highway to HEART BUTTE (L), 17 *m.,* known to the Sioux as *Ta canta wakpa Paha* (Heart River Butte). From this elevation the surrounding country is visible for 20 miles in all directions, and in early days ranchers used the hill as a lookout when searching for strayed cattle or horses. The wooded valley of the Heart River is 4 miles to the S., although it appears much nearer. In the sandstone formation atop the butte is a cave formed by wind and water erosion. The route crosses the crest of Heart Butte Dam, an earth-filled structure 88 feet high and 950 feet long, which will impound 75,000 acre-feet of water. The lake above the dam will provide water for flood control, irrigation, and for recreational areas.

East of Elgin on ND 21 is the junction with a graveled county road, 88 m.

Right on this road is LEITH, 4 m. (2,353 alt., 166 pop.), named for Leith, Scotland. It is on the Milwaukee R.R.

South of Leith on an unimproved county road to the junction with another dirt road, 6 m.; R. on this road to another junction at 7 m., where a vast deposit of small sea shells covers approximately one square mile to a depth of 4 feet, visible evidence that ages ago this region was the bed of a large sea. Only a thin layer of rich black soil covers the deposit, and in plowed fields the shells are easily seen. The practical-minded farmers of this region have found a good use for this gift of the prehistoric sea; they pulverize the shells and feed them to their poultry to provide the calcium in their diet.

CARSON, 92 m. (2,289 alt., 473 pop.), is a compact little town on the slope of a hill, dominated by the large, white frame courthouse at the high end of the main street. It is named for two early settlers, Frank Carter and Simon Pederson.

Left from Carson an unimproved county road leads to the HEART RIVER, 12 m.

Right on the south bank of the stream to a good camping place, 1 m. The river, free from rocks at this point, is deep enough for swimming.

Across the river (L) to the G. A. Johnson home. On a slight rise in the pasture back of the house is a row of evenly spaced piles of four or five stones, about one fourth mile long, placed at a right angle to the brink of the hill. This is believed to have been an Indian BUFFALO RUN, in which the Indians placed banners of red cloth or buckskin between the piles, then drove the hunted buffalo toward them. The animals, frightened by the banners, would swerve toward the crest of the hill where in their rush they would stumble down the incline and fall easy prey to the arrows and spears of the hunters.

At 101 m. is the junction with ND 31, a graveled highway, which unites with ND 21 to 106 m., where ND 31 branches R.

Right on this highway to the DOG TOOTH BUTTES (R), 2 m. From a distance their outlines indicate that they are well named. These buttes were a landmark on the Bismarck-Deadwood trail during the Black Hills gold rush from 1876 to 1884. The stagecoaches with their four-horse teams, and the lumbering ox teams pulling heavily loaded freight wagons, passed just SE. of here, leaving deep ruts which are still visible where ND 31 crosses them immediately S. of the buttes.

At 6 m. on ND 31 is RALEIGH (2,038 alt., 101 pop.), a German community, originated as Dog Tooth Post Office on the Bismarck-Deadwood trail. Purebred livestock is raised on many of the farms in this vicinity.

Left at 8 m. are THREE BUTTES. From the tallest of these peaks a far-reaching view is presented. On a clear day Mandan, 50 m. to the NE., is visible.

FLASHER, 110 m. (1,905 alt., 387 pop.), its residence district scattered over the south slope of a hill and its business street at the foot, is a Russo-German community named for Mabel Flasher, niece and secretary of William H. Brown, head of the land company that owned many of the town sites along the N. P. Ry. branch.

At 126 *m.* is the junction with ND 6 (*see Tour 8C*), 26 miles S. of Mandan (*see Tour* 8).

✧✧✧

Tour 5

Junction US 81—Cavalier—Rolla—Belcourt—Dunseith—Bottineau—Mohall—Crosby—(Scobey, Mont.); ND 5.
Junction with US 81 to Montana Line, 328 *m.*

Soo Ry. branch roughly parallels route from Flaxton to Montana Line; G. N. Ry. branches touch route at intervals between junction US 81 and Lignite, and branch parallels route between Lignite and Crosby.
Graveled roadbed 155 *m.,* bituminous surface 173 *m.*
Usual tourist accommodations in principal towns.

This route, paralleling the international boundary 10 to 15 miles to the north, passes through some of the oldest and some of the newest towns in the State. In the eastern section, where the country is more productive and settlement first began, are towns established in the 1870's, while in the western area, where occupation was slower, are a number of towns founded in the twentieth century. The route begins in the low, level wheatlands of the Red River Valley, at one time the bed of glacial Lake Agassiz, and soon doubles its altitude by rising 800 feet upon the broad, rough, less thickly settled Drift Prairie, which stretches away approximately two thirds of the distance across the State. This wide section, which includes the wooded Turtle Mountains and the level bottom of another glacial lake, Lake Souris, was once a hunters' paradise—a prize which involved the Chippewa Indians, who long held it, in frequent conflict with their enemies the Sioux. With the coming of the whites the region saw new rivals, as the XY, North West, and Hudson's Bay Companies struggled savagely and often bloodily for domination of the fur trade. Most of the Chippewa in the State now live on the Turtle Mountain Indian Reservation, through which the route passes.

Over the bed of ancient Lake Souris, west of the hills, once roamed hordes of buffalo; later, during early white settlement, this region was the feeding ground of great numbers of horses and cattle. After crossing the Souris (*Mouse*) River twice and the long, narrow Upper Des Lacs

Lake, the route ascends 300 to 400 feet to cross the Missouri Plateau, an open, rugged country, marked here and there with the homes of ranchers and farmers, and pitted by the strip mines extracting the huge lignite coal deposits that underlie the plateau.

HAMILTON, 0.0 *m.* (*see Tour* 1), is R. of ND 5 where it branches W. from US 81 (*see Tour* 1).

At 5 *m.* is the junction with ND 18, a graveled highway.

Right on this highway to the junction with a graveled spur, 5 *m.*; R. on this spur is BATHGATE, 8.5 *m.* (828 alt., 312 pop.), pleasantly situated in a bend of the TONGUE RIVER. At the southern side of town on a 40-acre tract of meadow and hayland are the buildings of the STATE SCHOOL FOR THE BLIND, established in 1908. Thirty-five to forty children attend each year for a nine-month period.

CAVALIER, 9 *m.* (894 alt., 1,105 pop.), Pembina County seat, was named for Charles Cavileer, one of the first white men to make a home within the borders of the present State. Usage has changed the spelling of the name. The town was established in 1875 by settlers who came overland from Missouri in a train of 10 covered wagons. The members of the train intended settling in Manitoba, Canada; but, not liking the country there, they returned to the United States, two of the families founding the Tongue River Settlement, which later became Cavalier. They came from Canada by way of Pembina over the old Fort Totten Trail, which ran where Main St. now passes and was one of several trails used by trappers, hunters, and traders as they journeyed between the hunting grounds and the trading posts. Over these trails often moved long caravans of creeking, fur-laden Red River oxcarts, on their long trek to St. Paul. Some trains are said to have contained as many as 1500 carts.

The jog in Cavalier's Main St. results from the fact that the land for the street, contributed by two men who owned adjoining farms, did not meet exactly. This complication was not discovered until after some buildings had been erected, but by that time it would have been too costly to change the route.

AKRA (Icelandic, *fields*), 14 *m.* (980 alt., 37 pop.), is near the southern edge of the Pembina Mountains (*see Tour* 5A), whose wooded height ahead abruptly marks the western edge of the level Red River Valley and the eastern edge of the Drift Prairie. The town is one of a group of communities comprising what is believed to be the largest Icelandic settlement in the United States (*see below*).

At 16 *m.* is CAMP COMFORT, an acre of beautifully wooded grounds (*good camping and picnicking facilities*). Camp Comfort marks the point at which the old Hunters Trail of fur-trading days crossed the Tongue River.

HALLSON, 19 *m.* (1,020 alt., 8 pop.), founded in 1878 and named for Johan Hallson, the first settler, is the oldest of the Icelandic settlements (*see below*).

At 21 *m.* is the junction with ND 32, a graveled highway.

Left on this highway is MOUNTAIN, 5 *m*. (1,030 alt., 205 pop.), so named because of its elevation. It is one of the larger Icelandic towns. A log church here, built in 1886, is said to be the oldest Icelandic church on the North American continent. When the Icelanders first came to America in 1874, they settled at Gimle, Manitoba, Canada. Later, possibly because the rough topography of the country reminded them of the fjords and cliffs of their native land, they colonized here near the headwaters of the Little Tongue River. At present their settlement includes the towns of Hallson, Mountain, Akra, Svold, Hensel, and Gardar. From the first they have engaged in diversified farming and therefore have usually known a fair degree of prosperity. An artistic and deeply imaginative people, perhaps because of the Celtic infusion received when their Norwegian ancestors fled to Ireland upon the ascendency of Harald the Fair-Haired, they still retain many of their old Icelandic traditions and arts, and their folklore is replete with weird and highly colored sagas. They take great pleasure in preserving their native culture and often present plays and pageants showing the dress and customs of Iceland.

Icelanders are particularly adept in gold and silver filigree work and in hand-carving. Almost every home has its treasures brought from far-off Iceland—beautifully hand-carved riding whips adorned with silver and gold ferrules, toys and spoons made from cowhorn, and bread boards carved with leaves and grapes.

The little community has produced many distinguished men, including Sveinbjorn Johnson (1883–1946), former professor of law in the University of Illinois and State supreme court justice (1922–8); Stephen G. Stephenson, poet honored by the Icelandic Government; Emile Walters (1893–   ), whose paintings have been shown at Eastern art centers; and Vilhjalmur Stefansson (1879–   ), scientist and explorer.

Recently large deposits of fuller's earth have been discovered near Mountain. It is estimated that approximately 5,000,000 tons lie in one 200-acre plot. This clay is used for reclaiming motor oil and for purifying animal and vegetable oils. The deposit in this area lies along the valleys of streams from the Canadian boundary to about 10 miles S. of Mountain and W. for an unknown distance.

At 24 *m*. is the junction (R) with ND 32 (*see Tour 5A*). At this junction is OAK LAWN HISTORIC SITE, a small park owned by the State historical society, in which is a weathered old LOG CHURCH, built in 1885 and for many years a landmark in the area.

At 24.5 *m*. is the junction with a county road.

Left on this road is CONCRETE, 1 *m*. (1100 alt., 38 pop.), named by Mrs. Webster Merrifield, whose husband, for many years president of the State university at Grand Forks, was one of the owners of the cement mines once operated here near the source of the Tongue River. At the height of production 500 bbl. were turned out per day, but operations were discontinued when a cheaper type of cement was imported.

Left at 43 *m*. is a small AGRICULTURAL EXPERIMENTAL STATION, a substation of the State agricultural college at Fargo.

LANGDON, 44 *m*. (1,612 alt., 1,546 pop.), became Cavalier County seat in 1884, through the efforts, it is said, of a dozen bachelors who, working hard and changing names and apparel often on election day, voted all the sod shacks—whose owners were either absent or not taking time to vote—for miles around. Originally called McHugh for a prominent early settler, the town later adopted the name of Langdon in honor of the man who made the survey for the local branch of the G. N. Ry. and who presented the village with a bell for the school soon to be built.

An unusual enterprise in Langdon is the Haymow Theater, a children's organization that has presented plays annually for more than a quarter of a century. Children of some of the first members of the company are now taking part in the plays. Performances are held (*adm.* 10¢) during the summer in the loft of the R. T. BURKE BARN (*for directions inquire at post office*).

CLYDE, 69 *m.* (1,618 alt., 80 pop.), is named for the Clyde River in Scotland.

At 86 *m.* is a junction with US 281 (*see Tour 2*), which to 91 *m.* unites with ND 5.

ROLLA, 108 *m.* (1,817 alt., 1,008 pop.), forms the eastern gateway to the lakes and hills of the TURTLE MOUNTAINS, a rolling plateau rising 300 to 400 feet above the surrounding country. It stretches 40 miles to the W. and about 30 miles N. and S., and is bisected by the international boundary. The mountains were named by the Indians, to whom their outline suggested the form of the sacred turtle. Rolla is the Rolette County seat, and its name is believed to be a contraction of the county name. At Rolla in 1889 was established the short-lived Rolla University, which opened its doors to 45 students, and closed them when lack of funds became pressing. During 15 years of his young manhood John Burke (1859–1937), three times Governor of the State (1907–13), former United States Treasurer (1913–21), and former chief justice of the State supreme court (1935–7), lived in Rolla. Here is the office of the secretary of the International Peace Garden, Inc. (*see below*), where most of the business of the corporation is transacted.

At Rolla is the junction with ND 30, a graveled highway.

Right on this highway is ST. JOHN, 8 *m.* (1,944 alt., 517 pop.), named for the eastern Quebec parish from which came the Reverend John Malo, early missionary to the Indians. The town is a port of entry from Canada and is the oldest white settlement on the eastern edge of the mountains. Because of its position near some of the most attractive lakes of the region, it has a fair tourist trade during the summer months. St. John's Day, honoring St. John the Baptist, patron saint of the French Canadians who settled the region, is celebrated June 24.

Left from St. John on a graded dirt highway, to the junction with a county road, 9 *m.*; R. here 0.5 *m.* to ST. CLAUDE STATE PARK, established to commemorate the founding of one of the first permanent white settlements in the Turtle Mountains. The colony grew up about a school and church inaugurated by Father Malo in 1882. As it developed it gradually moved S. and became the town of St. John.

At 13 *m.* on this road is the junction with a county road; R. here 1.8 *m.* to the frame buildings of a STATE GAME AND FISH RESERVE, an 800-acre tract containing OAK, GRAVEL, and LONG LAKES. Five hundred acres are fenced to confine herds of elk, deer, and buffalo. Impure water in the lakes, caused by the recession of the water level, has necessitated the abandonment of the fish hatchery near Gravel Lake. In the MUSEUM across the road from the hatchery is a good mounted display of the game birds, fish, and wild animals of the Turtle Mountains.

LAKE UPSILON, 14.5 *m.*, is the largest lake on the eastern side of the mountains, named for its resemblance to the Greek letter 'Y.' It is one of the most attractive and most popular lakes of the Turtle Mountains group.

BELCOURT, 114 *m.* (1,619 alt., 6,650 pop., including Indian reservation), agency headquarters for the Turtle Mountain Indian Reservation, lies in a shallow valley on the southeastern border of the hills. It was named for the Reverend George Antoine Belcourt, a priest prominent in the establishment of the community. The Indians, about 95 per cent of whom are of mixed Chippewa Indian and French blood, make their homes in crude cabins on small farms out in the reservation. Academic and vocational training for the children is provided by the large consolidated school in Belcourt. The Chippewa are woods Indians who when first encountered by the whites dwelt in the region of the Great Lakes. From here they pressed W., often warring with their enemies the Sioux, until ultimately their hunting grounds included the Turtle Mountain region. With the white occupation of the West their range in North Dakota was reduced until finally it was limited to this small and crowded reservation of 72 square miles. (*See* INDIANS AND THEIR PREDECESSORS.)

Each year the Indians hold a sun dance (*June; approx. 5 m. NE. of Belcourt; no set date or place*). The ceremony lasts for several days. At the fairgrounds in Belcourt an Indian fair is conducted (*Oct.*).

Since 1896 the week of St. Ann has been the occasion of a retreat at Belcourt for the people of the mountains, for whom St. Ann is the patron saint. Many of the Indians bring their tipis in which they live during the retreat. The week is culminated with the feast of St. Ann (*July 26, if it falls on Sun. or on Sun. following that date*). On the feast day a procession is held, with hundreds participating. Many cures—none, however, authenticated by the Roman Catholic Church—have been attributed to the shrine at the Belcourt church.

DUNSEITH, 131 *m.* (1,715 alt., 719 pop.), scattered over level land at the edge of the Turtle Mountains, is the southern entrance to these hills. Its name means *city of peace* and was selected to honor the first white man in the vicinity and also the city of Dunseith in Scotland. The town is the terminus of a G. N. Ry. branch from the main line at York (*see Tour* 6).

The Dunseith Gristmill was built on Willow Creek in 1887 of lumber hauled from Devils Lake by ox teams. It continued to grind for several years after steam boilers and modern machinery had come into general use, but in 1913 it was damaged by fire and has never been repaired.

Dunseith may have a buried treasure somewhere in the foothills. In 1893 its Turtle Mountain Bank was robbed, and the robber had time to bury his loot in the hills before he was shot by a posse. The stolen money was never found, and the bank was forced to close.

At Dunseith is the Junction with ND 3, a bituminous highway.

Right on this highway to the junction with a bituminous road, 2 *m.*
Right on this road to SAN HAVEN, 0.5 *m.*, State tuberculosis sanatorium, situated in a 2500-acre game reserve on the southern slope of the mountains overlooking a vast expanse of prairie.
North from the junction with the paved road, ND 3 runs over ridges and

past little lakes, into the Turtle Mountains, whose hills are the habitat of hundreds of deer in addition to many varieties of song and game birds.

On ND 3 is the INTERNATIONAL PEACE GARDEN, 12.5 *m.*, a memorial to the peace that has prevailed between this country and Canada for more than 130 years. The garden lies partly in North Dakota and partly in Manitoba. On the international boundary stands a stone cairn with a plaque bearing a pledge of peace:

'To God in His Glory
We two Nations do pledge ourselves
That so long as men shall live
We will not take up arms against one another.'

A formal garden, one mile square, is being developed by the State of North Dakota and the province of Manitoba, with the aid of the U.S. government, on the International Line. It will center about a peace fountain around which a circular garden plot will form a visible ring of friendship between the two nations. The memorial has attracted wide attention because of its noble purpose, and several foreign countries have expressed a desire to aid in its development. It is rededicated with appropriate ceremonies each year (1st *wk. in Aug.*).

To the S. and W. of the hills and also in the northeastern section of the State a great number of the settlers were of Scottish descent, and each year in connection with the ceremonies at the Peace Garden a Highlanders' Frolic is held with old-fashioned Scotch music, dances, and games.

At 138 *m.* is the junction with a partly improved dirt road.

Right on this attractive road to BUTTE ST. PAUL PARK, 3 *m.*, plainly marked by Butte St. Paul (2500 alt.), highest point on the southern edge of the Turtle Mountains. A steep climb up the eastern slope leads to the 15-foot stone cairn commemorating the work of the Reverend G. A. Belcourt, missionary to the Indians, who on his first visit in 1853 placed a wooden cross where the cairn now stands. From the top of the butte a beautiful scene stretches away to the tree-covered plateau on the N. and E. and to the prairies on the S. and W.

BOTTINEAU, 149 *m.* (1,645 alt., 1,739 pop.), was named for Pierre Bottineau (*c.*1812–95), most noted of Dakota guides (*see* HISTORY). It lies beside tree-bordered OAK CREEK on a gently rolling plain. Most of its settlers were of Scottish descent, but the western end of the mountains was long nicknamed Little Norway, and until recent years Norwegian was heard there more often than English. From 1883–4 a stagecoach line connected the town with the nearest railroad point, Devils Lake (*see Tour* 6), 120 miles to the SE., whence settlers hauled supplies with oxen.

Originally Bottineau was situated a mile farther N. When the G. N. Ry. survey was made, it became evident that the permanent site would be farther S. Business houses were soon moved, but the Bottineau County Courthouse could not be legally moved without recourse to legislation. Accordingly, one morning the building was found reposing in the new settlement. As no one was supposed to know how the transfer had been effected, no one could be prosecuted, and the expense of returning the building to its former site provided a convenient and practical argument against that action.

A catastrophe long remembered by the early residents of Bottineau was a huge prairie fire in 1886 that swept 500 square miles of territory NW. of town, destroying hay and buildings.

The Indians of the region were not hostile to the white settlers, but there were Indian scares now and then, and the white men were inclined to be cautious. An old French settler living near Bottineau tells the story of being lost with two companions. They asked some Indians for directions, and were invited to a meal, which they accepted to avoid giving offense. They were almost enjoying the meal, when an old squaw, who had been stirring the stew which they had been eating, urged hospitably, 'Dig down deep; pup in bottom.'

The STATE SCHOOL OF FORESTRY, in the northeastern part of Bottineau on Oak Creek, offers a two-year junior college course in forestry. In the botanical garden or arboretum are about 30 varieties of foreign trees, obtained on a reciprocal basis from other countries, to be tried out in this climate. Plantings established under direction of the school are found on farms in every county in the State. The annual output of the nursery at the present time (1949) is over 500,000 seedlings.

At Bottineau is the junction with a graveled highway called the Lake Road, which leads NE. into the hills to Lake Metigoshe, one of the State's best-known summer resorts.

Right on this road, at the southern approach to the bridge over Oak Creek, to the junction with a trail, 1 m.

Left on this unusually delightful 5-mile trail, along the western bank of the creek. At about 0.5 m. is the junction with a less well-defined trail; L. here on the western side of the creek to a stone cairn marking the SITE OF THE FIRST WHITE MAN'S HOME IN BOTTINEAU COUNTY and the original site of the town of Bottineau, 1 m. Farther on the country becomes hilly, and at 2.3 m. a faint wagon trail leads R. through a wire gate down to the GORGE, a pleasant spot where the creek flows through a heavily wooded ravine, an excellent place for picnicking. Crossing the stream, the trail follows the eastern side of the creek back toward town. At 2.5 m. is the STATE GAME FARM, temporarily (1938) used as the Bottineau Country Club; here is a junction with the Lake Road (L) which may be followed S.; along the side of the creek, a much more attractive route, at 4 m. the trail joins the Lake Road following the creek to the CCC DAM, 4.3 m., just N. of the WILLOW VALE DAIRY FARM. Here the trail crosses to the western side of the stream and rejoins the trail on which it began.

Right on the Lake Road to the 675-acre LAKE METIGOSHE STATE PARK, 14.5 m. In the park lodge is the HENRY KLEBE COLLECTION (open) of Turtle Mountain fossils, Indian artifacts, and geologic formations.

Left on the Lake Road 15 m. to the center of activity on LAKE METIGOSHE, largest and scenically one of the most attractive of the Turtle Mountain lakes. It has 70 miles of shore line and extends across the border into Canada. Its name comes from metigoshe washegum (Chippewa, clear water lake surrounded by oaks). There are 6 resort parks (stores, hotels, cottages, bathing beaches, boat landings; 12-mile motorboat trip crosses into Canada, not permissible to land on Canadian side). About 1 mile from shore is MASONS' ISLAND, where Masonic groups hold annual summer meetings. The Congregational Conference of North Dakota has a summer Bible camp on the lake, and the Great Plains Area of the Boy Scouts of America holds an annual encampment here.

West of Bottineau the route proceeds over the extraordinarily level country formed by the bed of glacial Lake Souris. At 161 m. is the junction with ND 14, a graveled highway.

Left on this highway is KRAMER, 9 *m.* (1,460 alt., 220 pop.), believed to have been named for one of the surveyors of the Soo Ry., which passes through the town. The Kramer Equity Cooperative Elevator, with a capacity of 110,000 bu., all under one roof, is one of the largest co-operative elevators in the State.

Right from Kramer 2 *m.* on an improved county highway to a junction with a road; L. on this road to the junction with another road, 3 *m.*; R. here to the site of a former CCC CAMP, 4 *m.*, whose workers constructed dams on the Souris River and worked on the LOWER SOURIS MIGRATORY WATER-FOWL REFUGE, an area of 48,000 acres, largest project of the U. S. Fish and Wildlife Service in North Dakota and one of the most important refuges in the country.

At 13 *m.* on ND 14 the route crosses the Mouse, or Souris, River, remnant of Lake Souris. At 14.5 *m.* are the headquarters of the refuge, where the ADMINISTRATION BUILDINGS are. The 100-foot observation tower is used in studying bird life (*open, children must be accompanied by adults*).

UPHAM, 18 *m.* (1,461 alt., 243 pop.), is believed to have been named by the G. N. Ry. town-site company. Left from Upham at 22 *m.* on an improved county road to the largest dam on the lower Souris Refuge, with a retaining dike approximately 3 miles long.

At 165.5 *m.* the highway dips slightly and crosses the Souris River, here resembling a canal, and running almost bank full. At 175 *m.* is a junction with US 83; between this point and 192 *m.* the two roads coincide (*see Tour* 3).

MOHALL, 202 *m.* (1,646 alt., 687 pop.), seat of Renville County, was named for M. O. Hall, publisher of the first newspaper. Platted in 1903 as the terminus of the railroad, its growth for the first few months was rapid. The Renville County *Tribune* of December 3 of that year said that the G. N. Ry. agent estimated that during the preceding week 125 carloads of material had been shipped into the new town, in addition to 175 cars lying on sidetracks along the line and billed for Mohall. Four tracks were crowded with cars and eight dray lines were kept busy transferring the material to the lumberyards and points of construction. One hundred and seventy-five carpenters were employed, and then the demand was only half met. At that time the place had nine grain buyers.

Dick Grace, motion-picture stunt flier, lived here for a time.

At 205 *m.* the route passes between two farms lighted by natural gas from wells drilled on the premises. Although natural gas in large quantities has been found in Montana, and a number of small wells have been opened in North Dakota, there has never been a sufficient amount in this State to form the basis for a permanent commercial enterprise.

At 214 *m.* the route leads down into the mile-wide Souris valley. The stream here is lined with box elder, elm, and small fruit trees.

At 215 *m.* is the junction with a graveled county road.

Right on this road to the 480-acre MOUSE RIVER PARK (*boating, swimming, roller skating, golf; store, dining hall, auditorium, cottages*), 2 *m.*

At 228 *m.* is a junction with US 52, a bituminous highway, which unites with ND 5 between this point and 257 *m.* (*see Tour* 7).

At 258 *m.* is the junction with a graveled county highway.

Left on this road is LIGNITE, 1 *m.* (1,979 alt., 235 pop.), which was to have been named Kincaid, for an agent of the G. N. Ry., but through an error of the town-site company was given the name intended for the neighboring town, a lignite mining center, which was consequently named Kincaid.

At 8 *m.* BIG BUTTE (2200 alt.), a large grassy hill, covers about two sections of land, rising more than 200 feet above the surrounding prairie. At the foot of the butte was once a spring of excellent water, frequented by Indians passing along the old White Earth Trail from the Turtle Mountains to the Missouri River. Circles of stone and Indian mounds are found on the northern side of the butte. In early days there was a ranch with 300 head of horses near the spring, but the owner lost all his stock to smugglers. Somewhere in the vicinity of Big Butte may be the hiding place of $40,000. A story, not generally credited, relates that in the late 1870's a Hudson's Bay Company paymaster, on his way to pay employees of the company at the several trading posts in the territory, was robbed of this amount near Estevan, Canada. The robber was apprehended in the neighborhood of Big Butte, but not before he had found a place to cache his loot. Taken to Portal, he died under torture while an attempt was being made to force his secret from him. On the tanned side of his fur coat was found a diagram believed to show the hiding place of the treasure, which has since been the object of many searches. The accidental unearthing of a stone bearing the inscription '1877' inspired fresh digging. At another time the Royal Mounted Police of Calgary are said to have sent men to the locality in an attempt to recover the money. So far, however, all efforts have proved unsuccessful. Some believe the treasure was found and taken away; others think it is still in the vicinity of Big Butte; and a few skeptics disdain the idea that it was ever buried here at all.

At 268 *m.* is the junction with a graveled road.

Right on this road is COLUMBUS, 0.5 *m.* (1,930 alt., 506 pop.), clumped together on the flat prairie. First settled in 1902, it was moved to the railroad in 1906 when the Soo Ry. was extended through this part of the State. The first postmaster, Columbus Larson, gave his Christian name to this town, and his surname to the next town W.

At 269 *m.* is a junction with ND 40, a graveled highway, which unites with ND 5 to 279 *m.*

Left on this highway 3 *m.* to a junction with an improved road; R. here to the MONTANA-DAKOTA POWER PLANT, 2 *m.*, in the heart of the lignite coal field. The plant was opened in 1928, and today is a $300,000 enterprise, supplying electrical energy to the towns of northeastern Montana and northwestern North Dakota.

At 4 *m.* on ND 40 is a junction with a second improved road; L. here to the TRUAX-TRAER LIGNITE STRIP MINE, 4.5 *m.*, the oldest strip mine in North Dakota. The big shovels that have been stripping the earth overburden since 1919 have piled ridges of earth so vast that they resemble miniature mountains. The eight-cubic-yard shovel saw service in the construction of the Panama Canal. It is supplemented by another of four-cubuc-yard capacity. About 150,000 tons of coal are taken out annually. Huddled on a small piece of unbroken ground between the artificial buttes are the frame homes and store buildings of the little community of miners.

At 273 *m.* is the junction with a graveled spur.

Left on this road is LARSON, 0.5 *m.* (1,931 alt., 79 pop.), a small Scandinavian town, named for the first postmaster of Columbus.

West of Larson the route ascends the hills of the Missouri Plateau. At 278 *m.* is the junction with a graveled road.

Left on this road to the BAUKOL-NOONAN COAL MINE, 1 *m.*, third largest lignite strip mine in the State. The mining operations cover an area of 1,040 acres adjacent to the town of Noonan, and the lignite vein, which lies beneath a 30-foot overburden, averages 7 to 9 feet in thickness. The huge, molehill-like hummocks of earth tossed up by the giant steam shovels spread fanwise from a central, electrically operated tipple. Loading and screening facilities at the tipple permit the filling of four cars at the same time, each with a different grade of coal. During 1948 more than 230,000 tons of coal were taken out.

NOONAN, 279 *m.* (1,959 alt., 520 pop.), named for an early settler, has its white buildings scattered over the northern slope of a small hill. When the town was platted in 1906, contracts stipulated that buildings should be painted white in order that the community might live up to its advertised name of the *White City*.

CROSBY, 293 *m.* (1,962 alt., 1,404 pop.), dominated by the dome of the Divide County Courthouse at the northern end of Main St., was named for a member of the town-site company of Portal (*see Tour* 7). It sprang up at the junction of the Soo and G.N. branch lines, a strategic rail position that soon established it as a focal point for trade in the northwestern corner of the State.

Straight ahead (N.) from the fairgrounds on a graveled road to the CROSBY CITY RECREATION PARK (*swimming pool, golf course, tennis and horse-shoe courts, ski jump, camping ground*), 5 *m.*, developed along the Canadian border.

At 301 *m.* an improved road (old US 85) branches R.

AMBROSE, 3 *m.* (2,060 alt., 294 pop.), on this road, named for a Soo Line right-of-way employee, in its early history was one of the greatest primary grain markets in the Northwest. With 5 elevators, and many hawkers buying on the track, as many as 300 grain wagons often crowded the streets, sometimes remaining several days before they could deliver their loads. Before the railway was extended W. of Ambrose, the town was a shipping point for horses, sheep, and cattle from the ranch country of eastern Montana and western North Dakota. Ambrose has two parks and a swimming pool.

At 311 *m.* is a junction with US 85 (*see Tour* 4), which unites with ND 5 to 313 *m.*

At 328 *m.* the route crosses the Montana Line, 69 *m.* E. of Scobey, Montana.

Tour 5A

Junction ND 5—Walhalla—Leroy; ND 32, ND 55, and an unimproved road.
Junction ND 5 to Leroy, 25 *m.*

Branch of G. N. Ry. touches at Walhalla.
Graveled roadbed.
Accommodations in Walhalla.

This route runs through the Pembina Mountains, a scenic region rich in historical associations. From Walhalla, one of the oldest towns in the State, the route turns east to the settlement of the metis, descendants of those French-Chippewa who conducted the famous Pembina hunts of the middle nineteenth century.

ND 32 branches N. from ND 5 at Oak Lawn Historic Site (*see Tour* 5), 0.0 *m.*

At 8 *m.* the graceful wooded PEMBINA MOUNTAINS are visible on the horizon. The nearest elevation, 250 or 350 feet higher than the country to the E., is known as Second Pembina Mountain and is a portion of the Pembina Escarpment, a high ridge extending from Canada through North Dakota into South Dakota and southwestern Minnesota. In the southern part of North Dakota it is known as the Coteau des Prairies. First Pembina Mountain, lying SE. of Second Mountain, is the prehistoric delta of the Pembina River, formed when that stream drained the melting ice sheet into Lake Agassiz (*see* NATURAL SETTING *and Tour* 1). First Pembina Mountain has an average height of 150 feet, and its eastern edge shows the various shore lines of Lake Agassiz as it receded in post-glacial times.

To the first white explorers and trappers the Pembina Mountains were known as the Hair Hills, coveted hunting ground held by the Chippewa, whose ownership was often hotly contested by the Sioux. During the early nineteenth century, white and half-breed hunters roamed the hills, gathering furs to be loaded on lumbering, squeaking oxcarts and sent to eastern trading posts.

It was in this vicinity that Charles Cavileer (*see Tour* 5), one of the most prominent settlers of the State, in the 1860's while making a trip with a party from Pembina to Devils Lake, saw a herd of buffalo like a black cloud on the horizon. The party immediately arranged their carts in a semicircle and prepared for an onslaught. The bison came on with a rumble like thunder, the rumble became a roar, and the earth trembled; but when they reached the carts the herd parted and swerved on either side, upsetting only the outside row of the improvised stock-ade. Not until the second day could the journey be resumed, and even then there were buffalo in sight for another day. The herd was believed to number two or three million, and in its wake was an area, several miles in width, entirely devoid of vegetation.

At 9 *m.* (L) are the SAND SLIDES, where steep sand and gravel slopes form a precipitous funnel-shaped valley down to the PEMBINA RIVER. This stream once drained prehistoric Lake Souris into Lake Agassiz, and its rushing waters cut into the Pembina Mountains, creating the present canyon 350 to 450 feet deep.

At 12 *m.* (R) is WALHALLA (966 alt., 1,138 pop.), attractively situated in the wooded river valley on the slope of Second Pembina Mountain. In 1848 Father G. A. Belcourt established St. Joseph's Mission here for the Chippewa Indians. By 1860 the settlement had become an important fur trading post, with a population of 1800; but good furs became scarce, the bison virtually disappeared, and by 1871 'St. Joe' was inhabited only by a priest, the U.S. customs inspector, and some 50 metis or half-breeds, who remained only as long as the hunting was good. The town revived and was platted in 1877 and renamed Walhalla, for the palace of immortality in Norse mythology.

The old bell in the Catholic church belfry, known as the ANGELUS BELL, was brought to Father Belcourt's mission when it was opened, and was the first church bell erected on the plains of North Dakota. It was cast in 1845, and a wreath of raised figures around the top represents science, art, music, mechanics, and astronomy. The bell is believed to have been brought down the Red River by boat, thence to St. Joseph by oxcart. Its tone is similar to that of the old mission bells of California.

Right from Walhalla crossing the railroad tracks on a graveled road; L. on a graveled road to a METIS SETTLEMENT, 4 *m.* Here, in the foothills of the Pembina Mountains, live descendants of half-breed French Canadians and Indians of earlier days. The metis are found throughout the northeastern corner of North Dakota (*see below*). In this particular settlement they operate small farms, gaining their livelihood by selling garden produce, berries, and cordwood. The graveled road turns L. at 5 *m.*, to Leroy (*see below*), 7 *m.*

Also at 12 *m.* is WALHALLA STATE PARK (L), on the eastern slope of the Pembina Mountains. The wooded 5-acre tract contains the SITE OF ALEXANDER HENRY, JR.'S TRADING POST, a temporary depot established in 1801, one of the first posts in present North Dakota; also the KITTSON HOUSE, erected in 1851–2 as a trading post and warehouse under the supervision of Norman Kittson, who became the first postmaster in North Dakota. This building was originally built near by and was moved to the park in 1915. Often locally designated as Old Settlers' Park, the area is the scene of the annual meeting and picnic of the Pembina County Old Settlers' Association (*July*).

Left from the park on a winding graveled road to the PROTESTANT CEMETERY, 0.4 *m.*, where are buried two missionaries killed by Indians in the early 1850's and hence known as the Martyrs of St. Joe. At 1.4 *m.*, at the summit of the mountain, LOOKOUT POINT affords a fine view of the deep Pembina River valley below and the Red River Valley farming area, dotted with villages and farmhouses, which stretches away in the distance. The point is the property of several Masonic lodges in this area, and they hold an annual picnic here.

At 15 *m.* on ND 32 is the junction with ND 55, on which the route continues. At 22 *m.* is the junction with a graveled road. After crossing the Pembina River, the highway at 25 *m.* enters LEROY (890 alt., 100 pop.). The inhabitants of the town are chiefly metis, and their log cabins are scattered in the timber along the river. From the time the Hudson's Bay Company began operations in 1670, French Canadians migrated westward, intermarrying with Chippewa women. Their children were known as metis or mixed-bloods. Inheriting the characteristics of both the Indian and the French-Canadian woodsman, the metis became adept *voyageurs,* and their part in the early fur trade of the Middlewest was very important. They were excellent hunters, trappers, and couriers, and it is said they loved the 'musical' sound of the Red River oxcarts, which, with their unlubricated wooden axles and hubs screeching across the plains, brought furs E. from the trading posts.

When this region began to be settled the metis were the first mail carriers, since their stamina and knowledge of the frontier made them 'brave and bold, and the most reliable men to be had.'

The early metis of North Dakota, ancestors of the present metis, enjoyed life with true appreciation. They were fond of good dress, and their clothes were made of the finest imported merinos, cashmeres, and broadcloths, bought at the trading posts. The men wore black broadcloth redingotes, long and double-breasted and trimmed with large brass buttons. At the collar was a *capuchon* or hood, which was never worn but served merely as an adornment. A bright sash about the waist, beaded moccasins, and a beaded tobacco pouch, used much as a French courtier used his snuff box, completed the costume. The women wore the tight basque and flowing skirt, and, in summer as well as winter, a half-dozen gaily colored petticoats, which created quite a dazzling array when the wearer stooped to tie the lace of a beaded moccasin. A black silk kerchief was tied about the head, and over this went a large square of black broadcloth which wrapped about the entire body and served as a cloak.

The metis were, and still are, fond of music and dancing. Their songs came down from their French ancestors or were learned from the mission priests. One favorite was *Au clair de la lune* (*By Moonlight*) and another was *Marlbrouck s'en va-t-en guerre* (*Marlborough Goes to War*). Square dances, the Red River Jig, Pair O' Fours, and Reel O' Cats were favorite dances, and some of them are still performed.

The most important event in the year for the metis, in the first half of the last century, was the Pembina buffalo hunt. For this, white and metis hunters would meet at Pembina on an expedition that sometimes took them as far as Fort Union on the Missouri (*see Tour 6B*). Not only men but also women and children went on the hunt, and even the priest went along to counsel and advise. Equipment was carried in stridently creaking oxcarts. It was like a good-sized town on a tour. On the hunt of 1840, probably the largest ever held, there were 1,630 people and 1,210 oxcarts, and the cost of the expedition has been estimated at $120,000. The camp was organized under a chief, with 10 captains under him, and 10 soldiers under each captain to enforce the camp regulations. For a first violation the saddle and bridle of the offender were cut up; for a second, his coat was destroyed; and for a third, he was flogged. A thief, even if he stole something of no greater value than a buffalo sinew—a common article of barter in the Red River country—was publicly cried 'thief.' Hunting was not always good; hot weather or storms delayed parties, and sometimes prairie fires were encountered. Eventually encroaching civilization put an end to the buffalo hunts, but while they were held, and when they were successful, the hunters lived in plenty. The 1840 expedition took home more than a million pounds of meat in their oxcarts.

The main food of the early metis was pemmican, or dried buffalo meat, but wild game was also plentiful. *Galette,* an unleavened bread made by mixing flour with water, salt, and shortening, was preferred to white man's bread.

Great respect for old age and deep affection for relatives characterize metis family relationships. Concerning birds and animals, they have many unusual beliefs: a hungry beast coming to the door is regarded as a sign of poverty, a woodpecker pecking at a window is said to be a sign of death in the family, and snakes are believed to be symbols of quarrels and enemies.

✿✿

Tour 6

(Duluth, Minn.)—Grand Forks—Devils Lake—Minot—Williston—(Glasgow, Mont.); US 2.
Minnesota Line to Montana Line, 367 *m.*

G. N. Ry. roughly parallels entire route.
Entire route paved or hard-surfaced.
Accommodations in principal towns.

This route reveals a cross section of the agricultural life of the State. In the east the flat, fertile lands of the narrow Red River Valley, which formed the bottom of glacial Lake Agassiz, blend into the uneven, farm-dotted surface of the broad Drift Prairie, bordered on the west by the rougher, more sparsely settled grazing areas of the Missouri Plateau. The route touches on Devils Lake and crosses the level loop of the wooded Mouse River, a region at one time covered by Lake Souris, another extinct creation of the glacial epoch. Midway across the State is the geographic center of North America. The western half of the route is through a rich, though largely undeveloped, lignite coal area, formed ages ago by the inundation of prehistoric forests.

GRAND FORKS, 0.0 *m.* (834 alt., 20,228 pop.) (*see* GRAND FORKS).

At Demers Ave. and 5th St. is a junction with US 81 (*see Tour* 1), which unites with US 2 to the intersection of Skidmore Ave. N. and N. 16th St.

West of Grand Forks US 2 passes through the western half of the Red River Valley, part of the bed of ancient Lake Agassiz.

At 9 *m.* is the junction with a county dirt road.

Left on this road to tiny OJATA, 1 *m.*, the remains of a once-thriving boom town known as Stickney. In its heyday it was a railroad terminus and for a time rivaled Grand Forks in trade. Since the site is swampland, each heavy rain makes it a quagmire, and residents, considering the first name too literal, soon changed it to Ojata. The place declined when the railroad was extended W. At one time a farmer acquired the entire village in exchange for a stallion.

At 22.5 *m.* is the junction with a county graveled road.

Right on this road to TURTLE RIVER STATE PARK (*swimming, picnicking, camping*), ½ *m.*, where a picturesque ravine, cut by the once swift-flowing waters of the TURTLE RIVER, offers a pleasing variation to the level surrounding country. The river is named for the many small terrapin found on its banks. Just W. of the entrance are 15 tumuli (mounds) built by prehistoric Indians. Excavations by Dr. A. E. Jenks of the University of Minnesota have yielded copper instruments, an ivory pipe, and other artifacts. Unlike the mounds in other parts of the State (*see Tours 8A and 8B*), these have been plowed over and cultivated until they are only small humps on the prairie. The few tumuli opened have been easily excavated because they lie in a gravel deposit.

Right on this road to ARVILLA (1,019 alt., 60 pop.), 1 *m.*, named for the wife of a bonanza farmer. The Arvilla Academy and North Dakota Conservatory of Music, the first private college in the State to maintain a music department, was founded in 1886 by Reverend John Allen Brown, Presbyterian pastor at Arvilla. Miss Sadie P. Brown, daughter of the founder, and a graduate of the Boston Conservatory of Music, headed the music department. The existence of the academy was brief, for the building was destroyed by fire in 1893 and was never rebuilt.

The CRYSTAL SPRINGS STOCK FARM, 24 *m.*, consisting of 2,480 acres along the Turtle River, was a bonanza farm and then a stock farm, but now is known for the spring water bottled here for commercial purposes. In its early days the 20-room house, now dismantled, was the scene of a social life that rivaled the surrounding bonanza acres in expansiveness and amplitude. H. T. Hersey, a Minnesota millionaire, became interested in wheat farming and built the house. His wife installed a full staff of servants, and many parties were held for eastern friends. On several occasions James J. Hill stopped his special train here to visit the Herseys, and once a special train carrying members of the State legislature stopped while its passengers were entertained at this prairie palace. Eventually Hersey tired of his role of gentleman farmer and sold his farm to James Streeter, prominent Larimore real estate dealer and farmer.

At 27 *m.* US 2 unites with ND 18 as far as 31 *m.*

L. on ND 18, from the first junction, at 2.5 *m.* is LARIMORE (1,135 alt., 1,222 pop.), named for N. D. Larimore, stockholder and business head of the Elk River Valley Farm, which was once the world's largest farm under single management. Most of the bonanza farms were divided into a number of tracts, each under a foreman, but the Elk River Valley Farm had all operations centralized. Its huge proportions attracted the St. Louis World's Fair Foreign Commission, which visited the farm in 1904, at which time there were 11,000 acres under cultivation. From this visit a great influx of northern Europeans resulted, leading to the breaking up of the bonanza farms and the sale of small farms to the new settlers.

The CITY PARK (*wading pool, tennis courts, tourist camp*) is in the same block as the city hall.

At 33 *m.* the highway crosses the Turtle River, near a dam built by the Civilian Conservation Corps (*swimming, picnic grounds*).

McCANNA, 36 *m.* (1,142 alt., 100 pop.), was named for S. A. McCanna, owner of the McCANNA FARM (R), now the largest in the western part of Grand Forks County. Large modern buildings adjacent to the town on the NW., and the use of modern farm methods make it one of the show places in the area.

NIAGARA, 44 *m.* (1,443 alt., 179 pop.), was named for Niagara County, N. Y. Because of uncertainty where the railroad would pass, the town was first built on skids 1 mile E. of the present site, and was moved when the railroad came in 1882.

PETERSBURG, 49 *m.* (1,524 alt., 285 pop.), named for a pioneer clergyman in the community, has a population predominantly Norwegian, as has MICHIGAN CITY, 57.5 *m.* (1,520 alt., 491 pop.), platted on land of the James Lamb family, who were among early arrivals in the vicinity and have continued to be prominent in local affairs. The town was named in honor of the native State of many of its first settlers. In the early 1880's an error in billing sent here an entire trainload of iron ore intended for Michigan City, Indiana. The village officially retains its original name, but local usage has abridged this to 'Michigan.'

MAPES, 60 *m.* (1,530 alt.), once a prosperous grain-shipping center, was named for Emery Mapes, one of the men who worked out the formula for the nationally known Cream of Wheat.

At 67 *m.* is the junction with ND 1, a graveled highway (*see Tour 8B*).

LAKOTA, 67 *m.* (1,518 alt., 907 pop.), is the seat of Nelson County. Its name is derived from the Teton Sioux word meaning *allies,* which is the same as the Santee Sioux *dakota.* The many trees lining Lakota's streets are the result of experiments by a pioneer who believed trees could be grown on the barren prairies. The TOFTHAGEN LIBRARY AND MUSEUM (*open*), built in 1927, was a gift to the city from A. M. Tofthagen, Nelson County pioneer. It contains over 5000 volumes, and curios gathered by the donor in his travels.

BARTLETT, 71 *m.* (1,534 alt., 78 pop.), was named for Frank Bartlett of Larimore, who owned the town site. For a time Bartlett was the end of the rail line, a typical boom town, and had 21 saloons; one, the Diamond, employed a Negro piano player and singer who usually ended his performance in a burst of 'Bartlett, dear Bartlett, will be a dandy of Dakota yet.'

DOYON, 77 *m.* (1,512 alt., 150 pop.), was named for Charles H. Doyon, a bonanza farmer.

DEVILS LAKE, 95 *m.* (1,466 alt., 6,204 pop.), seat of Ramsey County, was at one time head of steamboat navigation on the then important inland sea of Devils Lake (*see Tour 6A*). The lake has receded 5 miles in the half century since the vicinity was settled, and the town now overlooks a dry bed and shrunken shore line. Fort Totten, which later became Fort Totten Indian Agency (*see Tour 6A*), was established on the southern shore of the lake in 1867 to place the Indians of the region on a permanent reservation. In 1882 the Government held that the Chippewa Indians had no claim to the lands N. of the lake, settlers began to come in, and Creelsburgh, or Creel City, 4 miles NW. of the present site of Devils Lake, became the first white community in the area. The town of Devils Lake was founded the following year and many Creel City citizens moved to the new town site.

One of the first settlers in Creel City was Captain Edward Heerman, who inaugurated steamboat navigation on Devils Lake. On July 4, 1883, the first train on regular schedule arrived in Devils Lake and was met by Heerman's steamboat, the *Minnie H.* The service was later augmented by two smaller steamers. Rails were laid on the wharf at Devils Lake so that all freight and passengers for Fort Totten, Minnewaukan, and other points across the lake were transferred directly from car to steamer. By 1909, however, the water of the lake had receded 4 miles from the city, 6 miles from Minnewaukan, and nearly 2.5 miles from the fort, so navigation came to an end. The shrinking of Devils Lake has been one of the arguments for the Missouri River Diversion project, which, it has been asserted, would raise the water level of the lake.

The STATE SCHOOL FOR DEAF is at 14th St. and 1st Ave., situated in expertly landscaped grounds. Established in 1890, the school has gained international recognition for its work in physical education for the deaf. An elaborate revue, known as a Rhythm Pageant (*public, June*), is presented annually at the school's graduation exercises, and motion pictures of this pageant have been made for study in similar institutions elsewhere.

At the eastern end of 2nd St. is the I.O.O.F. HOME, maintained by the North Dakota Grand Lodge of the Odd Fellows for its aged members and orphans of former members. It is a three-story brick building surrounded by landscaped yard and gardens.

The WORLD WAR MEMORIAL BUILDING, 504 4th St., is a community recreation center. Studios and transmitter of KDLR are in the Grayson Hotel building at the cor. 5th Ave. and 7th St.

At the W. end of 5th St. is the junction of ND 20, a graveled highway (see Tour 6A) and ND 19. Right at this junction is ROOSEVELT PARK (swimming pool, picnicking, camping), built as a WPA project.

North of Devils Lake ND 20 passes SWEETWATER LAKE, 9 m., a large body of fresh water that attracted pioneers.

CHURCHS FERRY, 114 m. (1,460 alt., 244 pop.), developed from a ferry established by Irvine Church across Mauvaise Coulee (Fr., bad streambed) in 1886, so named by French explorers because it was difficult to cross, the channel once drained a large territory into Devils Lake to the S. Although it has been dry for several years, in the 1870's and 1880's, until Church began his ferry, all goods for the area NW. and W. of Devils Lake had to be boated across or hauled around the southern shore of the lake.

Here is the junction with US 281, a graveled and bituminous-surfaced highway (see Tour 2), which unites with US 2 from this point to 115 m.

LEEDS, 125 m. (1,514 alt., 782 pop.), with a predominantly Scandinavian population, was established in 1884. It has paved streets and a park (swimming pool). Because many stockholders in the G. N. Ry. were Englishmen, several of the towns along the railroad, including Leeds, were given names of English towns. One of the first newspapers in this region, the Leeds News, founded in 1903, boosting the new community in the customary manner, lauded it with this characteristic humor: 'A man died and entered heaven. On his first walk about his new abode he noticed several men fettered in ball and chain. His inquiry of a passer-by brought the reply, "They came from Leeds, North Dakota, and if they weren't chained they'd go back." '

Left from Leeds on a county dirt road to LAKE IBSEN, 2 m., named for Henrik Ibsen, Norwegian poet and dramatist. It is said that about 1858 a peace agreement between the Sioux and Chippewa Indians was made at this lake, a treaty well observed by both tribes. Small islands in the lake were known to explorers of the region as Petites Isles Aux Mortes (Fr. small islands of the dead), owing to the fact that the Indians had buried many victims of a devastating smallpox epidemic here. They placed their dead on scaffolds, the wooden frames of which were visible from the lake shores.

YORK, 131 m. (1,612 alt., 325 pop.), is another town with an English name and a predominantly Scandinavian population.

KNOX, 137 m. (1,605 alt., 189 pop.), is named for John Knox, the Scottish religious reformer.

PLEASANT LAKE (good.camping, tourist accommodations, spring water), 142 m., is a small tree-fringed body of water which was called

Broken Bones Lake by the Indians who camped on its shores to dry their buffalo meats. They broke the buffalo bones to remove the marrow, which they sewed into sacks of skin and preserved for winter use. Evidences of an Indian burial ground are found on a hill to the N. These burials are not in mounds, and the only excavations are those made accidentally by farmers plowing the land.

At 143 *m.* is the railway station of PLEASANT LAKE (1,603 alt., 35 pop.), where tribal dances were performed on the town site by a group of Indians as recently as 1883. Some of the settlers feared that the ritual was a war dance, but the Indians did no harm.

At 151 *m.* is the junction with ND 3, a graveled and bituminous-surfaced highway. At this crossroads is a stone cairn marking the GEOGRAPHIC CENTER OF NORTH AMERICA. In 1931 the U.S. Geological Survey determined that the geographic center of the continent is in Pierce County, and the marker at the junction is in the approximate center of the county. The survey states, 'The geographic center of an area may be defined as that point on which the surface of the area would balance if it were a plane of uniform thickness, or in other words, the center of gravity of the surface. . . It would not be feasible, therefore, to specify for such a large irregular area as that of North America the exact section, township and range in which the geographic center lies.' Some years before 1931 Pierre, South Dakota, claimed to be the approximate center of the continent, based on the fact that two lines drawn from corner to corner of a map of North America intersected near Pierre.

Right on ND 3 is RUGBY, 1 *m.* (1,562 alt., 2,215 pop.), Pierce County seat, named for Rugby, England. It was platted in July 1885 and the first train arrived a month later. In the CITY HALL is a museum (*open weekdays, 9–5*) containing, among other things, Indian artifacts found in the county and Spanish-American War relics. ELLERY PARK and the tourist camp are in the western part of town. Rugby was the home of the late N. P. Lindberg, who is said to have originated the slogan, *Say It with Flowers*. It is said that in the course of a talk made at a national florists' convention in Chicago he remarked, 'In North Dakota we say it with flowers.' His words caught the fancy of his fellow delegates, who adopted them as a slogan.

TUNBRIDGE, 162 *m.* (1,509 alt.), and BERWICK, 174.5 *m.* (1,484 alt., 92 pop.), are small hamlets R. of the route. Although the latter town has a name of English origin, the Berwick *Post,* which suspended publication several years ago, was published partly in German for the large community of Russo-Germans living S. of the town.

TOWNER, 170 *m.* (1,478 alt., 918 pop.), named for Colonel O. M. Towner, one of the first ranchers in McHenry County, is the county seat. It lies in a bend of the SOURIS (Fr., *mouse*) RIVER, so named by French explorers for the numerous field mice found in the river basin. The river itself lies on a level plain that was at one time the bed of glacial Lake Souris, of which the stream is now the only remnant. Fully three fourths of McHenry County is on this plain, once principally cattle country, now devoted to diversified farming.

During ranching days in the 1880's the country was a rough frontier populated by an odd assortment of personalities. Among these were two English peers, each of whom acquired a ranch near Towner, built a large home, and settled down to the serious business of living lavishly on remittances from home. The community was excited when one of the men had a visit from his sister, a countess prominent in women's suffrage work in the British Isles, who arrived on a special train. The other exile also had a caller from home, an elderly woman who arrived unexpectedly to find him occupied with the entertainment of a houseful of guests. She departed without seeing him or even getting out of her carriage. Not long afterwards both Englishmen took their leave.

Towner is the junction with ND 14, a graveled highway, which unites with US 2 between this point and 174 *m.*

1. Left from Towner on a graveled county road to the SCHULTZ HERE-FORD RANCH, 1.8 *m.*, where registered Hereford cattle and Belgian horses are bred. Situated on the timber-flanked banks of the Mouse, the ranch has an air of early-day friendliness. Its huge barns and corrals reflect the large-scale ranching of pioneer days joined with the efficiency of a modern business—a combination typical of the present-day stock raising industry in the State.

2. Right (N) from Towner on a graveled county road to a GOVERNMENT NURSERY, 1.5 *m.*, where experimental work in connection with the shelterbelt project is conducted.

3. Right from Towner on ND 14 is BANTRY, 14 *m.* (1,469 alt., 150 pop.). Left from Bantry on ND 17, a graveled highway, to the LONG TURKEY RANCH, 20.5 *m.* At the age of six weeks the young turkeys are sent out on the 320-acre range in flocks of 700, and attain their full bone growth during the summer months. A few weeks before fall marketing the flocks are driven in to the ranch and the birds confined in large pens where they are fattened for market. More than 2000 turkeys are shipped from the Long ranch annually.

At 174 *m.* is a junction with ND 14.

Left on this graveled highway to the junction with a dirt road, 1.5 *m.*; R. here to the EATON DAM, 3.3 *m.*, which irrigates 6800 acres of meadowland. This water adds to the productivity of the heavy native grasses from which many hundreds of tons of hay are cut each year. At the close of the haying season the river bottoms are dotted with hundreds of small, moundlike haystacks resembling huge grain shocks in a field of giant wheat. In the time between haying and fall the grasses attain a second growth and cover the meadowlands around the stacks with a luxurious green carpet that contrasts with the dingy brown of the autumnal stubblefields through which the Souris courses.

At 183 *m.* (L) are the DENBIGH REFORESTATION PROJECT HEADQUARTERS. The feasibility of growing trees in poor, sandy soil and semi-arid climate is being tested on a 640-acre tract by the Northern Plains branch of the Lake States Forest Experimental Station. The results secured will serve as a guide for work in similar areas of other States.

GRANVILLE, 192 *m.* (1,513 alt., 443 pop.), named for Granville M. Dodge, G. N. Ry. civil engineer, is in a level agricultural area W. of the sand hills bordering the Mouse River. A condition common in homesteading days drew this worried comment from the Granville

Record in 1904: 'It is a great wonder this country has advanced and is developing as rapidly as it is with so many old bachelors who do not improve their places and so many old maids holding down claims. It ought to cause a blush of shame to mount the face of every bald-headed old bachelor in the vicinity.'

At 201 *m.* is NORWICH (1,529 alt., 40 pop.), named by the G. N. Ry. town-site company for an English town.

West of SURREY, 208 *m.* (1,627 alt., 250 pop.), the route begins the gradual descent to a second crossing of the Mouse River. In the distance to the W. and S. of the river, the hills rise to the Missouri Plateau.

MINOT, 216 *m.* (1,557 alt., 16,577 pop.) (*see* MINOT).

At Valley St. and 4th Ave. SE. is the junction with US 52 (*see Tour* 7), which unites with US 2 until 222 *m.* At 4th Ave. and 2nd St. SW. is the junction with US 83 (*see Tour* 3).

Just W. of Minot is the (L) HIGH STEEL TRESTLE (120 ft.) of the G. N. Ry., spanning Gassman Coulee. Early one morning in the 1880's a high wind blew down the wooden bridge which then stood here, and only the quick work of an engineer prevented an entire train from plunging into the deep coulee.

At 222 *m.* is the junction with US 52 (*see Tour* 7). A large tourist camp is L. The highway here makes an abrupt ascent to the level Missouri Plateau.

All towns along the route W. of Minot are populated principally by Scandinavians.

DES LACS, 231 *m.* (1,932 alt., 197 pop.), is named for Des Lacs River and Lake (*see Tour* 7). The little town received publicity in 1922 when it elected a complete ticket of women officials. One eastern newspaper wrote a glowing description of a campaign torchlight parade around the city hall and told of the enthusiasm which the men of the town felt over the winning ticket; but a writer for a women's magazine, sent out to look over the situation, was forced to report that there was no city hall, and that 'the men were not so enthusiastic now, perhaps because they did not like to have their own backyards cleaned up.'

LONETREE, 237 *m.* (2,002 alt., 70 pop.), was named by the railroad company for the one tree that was there when the rails were laid. This little town figured prominently in the Burlington-Minot battle for the seat of 'Imperial Ward' County in 1888, turning the election for Minot (*see* MINOT).

BERTHOLD, 239 *m.* (2,089 alt., 428 pop.), is the center of a certified seed potato raising area. In the late 1880's it was the nearest railhead to Fort Berthold on the Indian reservation to the S., hence its name.

At 248 *m.* the terrain becomes more rolling and from here to the Missouri River the route traverses the ALTAMONT MORAINE, a range of hills lying on the eastern portion of the Missouri Plateau, and marking the farthest advance of the western lobe of the last or Dakota Glacier.

TAGUS, 251 *m*. (2,189 alt., 140 pop.), was named for a rancher named Taguson.

Left from Tagus on an unimproved dirt road to CARPENTER LAKE (*swimming*), 6 *m*.

BLAISDELL (L), 259 *m*. (2,264 alt., 100 pop.), was named for Alfred Blaisdell, a settler who later became secretary of state of North Dakota.

PALERMO (L), 266 *m*. (2,201 alt., 178 pop.), is the namesake of a city in Sicily.

Right from Palermo in the rolling hills of the glacial moraine N. and E. of the town are several small lakes containing heavy deposits of sodium sulphate (*see Tour 4A*).

STANLEY, 274 *m*. (2,253 alt., 1,058 pop.), is named for one of the first homesteaders in the area. The MOUNTRAIL COUNTY COURTHOUSE (R), topped by a cupola, is at the northern end of town. Stanley is on a nearly level plateau, while both to the N. and to the S. the terrain is more rolling. There is a junction here with ND 8, a graveled highway (*see Tour 3A*). In 1906 the Stanley *Sun*, a usually conservative newspaper, joined other papers in the State in telling of the wonderful fertility of North Dakota soil: '. . . the most productive soil on earth, insomuch that if you stick a nail in the ground at night, it will grow into a crowbar before morning.'

ROSS, 282 *m*. (2,292 alt., 5 pop.), was named by the railway company. In 1902 a group of 20 Moslem families from Damascus, Syria, filed on homesteads SE. of Ross, and since 1909, when the Federal Government withdrew its objection to their naturalization, many of them have become citizens. They are Americanized in dress, although the women have a penchant for highly colored clothes. Many Old Country foods are still used; one Syrian dish especially well-liked consists of durum wheat boiled, sun-dried, ground, and screened, and stewed with meats and vegetables or sweet oils. The dried grain is ground in a large horse-powered machine resembling a coffee mill.

In 1929 this colony built a basement mosque, and each Friday a member of the congregation conducts services. Each person carefully washes his hands and feet before entering the temple; the sexes are segregated during prayer. During Ramadan—the ninth month according to the Mohammedan calendar, which is lunar—the people fast for 30 days, taking food only after dark; the month ends with a feast. The wedding ceremony of the group is unusual, for the bride is not present. Before the wedding she selects two witnesses to act in her behalf, who state the amount of money to be exchanged between the bridegroom and her parents—the bridegroom gives the parents this amount and they return the same amount to him. During the wedding ceremony the bride retires to another room; the father places his hand in that of the bridegroom, a large kerchief is placed over the clasped hands, and a member of the congregation reads the service. It is a custom of these people to shake hands at any chance meeting, no matter how recently they have met.

At 284.5 *m.* is the junction with a graveled road.

Left on this road is SANISH (Arikaran, *real people*), 23 *m.* (1,820 alt., 455 pop.), lying in a valley between bluffs bordering the eastern bank of the Missouri River. Spanning the Missouri here is the VERENDRYE BRIDGE, completed in 1927, the third highway bridge built across the river in the State. The site was known to the Indians from the earliest times as the Old Crossing because it was used as a ford by the large buffalo herds in their annual migrations. Adjoining Sanish on the S. is VERENDRYE NATIONAL MONUMENT, in which is CROW FLIES HIGH BUTTE, named for an Hidatsa Indian chieftain. On this butte is a monument dedicated to the Verendryes, who are believed to have visited one of the agricultural Indian tribes here on their exploratory trip into present North Dakota in 1738. The site discovered near Menoken in 1936, however, may be more definitely established as the village they visited (*see Tour* 8).

MANITOU (Chippewa, *the Great Spirit*), 286 *m.* (2,282 alt.), founded when the G. N. Ry. built through the territory in 1887, today consists of only a consolidated school, a store, and an elevator. It is part of Manitou township (pop. 128).

A county road beyond Manitou leads R. a few miles to WHITE EARTH (2,099 alt., 272 pop.), founded in 1891, probably named for the fine, white, clayey sand that has washed down into the White Earth River valley. It overlies the Laramie formation, which is exposed in many places on the sides of the valley, 150 feet deep here. While diversified farming predominates in the vicinity, traces of the Old West are still found on a few small ranches along the White Earth River between the route and the Missouri River to the S.

At 300 *m.* is the junction with ND 40 which goes N.

On ND 40 at 4 *m.* is TIOGA (Iroquois, *beautiful valley*) (2,241 alt., 385 pop.), which was founded in 1902.

RAY, 311 *m.* (2,271 alt., 579 pop.), named for Al G. Ray, chief special agent for the G. N. Ry. when the town was established in 1902, is scattered on level land along the railroad right-of-way. It was one of the first towns in the United States to adopt a commission form of city government (1910).

1. Right from Ray on a graveled county road to the WILLIAM SIMPSON FARM HOME, 8 *m.*, where there is an unusual COLLECTION (*open*) of South African oddities, collected by Simpson, a Scotchman, who during several years there obtained animal skins, beads, heads, and horns from the natives.

2. Left from Ray on a dirt graded county highway to the junction with another road, 10 *m.*; L. here to the first WELL AND DERRICK of the Big Viking Oil Company, on the Nesson Flats, 17 *m.*, a level bench just above the Missouri River opposite the mouth of TOBACCO GARDEN CREEK (*see Tour* 10). Interest in a prospective oil field here led to a 40-day $25,000 survey and the expenditure of $195,000 in test well drilling by the Standard Oil Company of California in 1937. More than 200,000 acres in oil leases were taken up in the vicinity in 1938, but no commercial quantities of oil were produced.

Opposite Nesson Flats near the mouth of Tobacco Garden Creek an attack upon a river steamer was made by a Sioux war party July 7, 1863. The Sioux, goaded to hostility by repeated violations of treaties and corrupt handling of annuity goods by governmental agencies, had met the *Robert Campbell* at Fort Pierre, South Dakota, to ask for the goods due them. When Samuel M. Latta, Indian agent in charge of distribution of the boat's cargo—a newcomer in the Indian service, arrogant and none too scrupulous—withheld one third of the goods, the Indians vowed to follow the boat up the river to Fort Benton, its destination. For 600 miles they harassed the steamer, pouring shots into it at every vantage point, attacking the crew at each woodyard, and making life miserable for all on board.

At that time the river at the mouth of Tobacco Garden Creek was quite narrow, and the Indians chose this spot for a massed attack. Joseph LaBarge, captain of the *Robert Campbell*, realizing the hazards of steaming through this point, made his boat fast to the opposite bank to prepare for a parley. The Sioux sent word that they wanted no trouble, only the annuity goods due them. Latta, however, refused to give up the goods, and suggested sending a yawl ashore to negotiate with the Indians. The Sioux consented, provided Latta came ashore. He, in turn, agreed to go, but when the yawl was ready he became conveniently ill in his cabin.

The yawl went ashore and had hardly landed when the Indians, angered by Latta's perfidy, attacked the crew. Three were killed and another wounded before the crew of the steamer opened fire, killing 18 Indians and 20 horses. The slain white men were buried next day on a bluff opposite the mouth of the Little Muddy Creek, where the city of Williston now stands (*see below*).

WHEELOCK, 318 *m.* (2,387 alt., 94 pop.), named for Ralph W. Wheelock, an editorial writer on the Minneapolis (Minnesota) *Tribune* in the early 1900's, is the highest point of elevation on the G. N. Ry. in North Dakota.

Left from Wheelock on an improved dirt road to the junction with an unimproved dirt road, 5 *m.*; L. here 3 *m.* to HUNGRY GULCH, a pleasant ravine on Tobacco Garden Creek. From the base of one hill bubbles a spring of clear water, and level areas under clumps of trees invite picnic spreads on the banks of the creek. Along the stream is a deposit of 'fool's gold,' or pyrite, which in 1902 had gold prospectors agog in anticipation of wealth. The story is told that, in the rush to stake claims here, James Moorman, on whose land the 'strike' was made, was the only person to benefit. He made a substantial profit selling the hungry prospectors his small stock of flour, in the form of pancakes, at exorbitant prices. When the supply was exhausted and appetites still were not satisfied, Moorman told them he would peel bark from the trees for them to eat. The ravine has since been known as Hungry Gulch.

South of the junction with unimproved road to SEVEN MILE HILL, 7 *m.*, a large, fairly level elevation over which passed the old trail used by fur traders, soldiers, and travelers between Bismarck and Williston. Blue Buttes, prominent peaks in the Badlands across the Missouri, are visible in the SE. on a clear day; N. and E. is an expanse of prairie; and to the S. and W. the Missouri, with its wooded banks and lowlands, winds to the horizon. Near the foot of the hill is CUSAC SPRINGS FARM (R), where a skirmish apparently unrecorded in military annals—possibly between Indians and soldiers—took place near a spring. Rifle pits are still visible, and rifle shells and human bones have been found in them.

EPPING, 324 *m.* (2,224 alt., 154 pop.), named for Epping in England, lies on the southern slope of one of the many rolling hills of the prairie.

Left from Epping on a graveled county road, formerly US 2, to the EPPING-SPRINGBROOK DAM, 5 *m.* Constructed as an FERA and WPA project, it was completed in 1936. This bulwark on STONY CREEK has created a lake covering 180 acres, which, including a strip of land around the water, has been made into a park devoted entirely to recreation.

At 334 *m.* the tableland of the Missouri Plateau comes to an abrupt end, and the highway descends into the valley of LITTLE MUDDY CREEK. From the top of the hill leading into this valley there is a panorama of level land dotted with farmhouses, and in the distance to the L. are the Missouri River and Williston.

At 335 *m.* is the junction with an unimproved private road.

Right on this road to the OASIS GARDENS, 0.5 *m.*, a private truck farm where irrigation has been successfully employed.

At 337 *m.* is the junction with US 85 (*see Tour* 4), a graveled highway. US 2 and 85 are one route to 352 *m.*

At 343.5 *m.* is the junction with a graveled driveway.

Left on this driveway to the twin artificial lakes known as LAKE MINNE-KOSH (Sioux, *twin waters*), 0.3 *m.* These lakes, built under a Federal project, are formed by dammed springs (*sand beaches, diving towers, bathing houses*).

WILLISTON, 347 *m.* (1,861 alt., 5,790 pop.), was named by James J. Hill, builder and first president of the G. N. Ry., for his friend S. Willis James of New York City, who was one of the stockholders in the company. The JAMES MEMORIAL LIBRARY, cor. 1st Ave. W. and 7th St., is a gift of the James family.

A large residential district and an active business section form the city, which is Williams County seat and the trade center for a large agricultural area in northwestern North Dakota and northeastern Montana. It lies on a gravelly terrace between the lowlands of the Missouri River and the hills and prairies. The river, which at one time flowed at the foot of Main St. and now has cut its channel nearly a mile to the S., has played a prominent part in the history of the locality. Up it came Lewis and Clark in 1805 on their historic expedition to the Pacific coast. In 1832 the *Yellowstone,* first steamboat to navigate the upper Missouri, passed the site, and by 1860 several boats were plying the stream. For 20 years after the gold strike in Montana in 1863 and 1864 the river was the major channel of communication to the Northwest.

The first white settler in the vicinity was Robert Matthews, employed by the post traders at Fort Buford to cut hay for the cavalry horses. In the 1870's he established himself some distance below the present town, near where Stony Creek flows into the Little Muddy. Here he kept a stock of goods for sale, and often hired crews of woodcutters to supply the demand for fuel for the steamboats. A post office known as Little Muddy was established on his ranch.

Although Matthews was the first permanent settler in the immediate Williston area, the first white man to settle in Williams County outside a trading or military post was George Grinnell. Born in Maryland, he served as a spy for General Philip H. Sheridan in the Army of the Potomac, was honorably discharged, and in 1865 accompanied a military wagon train from Fort Snelling, Minnesota, to Fort Berthold. The next year found him established as a 'woodhawk,' furnishing fuel to steamboats, near the mouth of Dry Fork Creek, where he operated a sawmill until advised that he was on Government property. Part of each year he hunted along the Missouri, and for a time in 1875 was with a party of gold seekers in the Musselshell country of Montana.

It was common practice of the period for hunters, traders, or trappers to select a 'woman of convenience' from among the Indians. In many instances these women were mistreated and even held in contempt by the very men who took them from their tribes. Grinnell was one of these men. In his earlier days along the Missouri he lived with a pure-blooded Indian woman, later discarding her for an educated and talented half-breed, Josephine Manuri. One bitter cold winter day Josephine's small son had wandered from the house and been lost. Several men were ready to search for the youngster but Grinnell, wishing to show his contempt for his wife, threatened to kill the first man to go after him. In the group was George Newton, buffalo hunter and pioneer Williston businessman, who replied, 'Then you've got me to kill,' and went out and brought the child back to his mother.

One day in 1888, coming from his saloon where he had been drinking heavily, Grinnell began to abuse his wife, who ran from him to a near-by field where several men were plowing. Too drunk to pursue her on foot, he mounted his horse and followed her to the field where, in an attempt to strike her down with the butt of his pistol, he fell from his horse, carrying his wife down with him. The two struggled for several minutes, none of the bystanders daring to interfere for fear of his gun. Suddenly Grinnell relaxed and lay quiet. He was in the habit of wearing around his neck a long leather watch thong with a sliding knot, and in the struggle his wife had clung to this thong and strangled him. After ascertaining that Grinnell was dead one of the onlookers remarked, 'Let's go get a drink,' and they all retired to his saloon, leaving the body as it was. Later a coroner's jury at Williston absolved the woman of all blame in the death of her husband with the unique verdict that Grinnell '. . . came to his death through an act of Almighty God, by the hand of His agent, Josephine Grinnell.'

With the coming of the railroad Williston was moved to higher ground farther W. It was only a tent colony and a few log cabins when the rails were laid into it in 1887, and it was said to have had a saloon on each corner of its one business block, with seven or eight others between. The late Joseph Stroud, pioneer Williston merchant, related that on the occasion of his first visit to the new town he was attracted by a large crowd of men on the street, engaged in rolling a man over a barrel. Inquiring of a bystander as to the cause of the man's accident, he was informed that the victim had taken a drink of water by mistake.

By 1900 a steady influx of homesteaders into the Williston area had

begun, and by 1910 the most desirable lands in the surrounding territory had been settled. Williston's population of 5000, which has
fluctuated little in the last 30 years, was attained by 1915.

An important factor in the rapid growth of the city was the location here of the division headquarters of the G. N. Ry. The roundhouse,
car repair shop, and huge ice house require the services of a large force
of men. The railroad stockyards E. of the city accommodate 93 carloads
of livestock, and have loading equipment for 23 cars; many trainloads
of western sheep and cattle are fed in transit annually. On several occasions a million bushels of grain have been handled at Williston in a
year. The city is an important primary turkey market, and thousands
of birds are shipped to holiday markets each year.

The Farmers Educational and Cooperative Union of America has
entitled Williston the *Cooperative City of North Dakota*. The FARMERS
UNION COOPERATIVE CREAMERY, rated as the largest enterprise of its
kind in the State, has its modern plant on W. Broadway. On W. 2nd
St. (US 2 and 85) is the FARMERS UNION OIL CO. PLANT, which maintains a wholesale department for oils, tires, and binder twine, and has
a tractor and farm machinery repair division. On W. 1st St. is the
FARMERS NATIONAL WAREHOUSE CORP. BUILDING, a concrete elevator
with 217,000 bu. capacity, said to be the largest co-operatively owned
primary grain warehouse in the United States. Newest of the co-operatives is the POULTRY PLANT on W. 2nd St. at the outskirts of the city.

In RECREATION PARK, between 2nd and 3rd Aves. W. and 4th and
5th Sts. W., are playground facilities, a bandstand, and a number of
cages of wild animals and birds; the larger animals are kept in WEST-
LAWN PARK, in the northwestern part of the city. HARMON FIELD (*baseball diamond, football gridiron, cinder track, swimming pool*), at the
northern end of Main St., was built under the Civil Works Administration. Two annual events in Williston are the Old Fiddlers Contest
(*Jan.*), and the Upper Missouri Band Tournament (*1st wk. in June*).

Left from Williston on E. Broadway on a graveled Scenic Highway, following
the route of the old overland trail between Bismarck and Fort Buford (*see Tour
3B*), to the junction with a graded dirt highway at 2.5 *m.*; R. here across
CRAZY MAN'S COULEE, 3 *m.* One day in the early 1880's Robert Matthews
(*see above*), the first settler in the region, was seated on the steps of his ranch
house just W. of the ravine when he saw a man, dressed in skins and with hair
falling to his shoulders, come out of the thickets in the coulee. Matthews knew
that no one lived in the country for miles around, and was interested in learning his identity. When the man saw the ranch buildings, however, he started
away, broke into a run, and disappeared into the brush along the creek running
through the ravine. About a year later a man similarly dressed, perhaps the same
person, came out of the brush and repeated the performance of the previous
year. Matthews remarked to his wife, 'That is surely Crazy Man's Coulee over
there. That's the second wild man who has come out of it.'

Left from Crazy Man's Coulee 1.5 *m.* on an unimproved dirt road to MEDI-
CINE LODGE SPRING (R), in the coulee farther to the E. An early homesteader bottled and sold the mineral water of the spring. However, the Indians
had discovered its health-giving qualities many years before, and used to come
long distances to camp here. One of their favorite camping places was MEDI-
CINE LODGE HILL, visible about a mile N. of the spring, from whose height

signal fires could be seen in all directions, and from which game or enemies could easily be sighted. Atop the hill are traces of Indian rings.

Southeast from Crazy Man's Coulee on the Scenic Highway to a junction at 5.5 *m.*; L. to 11.5 *m.*; R. to 13.5 *m.*; L. to 15.5 *m.*; R. to the Babcock Farm, 19 *m.* Right here on an unimproved trail to the Harm Arends place on SPANISH POINT, 22 *m.*

A short distance from the Arends farm is LAKE JESSIE (*boating, fishing, swimming*), an oxbow lake formed by the changing channel of the Missouri. The woods offer many natural camping places; the Upper Missouri District of the Great Plains Area, Boy Scouts of America, maintains a summer camp for boys here. Spanish Point was first known as the Spanish Woodyard, from the fact that two Mexicans in 1868 started selling fuel here to the steamers plying between St. Louis and the Montana gold fields. The Mexicans were joined by other woodcutters, and for a time the group prospered. A murder, two deaths at the hands of Indians, and other disasters, however, took their toll, and by 1870 the log cabin and stockade were deteriorating, and in a short time the river had washed away all traces of the woodyard.

West of Williston the MISSOURI RIVER (L) is bordered on the near side by timbered bottomlands, and on the far side by high, steep buttes.

At 352 *m.* is the junction (L) with US 85 (*see Tour* 4), and at 364 *m.* is the junction with a county graveled road (*see Tour 6B*). The route crosses the Montana Line at 367 *m.*, 132 *m.* E. of Glasgow, Montana (*see Montana Guide Tour* 2).

✿✿

Tour 6A

Devils Lake (city)—Camp Grafton—Devils Lake—Fort Totten Indian Agency—Sully's Hill National Game Preserve—Devils Lake (city); ND 20, ND 57, and Indian Service roads.
Devils Lake to Devils Lake, 33 *m.*

Graveled and bituminous-surfaced roadbed.
No accommodations along route.

This circular route from the city of Devils Lake along the beautifully wooded southern shore of the lake passes the homes of the Sioux and Chippewa Indians near the Fort Totten Agency, and many points connected with Indian life and legend.

ND 20 branches S. from US 2 in DEVILS LAKE, 0.0 *m.* (*see Tour* 6).

South of the city is level farming land, once the bed of a shallow glacial sea of which DEVILS LAKE, 5 *m.*, is a remnant. The name is the white man's misinterpretation of the Sioux name Minnewaukan, *mystery*, or *spirit water*. Approximately 30 miles by 10 miles, the lake is narrow and extremely irregular, with many little bays and peninsulas, and is surrounded by high morainic hills which, particularly along the southern shore, are heavily wooded. The clear water is strongly impregnated with sulphite, sodium carbonate, lime, magnesium, and iron— much like the water of oceans. It has been calculated that at the time of origin several thousand years ago the lake had a depth of 56 feet. A fall of 21 feet is shown between that time and the Government land survey of 1883, and a further fall of more than 26 feet in the half century since. At the time of the survey fish were plentiful in the lake, and each spring in the early 1880's the settlers caught them with pitchforks and took them away by the wagonload. In 1888, for some reason never clearly explained, the fish disappeared from the lake, and by 1909 the water level had fallen so far that commercial shipping on the lake was discontinued (*see Tour 6*). The sudden recession of the lake is attributed to the lack of ground and surface water in North Dakota, and constituted a strong argument for the Missouri River diversion project, which would store water from the Missouri and divert it for use in the eastern part of this State and South Dakota and in western Minnesota.

Many legends concerning Devils Lake have been handed down by the Indians. One tells of two Indian braves who were talking and smoking on the shore, when one of them idly thrust his knife into a large log lying on the water's edge. The log slid into the lake, and the men saw that it was a huge sea monster. Some say this serpent still lives in a hole in the bottom of the lake, and can be seen at times; that the water rises and boils when he comes out of his lair; that he leaves the lake at night to sleep on the shore.

Another story relates how a victorious party of Sioux warriors, who had attacked the Chippewa against the advice of Owanda the Seer, were swallowed up by the lake as they returned across its surface from the battle.

Phantom ships are the subject of a number of stories told by both white people and Indians. Under proper atmospheric conditions the waters of the lake throw off a vapor through which birds swimming on the surface can be seen from a distance highly magnified and resembling ships moving on the lake.

At 5 *m.* is a junction with a graveled road.

Right on this road is LAKEWOOD PARK (*cottages can be rented; due to low water level, lake unsuitable for bathing here; band concerts, dancing, baseball, and boating*), 1 *m.* (1,460 alt.), on an attractive arm of the lake known as Creel's Bay. The settlement grew up about a Chautauqua movement, which was inaugurated in 1892, continued for more than 35 years, and became the third largest in the country (1911). During Chautauqua season in the early days steamboats, including the *Minnie H* (*see Tour 6*), made daily excursions to points of interest on the lake. The Chautauqua association had its own railway from the park to Devils Lake, and on some occasions special trains were run on all lines leading into the city. The point is still a popular summer resort.

At 6 *m.*, at the 'Narrows' of the lake, which is now only about 400 feet wide, is a junction with a graveled road.

Right on this road to CAMP GRAFTON, 2.5 *m.*, where field training of the North Dakota National Guard has been conducted annually since 1904. Named for Lieutenant Colonel Gilbert C. Grafton, who died in the First World War, the camp covers 6 of the 180 square miles once occupied by Fort Totten military reserve. Two-week maneuvers are held in June, usually early in the month, with 21 units, totaling approximately 1100 troops, participating. The high light of the training events is Governor's Day, the second Sunday of the period, when the camp is put on dress parade for inspection by the chief executive of the State, who is commander-in-chief of its armed forces.

At 6.5 *m.* on ND 20 is a junction with ND 57, now the tour route.

Left on ND 20 to the junction with a graveled county road, 10 *m.*; R. here is TOKIO, 10.8 *m.* (1,501 alt., 112 pop.), near the center of the original Fort Totten Indian Reservation.

Right from Tokio 1.5 *m.* on a county dirt road to the DEVIL'S HEART, highest point in the Devils Lake area. For the Sioux it was a traditional meeting place to discuss war, hunting, or other ventures, and their name for it, in translation, means *center of the region.* Any promise made by an Indian on this hill is said to be sacred and must be conscientiously fulfilled. Father J. B. Genin, one of the earliest missionaries to the Indians of this region, erected a cross on the crest of the hill March 4, 1868, and at the same time announced that Devils Lake was to be known as St. Michael's Lake, but the change was never popularly adopted, and lake and town still bear the ancient mystic Indian name. From the top of Devil's Heart there is an excellent panorama of the entire lake region.

South from Tokio on the county graveled road to a junction at 11 *m.*; R. to 12.3 *m.*; L. to WOOD LAKE (*tourist and camping facilities; boating, fishing supplies*), 13.3 *m.*, a small wooded body of water. Fishing is good during open season (*May 15–Nov. 1 for perch, June 5–Nov. 1 for crappie*). In June and July a boys' camp is operated here by the Devils Lake Boy Scouts. On the northwestern shore is the BENSON COUNTY PARK (*picnicking and camping*), a 40-acre tract improved under the Works Progress Administration in 1937.

Between its junction with ND 20 and Fort Totten, ND 57 winds along the lake shore at the foot of the high, tree-clad range, and is known as the Burtness Scenic Highway, in honor of O. B. Burtness of Grand Forks (1884–   ), who as a Congressman from North Dakota (1921–7) was influential in obtaining funds for construction of the road.

At 11.3 *m.* on ND 57 is a junction with a trail.

Left on this trail to the SKI SLIDE, 0.5 *m.*, of the Lake Region Ski Club. Each year (*Feb.*) skiers from all parts of the United States participate in the tournament held here.

At 13.3 *m.* is a MONUMENT TO FATHER JEROME HUNT, who served St. Michael's Mission (*see below*) almost 40 years. With the help of a young Indian, Ignatius Court, whom he sent to the office of the Devils Lake *News* to learn the art of printing, he published a small newspaper, two prayer books, and Bible stories, all in the Siouan language.

FORT TOTTEN, 14 *m.* (1,470 alt., 1,306 pop., including town and reservation), with its uniform white agency buildings primly facing a central square, was originally a military post established in 1867 as a step in the plan to place the Indians of the region on a reservation. The reservation, named for General Gilbert Totten, then Chief, Engineer Corps, U.S. Army, was established through a treaty in 1867 with the Sisseton, Wahpeton, and Cut-Head Sioux. On July 17, 1867, General A. H. Terry, commander of the Department of Dakota, arrived on the southern shore of Devils Lake with three companies of the Thirty-First U.S. Infantry, to establish the post. The original fort was of logs and still stands half a mile S. of the brick buildings that replaced it in 1868. The bricks for the fort were made on the reservation, and, with the exception of present Fort Lincoln (*see Tour* 8), built much later, this is considered the best-built fort in the history of North Dakota.

Principally used as troops' winter quarters, the post sometimes had as many as five companies and at other times only one. Fort Totten troops acted as escorts for surveyors of the N. P. Ry. and for the International Boundary Line Commission, and participated in various campaigns in Dakota and Montana, returning to the fort for the winter.

Although the Indians of the region were usually quite peaceable, there was occasional trouble with them, particularly on the route to Fort Stevenson along the Missouri (*see Tour* 10). This trail constituted the main channel of transportation and communication for Fort Totten in its early days. An anonymous poem describes what is said to have been an actual occurrence (although the date given is not correct) in which Josh Murphy and Charlie Reynolds—General Custer's scout on the Black Hills expedition, who died with Custer at the Little Big Horn (*see* HISTORY)—are carrying the mail into Fort Totten.

> It was in the spring of sixty-four,
> Just a little while ere the war was o'er,
> That 'twas mine the mail bags to transport
> From Stevenson Pass to Totten fort;
> Through the rugged passes the route to take
> O'er the mountains that frown on Devils Lake;
> Those canyons alive with skulking crews
> Of the Chippewas and the savage Sioux;
> But my heart felt light and my arm felt strong
> For brave Josh Murphy rode along.

Josh is shot by Indians and begs his companion to prevent them from taking his scalp. Charlie lifts the dying man to his saddle and Josh's pony dashes into the night.

> We sought for Josh and we struck his trail
> In the dew damp notes of the scattered mail;
> And we found him at last, scarce a pistol shot
> From the picket wall of the fort he sought.
> There he proudly lay with his unscalped head
> On the throbless breast of his pony—dead!
> And the route from the pass to the cedared hill
> Is known as the 'Deadman's Journey' still.

The garrison was withdrawn from Fort Totten in 1890, and the mission school, which had been conducted by the Grey Nuns of Montreal since 1874, was consolidated with the Indian Industrial School and housed with the agency offices in the fort buildings. Approximately 1000 Sioux and a small number of Chippewa—many of both tribes are now of mixed blood—are under jurisdiction of the agency. At the school here the boys are taught dairying, gardening, carpentry, shoe repairing, steam and electrical engineering, baking, and tailoring; and the girls, sewing, laundering, cooking, and housekeeping.

At the auditorium (*last wk. Feb.*) is held the annual Midwinter Fair. Another annual fair is held (*1st wk. Sept.*) on the fairgrounds adjoining the agency on the NW. To both of these a few Indians bring handicraft work for sale; elsewhere such work is scarce, though beadwork and certain primitive musical instruments—flutes of red cedar, whistles of bone, large drums, tom-toms, rattles, and string bells—can be obtained at some of the homes.

The reservation, with its wooded hills and ravines, and its numerous lakes, is a beautiful region. Originally covering 360 square miles, it has been reduced to 137,000 acres. The land is allotted in 60-acre tracts to a family, and some farming is done. The economic status of the Indians here is poor, however.

At Fort Totten is the junction (L) with a graveled Indian Service road, from this point the tour route.

Right from Fort Totten on ND 57 to the INDIAN RESETTLEMENT TRACT (R), 0.5 *m.*, where the Government has constructed 13 new homes for the Indians.

At 2 *m.* on ND 57 are the DEVIL'S EARS, two long hills through which the highway runs. A man passing between these hills loses his mind, according to Indian legend, but regains it as soon as he comes out of the valley. The Indians are reluctant to discuss these hills with strangers; for while their pre-Christian philosophy included no devils, the hills were believed to have some connection with the Great Mystery or Great Spirit.

On the graveled Indian Service road is the 800-acre SULLY'S HILL NATIONAL GAME PRESERVE, 15.5 *m.* (*no admission charge; picnic shelters, playgrounds, pure water, camping facilities; vehicles not allowed within fenced area*). Trees and shrubs cover the hills of the park almost to their peaks, and tiny lakes dot the valleys, making this a beautiful spot. The park and its highest point, Sully's Hill, are named for General Alfred H. Sully, to commemorate his Indian expeditions into North Dakota. A high woven-wire fence encloses small herds of buffalo, elk, and deer, also wild fowl. Some of the animals are quite tame and amuse visitors with their antics. More than 14,000 people visited the park in 1935.

The DEVIL'S TOOTH (L), 17 *m.*, a boulder about 6 feet high and 5 feet square at the base, resembles a tooth with its roots upward. This rock is greatly revered by the Indians, who tell that an Indian mother wandered over the hill one day carrying her child and disappeared. Searchers, looking for her in vain, found this large stone, which had not been here before, and concluded it was the spirit of the woman and child. The stone has since had a reputation of connection with evil spirits. Gifts are often left here by Indians when a relative has died, but it is said that other Indians sometimes appropriate these offerings. It is an old custom for an Indian to give away part or even all of his possessions after the death of a loved one.

At 19 *m*. L. on a graveled Indian Service road.

At 21 *m*. (R) is small, attractive COURT LAKE (*charge of* 10¢ *per day or* 25¢ *per wk. for use of bathing beach*), named for Ignatius Court, the Indian who helped Father Hunt print a Siouan newspaper in the early days of St. Michael's Mission, and who served for many years as official interpreter at the Fort Totten Agency.

At 21.8 *m*. is a junction with a graveled Indian Service road (L), now the route.

> Right on this road is ST. MICHAEL, 2 *m*. (1,470 alt., 35 pop.), at the foot of Mission Hill, which affords a good view of the surrounding country. Here is St. Michael's Mission, established in 1874 by the Grey Nuns order of the Roman Catholic Church, through the efforts of Major William H. Forbes, first Indian agent on the reservation. At the mission lived and worked Father Jerome Hunt (*see above*). The old mission church is still standing.

Left from the St. Michael junction to ND 57 at 22.5 *m*.; R. here to Devils Lake, 33 *m*.

✿✿

Tour 6B

Junction US 2—Buford—Fort Buford State Park.
Junction with US 2 to Fort Buford State Park, 9.5 *m*.

Unmarked graveled road 8.5 *m*., unimproved road 1 *m*.
No accommodations.

The remains of Fort Buford, at the end of this route, evoke memories of the once-feared Indian chieftains Sitting Bull, Gall, and Joseph, and of the notable military leaders General Hugh E. Scott and General William H. Hazen.

The route, an unmarked gravel road, branches S. from US 2 (*see Tour* 6) 17 *m*. W. of Williston. At 8 *m*. is BUFORD (1,950 alt., 35 pop.), a little village named for the old fort. At 8.5 *m*. is the junction with an unimproved road; L. here.

On the SITE OF FORT BUFORD, 9 *m.*, a stone powder house and the regimental headquarters buildings still stand; the military cemetery is to the S.

In 1828 John Jacob Astor's American Fur Company built its principal post on the upper Missouri, Fort Union, 3 miles up the Missouri from the mouth of the Yellowstone, a few hundred yards E. of the present Montana Line. For almost 40 years Fort Union was the most important trading post in the Dakotas. Unfortunately, the traders at the post were more interested in getting furs cheaply than in preserving the morale of the Indians of the region. Whiskey, although prohibited, flowed freely. Quarrels between the Indians and the white men were frequent. Conditions were so bad in 1864 when General Alfred Sully made a visit to the post following his campaign against the Sioux (*see Tour 8 and Tour 8D*), that he recommended Government control of the trading posts if peace were ever to be made with the Indians. Upon his recommendation, therefore, Fort Buford was established in June 1866 opposite the mouth of the Yellowstone. Fort Union was dismantled and its materials were brought here for use in building the new post.

Because of its strategic position, the new fort, named for General John Buford, who distinguished himself at Gettysburg, commanded the water routes to the Northwest, and for more than 25 years was one of the country's vital Army posts. The fort was garrisoned partly by ex-Confederate soldiers, prisoners of war who had been paroled on oath that they would not again bear arms against the Union and on agreement to enlist for service in the outposts of the West. It played an active part in the settlement of the Indian troubles, and in establishing the Indians upon the reservations.

When Chief Joseph and his Nez Perce followers from Oregon finally surrendered in the Bear Paw Mountains of Montana in 1877 after leading their pursuers a merry 2000-mile chase through the Rockies for more than a year, he was brought to Fort Buford before being placed on a reservation in Washington. Sitting Bull and his band of Sioux, after their flight into Canada in a vain attempt to avoid confinement on the reservation, also came to Fort Buford in 1881, and it was before the regimental headquarters building, the southernmost of the group now standing, that the chief surrendered. Gall had preceded him by a few months, also coming to Fort Buford to give himself up.

Telegraphic connections with Fort Lincoln were established in 1873, and a wagon road, used until 1881, connected Fort Buford with the Custer post and with the railroad, which at that time ended in Bismarck. It followed the eastern side of the Missouri and is still in use in some places (*see Tour 3B*). Except for goods sent by steamboat, all supplies and mail were freighted over this road.

Fort Buford was sold at public auction in 1895. The 20-room residence of the commanding officers was purchased by John Mercer, who maintained it as a museum until its destruction by fire in 1937.

South of the old buildings is FORT BUFORD STATE PARK, 9.5 *m.*, including the military CEMETERY OF THE FORT. The unkept graves, some marked with marble slabs, some with wooden markers on which the inscriptions have lost all legibility, are sunken and overgrown with grass.

About a quarter of a mile SE. of the buildings by the river, in the 1830's and 1840's, stood a trading post known first as Fort William and later as Fort Mortimer. When William Sublette and Robert Campbell built Fort William in 1833, they found themselves treated as intruders by the monopolistic American Fur Company post at Fort Union. The policy of the American Fur Company, in its fight against competition, was to try every kind of tactics, from rate wars to the instigation of killings by the Indians. On a typical occasion a band of Blackfeet Indians, coming to trade, was met by a procession from Fort Union headed by a band in full uniform, with the traders following, bearing articles of barter. That day the impressionable aborigines traded at Fort Union. Another time a Fort William expedition to the Crow Indians was robbed of everything, including horses, by marauders believed to have been sent by the neighboring post.

The power of liquor as an article of trade was unbelievably great. Charles Larpenteur, who was at Fort William, tells in his memoirs of going into an Indian camp in weather so cold that his mules froze to death in the shelter provided for them, and obtaining 180 buffalo robes for 5 gallons of alcohol, which sufficed to make everyone in the camp drunk twice. The use of liquor was a sore point between Fort Union and Fort William, for, although it was illegal in Indian country, Sublette had been able to get a supply into Fort William, while every similar effort at Fort Union had been defeated. Larpenteur describes the opening of trade at Fort William thus:

The liquor trade started at dark, and soon the singing and yelling commenced. The Indians were all locked up in the fort, for fear that some might go to Fort Union, which was about two and one-half miles distant. Imagine the noise. Five hundred Indians with their squaws, all drunk as they could be, locked up in that small space. [The stockade was 150 feet by 130 feet.] The debauch continued during that entire night and well into the next day. . . Indians in stupor from drink lay in every direction.

Competition grew keen. Beaver skins, which ordinarily were worth $3, brought as much as $12. It was the policy of the American Fur Company, however, to buy out its competitors if it could not frighten them out. Accordingly, after a year of bitter rivalry, an agreement was reached whereby Sublette and Campbell sold Fort William to the Astor concern and moved W., leaving the profitable upper Missouri valley trade to Fort Union.

In 1842 a new post, called Fort Mortimer, was built by Fox, Livingston & Co. a short distance back from the bank at the Fort William site. The new traders did not long survive the competition of Fort Union, and in 1846 found it expedient to sell out to the American Fur Company. Some 12 years later an adobe trading post was erected here, but little is known of it other than that it was abandoned in 1858 and was finally torn down in 1866, its materials being used in the building of Fort Buford.

❖❖❖

Tour 7

Carrington—Minot—Bowbells—Portal—(Estevan, Sask., Can.); US 52.
Carrington to Canadian border, 235 m.

Soo Ry. roughly parallels entire route.
Bituminous-surfaced highway except 19 m.
Accommodations in principal towns.

US 52, pursuing a diagonal course northwest across the State, provides a direct route between the Canadian Rockies and the Middle West. It traverses a diversified farming area and passes through the fertile Souris River valley and the treeless valley of the Des Lacs River. In the green panorama of spring the prairie grasslands, dotted with small grazing herds of white-faced Herefords or black and white Holsteins, alternate with tilled fields. By late summer, tones of yellow dominate the landscape, which after the harvest is left a scarred, grimy tan.

At CARRINGTON, 0.0 m. (see Tour 2), is the junction with US 281 (see Tour 2).

At 9 m. on US 52 is the junction with ND 30, a graveled road, which unites with US 52 to 13 m.

Left on this road to the HAWKSNEST, 9 m., a high, flat-topped hill with well-timbered slopes rising 400 feet above the surrounding plain. Near its top is a crystal-clear spring. It was named in 1873 by a party of surveyors who saw a great number of hawks swarm from the trees. On top of the hill is a large serpentine mound. After the coming of the white man the hill was a camping place for Sioux Indians traveling between Fort Totten and Fort Yates. They called the hill Huya Wayapa ahdi (where the eagle brings something home in his beak). According to Indian legend a large band of Sioux once camped near the hill but were unable to ascertain the whereabouts of a war party of Chippewa which they suspected to be near. One of the Sioux, however, observed that an eagle flying into the trees carried in its mouth what appeared to be a piece of meat cut with a knife. From the direction in which the eagle had flown the Sioux were able to find the enemy. The legend is silent on the outcome of the warriors' meeting.

Left from the Hawksnest 3 *m.* to CAMP KIMBALL HISTORIC SITE, where Sibley camped July 22 and 23, 1863. It was from this point that the expedition moved SW. to engage in the Battle of Big Mound (*see Tour 8*).

At 13 *m.* ND 30 branches N.

R. on this road is SYKESTON (1,233 alt., 273 pop.), a German community named for Richard Sykes, who platted the town in 1883 on the banks of the PIPESTEM RIVER and artificial LAKE HIAWATHA. Sykes Park provides good camping. Buffalo favored this vicinity as a grazing spot before the coming of settlers, but the semi-annual hunting expeditions of the metis (*see Tour 5A*) destroyed many, and after the cattlemen arrived only an occasional specimen was sighted. The library of an Inverness, Scotland, home is adorned with the head of what was probably the last buffalo killed in this vicinity. A party of guests at the Sykes ranch in 1881, including Ewen Grant of Inverness, learned that a buffalo was grazing with the Sykes cattle, and in the exciting chase to bag the animal Grant had the good fortune to despatch him.

FESSENDEN, 37 *m.* (1,610 alt., 902 pop.), named for Cortez Fessenden, surveyor general of Dakota Territory from 1881 to 1885, was originally settled by a group of Welsh farmers, though the population is now predominantly Scandinavian. Fessenden was platted in 1893, and in the election of 1894 was named Wells County seat. Its citizens journeyed by teams and wagons in the still hours of the night to Sykeston, first county seat, seized the county records, and hauled them to the new location. Each year (*March*) Fessenden holds an agricultural exposition culminating in the coronation of an Alfalfa Queen.

HARVEY, 61 *m.* (1,596 alt., 1,851 pop.), named for Colonel James S. Harvey, a former director of the Soo Line, is on the banks of the SHEYENNE RIVER. It is a division point on the Soo and is the largest town on the route with the exception of Minot.

Right from Harvey on ND 3, a graveled road, to junction with a dirt road at 4 *m.*; R. on this road to BUTTE DE MORALE, 7 *m.*, an ancient landmark rising 300 feet above the surrounding prairie. It was to this region that the metis, or French-Indian half-breeds, came in the 1840's on their buffalo-hunting expeditions (*see Tour 5A*). It is said that on one occasion a party of 1,390 people with 824 wagons and 1200 animals camped here and slaughtered 250 buffalo in a single day. In 1853 the surveying expedition of Governor I. I. Stevens passed the hill, and in 1862–3 Captain James L. Fisk led two expeditions of Montana gold seekers through the vicinity.

MARTIN, 71 *m.* (1,589 alt., 228 pop.), known in early days as Casselman, was later renamed for a Soo official in order to avoid confusion with other towns of similar names. A group of Rumanians from Regina, Sask., settled here in 1893, but the population is now predominantly German, as is that of ANAMOOSE (from Chippewa *uhnemoosh*, dog), 79 *m.* (1,620 alt., 478 pop.)

DRAKE, 87 *m.* (1,634 alt., 654 pop.), named for an early settler, Herman Drake, is on the watershed between the Mouse and Sheyenne Rivers in a diversified farming and dairying area. A small railroad center, it has become a wholesale distribution point; a $20,000 co-operative creamery is operated here.

Northwest of Drake the route traverses rolling tree-dotted hills that begin to slope toward the Mouse River valley.

BALFOUR, 95 *m.* (1,613 alt., 193 pop.), named by the town site company, and VOLTAIRE, 113 *m.* (1,587 alt., 101 pop.), believed to have been named for an early settler, are both young villages incorporated in 1929.

The road makes an abrupt descent into the flat, trough-like Mouse River valley at VELVA, 118 *m.* (1,511 alt., 1,017 pop.), which is at the southwestern point of the loop of the river, near a camp site of the Sully expedition of 1865. The park-like little town is on the flood plain of the river which flows through it. First known as Mouse River Post Office, it was given its present name after organization of the town site in 1891–2. A park in the northern part of the town offers recreational facilities and contains the FIRST DWELLING IN VELVA, a log hut built in 1885.

1. Right from Velva on a dirt road winding down the Mouse River valley is VERENDRYE, 11 *m.* (1,554 alt., 54 pop.). First known as Falsen, the town was given its present name in honor of Pierre de la Verendrye, earliest known white explorer in the region. Right from the town pump 0.5 *m.* to the globular masonry DAVID THOMPSON MEMORIAL, erected by the G. N. Ry. in 1925 on a high point overlooking the river valley. On the base of the monument is the inscription: '1770—David Thompson—1885, Geographer and Astronomer passed near here in 1797 and 1798 on a scientific and trading expedition. He made the first map of the country which is now North Dakota and achieved many noteworthy discoveries in the northwest.' Thompson made his explorations while an employee of the North West Fur Company.

2. Left from Velva on a graded dirt road to a junction with another graded road at 4 *m.*; R. here to another junction at 8 *m.*; L. here to a STRIP MINE, which is one of the larger lignite operating units in the United States, 10 *m.* Here, in order to reach a vein of coal averaging 14 feet in thickness, great shovels strip the 40- to 50-feet overburden and pile it into fantastic high mounds and ridges resembling the work of a giant mole. Near by is a small community of some 40 homes of miners.

Northwest of Velva the route follows the foot of the hills bordering the valley to SAWYER, 124 *m.* (1,525 alt., 271 pop.), believed to have been named for a Soo Ry. official.

MINOT, 140 *m.* (1,557 alt., 16,577 pop.) (*see* MINOT).

At Valley St. and 4th Ave. SE. is a junction with US 2 (*see Tour 6*), which unites with US 52 to 146 *m.* At 4th Ave. and 2nd St. SW. is the junction with US 83 (*see Tour 3*).

Left of the junction at 146 *m.* is a large tourist camp.

BURLINGTON, 148 *m.* (1,590 alt., 200 pop.), named for Burlington, Iowa, under the North Dakota Rural Rehabilitation Corporation became the scene of the State's first SUBSISTENCE HOMESTEAD PROJECT. Here, in the wooded valley at the confluence of the Mouse and the Des Lacs Rivers, a model village of comfortable homes arose (1937) to replace the former dwellings of the miners who have part-time employment in the lignite mines of the vicinity. The project was then transferred to the Farm Security Administration and in 1946 to the State of North Dakota, acting through the Industrial Commission of North Dakota. Its purpose is to provide homes for disabled war veterans and at present 35 families are accommodated by the project. A concrete dam and bowl spillway on the Des Lacs River will irrigate more than half the 600 acres included in the project.

A camp fire unwittingly built upon an outcropping of lignite at Burlington in the spring of 1883 is credited with first having acquainted pioneers here with the possibilities of developing the fuel on a large scale. Three men camped at the fork of the Mouse and Des Lacs Rivers were surprised one morning to find their camp fire of the previous night still burning. Upon investigation they learned that their wood fire had ignited a blackish mineral—lignite—in the earth beneath it. All lignite mines in the Burlington vicinity are underground (*open on application at mine office in Burlington*).

Northwest of Burlington the route follows the Des Lacs River valley to FOXHOLM, 159 *m.* (1,657 alt., 175 pop.), named for Foxholm, England, and CARPIO, 168 *m.* (1,696 alt., 322 pop.), which touches the hills on both sides of the narrow valley. One story has it that Carpio was named by the wife of one of the railroad officials; another that the name was suggested by the fact that the first post office was a freight car on which was posted the sign 'P. O.'

Right from Carpio on a graveled county road to the UPPER SOURIS MIGRATORY WATERFOWL PROJECT, 7 *m.*, one of the largest of its type undertaken in North Dakota by the U.S. Fish and Wildlife Service. Here a marshland along the Mouse River has been purchased and a large dam constructed to impound a lake 26 miles long. A series of smaller dams farther down the river will control the flood waters of the Souris and will aid in restoring the marshes to suitable breeding and nesting grounds for migratory waterfowl. The low, chalky white, red-roofed buildings E. of the dam are PROJECT HEADQUARTERS.

DONNYBROOK, 177 *m.* (1,760 alt., 215 pop.), named by its founders for Donnybrook, Ireland, is at the foot of the hills bordering the western side of the Des Lacs valley.

At 185 *m.* the route passes S. of DES LACS LAKE, a remnant of a glacial stream, now divided into three parts and drained by the Des Lacs River. The U.S. Fish and Wildlife Service has a large migratory waterfowl project on the lower lake, and as the road winds along the eastern shore the nesting islands and several dams built by the survey are visible.

KENMARE, 193 *m.* (1,799 alt., 1,528 pop.), believed to have been named by the wife of a Canadian Pacific Ry. official for a community in Ireland, lies on a hillside facing MIDDLE DES LACS LAKE. In the steep sides of the lake valley near by are a number of lignite mines.

Opposite Kenmare are the ADMINISTRATION BUILDINGS of the Des Lacs Lake Migratory Waterfowl Project—low white structures with red tile roofs.

At Kenmare the highway leaves the valley for the Drift Plain, which stretches away to the E. to meet the flat bed of glacial Lake Souris, beyond which lie the Turtle Mountains. To the W. against the horizon rises the eastern edge of the great Missouri Plateau topped by the Altamont Moraine, the height of land between the Missouri and Souris Rivers.

At 199 *m.* is the junction with ND5, a graveled highway (*see Tour* 5). US 52 and ND 5 are one route to 228 *m.*

At 204 *m.* the highway dips into a large cut to cross UPPER DES LACS LAKE, which was once the scene of steamboating. In early days it was navigable across the Canadian border near Northgate, and grain from points in Canada and along the lake in North Dakota was shipped via the water route to Kenmare for trans-shipment by rail to eastern markets.

BOWBELLS, 208 *m.* (1,961 alt., 787 pop.), named by English stock-holders of the Soo Line for the famous Bow Bells in St. Mary-le-Bow Church in London, is the Burke County seat. Almost treeless, its squat appearance blends into the flat terrain, with the tall water tower, the only notable feature of the town, visible for miles on the level prairie.

FLAXTON, 221 *m.* (1,940 alt., 362 pop.), was given its present name because the town site was a field of flax when application for a post office was made.

At 228 *m.* is a junction with ND 5 (*see Tour* 5).

PORTAL, 235 *m.* (1,954 alt., 499 pop.), is an important international port of entry, hence its name. It is an airport of entry, and also a division point on the Soo, much of the traffic to the Canadian Northwest passing through its custom offices. The U.S. CUSTOM AND IMMIGRATION HOUSE (*for custom regulations see* INFORMATION FOR TRAVELERS), on Boundary and Railway Aves., is a two-story brick building in Colonial style. A large canopied driveway at the front of the building permits inspection of three automobiles at once. The Canadian custom offices are directly across the avenue, which is bisected by the international boundary. Portal is the home of many sports enthusiasts, and most of its games have an international aspect. Unusual in sports is the international golf course, on which in August 1934 a young Portal golfer, George Wegener, made an international hole-in-one, driving from the eighth tee, which is in Canada, 125 yards into the cup on the ninth green, in the United States. The curling club here is also international, being composed of both Canadian and United States citizens in the border cities of Portal and North Portal. They play this winter sport in a specially constructed domed building.

US 52 crosses the Canadian Line at the customhouses in the city of Portal, 28 miles S. of Estevan, Saskatchewan.

Tour 8

(Minneapolis, Minn.)—Fargo—Valley City—Jamestown—Bismarck—
Mandan—Dickinson—(Glendive, Mont.); US 10.
Minnesota Line to Montana Line, 370 m.

N. P. Ry. and Northwest Airlines parallel route across State.
Paved or bituminous-surfaced roadbed all hard-surfaced.
Accommodations chiefly in towns.

US 10, rising steadily toward the foothills of the Rocky Mountains, with a gain of 1,852 feet in altitude in crossing the State, traverses the three main topographic divisions of North Dakota (*see* NATURAL SETTING), from the low, flat Red River Valley, across the rolling Drift Plain and out upon the Missouri Plateau. Near the end of the route are the strange and beautiful Badlands.

Most of the country along the road is cultivated, and in the fields the cycle of farming operations—plowing, seeding, cultivating, harvesting—repeats itself as the seasons progress. During the growing season, stretching far across the flat plains and over the sloping hills, the varying greens of the grains blend with the blue flax fields and the invading yellow patches of mustard. In the fall the prairies have a somber, peaceful air as their tawny stubblefields and newly plowed black acres await the first snowfall. When winter comes the never-ending expanse of white is broken by the dark pattern of roads and an occasional lead-colored clump of trees, bare and shivering in the wind, while at the distant horizon the whiteness unites with the pale blue of clear winter skies.

West of the Red River Valley trees are few except along the rivers. Yet, according to legend, this country was once heavily forested—until Paul Bunyan, the master woodsman, had his men log it off, just before his famous fight with his foreman, the Bull of the Woods, on top of the bottom of the Mountain That Stood on Its Head. As a matter of geologic fact, the area traversed by the route has been largely treeless since the gradual cooling of the climate, incident to the ice age, destroyed the tropical plant and animal life that once was profuse here.

FARGO, 0.0 m. (907 alt., 32,580 pop.) (*see* FARGO).

At Front and 13th Sts. is the junction with US 81 (*see Tour* 1).

WEST FARGO (R) (907 alt., 117 pop.) and SOUTHWEST FARGO (L) (907 alt., 707 pop.), 5 m., suburbs of Fargo, are the center of North Dakota's meat-packing industry. An ARMOUR & CO. PLANT (*open; tours at* 9:30 & 11 *a.m.,* 1 & 3 *p.m. Mon.–Fri.,* 10:30 *a.m. only on Sat.; no children under* 10) and a large livestock market employ the majority of the residents of these two young villages, incorporated in 1931 and 1937 respectively. Armour's plant, housed in a four-story brick building, employs more than 400 people. Connected with it is the Union Stockyards, where representatives of commission firms buy livestock from North Dakota farmers. Included in the yards is an exchange building that houses offices of the company, dealers, and commission firms, and State and Federal agencies supervising market operations.

At 12 *m.* is the junction with a graveled county highway.

Right on this highway is MAPLETON, 1 *m.* (904 alt., 180 pop.), one of the oldest towns in the State, organized about 1870. It is named for the MAPLE RIVER, which flows through it, one of the many meandering tributaries of the Red.

At 20 *m.* is the junction with ND 18, a graveled highway.

Right on this road is CASSELTON, 2 *m.* (936 alt., 1,358 pop.), named for Major G. W. Cass (1810–88) of Minneapolis, stockholder in the N. P. Ry. and proponent of the railroad nursery that propagated the poplar trees that today line the streets. It was the boyhood home of William Langer (1886–   ), Governor of the State (1933–4; 1937–9) and a storm center in Nonpartisan League politics (*see* HISTORY).

During the bonanza farm era (*see* AGRICULTURE AND FARM LIFE) Casselton was headquarters of the huge Dalrymple farm, which made it a metropolis of the Red River Valley. One of the earliest practical uses of the telephone in the United States, and what may have been the introduction of the instrument into this State (*see Tour* 1), was made in 1876 on the Dalrymple farm. Oliver Dalrymple had taken advantage of low prices occasioned by the panic of 1873 to buy 100,000 acres of Red River Valley land owned by the N. P. Ry. and had set out to demonstrate that the land was valuable for farming. The first year he seeded 1,280 acres and harvested 32,000 bushels of wheat. By 1878 he was farming 13,000 acres and by 1895, 65,000 acres. His land was divided into subfarms, each with a superintendent and foreman, and all using the most modern farm equipment obtainable. Dalrymple, on a visit to the Philadelphia Centennial in 1876, became interested in the newly invented telephone, and at the close of the fair purchased several of the instruments for installation on his subfarms and headquarters farm at Casselton.

Among the churches in Casselton is one maintained by a small group of Moravians, a German religious sect that came to the State during the early years of settlement.

On ND 18 at 18 *m.* to the D. H. HOUSTON FARM, where the principle of the roll-film camera was developed. Houston, a native of Wisconsin, had already invented one camera when he homesteaded in North Dakota in 1869. Although he acquired 6000 acres of land and became one of the early bonanza farmers, he continued his experiments in photography, and in 1881 developed the principle of the roll-film camera, selling his patent to George Eastman. It has been said that Houston named his device 'kodak' for North Dakota, but the generally accepted story is that Eastman himself coined the word because he desired a catchy, easily remembered name that could be used in any language. Houston's inventive interests included agricultural improvements, and in the 1880's he developed an improved bluestem wheat which, producing four to five bushels more per acre than other varieties, was soon in great demand throughout the Wheat Belt. He also patented improvements on the disc plow.

At 26.5 *m.* is the junction with a graveled road.

Right on this road is WHEATLAND, 2 *m.* (991 alt., 112 pop.), a quiet, pretty village named for the vast wheat acreage formerly seeded on the bonanza farms in the area.

At 30.5 *m.* the highway passes over a noticeable rise of land. This is Herman Beach, the western shore of ancient Lake Agassiz, which in glacial times covered 100,000 square miles and lay over the eastern portion of the State, reaching from Lake Winnipeg in Canada to Lake Traverse in South Dakota. It is estimated that when this gravelly ridge was formed by the waves of the lake, the water at the present site of Fargo was 175 feet deep.

BUFFALO, 38 *m.* (1,201 alt., 245 pop.), is named for Buffalo, New York.

Left from Buffalo on a graveled highway is ALICE, 11 *m.* (1,124 alt., 181 pop.), named for a relative of a railroad superintendent.
At the Multz Café is a COLLECTION OF INDIAN ARTIFACTS (*open*).

At 40 *m.* is BUFFALO CREEK HISTORIC SITE (R). A marker reads: 'August 16, 1863. General Sibley marched over this spot with 3400 soldiers on his return after driving the Indians across the Missouri River.'

TOWER CITY, 44 *m.* (1,169 alt., 364 pop.), in a grove of trees, is named for Charlemagne Tower (1848–1924), a Philadelphia capitalist and diplomat, who owned much land in the vicinity. He made the foundation plantings of the trees of the city and also donated the first books to the local public library. In 1886 Baptist leaders selected this city as the site of a proposed church college to be named Tower University. Excavations had actually begun, with the expectation that Tower would be its benefactor to the extent of $100,000. Because of some misunderstanding of the preliminary arrangements, however, the endowment fund was not forthcoming. Tower offered the use of a school building, but the school, being unable to continue without financial assistance, closed its doors two years later.

At 49 *m.* is the junction with ND 32, a graveled highway.

Right on this highway is ORISKA, 1 *m.* (1,267 alt., 217 pop.), once the center of a wide wheat-growing area. The name is believed to have been that of the heroine of an old book of western poems.
At 5 *m.* on ND 32 to CAMP ARNOLD HISTORIC SITE, where in 1863 the Sibley expedition made one of its many overnight camps.

At 56 *m.* is the junction with a graveled road.

Left on this road to CAMP SHEARDOWN HISTORIC SITE, 3 *m.*, another stopping place of the Sibley column. A few rifle pits dug for camp protection are still visible, and a bronze tablet marks the site. No engagement took place here, the rifle pits being evidence of Sibley's precautions against Indian attack.

VALLEY CITY, 59 *m.* (1,220 alt., 5,917 pop.), seat of Barnes County, lies sheltered and hidden in the deeply wooded Sheyenne River valley. Originally known as Worthington, it was given its present name when incorporated as a city in 1881.

The city's first settlers came with the N. P. Ry. in 1872, but Jay Cooke & Company, financiers of the railroad, crashed in the nation-wide panic of 1873, and the next five years brought a suspension of business and immigration. From 1878, however, the city had a steady growth; today it is the center of a large area of diversified farming, with flour milling and the processing of dairy products the chief industries. One notable asset of the city is a municipal light plant, which supplies electrical energy at the lowest rates prevalent in the State and provides an excellent street-lighting system without taxation. The studios and transmitter of KOVC, Valley City, are at 312 5th Ave.

On an attractive campus at the southern end of 5th Ave. is the VALLEY CITY STATE TEACHERS COLLEGE, established in 1890. In 1895 Governor Roger Allin vetoed State appropriations for the university and colleges, and, like other State educational institutions, the Valley City college was kept open by popular subscriptions for the biennial period. One of the outstanding alumni of the school is Paul Fjelde, a former student of Lorado Taft, who was commissioned to do the bust of Abraham Lincoln that North Dakota presented to Norway in 1914. A copy of this work has been placed in the auditorium of the college.

Near the college campus on 1st St. is CITY PARK, which contains recreational facilities and a small zoo. CHAUTAUQUA PARK (*swimming pool, playgrounds, large auditorium*) is in the northeastern part of the city.

In the BARNES COUNTY COURTHOUSE, 6th St. bet. 3rd and 4th Aves., is a small museum, which includes the Indian collection of Vernon Gale, an amateur archeologist. Among his exhibits are several stone hearts, which have been found only in the valley of Spiritwood Lake (*see below*).

The N. P. Ry. HIGH BRIDGE, known as the 'Hi-Line,' casts its long shadow across the river valley N. of Chautauqua Park. Including the approaches, it measures 1 mile—a long railroad trestle for its height, which is 148 feet above the water level of the Sheyenne.

> Right from Valley City on Chautauqua Blvd., which becomes a graveled road leading to a spot still known as ASHTABULA, 17 *m.*, the name of a post office once operated here. A ford in the Sheyenne at this point, Sibley's Crossing, was used by Captain James Fisk's immigrant trains to the Montana gold fields in 1862 and 1863, and twice by the Sibley military expedition in 1863, and later was on the Fort Ransom-Fort Totten trail. Deep ruts of wagon trains are still visible and can be traced across the valley. About 11 *m.* N. of Valley City is the Baldhill Dam and Reservoir. This earth-filled structure is 57 feet high and 2000 feet long and will maintain a normal pool level at an elevation of 1266. It will be an important recreational area.

At Valley City is a junction (L) with ND 1, a graveled highway (*see Tour 8A*), which unites with US 10 to 64 *m.*, where ND 1 (*see Tour 8B*) branches R.

On US 10 at the western end of the city is PIONEER PARK (R), where an outdoor amphitheater has been built. The park also contains a small

frame schoolhouse, typical of the pioneer period, which was moved from
its site four miles west of the city.

SANBORN, 71 *m.* (1,443 alt., 366 pop.), named for J. N. Sanborn,
a Fargo pioneer, was at one time a booming trade center, and seemed
destined to become important, until two severe blows retarded its
growth. First, in 1880, after a hot campaign, it lost the county seat election to Valley City; and then, in 1882, the county treasurer, whose bond
had been furnished by the businessmen of the town, absconded with the
county moneys, including a special fund for the erection of a courthouse. Among the early settlers of Sanborn was I. W. Barnum, brother
of P. T. Barnum of circus fame.

ECKELSON, 76 *m.* (1,472 alt., 80 pop.), was named for A. O.
Eckelson, a N. P. Ry. civil engineer of the 1870's, and was first platted
a mile E. of its present site. Because of the steep incline of the railroad
at that point, however, trains were unable to stop and the town had to
be moved to more level ground.

SPIRITWOOD, 83 *m.* (1,475 alt., 286 pop.), is named for the lake
16 *m.* NW.

At 94 *m.* is the junction with ND 20, a bituminous-surfaced highway.

Right on this highway to the junction with a county graveled road, 10 *m.*;
R. here to SPIRITWOOD LAKE (*bathing beaches, boathouses, cottages, golf
course, and two pavilions on the southern shore*), 16 *m.*, an attractive resort in a
wooded valley. It is known to the Sioux as Minneskaya (*water with white foam
on top*). According to an Indian legend, a grief-stricken girl plunged into its
waters to join her drowned lover, and her spirit still resides in the lake.

On the northern shore of the lake the State Game and Fish Commission maintains an AVIARY where Mongolian pheasants are confined for breeding purposes.
Eggs are hatched on near-by farms and the poults are then returned to the
aviary for distribution throughout the State.

In the vicinity of Spiritwood Lake have been found several heart-shaped
stones marked with a small cross, probably representing a star. This is the only
locality in the State where these stone hearts have been found, and archeologists
believe they are the product of the early Indians. Specimens are on display at
the State historical society museum (*see* BISMARCK) and in the Vernon Gale
Collection (*see* VALLEY CITY above).

JAMESTOWN, 96 *m.* (1,405 alt., 8,790 pop.), Stutsman County
seat, lies in the fertile valley of the winding JAMES RIVER, described as
the longest unnavigable river in the world. The story is told that the
stream received its name from a French-Indian hunter-trapper who,
having lost his way, was overcome with joy upon discovering the little
river and gave it his own name—Rivière de Jacques.

The first settlement at Jamestown was made in the fall of 1871,
when a corps of five or six N. P. Ry. engineers spent the winter here in
order to be in readiness for work in the spring. Soldiers from Fort
Ransom (*see Tour 8A*) acted as a guard for the engineers, and in June
a military post, Fort Cross (later Fort Seward), was established. During the summer settlers and businessmen came to the community, and
a brisk trade was carried on with the 500 railroad workers and the 3
companies of soldiers stationed at the fort.

On Sept. 13, 1872, the first train to enter Jamestown crossed the river into the city. Less than a month later construction crews, incensed because of unpaid wages, stopped work, and even began tearing up the newly laid tracks. Soldiers from the fort quickly quelled North Dakota's first strike.

Railroads played an important role in Jamestown's inception and growth. At one time there were prospects that two other railroads besides the N.P. would come into the city, and hope was high that the place would become an important railroad center. Although these plans did not fully materialize, one of the new roads, the Midland Continental, did make the city its home office. Financed by English capital, the Midland began to build in 1913, with plans for a line connecting Winnipeg, Manitoba, with the Gulf of Mexico. World War I intervened, foreign support was withdrawn, and operations ceased after completion of only 70 miles of road, from Edgeley to Wimbledon.

The first church services here were held in a schoolhouse, and a pioneer tells of how these meetings were faithfully attended by an old Indian 'clad in great dignity and an old nightshirt.' Jamestown's first church, the Presbyterian, was erected in 1881. The first resident Roman Catholic priest arrived the same year, and resided in a rectory that measured 14 by 22 feet. Although there were many places in the State where Catholic church services had long been held, Jamestown in September 1889 became the first seat of the diocese of North Dakota.

In 1879 a group of local businessmen organized the James River Navigation Company. Of their first steamer, the *Belle of Richmond,* the St. Paul *Pioneer Press* said, 'The craft is composed of a steamwhistle, an engine the size of a teakettle and a little boat under it.' Ice put a stop to river navigation that fall, and in May the following year the initial trip of a new boat that had been built during the winter proved unsuccessful.

The fertile James River Valley land has produced such bountiful crops that between 1875 and 1900 farmers often paid for their lands in two years. A writer of that time says that 'though North Dakota didn't have granite bluffs and waterfalls for its beauty, a land that would yield twice its cost in the first year would look rather beautiful to most men.'

Maxwell Anderson (1888–   ), Pulitzer Prize playwright (1933), and Curtis D. Wilbur (1867–   ), Secretary of War in President Coolidge's cabinet, once attended school in Jamestown.

The two leading institutions of Jamestown overlook the city from the river bluffs on both sides of town. To the SE. is the STATE HOSPITAL FOR THE INSANE, with its handsome buildings and beautifully landscaped grounds, a little city within its 2000 acres of farm land.

JAMESTOWN COLLEGE, on high bluffs (L) on the northeastern edge of the city, is the oldest and most important private college in North Dakota. Founded by the Red River Presbytery in 1883, it was the first school in the State to offer normal-school training for teachers. A plan for construction in semi-Gothic style has been followed, with the result that the buildings present a pleasing and uniform campus group.

On the campus is Voorhees Chapel, one of the finest college chapels in the Midwest; it is built of reinforced concrete, Bedford stone, and mat-faced Menominee brick. The interior is constructed with huge hammer beams of Gothic type, and there are two high Gothic windows. The chapel is also used for musical and dramatic performances, as the intent of the institution is to make this building the center of college life and associations.

KLAUS PARK, at the southwestern edge of the city, with entrances on Elder and Willow Aves., consists of 26 acres of heavily wooded land lying between the James River and Pipestem Creek. It was donated to the city by the heirs of Anton Klaus, prominent pioneer affectionately known as 'the father of Jamestown.' An outdoor swimming pool is supplied with warm artesian water. Preserved in the park is one of the original millstones used in Jamestown's first flour mill built by Anton Klaus in 1879.

NICKEUS PARK (equipped playgrounds), at the northern end of 5th Ave., is in a loop of the James River. It was donated to the city as a memorial to a pioneer Jamestown attorney, by Mrs. Fannie B. Nickeus, his widow.

CITY PARK (municipal tourist camp, ball park, fairgrounds, and tennis courts), at the southern end of 4th Ave., consists of a 52-acre tract along the wooded James River. The Park Auditorium, completed in 1936 as a WPA project, is a domical building, the design of its façade carried out in the straight lines and angles of modern architecture. Constructed with laminated truss-type arches that support the entire roof load, the auditorium has 25,000 square feet of floor space unobstructed by supporting columns. Its acoustics are excellent, owing to the vaulted shape of the roof and the absorbing quality of the timbers in the arches.

KRMC, Jamestown's radio broadcasting station, has its studios in the Gladstone Hotel building at 412 Front St. W.; its transmitter is just across the James River S. of the city.

The ALFRED DICKEY LIBRARY, corner 5th Ave. S. and Pacific St. W., is built of red Hebron (North Dakota) brick. Its style shows a Byzantine influence.

The SITE OF FORT WILLIAM H. SEWARD is indicated by a marker on US 281 at the foot of the bluffs on the northwestern outskirts of the city. The post, named for President Lincoln's Secretary of State, was abandoned in 1877, and in 1925 the N. P. Ry. donated the site, which is on the bluffs S.W. of the marker, as a State park.

Left from Jamestown 2 m. on Monroe St. to HOMER STATE PARK, a five-acre tract along the James River that was the site of an unidentified skirmish between white men and Indians.

ELDRIDGE, 104 m. (1,538 alt., 67 pop.), named for a pioneer family, is the most westerly town on the route lying within the Central Lowland of the Interior Plains. Between Eldridge and WINDSOR,

112 *m.* (1,839 alt., 74 pop.), whose name was suggested by that of Windsor, Ontario, there is a rise of 300 feet, which marks the division between the Central Lowland and the Great Plains. The Missouri Plateau, as this section of the Great Plains is called, extends beyond the western border of the State. As the route continues into the plateau, the altitude rises slightly to the village of CLEVELAND, 116 *m.* (1,849 alt., 246 pop.)—named for Cleveland, Ohio—only to fall away gradually and then rise once more in topping the Altamont Moraine (*see below*).

MEDINA, 125 *m.* (1,791 alt., 500 pop.), named for Medina, New York, has a strongly Russo-German population. It was originally known as Midway for its position halfway between Jamestown and Steele, and during the first two decades of the century was an important commercial point in the area.

At 127 *m.* is the junction with ND 30, a graveled highway.

Left on this highway to the junction with a graded dirt road, 12 *m.*; R. here to the junction with another dirt road, 17 *m.*; R. to another junction, 18 *m.*; and L. to Lake George, commonly known as SALT LAKE (*swimming*), 19 *m.*, because of its heavy impregnation with natural salts. It is said to be one of the deepest lakes in the State. The southern shore has an excellent sand beach. Northeast of the lake are fresh-water springs; here, on land controlled by the U. S. Fish and Wildlife Service through an easement, dikes and dams have been built to create a fresh-water feeding and nesting ground known as the LAKE GEORGE MIGRATORY WATERFOWL PROJECT. On the southern shore is STREETER MEMORIAL PARK, a First World War memorial.

At 132 *m.* are CRYSTAL SPRINGS LAKES. A cairn (L) houses a spring (*good water*). The lake offers fine opportunity to study varieties of shore birds, as the marshes of the spring-fed waters provide attractive breeding places. CRYSTAL SPRINGS, 133 *m.* (1,777 alt., 55 pop.), is named for the neighboring lakes.

West of Cleveland (*see above*) the route descends in a gentle grade to TAPPEN, 141 *m.* (1,764 alt., 323 pop.), named for an early settler.

Right from Tappen on a country trail, unsuited for trailers, to McPHAIL'S BUTTE HISTORIC SITE, 10 *m.* It was from here that Colonel Samuel McPhail directed the movement of his regiment of Minnesota Rangers July 24, 1863, in the Battle of Big Mound, one of the Sibley expedition encounters with the Sioux. After having been harried by the white soldiers, a small group of Sioux had asked to talk with a delegation of the enemy, and the meeting was apparently proceeding in an amicable manner when without warning a young Indian shot Dr. J. S. Weiser, one of the party, in the back. The Battle of Big Mound was precipitated, and the Sioux were forced to retreat farther W. Northeast of the battle site is BURMAN HISTORIC SITE, 2 *m.*, where Dr. Weiser is buried.

DAWSON, 147 *m.* (1,736 alt., 263 pop.), named for the town-site owner, Dawson Thompson, is in a fertile subirrigated area. A route for migratory birds crossing the United States passes through the Dawson vicinity, and a U.S. game reserve is 7 miles S. of the town on ND 3. At Dawson is one of the six Department of Commerce intermediate lighted airports in the State.

Left from Dawson on ND 3, a graveled highway, to LAKE ISABEL, 5 *m.* Here is CAMP GRASSICK, a children's summer camp formerly operated by the North Dakota Anti-Tuberculosis Association. In 1947 it was acquired by the State Elks Association and is operated by the Division of Child Welfare of the Public Welfare Board for handicapped and underprivileged children. It is named for Dr. J. Grassick, pioneer Grand Forks physician. Just E. of Lake Isabel are the LODGE AND GAME RESERVE formerly maintained by G. L. SLADE. Slade, a son-in-law of the late James J. Hill, the railroad builder, maintained breeding and nesting grounds for pheasants and waterfowl—even created his own Lake Slade by pumping water from deep wells. The game reserve has been transferred to the U.S. Fish and Wildlife Service, and the lodge has been leased to North Dakota 4-H clubs.

At 25 *m.* is NAPOLEON (1,955 alt., 982 pop.), seat of Logan County, named for Napoleon Goodsill who was president of the town-site company. The first business establishment (1886) was a supply store operated jointly with a newspaper, the Napoleon *Homestead,* which is still in operation. Two pigeon-holes in a desk in the *Homestead* office served as boxes for the first post office in Napoleon.

BURNSTAD, 40 *m.* (1,963 alt., 80 pop.), was formerly the trade center of a large cattle industry. C. P. Burnstad, for whom the town was named, was known as the 'Logan County Cattle King,' and grazed as many as 5000 cattle on 54 sections of land.

Left from Burnstad 2 *m.* on a graded dirt road to BEAVER LAKE STATE PARK (*swimming, picnicking*), a recreational area developed by WPA labor. A game refuge surrounds the lake.

At 53 *m.* on ND 3 is WISHEK (2,010 alt., 1,112 pop.), where, as in many of the neighboring towns, Russo-Germans make up the greater part of the population. The town is named for J. H. Wishek of Ashley, who owned the town site and donated lots for churches, parks, the town hall, and a bandstand.

Left from Wishek 6.5 *m.* on a graveled road to DOYLE MEMORIAL PARK on GREEN LAKE (*swimming, picnicking*). The land for this recreational area and memorial to pioneers was given to the State by Mr. and Mrs. John J. Doyle of Wishek.

At 65 *m.* on ND 3 is DANZIG (2,029 alt., 40 pop.), named for the Free City of Danzig in Europe.

ASHLEY, 77 *m.* (2,001 alt., 1,345 pop.), began as the town of Hoskins on the shore of near-by Hoskins Lake. Originally the town as well as the lake was given the maiden name of the wife of Colonel C. A. Lounsberry, historian, and at that time editor of the Bismarck *Tribune.* In 1888, to be on the railroad, Hoskins was moved bodily to the present site and was renamed in honor of Ashley E. Morrow, a member of the railroad construction company. In the rotunda of the MCINTOSH COUNTY COURTHOUSE is a series of pictures of pioneer life. A library founded in 1912 by the Ashley Women's Club is also in the courthouse.

Right from Ashley 4 *m.* on ND 11, a graveled highway, to LAKE HOSKINS (*swimming*), a summer recreational center.

On ND 3 at 85 *m.* is the South Dakota Line, 84 *m.* N. of Aberdeen, South Dakota.

STEELE, 156 *m.* (1,855 alt., 721 pop.), granted a city charter by the Territorial legislature in 1882–3, claimed at the time of its incorporation to be the smallest city in the United States. It is named for Colonel W. P. Steele, one of the original town-site owners, who in 1889 sent the first legislature a certified check for $100,000 with his bid for locating the State capitol at Steele. Colonel Steele liked riding on railroad trains and meeting strangers to whom he could talk of the glowing possibilities of North Dakota. At one time he procured passes on many of the large railroads in exchange for passes on his own road, the Steele-Alaska Northwestern, which despite its impressive title was only a half-mile spur from the Northern Pacific to his brick plant NE. of Steele. When his hoax was discovered and he was hailed before a group of directors of the larger lines, he justified his position with the statement, 'While my line is not as long as yours, I want it understood that it is every bit as wide.'

Left from Steele on a graveled road to the junction with a dirt road, 12 *m.*; R. on this road to PURSIAN LAKE (*swimming, picnicking*), 15 *m.*, a haven for migratory waterfowl.

DRISCOLL (L), 167 *m.* (1,870 alt., 200 pop.), is named for a N. P. Ry. stockholder.

Right from Driscoll on a road unsuitable for trailers to the junction with a country trail, 3 *m.*; R. here to CHASKA HISTORIC SITE, 4 *m.*, the grave of Chaska, a Sioux Indian scout with the Sibley expedition, who died during the campaign. Chaska is said to have been one of the two friendly Indians who warned the missionaries at the Yellow Medicine (Minnesota) Agency and led the whites to safety from the vengeful Sioux in the uprising of 1862.

West of Driscoll the route begins the ascent of the ALTAMONT MORAINE, the terminal moraine formed during the last advance of the Dakota lobe of the great continental ice sheets.

At 176 *m.* is the junction with US 83 (*see Tour 3*). The two highways form one route between this point and Bismarck, 200 *m.* Just W. of the junction the highway passes over a crest of the moraine, from which on a clear day the distant outline of the 19-story State capitol is visible, 24 miles W. The highway descends the western slope of the moraine in a gradual incline toward the Missouri River valley.

McKENZIE, 182 *m.* (1,700 alt., 100 pop.), is named for Alexander McKenzie, early-day political boss in North Dakota.

At 187 *m.* is the junction with a dirt road.

Right on this road to MENOKEN INDIAN VILLAGE SITE, 1 *m.*, believed by many historians to be the point at which in 1738 Pierre de la Verendrye, earliest white explorer of present North Dakota, first visited the Mandan Indians. Prior to the investigation of this site in 1936 it was generally supposed that Verendrye's first contact with the Mandans had been made near Sanish, and a monument commemorating the meeting had been erected at that place (*see Tour 6*). The Menoken site shows clearly the position of the bastions and moat of the old fortifications, and saucer-shaped depressions indicate where the earth lodges once stood. In addition, pottery, flint chips, and other artifacts have been found. Verendrye's journal states that he presented a leaden plate, bearing the name of the exploring party, to the Mandan chief at the village he visited. A similar plate was given to the Indians by Verendrye's sons on an expedition farther S. in 1741, and was found buried in the earth near Fort Pierre, South Dakota, in 1913. The first plate, however, has not been recovered and may now lie buried somewhere in the Menoken site.

MENOKEN, 187 *m.* (1,720 alt., 75 pop.), has had a number of names and still retains two officially. In early railroad days it was known as Seventeenth Siding, and later as Blaine. For transportation purposes it is now called Burleigh, to distinguish it from several other towns on the N. P. Ry. which have names beginning with *M*.

At 188 *m*. is the junction with a county graded dirt road.

Right on this road to the TRANSMITTING PLANT OF KFYR, 1.5 *m*., Bismarck's broadcasting station. The 704-foot all-steel vertical radiator, one of the three tallest self-supporting aerials in the United States (1938), can be seen for many miles.

Between Menoken and Bismarck the route crosses and recrosses APPLE CREEK, along which Sibley's army traveled for some distance. In ancient times this small, meandering stream was a great rushing glacial river.

At 198.5 *m*. (L) loom the brick walls of the STATE PENITEN-TIARY (*tours daily exc. Sat. and Sun. at 9, 10, and 11 a.m., 2, 3, and 4 p.m.*). When the prison was built (1885–9), the walls were of cotton-wood logs wired together at the top. The present walls, 27 feet high and 1,650 feet long, and made of bricks from clay found in the vicinity, were constructed by prison labor in 1889. The island-type of prison architecture has been employed, and there are two cell blocks of 160 cells each, all locked by a master control. Inmates are employed in the twine plant, which has an annual output of more than 4 million pounds; on the 950-acre farm; and in the auto license and tag plant.

The fact that most criminals come from large centers of population is given as the reason that North Dakota, an agricultural State with no large cities, has a low prison population. In 1937 it was only 270.

At 199 *m*. is the junction with a paved road.

Left on this road to FORT LINCOLN, 3 *m*., which covers an area of 900 acres and has buildings of modified Colonial design. It was first occupied in 1903, although established as a military reservation in 1895. In 1913 its garrison was removed, but in 1917 it was used as a concentration camp for midwestern troops headed for France. After the First World War it was not garrisoned until 1927, when Companies I, K, L, and M of the Third Battalion, Fourth Infantry were ordered here. Including detachments of Headquarters, Quartermasters and Service Corps, Medical Corps, and Signal and Finance Corps, the post numbered 426 enlisted men and 20 officers in 1937. It is now the headquarters for the U. S. Army Engineers of the Garrison Dam District.

At 4 *m*. is a junction with a dirt road; R. here to another junction, 4.8 *m*.; L. to SIBLEY ISLAND PARK (*shelters, tables, and benches*), 7 *m*. Sibley Island was actually an island when General Sibley fought the Sioux here in 1863, but now, because of the changing river channel, is a part of the river lowlands. The Indians, fleeing before the advancing column, were here forced to abandon large quantities of supplies and equipment, and to hurry across the Missouri. Two Sibley men, carrying orders to detachments in the woods, were ambushed and killed, and the Masonic burial given one is believed to have been the first instance of the use of this funeral rite within the borders of the State. The bodies were removed later, but the position of one grave is still indicated by a marker. Prior to the Sibley encounter the island was known as Assiniboine Island, from the fact that the *Assiniboine,* a river steamer carrying Prince Maximilian's Indian Collection, was destroyed by fire near here (1834).

BISMARCK, 200 *m*. (1,672 alt., 15,496 pop.) (*see* BISMARCK).

At Main Ave. and 6th St. is the junction with US 83 (*see Tour* 3).

At 201 *m.* US 10 crosses the MISSOURI RIVER on the $1,358,000 LIBERTY MEMORIAL BRIDGE, erected in 1922, first highway span across the river in North Dakota. At each end are large natural boulders bearing bronze plaques dedicating the bridge to men and women who served in the First World War.

Natural gas from the fields at Baker, Montana, is piped to Bismarck through a line crossing the Missouri on this bridge.

At the Bismarck end of the bridge is the junction with a county graveled highway (*see Tour 3B*).

Thoroughfare of early exploration of western North Dakota and Montana, the Missouri is still known to the Sioux Indians native to this region as Wakpa Hehanka (*elk river*). According to Sioux legend, once, during the great spring break-up, a large herd of elk were crossing the stream when the ice broke beneath them, precipitating them into quicksand. They perished, and when the ice had floated down the river the antlers of the elk were left protruding like branches from the sand bar.

The time changes from central to mountain standard W. of the river; watches and clocks of west-bound travelers should be turned back one hour, those of east-bound travelers should be set an hour ahead.

Along the highway on the flat lowlands between Bismarck and Mandan are several tourist camps and night clubs.

MANDAN, 205 *m.* (1,642 alt., 5,685 pop.), its business section stretched along one side of its long main street, lies crowded between the N.P. railroad yards and the hills bordering the Heart River valley near the confluence of the Heart and the Missouri.

Named for the agricultural Mandan Indian tribe, this western, overgrown small town is in the area they once occupied, and near two of their ancient village sites. One, Crying Hill Village, is on the bluffs along the Missouri, NE. of the city; the other, known as the Motsiff Site, 2 miles S. on the banks of the Heart. The town itself is so young that many of the original false-front frame or ornate red-brick buildings are still standing. A village grew up here quickly when the railroad crossed the Missouri in 1881, and incorporation as a city followed in 1883. With the settling of the adjoining territory, which began within two years after the founding of the town, development was rapid. Early ranching in the region has given way to grain raising, dairying, and diversified dry farming, and the city has become a wholesale and retail distribution center serving a large agricultural area.

One of the principal economic supports of the city is the N. P. Ry., which maintains a division point here. The RAILWAY DEPOT in red brick is modeled after Washington's Mount Vernon home. In the railroad park, in an ellipse formed by the driveway, stands a small bronze STATUE OF THEODORE ROOSEVELT as a Rough Rider, a reproduction of a large monument in a Minot park (*see* MINOT). On the depot platform, during the summer months, Yanktonai Sioux perform bits of native dances for the benefit of tourists on the fast trains.

On this platform Nov. 1, 1926, Queen Marie of Rumania, making a transcontinental tour, was adopted by the Sioux.

The RAILROAD YARDS are unusual in that their accommodations facilitate handling and housing of the large Pacific-type locomotives known as Five Thousands, so called because they are numbered above 5000. Because of their great length, 125 feet, and their weight, 550 tons, they cannot be used on the sharp curves of the Rocky Mountains; they are therefore employed exclusively on the steep Mandan-Billings, Montana, run. Five Thousands are used only for heavy freight traffic. The largest turntable on the N.P. system, 126 feet long, handles these giants of the rails.

At 1st St. and 2nd Ave. NW. is the MEMORIAL BUILDING, which has the largest indoor swimming pool in the State. The building was constructed under a Federal project.

The J. D. ALLEN TAXIDERMIST SHOP, formerly located at 302 5th Ave. NW., contained a rare collection of Indian relics and a variety of mounted specimens of animals, birds, and fish found in the State. In the hodgepodge of his workshop, Allen, who came to Mandan as a youth in 1881 and remained there until his death in 1947, mounted thousands of specimens, and worked for Theodore Roosevelt and for members of European nobility. His hobby was painting, and, although self-taught in his avocation, he captured the spirit of early North Dakota scenes as have few trained artists. Several of his canvases hang in the museum of the State historical society (*see* BISMARCK).

KGCU, with studios and transmitter in the Kennelly building, is at 205 1st St. NW.

CHAUTAUQUA PARK (*picnic grounds, tourist camp, golf course, clubhouse, tennis and horseshoe courts*) in the southwestern part of the city is on ND 6.

Left from Mandan 1.3 *m.* on a graveled road to the STATE TRAINING SCHOOL, to which modern buildings and well-landscaped grounds give the appearance of an up-to-date preparatory school rather than an institution for delinquent juveniles. The school, which houses both boys and girls, offers a four-year high school course and teaches farming, carpentry, cooking, laundering, and sewing.

On the high bluffs on the south edge of the city is the U.S. NORTHERN GREAT PLAINS FIELD STATION (*see Tour 8C*).

At Mandan is the junction with ND 6, a hard-surfaced highway (*see Tour 8C*).

Left from Mandan on 6th Ave. SE., which becomes a county graveled road and crosses the HEART RIVER, 1 *m.*, which in Sioux translation is called Tacanta Wakpa Tanka.

FORT ABRAHAM LINCOLN STATE PARK, 4.5 *m.* (*see* FORT ABRAHAM LINCOLN STATE PARK).

The graveled road proceeds S. over the benchland of the Missouri to SCHMIDT, 11 *m.*, an elevator and railroad siding. Here the route becomes a graded dirt road, and continues S.

At 18 *m.* the road cuts through an extending clay ridge, which protrudes like an eagle's beak from the Badlands-like formation to the R. To the W. here rises a flat-topped steep cliff jutting away from the other hills and connected with them only by a narrow neck. On this mesa once stood the Eagle's Nose Village of the Mandans, believed by some to have been built by the great Mandan tribal hero Good Furred Robe, although this origin has also been attributed to the Huff Site (*see below*). To reach the old village site one must ascend the SW. side of the hill. From the top there is a far-reaching view of the beautiful Missouri valley, stretching S. from the gray outlines of the capitol at Bismarck and the blockhouses on the hill at Fort McKeen.

At 20 *m.* is HUFF, a store and railroad station. At 20.5 *m.* (L) is the HUFF INDIAN VILLAGE STATE PARK, site of a Mandan village. According to legend the Mandan people at one time lived underground, but under the leadership of four chiefs, headed by Good Furred Robe, they climbed a vine to enter this world through an opening in the ground to the surface. Good Furred Robe then laid out their first village, placing the houses in rows like corn. This legend is believed by some Indians to refer to the Huff Site, whose heavily sodded lodge rings suggest great age. The reason for the somewhat rectangular shape of some of the depressions has not yet been determined.

South of Huff to FORT RICE STATE PARK, 29 *m.*, the site of a fort established by General Alfred H. Sully on his Indian expedition in 1864. It served as a military post until 1877, when it was succeeded by Fort Yates down the river. In 1868 Fort Rice was the scene of a peace council with the Sioux. Sitting Bull and some five thousand followers, resentful of the appropriation of their lands by the white settlers, had refused to go on reservations and had moved to the Powder River in present Wyoming, where they lived the free, open life to which they were accustomed. They harbored a bitter hatred for the white people, but there was one white man whom Sitting Bull trusted. He was Father Pierre Jean De Smet, a Jesuit missionary who had spent years among the Indians of the western plains and was sincerely interested in their welfare. He was known to the Sioux as 'Black Robe.' The War Department and the Indian Bureau, eager to negotiate with the Sioux, sent Father De Smet to lead a delegation to Sitting Bull's camp. Many of the hostile Indians had vowed to kill any white man on sight, but their leader learned that it was 'Black Robe' who was approaching, and welcomed him heartily. During the council that followed, Father De Smet gave Sitting Bull a brass and wood crucifix, which the Sioux leader, although he never professed Catholicism, prized highly all his life. At the instigation of the priest, Sitting Bull, while refusing to attend a peace council himself, sent two representatives, Chief Gall and Bull Owl, whom he instructed to say, 'Move out the soldiers and stop the steamboats and we shall have peace.' The peace council was held at Fort Rice and led to the Laramie Treaty later that year, which unfortunately was violated in 1875 by the Indian Bureau and the War Department, precipitating the hostilities that ended in the disastrous Battle of the Little Big Horn in June 1876 (*see* HISTORY).

West of Mandan US 10 enters that part of the Missouri Plateau known locally as the Missouri Slope, and proceeds over the rolling grasslands typical of this area. As the route progresses through the Slope region, buttes jutting up from the prairie become more numerous. Many are crowned with brick-red scoria (clay baked in the earth by the heat of burning lignite beds lying adjacent), and others have scoria formations protruding from their sides.

At 209 *m.* is the junction with ND 25, a graveled highway (*see Tour 8D*).

At 231 *m.* (L) is the WRONG SIDE UP MONUMENT, a four-foot natural boulder bearing a bronze plate, commemorating an incident to which the New Salem Holstein Breeders' Circuit, nationally known dairy organization, credits its success. As one of the early settlers was breaking land preparatory to seeding it for the first time, a Sioux Indian and his son approached. The father, turning a piece of the sod back into its natural position, remarked, 'Wrong side up.' His son explained that the father believed the soil should not be plowed. The farmer, heeding his advice, grazed cattle on his land instead. Neighbors followed his example, and today NEW SALEM, 232 m. (2,163 alt., 875 pop.), is the center of an extensive dairying area. The town was named by members of the Evangelical Lutheran Church for the Biblical city of Salem.

GLEN ULLIN, 253 m. (2,065 alt., 976 pop.), a Russo-German community, has a name suggested to a railroad official by the Scottish ballad *Lord Ullin's Daughter*. An intermediate lighted airport is maintained here by the Department of Commerce. Levon West, the etcher, once attended Glen Ullin high school.

HEBRON, 265 m. (2,155 alt., 1,267 pop.), is in a small valley just W. of the divide between the Heart and Knife Rivers. Like New Salem, its name is of Biblical origin. The town has more brick-faced buildings in its business district than most towns of similar size because of the proximity of the $250,000 Hebron BRICK PLANT (*for directions inquire at post office; open weekdays 9–5*). Clay deposits suitable for brick manufacture, discovered here in 1904, led to the development of the field. The plant, on the eastern outskirts of the town, ships its products to all parts of the Northwest, the Pacific Coast States, and Canada.

Just NW. of the town, where a cemetery now lies, FORT SAUERKRAUT was built at the time of a false Indian scare in 1892. There is no record of why it was given its odd name.

Right from Hebron on a country trail to CROWLEY FLINT QUARRY STATE PARK, 22 m. Here the Indians obtained flint from which to make arrow and spear heads. The process of making an arrowhead or spear point was tedious, the only tool being a piece of bone or horn that had been buried two weeks in wood ashes to remove grease and temper the material. On the palm of one hand was placed a buckskin covering, and on this was laid the flint, held in place by the fingers of the same hand. Using the bone tool in the other hand, the worker began flaking chips from the flint, first up one side and then the other, until the stone assumed the shape wanted. Today unfinished or broken arrowheads and spear points are occasionally found in the quarry.

West of ANTELOPE (L), 273 m. (2,410 alt., 17 pop.), the route follows closely the trail made by Custer's Seventh Cavalry in June 1876, on their way from Fort Abraham Lincoln to the Little Big Horn country in Montana, to meet death at the hands of the Sioux they pursued (*see* HISTORY). The deep ruts cut in the prairie by the military wagons of the expedition, and later by those traveling over the same trail to Fort Keogh, Montana, are visible R. and parallel to the highway where it passes S. of YOUNG MEN'S BUTTE, 275.5 m. According to legend, when the Arikara Indians were still living on the Grand River, in what is now South Dakota, a group separated from the tribe and set out toward the northwest to seek a new home. Two young men in the party, however, grew lonesome for the sweethearts they had left behind, and when they reached this butte they decided to return to their old home. The remainder of the party continued on the journey, and was never heard from again.

Left from Antelope an unimproved dirt road leads to the Heart River, 8 *m.*, and the SITE OF GENERAL SULLY'S TEMPORARY BASE CAMP for the Battle of Killdeer Mountains. On his march to the Yellowstone River, in 1864, Sully corralled his wagon train at this camp, and, traveling light, moved quickly N. to the Killdeer Mountains to make a surprise attack on a camp of 5000 Sioux (*see Tour 8D*).

RICHARDTON, 279 *m.* (2,465 alt., 682 pop.), is the home of As-SUMPTION ABBEY of the Benedictine order. The buildings, of Gothic and Romanesque styles, give the impression of having been transplanted from ancient Europe to the North Dakota prairie. Twin red-roofed steeples raise burnished crosses above the buildings, which are constructed in a square around a garden court. The abbey, completed in 1910, includes St. Mary's Monastery, St. Mary's Church, and a high school and junior college for boys. The library contains over 14,000 volumes, among which are several books dated 1720 and bound in pigskin. The town is named for C. B. Richardton, official of a steamship company that sought homes for German immigrants, and is predominantly Russo-German.

At 285 *m.* is TAYLOR (2,487 alt., 251 pop.). South of here along the Heart River are large deposits of bentonite, a clay used for commercial manufacture of paints, cleaners, linoleum, cosmetics, and other products (*see* INDUSTRY AND LABOR).

At 300.5 *m.* is the junction with a graveled road.

Left on this road is LEHIGH, 2 *m.* (2,347 alt.), named for Lehigh, Pennsylvania, because both are mining towns. Here is a BRIQUETTING PLANT (*open to large parties and school or college groups; guides*). This is the only plant in the United States producing lignite briquets with a B.t.u. (*British thermal unit: 778 foot-pounds energy*) rating of 15,000. Raw lignite has a B.t.u. rating of about 6500. Eighteen thousand tons of briquets are produced annually by the million-dollar plant. The work of the late E. J. Babcock of the State university has been of great importance in adapting the lignite briquetting process to North Dakota coal. The chief byproduct of the plant is creosote, of which about 70,000 gallons are shipped to eastern markets each year. Research conducted on activated carbon, a lignite product used in the manufacture of tires and for filtration purposes, points to commercial development of this byproduct (*see* INDUSTRY AND LABOR).

DICKINSON, 304 *m.* (2,305 alt., 5,839 pop.), principal stock and wheat shipping point in the central Missouri Slope area, and Stark County seat, is on the slope of a hill overlooking the Heart River, which cuts through the prairie S. of the city. The town is still young enough to retain much of the friendly atmosphere of the early West.

When the railroad reached this point in 1880, the site was known as Pleasant Valley Siding, but in 1883 the name was changed by H. L.

Dickinson, the town's first merchant, to honor his cousin Wells S. Dickinson, a New York State senator.

The town defeated Gladstone and Belfield for county seat in 1884, and the same year saw its development as a forwarding point for freight to the booming Black Hills gold fields. On April 15 alone, more than 220,000 pounds of freight destined for the Hills were received at Dickinson.

In 1886 the Dickinson *Press* reported:

The first Fourth of July celebration attempted in Dickinson took place last Monday. It exceeded the anticipation of all and proved to be a grand success—a day that will long be remembered. The day dawned bright and cool. Early in the morning people began to arrive and by ten o'clock the largest crowd ever assembled in Stark County lined the principal streets. The train from the west brought a number of Medora people. Amongst them was Hon. Theodore Roosevelt, the orator of the day. The celebration consisted of: A Parade, Addresses by Hon. Theodore Roosevelt and Hon. John A. Rae, Races, Fire Works, and a dance in the evening.

Russo-German immigrants seeking homes in this country were early attracted to Dickinson by the Catholic mission established there by Bishop Martin Marty of St. Paul, and today the southern part of the city is a Russo-German settlement, almost a town within a town. Although the younger generation is Americanized, the older women still wear old-fashioned, long, dark dresses, and cover their heads with dark scarfs or *tuecher*. There are halls for social functions and for the gala wedding dances, which often last several days.

In the northern part of the city are the DICKINSON COUNTRY CLUB (*golf*), WHITNEY SWIMMING POOL (*open June-Sept.; nominal fee*), and ATHLETIC FIELD (*gridiron, baseball diamond, running track, and tennis courts*), and ROCKY BUTTE PARK (*picnicking*).

Atop a knoll on 10th Ave. W. is the campus of the DICKINSON STATE NORMAL SCHOOL. Its buildings, in English Tudor style, constructed of Hebron brick with white sandstone trim, were not occupied until 1924, although classes were held in the Dickinson Elks building as early as 1918. On the top floor of May Hall is a natural history museum.

Left (S) from Dickinson on ND 22 to a U. S. Department of Commerce intermediate AIRPORT, 6 m.

At 305 m. is a junction with a graveled road.

Right on this road to the DICKINSON SUBSTATION AND NORTH DAKOTA AGRICULTURAL EXPERIMENT STATION, 2 m. Here, under State and Federal supervision, experiments are conducted in fruit production, dry land farming, and the raising of forage and cereal crops. The Dickinson Dam, an earth-filled structure on the Heart River 45 feet high and 1600 feet long, is located 2 m. W. of Dickinson and S. of US 10. It will furnish a dependable water supply for Dickinson and will also be used as a recreational area.

At 322 m. is the junction with a graveled spur.

Left on this spur is SOUTH HEART, 1 m. (2,474 alt., 70 pop.), so named because of its position on the southern branch of the Heart River. One mile W.

of the town the trail made in 1864 by General Alfred Sully and his troops on their return from the Battle of Killdeer Mountain is plainly visible. South of the town on a country trail is CUSTER HILL, 7 *m.*, where Custer made camp on his way to the Big Horn country in Montana in 1876. Breastworks thrown up as a protection are still visible.

BELFIELD, 324 *m.* (2,578 alt., 870 pop.), is in a small valley along a tributary of the Heart River. The Dakota Colloidal Corp., which operates the only BENTONITE PLANT (*open weekdays* 9–4) in the State, procures the mineral from a clay found N. of town and uses it in the manufacture of soaps and washing powders. Here is a junction with US 85 (*see Tour* 4).

At 332 *m.* the route comes dramatically upon the BADLANDS, cut into the heart of the plateau. In every direction stretches a confusion of bare, grotesque, garish buttes, their tops level with the surrounding prairies. Down their sides broad earth strata—brown, ash-gray, sulphur-yellow, and salmon—deposited through geological ages, have been exposed by years of erosion. French explorers named this region *mauvaises terres à traverser,* or bad lands to travel through.

Right at 334 *m.* is PAINTED CANYON with its jumble of gorges and superb buttes. Spread as far as one can see toward the northern horizon is a magnificent display of buttes, showing in varying light and shadow the great charm of this never-monotonous country. A drive lined with a wall of brick-red scoria (*see* NATURAL SETTING), mottled with green, like weathered bronze, parallels the highway, providing a good point from which to take photographs.

As the highway descends into the Badlands, it twists through ravines and valleys. At 337 *m.* is the eastern entrance to the THEODORE ROOSEVELT NATIONAL MEMORIAL PARK.

MEDORA, 343 *m.* (2,265 alt., 175 pop.), seat of Billings County, lies along the eastern bank of the Little Missouri River, at the foot of a steep wall of yellow clay cliffs. Now a center for tourists attracted by its history and the scenic beauty of the surrounding area, it was formerly such a bustling cattle town that on one occasion a thousand Texas steers stampeded across the tracks and stopped a train. In the same era, it is said, the more or less adequately named son of the plains, Hell-Roaring Bill Jones, saw an old gentleman in a derby get off the train here. Derbies and plug hats were especially scorned by the cowboys, so with a grunt of disapproval Bill shot off the offending bit of haberdashery. The gentleman hastened to re-enter the train, leaving his dismantled headgear to the West. But not so Bill Jones: 'Come back!' he roared in tones that compelled obedience. 'We don't want the blinkety-blank thing in Medora.'

In 1879 a military camp named Little Missouri Cantonment (*see below*) was established on the opposite bank to protect workers of the N. P. Ry. from Indian attacks. This typically rough frontier post saw the arrival in 1883 of two notable young men of almost the same age. Theodore Roosevelt, a young New York assemblyman of 25, traveling for his health and also to forget his recent loss of both mother and

wife, already displayed the rugged, direct personality that later characterized the wielder of the 'big stick.' Because of his eastern dress and
his heavy glasses he became known as 'the four-eyed dude from New
York,' or, more briefly, 'Four-eyes'—until one evening with his naked
fists he knocked out and disarmed a bully. Thereafter his nickname
was subtly changed to 'Old Four-eyes.'

The other young man was the Marquis de Mores, a handsome, spirited
Frenchman. Arriving in America about six months earlier with his bride,
the rich and charming Medora Von Hoffman of New York, he had
made a hunting trip to the West and, with characteristic dash, decided
to build a packing plant in the cattle country to capitalize on the advantage of avoiding the cost of shipping live animals to eastern abat-
toirs. Wealthy in his own right and backed by his millionaire father-in-
law, de Mores came to the wild Badlands to build the plant that was
to be the center of operations for the Northern Pacific Refrigerator Car
Co., incorporated to operate in five Territories and nine States, and to
do a general transportation business.

Because of some disagreement over contemplated real-estate purchases in Little Missouri, de Mores bought a huge tract of land on the
east side of the river, where he built his packing plant and with it a
town, named Medora for his wife.

In the middle 'eighties Medora, together with Mingusville (present
Wibaux, Montana), had become the center of a new, rich, cattle-grazing
section. The round-up area extended to a radius of 75 miles, and in
some round-ups as many as 100 men were employed. Large outfits ran
probably 100,000 head, and ranchers like Roosevelt, who grazed 2000
to 3000 head, were considered small cattlemen.

Many factors operated against the success of de Mores' packing plant,
which opened in the fall of 1883. He himself was young, rash, inexperi-
enced, and often ill-advised. His friends found him honest and confid-
ing, and less open minds than his took advantage of him. There were
costly mistakes, and many hundreds of thousands were spent before
any meat was sold. Moreover, eastern packers undersold de Mores and
forced ruinously low prices. Since he had to depend on grass for feed, he
could supply his trade from his own stock only at certain seasons, and
at the other times had to buy from outside parties, who took advantage
of the situation to charge him high prices. A plan to feed cattle at
Medora never materialized. De Mores ran sheep, but hundreds died. To
cap it all, the public apparently did not like grass-fed meat.

Another ill-starred enterprise was the Medora-Deadwood stage line,
begun in the fall of 1884 with the idea of securing a mail contract and
some of the passenger and freight traffic going to the Black Hills gold
fields by way of Dickinson. The route from Medora to Deadwood was
shorter than that from Dickinson, but it was also rougher. De Mores'
horses were wild and often broke up equipment. In addition, the mail
contract failed to materialize; the shift from placer to deep mining
lessened the flow of transients into the Hills; and after one trip over the

rough road, freight shippers usually chose the Dickinson route. The line was ordered discontinued in the spring of 1886, ending another of the marquis' dreams.

Many people of the Little Missouri Valley did not like de Mores. They doubted his claim to the peerage, or, if they believed it, regarded it as an affront to their almost belligerent democracy. Such things as his special car on the N. P. Ry. and his occasional trips East or abroad irked them. Worst of all, he began to fence his land—a glaring infraction of wide-open range etiquette. His fences were cut; he had them mended. They were cut open again. Things went from bad to worse. Stories were carried to de Mores of threats against his life. He appealed to the sheriff at Mandan for the arrest of the trouble-makers. When the deputy sheriff arrived, they bluffed him out, and de Mores, thinking the deputy overpowered or perhaps killed, endeavored to make the arrest. There was shooting, and when the smoke cleared, one man was dead.

This was in June 1883. Twice dismissed by lower courts, the charge against de Mores was finally brought in district court in Bismarck in September 1885. He was acquitted. About a year after the trial, realizing that his packing plant was not to be a success, he closed its doors and took his family to Europe. At the age of 38, while on an expedition to Africa, he was ambushed and killed by native guides.

Except for his neighbor Roosevelt, the Badlands have never known a more notable figure than this Frenchman with his dreams of their industrial development.

Theodore Roosevelt was a frequent visitor at the de Mores' chateau (*see below*) during the months he spent in Dakota Territory. On his first hunting trip here in 1883 he was so attracted by the wild country that he made arrangements to become a partner in a ranching enterprise, and for the next six years he spent part of each year here, first at the Maltese Cross, or Chimney Butte Ranch (*see* BISMARCK), 7 miles up the Little Missouri, and later at the Elkhorn, 35 miles downstream (*see Tour* 10). Both ranch sites are difficult to reach, and little is to be seen at them other than the sites where the buildings stood.

Roosevelt's ranching ventures were not financially successful; he ran small herds, and was interested more in the condition of his health than that of his fortune. His keen delight in hunting and the rough cowboy life, however, won him many friends. In the spring of 1884 he acted as chairman of the local Stockmen's Association, and the same year he was the principal speaker at Dickinson's first Fourth of July celebration. One day a cowboy overheard someone say, 'That fool Joe Ferris [a Medora storekeeper] says Roosevelt is going to be President.' Seventeen years later the cowboy told this to Ferris; the death of McKinley had just made Roosevelt President.

In company with the other stockmen of the valley, Roosevelt lost heavily in the severe winter of 1886–7. It is said that scarcely a rancher did not lose at least half his stock—the Hash-Knife, a large outfit, lost 65,000 head.

Roosevelt's trips to the West thereafter were of shorter duration. One of the strongest links that bound him to this country was his famous Rough Riders, made up mainly of western men, who served under him in the Spanish-American War. Roosevelt visited Medora in 1900, on a campaign tour, and again in 1903, and was warmly received each time by his old neighbors and friends.

Medora was briefly the home of Tom Mix, screen actor, who was married here to Olive M. Stokes, Jan. 19, 1909. Mix, then a circus performer, and Miss Stokes had just completed contracts with the Miller Brothers' 101 Ranch Wild West Show.

Right at the entrance to Main St. is the little buff brick ATHENAIS CHAPEL, built for the marquise by her husband in 1884, and named for their daughter. It was presented to the village in 1920 by members of the de Mores family, and is still in use as the Roman Catholic church of the community.

Fronting Main St. is the ROUGH RIDERS HOTEL, erected by de Mores in 1884. It served as headquarters for cattlemen and cowpunchers of the day; and although it was built a year after Theodore Roosevelt came to Dakota, the story is told that his first night in Medora was spent here. Doubtless, however, he spent many nights in the hotel, which suggested to him the name of his Spanish-American War regiment.

One block down Main St. (L) is a bronze STATUE OF MARQUIS DE MORES, erected by the family in 1926. It stands in a small plot that is part of De Mores State Park, three tracts comprising about 128 acres, deeded to the State Historical Society of North Dakota in 1936 by Louis, Count de Vallombrosa, eldest son of the marquis. On a second unit of the park, in the northwestern part of town, is the SITE OF THE DE MORES PACKING PLANT. The abandoned buildings, with mammoth refrigerators and machinery and mysterious dark passages, long bore the legend, 'Rent free to any responsible party who will make use of them.' Fire destroyed them in 1907; all that remains today is a tall, gaunt, yellow brick chimney.

Left from Medora on a winding graded county dirt road to the CUSTER TRAIL RANCH, 5 m., named by its founders, Howard, Willis, and Alden Eaton, for its position on the trail of the fatal military expedition to the Little Big Horn in 1876. It is at the confluence of the Little Missouri River and Davis Creek, where a Custer camp erected parapets for protection from possible Indian attack. Deep ruts cut by the wagons of the expedition are still visible near the ranch buildings. This ranch was established in the late 1880's and is the first of the 'dude ranches' which have become so popular in the West. The owners were neighbors of Roosevelt, whose Chimney Butte Ranch was 2 miles upstream. In 1897 Ernest Thompson Seton, naturalist and author, while gathering material for his books *Lives of the Hunted* and *Coyotito,* spent the month of September here with the Eatons. The ranch still has its quota of summer visitors, but in the early 1900's the Eatons transferred their activities to the vicinity of the Big Horn Mountains.

At 343.2 *m.* the route crosses the bridge leading over the LITTLE MISSOURI RIVER. Except in times of flood the stream, which is narrow here, is shallow and sluggish.

At 343.3 *m.* is the junction with an improved road.

Left on this road to the third unit (111 A.) of the De Mores State Park, the DE MORES CHATEAU, 0.5 *m.*, commanding an excellent view of the river, the bluffs, and the village. The chateau is a 28-room, 2-story frame structure with a wide veranda, and windows guarded by old-fashioned shutters.

Deserted by its wealthy young owners and their retinue of servants, and subjected to the aging of half a century, it presents a vastly different picture from that of 1883, when the ambitious Frenchman built it for his red-haired bride.

Although the establishment of the packing plant was de Mores' chief reason for being in Dakota, he and the marquise led an active social life, entertaining settlers of the region and also many distinguished guests from the East and from Europe, who came to hunt. An item in the Bismarck *Tribune* of Sept. 4, 1885, read:

'She Killed Three Bears

'The Marquise, wife of Marquis de Mores, has returned from her hunt in the Rocky mountains, where she killed two cinnamon bears and one large grizzly bear. The accomplished lady, who was a few years ago one of New York City's popular society belles, is now the queen of the Rocky mountains and the champion huntress of the great northwest.'

During their residence in America two children were born to the de Mores, a son, Louis, and a daughter, Athenais. A third child, Paul, was born in France soon after the family left Medora. The marquise died in 1920 as the result of an injury received while serving as a nurse in the First World War. Although she returned to Medora only once (1903), she removed nothing from the chateau to which she came as a bride. It was left in the hands of a caretaker until its transfer to the State historical society in 1936.

At 343.4 *m.* (L) are the partly filled cellar holes that mark the SITE OF LITTLE MISSOURI, Medora's predecessor. The story is told that, during the heyday of the town, passengers on a train pausing opposite a hotel here heard the sound of shots. Presently, to their horror, the door opened and a group of cowboys carried out a limp body. Soon there were more shots, and another body was brought out. Before the train left the cowboys figured they had given the 'dudes' an eyeful. The 'bodies' all belonged to the same man, and the shots had been aimed so as to do no harm.

At 345 *m.* is the junction with a graveled road.

Right on this road to the sandstone pillars marking the western entrance to the north section of the Theodore Roosevelt National Memorial Park, 0.1 *m.* (*see* THEODORE ROOSEVELT NATIONAL MEMORIAL PARK).

At 349 *m.* is the first glimpse of FLAT TOP BUTTE (L), sometimes known as Square Butte, whose mesa-like top contains nearly a section of land. On a slope of this butte occurred a skirmish between Sully's punitive expedition of 1864 and a band of Hunkpapa and Sans Arc Sioux led by Sitting Bull. Harried by a sniping fire from the Sioux, the 2200 soldiers, on quarter rations because of insufficient supplies, and burdened with an immigrant train of 600 people and 120 oxcarts, had sweltered through a hot August day. Just as darkness was closing over the Badlands they discovered a spring on the northeastern slope of Flat Top Butte, only to have Sitting Bull, who realized their need of the water, suddenly pour in a heavy fire from the near-by hills. The firing continued intermittently all night. In the morning, however, the Sioux withdrew and went hunting. Several Indians were killed during the encounter and many soldiers wounded.

At 357 *m.* the highway reaches the level prairie after a gradual rise out of the Badlands. From here is visible (L) Sentinel Butte (3,350 alt.), second highest point in the State, a large flat-topped mesa in the distance. Right is the CAMEL'S HUMP, a peculiarly rounded, grass-covered hill.

At 360 *m.* is the village of SENTINEL BUTTE (2,706 alt., 256 pop.), which was named for the near-by mesa to the S. The Sully expedition, following its encounter with the Sioux at Flat Top, passed over the present town site.

Left from the town on a graveled road to the junction with a county dirt road, 3 *m.*; L. here to a gate (L) at 4.3 *m.*; follow rutted trail to foot of southern slope of SENTINEL BUTTE, 5 *m.* In a pass at the top of this slope are two supposed graves of sentinels killed while on guard. Conflicting stories are told of the sentinels' identity. One Indian legend says romance was involved in the slaying of the two; another, that they were Arikara scouts surprised by a Sioux war party. Nearly 80 acres of grassland are on the flat top of Sentinel Butte, and its precipitous sandstone cliffsides rise 719 feet above the surrounding prairies. From the eastern rim of the butte on a clear day is a panorama of the Badlands, with Flat Top Butte in the foreground and the diggings of several private lignite coal mines visible in the slopes of the neighboring hills. To the S. and W. the plain stretches away into the distance: nicely squared patches of green in the spring and early summer, rippling areas of gold during harvest, and squares of plowed black earth etched against patches of grimy yellow stubble in the fall.

BEACH, 367.5 *m.* (2,755 alt., 1,178 pop.), is named for Captain Warren Beach of the Eleventh Infantry, who accompanied the Stanley railroad survey expedition in 1873. Beach is Golden Valley County seat, center of a large agricultural area in western North Dakota and eastern Montana, and a grain shipping point. John M. Baer, the political cartoonist, was postmaster in Beach from 1913 to 1915, and later became a North Dakota Congressman.

US 10 crosses the Montana Line, 370 *m.*, 38 *m.* E. of Glendive, Montana (*see Montana Guide Tour* 1).

◊◇◊

Tour 8A

Valley City—Oakes—South Dakota Line; ND 1.
Valley City to South Dakota Line, 75 *m.*

N. P. Ry. branch line roughly parallels route between Verona and Oakes, North
Western Ry. branch between Oakes and South Dakota Line.
Graveled roadbed throughout.
Accommodations in principal towns.

ND 1 south of Valley City traverses the rolling plain—part of the
Height of Land—that lies between the Sheyenne and the James Rivers.
The northern end of the route runs near the Sheyenne, while its southern course roughly parallels the James. Near the southern border of the
State the highway runs across the level bed of glacial Lake Dakota, a
small part of which extended into present North Dakota. This lake
existed before Lake Agassiz, in the valley of the James River, which was
in existence before the second ice age. Along the entire route pheasants
are plentiful.

ND 1 branches S. from US 10 at Valley City (*see Tour* 8).

At 19 *m.* is the junction with a graveled road.

Left on this road to BIRCH CREEK HISTORIC SITE (*picnic and camp
grounds adjoining*), 1 *m.* In the late 1830's the Federal Government sent its first
exploratory expedition into this area under Jean N. Nicollet and Lieutenant
John C. Frémont. Their party camped in this coulee on Birch Creek in 1839. In
August 1863 a detachment of the Sibley Indian expedition under Colonel Samuel
McPhail also camped here, naming the site Camp Johnson for one of the
officers. Later, in 1867–72, the Fort Totten-Fort Ransom trail crossed the coulee.

HASTINGS, 20 *m.* (1,453 alt., 150 pop.), was named by the N. P.
Ry. for Hastings, Minnesota, which in turn was named for General
Henry Hastings Sibley (1811–91), first Governor of Minnesota, and in
1863 commander of an expedition against the Sioux.

At 24 *m.* is the junction with ND 46, a graveled highway.

Left on this highway to the junction with an unimproved country trail, 7 *m.*;
R. here 0.5 *m.* to INYAN BOSDATA, or Standing Rock, one of two rocks within
the boundaries of North Dakota sacred to the Sioux tribes (*see Tour 8C*). The
Sioux are reticent concerning legends of the stone, saying only that it is *wau-
kan* (mysterious). About 4 feet high, it is roughly shaped like an inverted cone
and stands atop a circular mound, from which long, narrow mounds extend both
E. and W. The significance of the mound on which it stands is not definitely
known, but it is believed to be of ceremonial origin. Positions of skeletons and
types of artifacts found in the different strata of the few mounds excavated in
this area lead archeologists to believe that the mounds were built for burial purposes. Discoveries in the oldest stratum indicate that after the retreat of the

glacier the race that built the mounds was nomadic, living by the hunt and on edible tubers found in the region, while artifacts found in later strata reveal that the race had probably become agricultural and lived in permanent villages.

At 9 *m.* on ND 46 is the junction with an unimproved dirt road; L. here 1 *m.* to CAMP WEISER HISTORIC SITE, named for Dr. J. S. Weiser, surgeon with the First Minnesota Mounted Rangers, who was later killed in the Battle of Big Mound (*see Tour 8*). This was an encampment of the Sibley expedition the night of July 13–14, 1863.

At 31 *m.* on ND 1 is the junction with a graveled road.

Left here is FORT RANSOM, 7 *m.* (1,217 alt., 125 pop.), a quiet little village hidden in the trees at the foot of the hill on which are the RUINS OF OLD FORT RANSOM. Thousands of Civil War veterans, released from service, turned to the West for opportunity, crossing the plains to the gold fields in Montana and Idaho. To keep the hostile Sioux in check and to guard the immigrant wagon trains on their overland journeys, it was planned to establish a chain of forts across the prairies. Fort Ransom was the first of this chain, built in 1867 by General Alfred Terry and named for General Thomas Ransom, a Civil War officer. It was protected by sod and log breastworks 12 feet high, surrounded by a ditch 8 feet deep, a protection never greatly needed, for few Indians lived in the vicinity. In 1872 Fort Ransom was replaced by Fort Seward at Jamestown (*see Tour 8*). Remains of the breastworks of the fortification are visible. The site of Fort Ransom has been acquired by the State historical society.

Across the deep ravine running N. and W. of the fort a lookout post was situated on BEAR DEN HILLOCK, which the Sioux know as Matoti. On the slope of this hill is a large glaciated WRITING ROCK, on the surface of which are four deep grooves. These the Indians believe to have been written by spirits. Two legends are told of the stone: one, that a water sprite traced the markings with his finger, the other that two young women spirits came daily to write messages to the tribes, until the invasion of the white man, when they refused to send further messages. Several tumuli of the mound builders are on this hill.

At 37 *m.* on ND 1 is the junction with ND 27, a graveled highway.

Left here is LISBON, 19 *m.* (1,187 alt., 1,997 pop.), Ransom County seat, named by two settlers for their home cities, Lisbon, New York, and Lisbon, Illinois. The first settlers arrived in 1878, and two years later the town site was platted. Situated at the foot of the hills bordering the Sheyenne River, the town is scattered on both wooded banks of the stream. The red-brick buildings of the STATE SOLDIERS HOME, in landscaped grounds in the southern section of the town, accommodate 50 veterans. SANDAGER PARK in the northwestern part is a well-maintained recreational center (*short boat trips up river available in summer; reasonable fares*). W. D. Boyce (1860–1912), Lisbon newspaper publisher during the 1880's, who became publisher of the *Saturday Blade* in Chicago, is credited with bringing the Boy Scout idea to the United States from England, and a fine BOY SCOUT BUILDING AND PARK on Main St. are a memorial to him. R. N. Stevens (1852–1925), a Lisbon attorney and member of the State constitutional convention in 1889, later associated with Alexander McKenzie in Alaska, is characterized as the crafty attorney in Rex Beach's novel *The Spoilers*.

Left from Lisbon 1 *m.* on ND 32 to OAKWOOD CEMETERY, the land for which was a gift of William K. Thaw, a large landholder here in early days. It contains the graves of many soldiers. In the center of the area is a statue of a bugler in the pose of sounding taps, a memorial to the Civil War dead.

At 23 *m.* on ND 27 is the junction with a graveled road; R. here 2 *m.* to the junction with another graveled road; L. to another junction at 3 *m.*; R. to the SITE OF CAMP HAYES, 4.8 *m.* On the first bench above the level Sheyenne River flood plain General H. H. Sibley and his Indian expedition camped a week in July 1863 while awaiting supplies and mail from Fort Abercrombie. At each of his camps Sibley erected breastworks of some type, and remains of the ravine trenches at this site are still visible. Like giant anthills, several tumuli of the mound builders project against the sky line on the hills bordering the river opposite Camp Hayes. The largest of the hills along the river here is OKIEDAN BUTTE, meaning *place where they all rushed together,* famed in Sioux legend. At the foot of the hill, near a spring still flowing, a Sisseton Sioux war party is said to have attacked and killed a band of 30 Arikara Indians. At this same place in the early 1880's Brevet General H. M. Creel of the U.S. Regulars reported having his command entirely surrounded by so large a herd of bison that it stretched beyond the vision of his field glasses and took several hours in passing.

At 27 *m.* on ND 27 is the junction with an unimproved dirt road; R. here 3 *m.* to the CHEYENNE INDIAN VILLAGE SITE. A springhouse (L) stands at the entrance to the ear-shaped site. Depressions mark the position of the earth lodges that once stood here. A moat is still visible around the entire site. Many artifacts have been excavated, including traces of pottery. The homes of the Cheyennes were circular lodges, constructed of earth over a frame of logs, similar to those of the Mandan and Hidatsa Indians who lived along the Missouri River (*see Tour 3A and Tour 8*). In the eighteenth century the Cheyennes were forced into South Dakota and Wyoming by the continued attacks of the Sioux and Chippewa.

STRONG MEMORIAL PARK (*picnic and camp grounds*), 3.3 *m.,* is across the road (R) from the Indian village site. The land was given the State historical society by Frank Strong and is a memorial to him.

At 41.5 *m.* is the junction with ND 13, a graveled highway.

Left here is LaMOURE, 10 *m.* (1,304 alt., 990 pop.), named for Judson LaMoure (1839-1918), an early political power in the State. It is situated on the banks of the James River and is the center of a large dairying area. Its history dates from the arrival of the railroad in 1883. As the community grew, an intense rivalry was born between LaMoure and Grand Rapids (*see below*), a rivalry that did not end until LaMoure, in a hot fight in 1886, won the La-Moure County seat from Grand Rapids, which thereafter declined. Like other frontier towns, LaMoure had many gaming houses and saloons. Residences being scarce, one pious family was forced to live above a saloon. When it came time for the wife to entertain the weekly prayer meeting, the saloon closed out of deference, and the next issue of the LaMoure *Chronicle* mentioned the incident thus: 'There were spirits above and spirits below. The spirits below were spirits of wine, and the spirits above were spirits divine.' One year LaMoure had no speaker for a Fourth of July celebration, while a popular speaker, Dr. E. P. Robertson of Fargo, had been engaged by Grand Rapids. He arrived at Lisbon, the end of the railroad line, and was met by a fine four-horse team and the best carriage to be found. The driver shouted, 'All aboard for Grand Rapids! Right this way for Dr. Robertson!' and the unsuspecting doctor was driven to LaMoure, delivered a glowing address, was returned to Lisbon by the same rig, and reached home without having learned of his error. An occasion for excitement in LaMoure was the arrival of the steamer *Nettie Baldwin* in the late summer of 1883. The boat docked at a pontoon bridge, and some citizens had visions of the town's becoming an important river port. Of a second trip in 1884 the *Chronicle* recalls: 'The climax to speculation concerning a regular commercial route came suddenly and sadly. *Nettie Baldwin* couldn't cut the buck, or was it the mud?' The boat was left in the water, where it lay for many years.

At 13 *m.* on ND 13 is the junction with ND 63, a graveled highway; R. here is GRAND RAPIDS, 19 *m.* (1,320 alt., 30 pop.), named for the cataract in the James River at this point. The little village, once a prosperous county seat, lies at one of the widest points of the James River flood plain. It was the first organized town in LaMoure County, and until 1886 was the county seat. In that year it lost the position to LaMoure after a bitter struggle, although the editor of the LaMoure *Chronicle* dared to sympathize with Grand Rapids, to an extent that won him in his home city the title of 'Leper of LaMoure.'

On ND 63 to LAMOURE COUNTY MEMORIAL PARK (*picnic and camp grounds, playgrounds, swimming, horseshoe courts, athletic field*), 20 *m.*, is a 53-acre tract along the James River, established as a memorial to LaMoure County First World War dead. Many county gatherings are held here each summer.

ND 1 continues S. to VERONA, 42 *m.* (1,383 alt., 201 pop.), first settled in the spring of 1883, and named for the city in northern Italy.

ND 1, S. of Verona, continues over the level prairie. At 58 *m.* is a junction with ND 11, which unites with ND 1 between this point and 70 *m.*

OAKES, 58 *m.* (1,310 alt., 1,665 pop.), on a level rise of ground 1 mile E. of the James River, is at the extreme northern end of the bed of glacial Lake Dakota. The town site was platted in 1886 at the junction of the N.P. and North Western Rys., and was named for Thomas Fletcher Oakes (1843–1911), one-time vice president and general manager of the N. P. Ry. A short time later the Soo Line built into the new community, and these railroad facilities were a factor in the rapid growth of the town. It was incorporated as a city in 1888. The foresight of Oakes' first citizens is indicated by the exceptional width of the streets.

The million-dollar NORTH AMERICAN CREAMERY PLANT is the chief industrial plant of the town.

CENTRAL PARK, in the western part of town, contains a lighted ice-skating rink.

South of Oakes the low-lying hills of the Missouri Plateau (R) are visible in the distance, while a range of hills (L) marks the Height of Land between the Sheyenne and James Rivers. Rain falling on the western side of these hills finds its way into the James and the Gulf of Mexico via the Missouri and Mississippi Rivers, while that falling to the E. enters the Sheyenne and eventually makes its way to Hudson Bay through the Red River.

LUDDEN, 69 *m.* (1,303 alt., 150 pop.), was named by the town-site owner, Frank Randall, for Mr. and Mrs. J. D. Ludden of St. Paul, Minnesota, who had cared for him when he was an infant. First settled near by in 1883, the town was moved in 1886 to its present site on the railway. There are many Finns in the community who still use the *sauna*, or steam bath, of their native land. Early marriage is common among them; the Finnish tongue is usually spoken in the homes.

At 75 *m.* the route crosses the South Dakota Line, 48 *m.* NE. of Aberdeen, South Dakota.

Tour 8B

Junction US 10—Cooperstown—Junction US 2; ND 1 and 7.
Junction with US 10 to junction with US 2, 94 *m.*

N. P. Ry. branch line roughly parallels route between US 10 and Binford.
Graveled roadbed throughout.
Usual tourist accommodations in principal towns.

This route proceeds north over the smooth plain of the fertile black-
earth belt, through the hills of the upper Sheyenne River basin. First
the Indians and later the metis or half-breeds hunted the large herds of
buffalo that once roamed this lake-dotted region. Among the earliest
white comers here were the Nicollet-Frémont exploratory expedition in
the 1830's, the Stevens survey party in 1853, the Sibley expedition in
1863, and in the 1870's, the soldiers, scouts, and wagon trains following
the Fort Totten-Fort Abercrombie trail.

Bonanza farms flourished in this region during the last two decades
of the nineteenth century, but were subdivided eventually into smaller
farms taken up by Scandinavian immigrants who began to come here in
the 1880's. The first Norwegian community in North Dakota was established near this route, and the fine farms of the present-day Norse
residents are visible from the highway.

ND 1 branches N. from its junction with US 10, 5 *m.* W. of Valley
City (*see Tour* 8).

DAZEY, 22 *m.* (1,428 alt., 215 pop.), was named for the father of
Charles T. Dazey, author of the play *In Old Kentucky*. The elder Dazey
owned the town site.

Right from Dazey on ND 26, a graveled highway, to CAMP CORNING
HISTORIC SITE, 8 *m.*, where Sibley's expedition spent the night of July 16,
1863. The camp was named for an officer on the Sibley staff.

WALUM, 28 *m.* (1,429 alt., 30 pop.), was named in 1900 for a
prosperous landowner of this vicinity.

HANNAFORD, 31 *m.* (1,416 alt., 405 pop.), named for J. M. Hannaford, one-time vice president of the N. P. Ry., lies W. of Bald Hill
Creek, tributary of the Sheyenne River.

At 33 *m.* is the junction with a dirt road.

Right here 2 *m.* to the junction with another dirt road; R. here to CAMP
POPE, 2.3 *m.*, made by members of the Sibley expedition in August 1863 on
their return to Minnesota after driving the Sioux W. of the Missouri River.

At 36 *m.* the route crosses both the Sibley and the Fort Totten-Fort Abercrombie trails, although no traces of these routes are visible from the highway. The Sibley expedition, in pursuit of the Sioux believed to be responsible for the Minnesota Massacre (*see* HISTORY), had learned that the Indians were encamped near Devils Lake (*see Tour 6A*), so the long column of 4000 men, 1350 mules, 800 horses, and 225 wagons set out in a northwesterly course toward the lake from Lisbon (*see Tour 8A*). Before they arrived, however, they learned that their quarry had gone to the Missouri, so they changed their course to the W. The Sibley route toward Devils Lake was followed by the heavy traffic between Fort Totten and Fort Abercrombie in the next decade.

At 41 *m.* is the junction with ND 7, a graveled highway.

Right here is COOPERSTOWN, 2 *m.* (1,425 alt., 1,077 pop.). It was founded in 1882 by T. J. and Rollin C. Cooper, brothers who, flush with the profits of successful mining ventures in Colorado, arrived in this vicinity in 1880 and became bonanza farmers. They were instrumental in building the Sanborn, Cooperstown & Turtle Mountain R.R. (later an N. P. Ry. branch) into the town in 1883, and as terminal of this road Cooperstown grew rapidly.

Although old-fashioned, rambling houses set in spacious lawns and numerous old buildings fronting the business streets create an unhurried atmosphere, Cooperstown has contributed several progressives to the national picture. Gerald P. Nye (1892–   ), U.S. Senator from North Dakota, chairman (1936) of the committee for investigation of the munitions industry, was a weekly newspaper editor here when he was appointed to a vacancy in the Senate in 1925. Former Congressman James H. Sinclair (1871–1943), member of the Agricultural Committee (1925–35), and co-author of the Norris-Sinclair farm-relief bill, was superintendent of the Cooperstown schools (1896–8), and register of deeds (1899–1905). Thomas R. Amlie (1897–   ), Wisconsin Congressman, and Edward D. Stair (1859–   ), publisher of the Detroit (Michigan) *Free Press,* are also former residents.

Stair established Cooperstown's first paper, the *Courier,* the year the town was founded, and even before coming here had a hand in its history. He was feature writer for the Fargo *Argus* and was also working as a mail clerk on a railroad terminating in Hope at the time that Cooperstown, then only a small settlement, decided to contest Hope's right to the county seat. Stair learned that Hope was colonizing voters with a view to the coming county-seat election, and exposed the plan in a series of stories in the *Argus.* Hope residents were enraged, and warned him, if he wished to keep his skin unpunctured, to stay out of town, which was extremely difficult in view of the fact that his train made a lay-over of several hours there. His fellow mail clerk, a six-foot newspaper man, came to his support, and the two, with six-shooters dangling from their hips, sauntered about Hope unmolested but hungry, for the only hotel in town refused to sell food to the enemy. Cooperstown won the election, but Hope refused to concede victory, and it required two raids by Cooperstown residents to obtain the county records for the new county seat.

On the Griggs County Courthouse grounds stands the OPHEIM LOG CABIN, the first permanent white home in the county. Built in 1879 by Omund Nels Opheim on his claim NE. of Cooperstown, it was moved to its present site to become a pioneer memorial, and contains the hand-made furniture used by its former occupants.

East from Cooperstown on ND 7 to the junction with a dirt road, 3 *m.*; R. here to another junction, 7 *m.*; R. on a prairie trail to a circular group of five conical MOUNDS, 7.5 *m.* From excavations made in similar mounds along the lower Sheyenne River (*see Tour 8A*) archeologists believe that most of these tumuli were built for burial purposes.

ND 1 and 7 are identical between 41.5 *m.* and 48 *m.*, where ND 1 proceeds R. to enter the rounded, lake-dotted hills of the DOVRE MORAINE, seventh ridge formed by debris deposited during the halts of the retreating glaciers. The Nicollet-Frémont and Stevens expeditions, the Sibley column, and both a gold seekers' caravan and an immigrant train guided by Captain James Fisk crossed this moraine at various times, camping on some of the lakes.

At 53.5 *m.* is the junction with a prairie trail. At this junction is (R) CAMP ATCHESON HISTORIC SITE, commemorating establishment of Sibley's base camp July 18, 1863.

Left on the prairie trail to LAKE SIBLEY, 0.5 *m.*, a small morainic lake on the northeastern shore of which is the actual SITE OF CAMP ATCHESON. The camp was named for Captain Charles Atcheson of Sibley's staff. When General Sibley heard from friendly Chippewa Indians that the Sioux he was pursuing were fleeing from the Devils Lake region toward the Missouri River, he hastily ordered trenches dug and breastworks thrown up, and inside this fortification placed all his sick men, weak horses, the baggage train, the cattle, and the surplus of supply wagons. Leaving two companies of infantry to maintain the camp he started after the Sioux. The main column, traveling light, succeeded in driving them across the Missouri near Bismarck and returned to the base camp a month later. On a hill overlooking the lake from the NE. a marble marker denotes the grave of a private who died here.

At 57 *m.* is the junction with an unimproved dirt road.

Right here to LAKE JESSIE, 2.3 *m.*, where the bed of a once mirror-like body of water now blows with alkali dust. In the early 1900's the lake bed was covered by 12 feet of water, but in 1933 motorcycle races were run here. A heavy growth of timber, which has survived the lake, and a fine spring at its west end made it a landmark for explorers of the region. Nicollet and Frémont camped here in 1839, and Frémont named the lake for his fiancée, Jessie Benton. In 1853 Governor I. I. Stevens, guided by Pierre Bottineau (*see* HISTORY), camped on the lake on his way to become Governor of Washington Territory. In 1862 Captain James Fisk, guiding a party of gold seekers to the fields in Montana and Utah, camped on Lake Jessie, and again in 1863 stopped at the lake several days with an immigrant train he led through the State. The second Fisk expedition and the Sibley column, on Lake Sibley, were but a few miles apart, and the two camps exchanged visits.

BINFORD, 57 *m.* (1,518 alt., 311 pop.), was named for Ray Binford, attorney for the D. B. S. Johnston Land Co., which purchased and platted the town site. The company bought the homestead of Gilbert Gilbertson, an early settler. The many names used by Gilbertson illustrate the common Norwegian practice of changing the surname on arrival in this country, sometimes using the name of the father with 'son' affixed, and sometimes adopting the title of the home district as surname. To add to this, Americans thought these names too long or foreign to be practical and changed them for the newcomers. Gilbertson filed on his homestead as Gilbert Gilbertson, but was equally well known in his community as Gabriel Gabrielson, Gilbert Gabrielson, and Gabriel Gilbertson.

Left (NW) from Binford on a graveled road is MOSE, 6 *m.* (1,539 alt.). Here are the ANSONIA KENNELS, which raise white German shepherds. This is a remnant of an industry that reached its peak in Griggs County in 1924 when the nationwide fad for German police dogs was at its height. In that year as many as 400 farmers were breeding dogs in the county, and animals totaling a value of more than $100,000 were shipped to all parts of the United States, to South America, and to the Philippine Islands. The industry had its beginning in 1914 near Cooperstown when farmer Torkel Njaa imported a German shepherd for a watchdog. Njaa was so pleased with the animal that he imported two females. His success in raising and marketing dogs caught the fancy of other farmers and led to the establishment of the industry.

At 63.5 *m.* is the junction with a graveled spur.

Left here to RED WILLOW LAKE, 2 *m.* On the southern shore is a TOURIST PARK (*cabins, boats, swimming, camping, fishing*), part of a 1300-acre State game refuge. A pavilion (*seating capacity* 1500) serves for recreational purposes and is the scene of many conventions, including an annual Lutheran Bible Camp (*June*).

ND 1 crosses the wooded SHEYENNE RIVER at 69.5 *m.* and at 82.5 *m.* skirts the eastern end of STUMP LAKE, a body of water that once covered approximately 10,000 acres, but is now reduced to slightly more than 2000. The Sioux called the lake Wamduska (*serpent*), and believed it was once a great forest which the Great Spirit, in anger, allowed to be swallowed by water. On clear days logs can be seen below the surface, and where the water has receded many large stumps protrude from the ground, giving the lake bed the appearance of a timbered area logged off by beavers. Geologists believe that Stump Lake was once connected with Devils Lake, 10 miles W., and had an outlet into the Sheyenne River. The wooded area along the eastern shore has been transformed into a recreational park, and BIRD ISLAND, a 350-acre peninsula in the southwestern bay of the lake, has been set aside as a U.S. Fish and Wildlife Service game reserve.

At 87 *m.* is the junction with a graveled road.

Left on this road to the junction with an unimproved road at 2 *m.*; R. here to WAMDUSKA HOTEL, 2.5 *m.*, a lonely 75-room building that is a silent reminder of the village of Wamduska, platted, peopled, and abandoned because of a railroad survey. The town was founded in the 1880's when it was believed that the G. N. Ry. would be constructed along Lake Wamduska, as it was then called, but the survey was made 10 miles to the N., and Wamduska died. Today the old hotel is used as a farm storehouse.

At 94 *m.* is the junction with US 2 (*see Tour* 6) 2 *m.* E. of Lakota (*see Tour* 6).

Tour 8C

Mandan—Cannonball—Fort Yates—South Dakota Line; ND 6, 21, and 24.

Mandan to South Dakota Line, 72 m.

Graveled roadbed except 20 m. of bituminous surface.
Accommodations at Fort Yates only.

This route traverses the North Dakota section of the Standing Rock Indian Agency (*for history of the agency see* INDIANS AND THEIR PREDECESSORS), where Sitting Bull, Rain-in-the-Face, and Chief Gall, Father Pierre De Smet, and Major James McLaughlin made early history in the Dakotas. When organized in 1868 the reservation contained four million acres. The treaty with the Sioux in 1887, however, provided for white settlement, and when the area was opened for homesteading in 1910 the reservation was reduced to 1,343,000 acres. Today all of Sioux County constitutes the North Dakota portion of the agency. Here 1650 members of the upper and lower bands of the Yanktonai Sioux make their homes in an area of rugged brown hills, smooth grasslands, and rugged, distorted, gray-blue buttes. On the South Dakota side of the agency live 1100 Hunkpapa and Blackfoot Sioux.

ND 6 branches S. from its junction with US 10 at MANDAN (*see Tour 8*), crosses the Heart River, and passes the U.S. NORTHERN GREAT PLAINS FIELD STATION (*guides available at office*). At 4 m. is the U.S. NORTHERN GREAT PLAINS DAIRY STATION (R). Various crops, plants, trees, shrubs, methods of farming, breeds of cattle, and even buildings are tried, tested, and adapted to the dry farming of the Missouri Slope country at these two Government experimental stations.

As the highway gradually ascends from the river valley to the flowing prairies, high hills and buttes are outlined in a blue haze against the southwestern horizon. At 9 m. (R) is the CESKY ZAKOPNIK (pronounced *Chesky za-kop'neek*) or retreat of the Western Czechoslovakian Fraternal Organization, a social, benevolent, and protective society. The Cesky Zakopnik is a lodge hall and social center for the Czechs of Mandan and the vicinity. These people are thoroughly Americanized. Their dances (*public*), quite American in all other respects, have one unusual feature, the dancing of Sala Naninka De Zeli (*Annie Went to the Cabbage Patch*), a folk dance with intricate steps. It is usually performed once or twice during the evening, and the older people particularly enjoy it.

The sharp, high-pointed peak (L) of LITTLE HEART BUTTE (Sioux name, *Ta canta wakpa cikala paha*), an early-day landmark, is visible from a distance before the road passes it at 11 *m*. The Bismarck Weather Bureau uses the peak several times daily for observations of visibility.

At 15 *m*. is the junction with a graveled road.

Right here is ST. ANTHONY, 0.5 *m*. (1,790 alt., 98 pop.), a small community settled in 1887 by Roman Catholic German-Hungarians from Ohio. In 1906 a parochial school was opened, and despite the small size of the community this institution is still in operation, with an enrollment of more than 130.

The highway enters range country with few fences or farms. At 26 *m*. is a junction with ND 21 (*see Tour 4B*), which unites with ND 6 to 33 *m*. Here, as the highway begins to descend into the valley of the Cannonball River, there is a far-reaching view of country severe and imposing. Steep grass-covered hills and mesas give way to sharp, abrupt, gray clay cones and buttes that rise in confusion from the plain. The work of erosion in the creation of these formations is visible in many sidehills, where the top layers of earth have worn away to expose the bedrock strata beneath.

At 32 *m*. is the junction with a graveled roadbed.

Right here is BREIEN, 1 *m*. (1,694 alt., 14 pop.). Between the highway and the town is a natural park with camping facilities.

The CANNONBALL RIVER is crossed at 32.5 *m*. The river, its thin fringe of trees contrasting with the gray-brown of the valley, is so named because of the odd spheroidal formations found in its waters and in the steep banks of its valley. These concretions, believed to have been formed by the action of moisture within the Fox Hills sandstone, have been carried away in such large numbers by collectors that today only the small 'cannonballs' are found along the stream. The Cannonball was the northern boundary of the Standing Rock Reservation before the area was opened to white settlement in 1910, and now is the northern limit of jurisdiction of the agency.

Left at 33 *m*. on ND 21, an unimproved dry-weather roadbed; the route passes through rugged hills S. of the Cannonball, reaching SOLEN, 40 *m*. (1,671 alt., 250 pop.), on the riverbank.

The route continues through country occasionally dotted with the small frame buildings of white farmers and the log huts of Indian families.

At 49 *m*. is the junction with ND 24, a graveled highway; R. on this route.

Left from the junction with ND 24 on ND 21 to the junction with an unimproved road, 1 *m*.; straight ahead (N) 0.3 *m*. to the steep western slope of the HOLY HILL OF THE MANDANS (R). Almost every tribe of American Indians has a tradition of a great flood that covered all the earth. The Mandan legend tells that an ark came to rest on this hill near the Cannonball River, and after the waters subsided the First Man and First Woman stepped out on the hill. Mandan, Arikara, and Sioux all revere the place, and the older natives are reticent about approaching the hilltop.

While the hill is steep on its western slope, it rolls gently into the surrounding terrain to the E. Clustered at its top are four granite boulders. Carved into the face of the largest, a red stone, are many symbols: buffalo tracks, bear paws, thunderbird tracks, serpents, and turtles. The three smaller gray rocks also carry one or two symbols each. Through legend and story the existence of these writing rocks had been indicated for many years, but, because of Indian reticence regarding sacred objects, their exact location was not definitely established until early in 1937. For clearness and number of carvings they compare with the Grenora Writing Rock (*see Tour 4A*).

On ND 21 at 4 *m.* is CANNONBALL (1,607 alt., 200 pop.), on the slope above the first bench of the MISSOURI RIVER. This is a good place to observe the Sioux in his native surroundings. During the winter months he lives in a tiny log hut, clay-chinked and sod-roofed, heated with a crude open hearth or a modern heating stove, depending on his affluence. In the summer he takes to the cooler tents or brush wikiups. Sioux beadwork and other articles of handicraft can be purchased in the stores at reasonable prices. Many of the Sioux here are well educated and will talk freely with strangers on current issues, but they are decidedly reserved concerning information and legends of their people. This is, of course, typical of the entire agency; the Indian will pretend ignorance of the identity or whereabouts of any Indian about whom a white man may inquire, unless the white man is known to him.

The first Sioux sun dance in North Dakota in more than 50 years was held near Cannonball in July 1937.

Nearly opposite the mouth of the Cannonball on the eastern bank of the Missouri, according to legend, once stood a Sioux village where in early days a holy man prophesied the coming of the white people. This holy man saw a vision that made him very sad, but try as he would, he could not banish it or change it. Urged by his people to reveal what he saw, he told that a strange race of people was relentlessly moving westward toward them and would eventually claim their lands. He said these people had pale, hideous, ghastly skins, and their men had hairy faces like wolves. They had powerful weapons also, and the red men would not be able to withstand them when they came.

Right from Cannonball 13 *m.* on a graded dry-weather dirt road to an abandoned railroad bed, built when the N. P. Ry. planned a line to Pierre, South Dakota. Atop the old bed runs a trail through country teeming with upland game (*during open season excellent pheasant, chicken, and grouse hunting*). The trail turns R. at 20 *m.* and reaches ND 24 at 22 *m.*

South of Cannonball Corner the route proceeds on ND 24 to the junction with a graveled road at 61 *m.*

Right on this road at 0.5 *m.* are the SIOUX COUNTY FAIRGROUNDS where an annual Indian fair is held (*1st wk. Sept.*). Handiwork and produce are displayed, and bead, quill, and feather work can be purchased reasonably. A rodeo is usually a feature of the fair, with both white and Indian riders participating. Each evening there is dancing in costume, beginning with the true Indian dances and ending with the *kahomni,* or half-breed dances. There are also contests for the most skillful dancers.

At 0.7 *m.* is the unkept GRAVE OF SITTING BULL, covered with a concrete slab. This great Sioux chief was killed by Indian police on the Grand River in South Dakota during the Messiah trouble in 1890. Sitting Bull had long championed his people against the invasions of the white men and was one of the leaders in the Battle of the Little Big Horn. After the battle Sitting Bull, Chief Gall, and 300 followers, pursued by General Nelson A. Miles, took refuge in Canada, where they remained until 1881. Gall returned first, resigned himself to the ways of the white man, and lived out his life on the reservation. He is buried at Wakpala, South Dakota. A few months after Gall's surrender Sitting

Bull appeared at Fort Buford (*see Tour 6B*) followed by the tattered and hungry remnants of his faithful band, and gave himself up to the authorities. Although he never completely capitulated to the desires of his conquerors, he returned to the reservation and lived quietly there, except for a year he spent in Buffalo Bill's Wild West Show. In 1890, however, the Messiah craze arose. The Indians had been told a new Messiah was coming to restore their lands to them. They held ghost dances and planned for the repossession of their lands as soon as the Messiah appeared. To forestall the possibility of an uprising, the Indian police were sent to arrest Sitting Bull, who was believed to be a leader of the movement. In the half-light of a December early morning they entered his home and took him into custody. His followers were aroused and a battle ensued. At the first move from Sitting Bull's men the police shot him, and he fell, mortally wounded. Several of the police were also slain.

The bodies of the dead were taken to Fort Yates for burial, the Indian police being buried in the Roman Catholic cemetery, where today a monument marks their resting places. In contrast with the elaborate rites that attended the burial of the slain policemen, Sitting Bull's body was interred without ceremony in the military cemetery. Fort Yates was abandoned in 1895 and all military graves removed. Only the burial place of the famous Sioux leader was left.

FORT YATES, 61 *m.* (1,670 alt., 1,152 pop.), is INDIAN AGENCY HEADQUARTERS, and seat of Sioux County. A few soldiers were stationed at the Standing Rock Indian Reservation in 1873, but with the abandonment of Fort Rice in 1877 Fort Yates was established to protect the western frontier. It was named for Captain George Yates of the Seventh Cavalry, who was killed in the Battle of the Little Big Horn.

The superiority of railway transportation to that of the river boat led to the abandonment of Fort Yates in 1895 and the establishment of the new Fort Lincoln at Bismarck (*see Tour 8*).

It was at the Standing Rock Reservation that Rain-in-the-Face, a young Hunkpapa Sioux, was arrested by Tom Custer, brother of General George A. Custer, for the alleged slaying of two white men. Rain-in-the-Face was imprisoned at Fort Abraham Lincoln but made his escape and joined the band of Sitting Bull, who lived without benefit of agency. He gained his revenge by participating in the Battle of the Little Big Horn.

The town today retains much of the appearance and spirit of its frontier days, when it played an important part in the early Indian history of the State. On a flat plain overlooking the Missouri, its log huts and contrasting white frame buildings are scattered in a lazy fashion over a wide area, with the agency offices, schools, and the hospital as the core of the town.

Across the street from the agency office, overlooking the Missouri, is the famed STANDING ROCK (Sioux, *Inyan Woslata*), for which the agency was named. Originally sacred to the Arikara, it came into the possession of the Sioux. When the reservation was established the rock was on Proposal Hill, but it was later brought into town and mounted on a brick pedestal. It is of gray metamorphic composition entirely foreign to this area. If viewed from the correct angle, and with a discreet degree of imagination, the stone resembles the seated figure of a small, shawled woman. According to Dakota legend, a young Indian woman became jealous of her husband's second wife and refused to leave camp when the village moved. Thinking she would soon follow, the people of the village left her sitting before the fire with her child on her back. When she did not appear her husband sent his brothers-in-law to look for her. They returned to the deserted camp and found her and the child still seated before the fire—both transformed into stone. From that time the rock was carried with the tribe and occupied a position in the center of each village in which they lived. This rock is one of two revered by the Sioux. The other, Inyan Bosdata (*erect rock*), is on the Sheyenne River (*see Tour 8A*).

The population of Fort Yates is both white and Indian. The two great events of the year are the annual fair (*see above*), and the Fourth of July, when Indians from miles around come in to celebrate. On these occasions the fairgrounds present an unusual sight. Tall, graceful tipis rise above the squat, modern wall tents of the numerous camps that dot the level area around the race track, and back and forth is a bustling flow of dilapidated autos, sleek saddle ponies, running children, hobbling old warriors, and women dressed in bright colors. Except for their braided hair and their moccasins, the older men wear modern attire. The younger men, in keeping with the occasion, adopt western costume, high-heeled riding boots, blue denim trousers topped with wide, flashy belts, brightly colored shirts, and the ever-present 'ten-gallon' hat. Cotton dresses and large bright shawls form the costume of the women, and moccasins are also worn by the older women. The highly colored Sioux costumes are seen only during the native dances.

Memorial Day and Armistice Day are also holidays. On Memorial Day graves are decorated with crepe-paper flowers made by the women during the winter. The Indians are intensely patriotic, and it would be hard to find a fair, tribal council, or any other meeting over which the flag of the United States does not fly.

A trail runs NW. of the town past the Roman Catholic church to a GOLF COURSE, all nine holes laid out on the mesa-like top of Proposal Hill, where Standing Rock once stood. The hill in bygone days was a popular rendezvous for Indian sweethearts, hence its name.

Across the river from Fort Yates, in the heyday of the military post, there sprang up a little town called WINONA, a natural corollary of the restrictions of military life on an Indian reservation. By ferryboat in summer and over the ice by bobsled in winter went the soldier, trader, bullwhacker, Indian, and cowboy, to taste the 'night life' offered in the gaming houses with their expansive bars and amiable hostesses. In Territorial days no less than nine saloons were operating, and an excellent race track was the scene of many financial exchanges.

Like other western towns, Winona attracted a wide variety of inhabitants. One of the most colorful was 'Mustache Maude' Black. She came to the vicinity as a young school teacher, but, finding a more lucrative scope for her talents, entered the entertainment field. Tall, large, and angular, she was masculine in appearance, but wore women's clothing with the exception of her boots, which she had made to order, reputedly at $20 a pair. Because of her occupation the women of Winona ostracized her, but the men found her well educated, an astute business woman, a good poker player, and an excellent cook. By one of those quirks that make human beings as interesting as they are, Mustache Maude, the proprietor of many of Winona's most scarlet institutions, owned a good library and was an expert needlewoman. She married Ott Black, a rancher, and after the decline of her own business interests managed his ranch. She lived near Winona until her death.

There was another side of life in Winona, too. It was an enterprising business town, in the center of a growing ranching country. A Literary Society and Dramatic Club functioned for years. The Sunday school was organized by Mr. and Mrs. Thomas Spicer, who in 1897, together with four other members of their family, were killed by five drunken Indians, three of whom were subsequently lynched for the crime at near-by Williamsport.

Winona was so close to Fort Yates that at the time of the death of Sitting Bull and the Indian policemen the wailing of the squaws was clearly heard across the river. After the abandonment of Fort Yates, Winona began to decline. Today nothing is left of it but a few cellars and a solitary group of trees.

The route proceeds S. on ND 24, continuing through agency land. At 72 *m.* is the junction with ND 6; left here to South Dakota Line at 78 *m.*, 8 *m.* N. of McLaughlin, South Dakota (*see South Dakota Guide, Tour* 2).

Tour 8D

Junction US 10—Center—Beulah—Halliday—Killdeer—Junction US 85; ND 25.
Junction with US 10 to junction with US 85, 140 *m.*

N. P. Ry. branch roughly parallels route between Stanton and Killdeer.
Graveled roadbed.
Accommodations limited.

This route winds over the upper Missouri Slope, through grain-farming and grazing country, where infrequent farmhouses hide in the valleys. When ranching was the chief industry here, not long ago, the rough country provided shelter not only for the herds but also for rustlers. In the region adjacent to the route are some of the largest lignite mines in the State. Along the Missouri are numerous ancient Indian village sites. The Killdeer Mountains at the northern end of the route present some of the most charming scenery in North Dakota.

ND 25 branches N. from US 10 (*see Tour* 8) 4 *m.* W. of Mandan.

At 12 *m.* the highway crosses SQUARE BUTTE CREEK, named for the square-topped buttes to the E. (*see Tour* 3B). The stream parallels the route for several miles.

CENTER, 30 *m.* (1,760 alt., 509 pop.), was named for its geographic position in Oliver County. Its buildings, almost all of them white, are huddled in the narrow valley of Square Butte Creek. In the Oliver County Courthouse park is a Log Cabin Museum (*open*) erected in 1937 under the Works Progress Administration to house Indian and pioneer relics. Near by is the Miner Memorial, a granite marker of Gothic style, erected by former Governor L. B. Hanna, in commemoration of 16-year-old Hazel Miner. In 1920 Hazel and a younger brother and sister were lost in a raging March blizzard while driving home from school. When they were found the next morning, the two younger children were still alive, for Hazel had used her body to shield them and to hold down the blankets that kept them from freezing. The story of her life and death has been made part of the official records of the county.

North of Center the route encounters rougher country and turns NW. to follow the MISSOURI RIVER for a few miles.

At 40 *m.* is the junction with an unimproved county dirt road.

Right on this road to the junction with another unimproved road, 1 *m.*; L. here to FORT CLARK STATE PARK, 2 *m.*, site of a trading post established by the American Fur Company in 1829. The post was only a few feet S. of a village built by the Mandans about 1822, and later occupied by the Arikara. West of the depressions left by the earth lodges are the remains of a burial ground.

At 46 *m.* is the junction with a graveled road.

Right on this road is STANTON, 1.5 *m.* (1,722 alt., 370 pop.), on the first bench overlooking the Missouri, which it once served as a river port. The town was founded in 1883 and given the name of a pioneer mother of the vicinity. Partly within the Mercer County Courthouse yard is the site of an Indian Village, where excavations have revealed many artifacts.

Straight ahead from Stanton on a county road to the SITE OF SCATTERED VILLAGE, 2.5 *m.*, one of the three Hidatsa and two Mandan villages known to white traders and trappers as the Five Villages. Charbonneau, the French frontiersman, and his Shoshone wife, Sakakawea, were living here when Charbonneau was engaged by the exploring party of Lewis and Clark, in 1805, to accompany them on their hazardous journey to the Pacific coast. Sakakawea went with her husband and proved herself invaluable to the success of the expedition (*see* Bismarck). Scattered Village lies on the southern bank of the KNIFE RIVER, which was named by various Indian tribes who procured flint for their knives from pits along the river. The area about the mouth of the Knife is rich in Indian history.

West of Stanton the route moves roughly parallel to the combined courses of the Knife River and Spring Creek.

HAZEN, 57 *m.* (1,760 alt., 662 pop.), was named for A. D. Hazen, Third Assistant Postmaster General in 1884 when postal service was established here. An Old Settlers Monument, at the E. end of Main St. in a triangular plot known as Washington Memorial Park, consists of a concrete pyramid with a buffalo skull embedded in the top. Businessmen of Hazen have provided a Tourist Park (*camping facilities*) in a heavily wooded area along the Knife on the southern edge of the town.

At 64.5 *m.* (L) is the large underground LIGNITE MINE of the Knife River Coal Mining Co. (*Morning preferred for visiting; guides at mine office in* BEULAH, *see below.*) This mine is one of the largest in the State. The entrance is at the head of a little valley a few rods L. of the highway. It opens into a long tunnel, with a narrow-gauge trolley line extending down its center. Six electric locomotives are employed to draw a fleet of 450 mine cars over almost 30 miles of track which carry coal out of the mine to the processing plant. The entry has passages branching from it, leading to the veins from which the coal is taken. As the coal is taken out, tunnels or rooms are created, extending for miles through the underground darkness, in some places as much as 140 feet below the surface.

The coal is loosened by electric cutting machines and blasting powder, after which loading machines carry it upward to the mine cars; these are formed into trains to haul the lignite to the processing plant.

During an 8-hour shift 2500 tons of coal are mined, enough to fill more than 60 forty-ton cars. It is estimated that this particular field contains about 50,000,000 tons of lignite, enough to enable operations to continue for 50 years. Visitors to the mine are given electric lights fastened to stout fiber helmets, and get a novel ride on the underground train.

BEULAH, 67 *m.* (1,797 alt., 942 pop.), named for the niece of an official of the town-site land company, forms one main street along the Knife River just E. of its confluence with Spring Creek. The PROCESSING PLANT of the Knife River mine and an ELECTRIC PLANT of the Montana Dakota Utilities Company are in the eastern part of town. The electric plant uses lignite to generate the power with which it serves surrounding towns.

At 67.5 *m.* is the junction with ND 49, a graveled highway. What is believed to be the SITE OF CHARLES LE RAYE'S CAMP (L), used by the French explorer in 1803, has been marked by the Mercer County Old Settlers' Association. Le Raye, who was held captive three years (1801–4) by a band of Brulé Sioux, is said to have been the first white traveler to mention the Knife River. During his captivity he was taken through much of the area between the Mississippi and the Rockies, and was one of the first white men to become familiar with that region.

At 73.5 *m.* (L) is the large lignite strip mine of the Zap Colliery, one of the heaviest-producing mines in the State, with an annual production of 140,000 tons.

At 75 *m.* is the junction with a county graded dirt road.

Left on this road, a winding country trail unsuited to trailer travel, to MEDICINE HILL, 11.5 *m.,* from which flowed spring waters attributed with healing powers by the Indians. Chert, a mineral rock closely allied to flint, is found in the Slope area, and near the hill is a quarry from which natives took material for arrowpoints and knives.

GOLDEN VALLEY, 83 *m.* (1,946 alt., 400 pop.), was named for the fertility of the surrounding region.

DODGE, 91 *m.* (1,979 alt., 234 pop.), is in the valley of Spring Creek.

At 97 *m.* is a junction with ND 8, which unites with ND 25 to 99 *m.,* where ND 25 branches L.

Right on ND 8 at the confluence of Alkaline and Spring Creek is HALLIDAY, 0.5 *m.* (2,048 alt., 395 pop.), named for one of its first settlers.
At 19 *m.* is FOUR BEARS BRIDGE (*see Tour 3A*).

DUNN CENTER, 113 *m.* (2,191 alt., 238 pop.), is so named because it is near the geographic center of Dunn County.

At 120 *m.* is the junction with ND 22, a graded dirt highway.

Right on this highway is KILLDEER, 1 *m.* (2,233 alt., 650 pop.), named for the near-by KILLDEER MOUNTAINS, which rise clearly into view as ND 22 proceeds NW. from the town. The Killdeers are not mountains, but rather two lofty hills, extending NE. to SW. more than 10 miles, and at their highest points rising 600 feet above the surrounding prairie. The Sioux called them Tah-kah-o-kuty (*the place where they kill the deer*). The upper 300 to 400 feet of the hills belong to the geologic stratum known as the White River formation. This is the youngest of the various layers of bedrock underlying North Dakota, having been deposited by the last of the prehistoric seas which inundated this area. It is also the rarest stratum in the State, since, being at the surface, it has eroded until it is now found in only a few places. The White River formation is particularly rich in fossil remains ranging from fish and turtles to huge prehistoric mammals, although no specimens have been taken from the Killdeer Mountains.

At 4 *m.* to the junction with an unimproved county road; L. here to the junction with another dirt road, 7 *m.*

Directly ahead 2 *m.* on the dirt road to the junction with a prairie trail leading through a pasture gate. Right on this trail are the buildings of DIAMOND C RANCH, 4 *m.,* the little white ranch house, the red cattle barns, and the gray weathered wooden poles of the corrals all situated along the timbered ravine formed by FALLING SPRING, near which took place the Battle of Killdeer Mountains. The spring drops from a sandstone formation in a hillside to the rear of the ranch house, providing a steady flow of cool, clear water as it did one July day in 1864 when 5000 Sioux were encamped along it, hunting and preparing hides for clothing and food for the coming winter. General Alfred H. Sully, sent out to punish the Sioux for the Minnesota Massacre of 1862, learned that they were in the mountains. Rapidly moving his force of 2200 men he attacked the Indians on sight the morning of July 28. The Indians offered stubborn resistance despite the surprise of the attack and the confusion caused by the shelling of their camp, but were finally forced to make a hasty retreat over the mountain through DEAD MAN'S GULCH, a steep-sided ravine leading through the mountains back of Falling Spring, into the Badlands along the Little Missouri River. In their retreat the Sioux were forced to leave almost all of their belongings, and when five companies of troops set about demolishing the camp it is said they worked five hours destroying tipis, travois poles, cooking utensils, robes, and foods. Dried and drying meat estimated at 200 tons was destroyed. The Sioux loss was reported as 27 dead on the field in addition to many carried off by their comrades. Sully's loss in the encounter was 5 killed and 10 wounded, 2 of whom were pickets slain the second night. Two white marble slabs enclosed in a steel wire fence, a short distance S. of the Diamond C ranch house, mark their graves.

On the county road N. of junction with ranch road to a junction with a dirt road, 9 *m.*; L. here to OAKDALE, 9.8 *m.,* part way up the eastern slope of the southern mountain. Formerly a good-sized frontier town, it now has only a residence and a store and post office. It is a very pleasant spot, however, for its trees and many springs of clear, cold water flowing down from the mountain keep it several degrees cooler in summer than the dry, shadeless prairie. Oakdale is a good point from which to make hiking trips into the mountains, but the tourist accommodations are limited.

From the store is a two-hour hike over a precipitous trail up the mountain. Past oak, box elder, poplar, and scrub cedar trees, the path leads to the base of the limestone formation. Here the trail ascends the face of a steep cliff. In the upward climb it passes through a narrow cleft in the rock ironically called ELE-PHANT'S PASS, and comes at last to the level mountain top, where there is a magnificent view of the surrounding country, taking in 40 or 50 miles in three directions. To the N. and NE. lies the rough country along the Missouri and Little Missouri Rivers, while E. and S. stretches the vast pattern of cultivated fields and virgin grasslands. The table-like top of the mountain is 3,140 feet above sea level, highest elevation in the range. From here the trail skirts the southern rim of the cliff to MEDICINE HOLE, from which, according to Indian tradition, the first buffalo emerged upon the earth. Today the hole is little more than an elongated three-foot-deep depression in the flat limestone surface of the mountain top. It has been closed by the lodging, on the first ledge, of a number of large rocks thrown into the aperture by curious visitors trying to sound the bottom. It had been explored to a depth of 80 feet before it was closed, but the extreme cold encountered below that depth made further exploration difficult. In summer a cold draught of air formerly rose from the hole, and in winter a column of steam.

Just W. of Medicine Hole to SIGNAL ROCK, said to have been used as an Indian signal station. From the cliff top here the buildings of the Diamond C Ranch and the site of the Battle of Killdeer Mountains (*see above*) are visible to the S. Part way down the southern slope of the mountain, from E. to W. in the order named, rise the odd rock formations known as the THREE SISTERS, the COLISEUM, and SOLOMON'S TEMPLE. The Three Sisters are slender spires pointing upward from a common base; the Coliseum, which belies its name, is a tall pillar of sandstone shaped like an hourglass; and the Temple is a long, narrow, gray formation. Continuing W. along the rim of the cliff, the hike trail leads to EAGLE ROCK, so named because of the eagle nests once numerous here, and after touching the timbered edge of Dead Man's Gulch, retraces its route to Oakdale.

Few large wild animals remain in the Killdeer Mountains, but in 1848–9 John Palliser, an English sportsman, and his party killed five grizzly bears here. Deer were once plentiful also. Pioneer cattlemen still tell of the Wolf Leader, a savage animal, half wolf and half collie, that led a pack of wolves in depredations upon the herds of the region. Conspicuous because of the white ring around his neck, the Wolf Leader was the bane of ranchers for many years before he was trapped.

West of Killdeer the route proceeds along the valley of Spring Creek through the foothills of the Killdeer Mountains to the junction with US 85 at 140 *m.*, 24 miles S. of Watford City (*see Tour* 4).

✿✿

Tour 9

(McIntosh, S. Dak.)—Hettinger—Bowman—Marmarth—(Miles City, Mont.); US 12.
South Dakota Line to Montana Line, 95.5 *m.*

Milwaukee R.R. parallels route.
Graveled roadbed 37 *m.*, bituminous surface 58.5 *m.*
Accommodations in principal towns.

US 12 cuts across the southwestern corner of North Dakota through an area where herds of cattle and flocks of sheep graze on the hardy prairie grasses that grow in the small valleys between high, rough, brown mesa-topped buttes. The day of the pioneer homesteader and rancher is barely in the past here, and only within recent years has diversified farming gradually been adopted. Near its western end the route passes through the southern part of the Badlands, a strange land of fantastic enchantment where ever-changing combinations of color and shadow form a background of weird beauty (*see Tour* 8).

US 12 crosses the South Dakota Line at 0.0 *m.* on a railroad overpass at White Butte, South Dakota (*see South Dakota Guide Tour* 2).

At 1 *m.* the route passes through a level area adjacent to HIDDEN WOOD CREEK (L), also called Flat Creek. Along its course, approximately a mile apart and covered with brush, are two cutbanks known as BRUSHY BANKS, near which the Custer Black Hills expedition camped on the way from Fort Abraham Lincoln in 1874.

On Hidden Wood Creek in this vicinity in 1882 was situated the main camp of the Indians from the Standing Rock Reservation who took part in the last big buffalo hunt of the Sioux tribe, said to be the last large hunt in the United States, held under the direction of Major James McLaughlin, then Indian agent at Fort Yates (*see Tour* 8C).

In the years following the Custer episode in 1876 (*see* HISTORY *and* FORT ABRAHAM LINCOLN STATE PARK) many of the Sioux, except the faithful few who accompanied Sitting Bull into exile in Canada (*see Tours* 6B *and* 8C), returned to the reservations to assimilate the white man's civilization. Before the white man's restrictions had been placed upon them, the Plains Indians had been trained from childhood to the pursuit of the buffalo, for the buffalo was the staff of the Indian's life, providing food, shelter, and clothing. The hunt in 1882 caused much rejoicing among the tribesmen, offering them a temporary respite from the humdrum reservation life and a brief return to the activity that had once existed in this land that was rightfully theirs.

Long and extensive preparations were made for this hunt. Strict religious ceremonies invoked the blessing of the Great Mystery. Running Antelope, whose picture was on the old five-dollar Treasury notes, was generalissimo of the affair, while under him, leading the different bands, were such famed Indians as Gall, Rain-in-the-Face, John Grass, Fire Heart, Kill Eagle, Crazy Walking, Spotted Horn Bull, Gray Eagle, and Charging Thunder.

Approximately 2000 men, women, and children, including a few white men, made the 100-mile journey from Fort Yates to the scene of the hunt, and McLaughlin estimated that more than 600 mounted red men took part in the actual killing. The herd, said to number 50,000 head, was first sighted near White Butte, 10 miles S. of the present South

Dakota town of the same name, and covered the valley from that point to Haynes (*see below*). On the first day of the hunt 2000 buffalo were killed, and the second day was given to skinning and cutting up the dead animals. The third day found the Indians again on the chase, and this time 3000 bison were killed. The Hidden Wood Creek camp was maintained until all the meat was cured and ready to take back to the reservation. Years later when the railroad was built, many of the settlers made a nice profit shipping the bones of the buffalo carcasses left from this hunt.

HAYNES, 3 *m.* (2,540 alt., 210 pop.), on a road branching L. from US 12 at White Butte, was named for George B. Haynes, general passenger agent of the Milwaukee R.R. when it constructed its main line in 1907.

At 7 *m.* are the junctions with ND 8, a graveled highway, and with an unimproved county dirt road. US 12 turns L.

1. Right from the junction on the unimproved road to the rammed-earth home and garage of the SCORIA LILY RANCH, 5 *m.* The owner, Colonel Paul S. Bliss, naturalist and author of three books of North Dakota verse, has had the two buildings erected as an example of the practical use of earth for permanent, low-cost farm buildings. In the building process earth is packed into plank forms. After 'setting' it forms a durable, heat- and cold-resisting wall.

2. Straight ahead on ND 8 to the abandoned workings of the STATE MINE, 0.5 *m.* (R), an underground lignite mine once owned and used for experimental purposes by the South Dakota School of Mines. The mine was abandoned several years ago when the coal vein caught fire. The coal is still burning, and occasionally at night the red glow of this earthly furnace is visible where the tunnel timbering and earth have caved in, leaving the hillsides pockmarked and scarred. Near by on two short rails is a rusty railroad steam engine, its gears fast in the grip of rust and its wooden cab nearly eaten away by wind and rain. Deserted, it stands where it was last stopped before the rails of the spur from Haynes to the mine were taken up.

At 11 *m.* on US 12 is the junction with an unimproved county dirt road.

Left on this road to PRAIRIE SPHINX BUTTE (R), 2.5 *m.*, where the steep sandstone outcroppings at the top of the formation resemble the features of the Gizeh Sphinx.

HETTINGER, 15 *m.* (2,668 alt., 1,138 pop.), seat of Adams County, is at the foot of a high hill rising from the valley of Hidden Wood Creek. Adams County was formerly part of Hettinger County, named for Mathias Hettinger, a Freeport, Illinois, banker. When the counties were separated in 1907 each wished to retain the original name, and a compromise was finally effected whereby the new county could use the old name for its county seat. The new brick COURTHOUSE (R) was built in 1929.

Hettinger's first newspaper editor was a man of unusual enterprise. As he hauled his press overland from Dickinson, he stopped everyone he met to tell them about his forthcoming publication, and by the time he reached Hettinger he had procured nearly 100 subscriptions. In 1908 this paper, the Adams County *Record,* was appointed official paper for Hettinger, and in one of the first resolutions it published citizens were instructed to remove their buildings from the streets, where, in the rush of locating, they had built with little regard for the town-site plat.

BUCYRUS, 24 *m.* (2,778 alt., 117 pop.), was first known as Dolan, in honor of the contractor for the Milwaukee R.R. grade there. During the grading a new name was sought for the town, however, and Bucyrus, the trade name of one of the huge steam shovels in use, was suggested and adopted.

REEDER, 33 *m.* (2,810 alt., 263 pop.), was named for E. O. Reeder, who at the time of the founding of the town was chief engineer for the Milwaukee R.R. Alden Scott Boyer, now a well-known American and French cosmetics manufacturer, operated a drug store here in 1909–13.

Right from Reeder on ND 22, a graveled road, to LOOKOUT POINT, 2 *m.,* an elevation from which five towns, Reeder, Bucyrus, Gascoyne, Scranton, and Buffalo Springs, are visible.

WHETSTONE BUTTES (L), 9 *m.,* a high range of hills visible for miles, are topped by a peculiar sandstone formation, which is so hard that pieces from it were used by the Indians and early settlers for sharpening their tools and weapons.

GASCOYNE, 40 *m.* (2,759 alt., 48 pop.), is L. of the highway. North-west of town is a railroad RESERVOIR (*swimming and picnicking facilities*).

SCRANTON, 44 *m.* (2,773 alt., 277 pop.), is a namesake of Scran-ton, Pennsylvania, because both are coal-mining towns. The first mine here opened in 1907, preceding the railroad, which arrived late that year, and providing the impetus for the town that grew up. The dis-covery of suitable clay resulted in the establishment of a brick plant, the product of which can be seen in many of the buildings in the town. On each side of the highway as it passes the Milwaukee R.R. station are two round markers picturing the head of a Texas longhorn steer and carrying the legend, 'Comin' up the Texas Chisholm Trail.' The mark-ers indicate one of the trails by which cattle were brought to this part of the Great Plains. Although the Chisholm Trail is believed to have run no farther N. than Abilene, Kansas, the name has often been loosely applied to other trails running N. of that city, unofficial extensions of the original route from the Panhandle region (*see Tour* 4).

BUFFALO SPRINGS, 50 *m.* (2,850 alt., 25 pop.), was known briefly as Ingomar, but in 1907 received its present name, suggested by the near-by springs, which once served as a watering place for the bison that roamed the plains. East of town is a railroad RESERVOIR (*swimming, fishing*).

BOWMAN, 58 *m.* (*see Tour* 4), is the junction with US 85 (*see Tour* 4).

RHAME, 74 *m.* (3,184 alt., 283 pop.), named for M. D. Rhame, district engineer of the Milwaukee R.R. when it was established in

1907, has the highest elevation of any town in the State. It is in a high valley between two large, flat, scoria-capped buttes.

At 79 *m.* is the junction with an unimproved country dirt road.

Right on this road, across the railroad, to FORT DILTS STATE PARK (L), 2 *m.,* marking the site where Captain James L. Fisk's 80-wagon immigrant train, bound for the Montana gold fields, was corralled in defense formation for 14 days in September 1864. The expedition, accompanied by a cavalry detachment of 50 men, left Fort Rice in August and encountered no trouble until September 1, when a wagon overturned in crossing a steep-sided creek. Fisk detailed another wagon and a detachment of eight cavalrymen to remain and right the overturned vehicle. As soon as the main party was out of sight over a hill, a band of Hunkpapa Sioux—part of the group met by Sully at the Killdeer Mountains (*see Tour 8D*) and in the Battle of the Badlands (*see Tour 8*)—who were at that time engaged in hunting buffalo, attacked the detachment, killing nine and mortally wounding three. The expedition heard the rifle shots and returned to aid their comrades, but were too late to do more than rout the Indians. Just as the natives were being driven off, Jefferson Dilts, a scout for the expedition, returned from reconnoitering in the Badlands and rode directly into the fleeing band of Sioux and was killed.

The expedition moved 10 miles the next day, and when it broke camp the morning of September 3 a large box of poisoned hardtack was purposely left behind. The Indians swooped down and hungrily devoured it, and it is said that 25 died from the effects of the poison, more than were killed by the expedition's bullets. That day the wagon train advanced only 3 miles before going into corral and beginning to throw up a defense, which they called Fort Dilts. Oxen and plows were used to obtain sod with which a dirt wall 6 feet high and nearly 2 feet thick was built outside the ring of wagons. The cavalry was stationed between the wall and the wagons. That night 16 volunteers slipped through the Indian lines and after 3 days and nights of hard riding reached Fort Rice, whence Colonel Daniel J. Dill and a detachment set out at once. They arrived September 17, but by that time the Hunkpapa had departed for Cave Hills, South Dakota, where they had learned a large herd of bison was running. They had lingered only a day or two after the fortification was thrown up, sniping at it occasionally, before their interest waned.

The State park, which contains approximately 9 acres belonging to the State historical society, was dedicated to Jefferson Dilts in 1932. Within the fenced area are the remains of the sod fortification, and eight Government grave markers have been placed inside it in memory of those who lost their lives in the episode.

MARMARTH, 89 *m.* (2,709 alt., 626 pop.), is at the confluence of Little Beaver Creek, Hay Creek, and the Little Missouri River. Known as the 'city of trees,' Marmarth is almost an oasis in the treeless Badlands country. Its name is derived from the mispronunciation of her own name, Margaret Martha, by a small granddaughter of the president of the Milwaukee R.R. The town had its inception in 1902, and grew rapidly following the advent of the Milwaukee R.R. in 1907 and the establishment of a railroad division point here the next year. Proximity to the Little Missouri and its tributaries has not always been advantageous; the town has been flooded five times—1907, 1913, 1929, and twice in 1921. To prevent another flood a dam has been built on Little Beaver Creek W. of town, and dikes have been put up around the town adjacent to the streams.

Theodore Roosevelt killed his first grizzly bear a short distance W.

of Marmarth on the Little Beaver, and just N. of the town on the Little Missouri he shot his first buffalo. Many years later, when he was campaigning for the presidency, on an appearance in Minneapolis he met a Marmarth pioneer. When informed the man was from Marmarth, at the mouth of Little Beaver Creek, the President exclaimed, 'A town there? Do you have boats tied to your back doors?' He had visited the site only at times of high water.

Marmarth is a shipping point for cattle brought overland from range grounds in this State, Montana, and South Dakota. The stockyards, which cover an area of 45 acres, and contain 86 pens and 15 loading chutes, are built on the site of the old O-X (O Bar X) ranch. Near by, on Hay Creek, still stands the squat old ranch house in which Theodore Roosevelt was once a guest.

Activity in the Little Beaver Dome, an oil field near Marmarth (*see below*), brought the town a boom in 1936. Business buildings and residences that had long stood idle were quickly occupied.

Also at 89 *m.* is the junction with ND 16, an unimproved road.

Left on this highway to the junction with a country trail, 2 *m.*; L. here 1 *m.* to THE WOMAN IN STONE, a 50-foot rock that shows the head and face of a woman, even to the hairline, clearly outlined against the sky. The form of the sandstone is the result of countless years of weathering.

On ND 16 to a junction with a well-defined prairie trail, 16 *m.*; R. on this trail to the NUMBER TWO WELL of the Little Beaver Dome, 21 *m.* This well has not produced oil in any quantity, but results of the Number One Well, just over the State Line in Montana, show a crude oil apparently high in gasoline and kerosene content, very light, but darker in color, and with a somewhat different odor from that usually associated with midcontinent crude oils. The Little Beaver Dome is part of the Cedar Creek Anticline, a geologic formation of arched rock strata extending from eastern Montana into southwestern North Dakota. It is one of the greatest natural gas fields in the United States. The gas is piped into cities in the western part of the State, where it is used for heating and industrial purposes.

US 12 crosses the Montana Line at 95.5 *m.*, 95 *m.* E. of Miles City, Montana (*see Montana Guide Tour 17*).

✿✿

Tour 10

(WATER ROUTE)

Medora—South Roosevelt National Memorial Park—Beaver River—North Roosevelt National Memorial Park—Cherry Creek—Missouri River—Elbowoods—Stanton—Fort Clark—Washburn—Bismarck.

Route: Little Missouri and Missouri Rivers.
Medora to Bismarck, 350 *m.* (by river), 10 to 20 days.
N. P. Ry. parallels route from Stanton to Bismarck.

Note: The conditions encountered on Tour 10 will be materially changed when the Garrison Dam is completed. The valleys of the Little Missouri and the Missouri will be flooded from a point north of the Killdeer Mountains to the Garrison Dam. Points of interest that will be inundated include Elbowoods, Four Bears Bridge, Fort Berthold, Ree, Nichu, Manuel Rock, and Fort Stevenson. The higher water level will minimize some dangers of navigation, such as sand bars and snags, but it will necessitate a portage around the Garrison Dam.
Special equipment: Light duffle, including 7 x 7 tent, waterproof sleeping bags, waterproof duffle bags, complete change outdoor clothing; flat-bottomed boat capable carrying 1000 lb., of not more than 5 in. draft for party of three; complete camping gear. No accommodations available.
Food: Fourteen days' supply, carried in paraffin-treated bags; mainly canned goods—soups, meats, vegetables, and milk; flour, salt, sugar, coffee, and cocoa; dried fruits. Butter hard to keep. Biscuits can be made en route.
Water: Carry light water cask or bag. Refill at various ranch houses. Use chlorine or iodine in settled river water.
Warning: No trip for 'tenderfeet' unless accompanied by experienced guide and riverman; select night camps on high ground at safe distance back from river's bank; overhanging banks may cave in, creek and gully bottoms subject to suddenly rising water if rain falls; tie boats to trees on high ground; boat may be lost in sudden rise of river if tied too low; avoid drifting near overhanging cutbanks along stream; landslides dangerous to small boats occur occasionally; watch channels for snags; high, upstream winds dangerous on Missouri; carry antivenom serum for treatment of possible rattlesnake bites.
Seasons: Latter part of June or first weeks of July. Spring floods and early June rise make rivers treacherous; dry seasons of late summer may require portage of Little Missouri.
Maps: Highway Planning Survey, Bismarck, North Dakota, can furnish county maps.

For the experienced camper, for the seeker of adventure, for the lover of nature, this route offers much pleasure; it is on the Little Missouri River through the heart of North Dakota's Badlands and down the Missouri River to Bismarck. During past ages the Little Missouri has been the chief agent in cutting into the prairies of North Dakota the wide slash that is the Badlands region. Rain and surface waters have washed away the soft upper layers of the deposits made by successive prehistoric seas, and, continually seeking lower levels, in the slow process of erosion through the centuries have left a jumble of jagged buttes. The sides of these buttes expose the various strata, each the testimonial of one age in the geological history of the area.

Undoubtedly the Missouri and Little Missouri were navigated by many an Indian hunter in search of the big game that once roamed the region, and by many a brave seeking the scalp of some unwary opponent; but Baptiste Le Page, the French explorer who made the voyage from the Black Hills (which title then designated all the rough upland country W. of the Missouri here) to the mouth of the Knife River in 45 days in 1804, is believed to have been the first white man to journey down the tortuous Little Missouri into the Missouri, called Wakpa Hehanka (*elk river*) by the Sioux. Le Page joined the Lewis and Clark expedition at one of the Indian villages near the mouth of the Knife River.

While Le Page drifted down almost the entire course of the Little Missouri, the modern would-be explorer following this route slips his boat into the historic waters more than halfway down the stream at MEDORA (2,265 alt., 175 pop.) (*see Tour* 8), and heads downstream with the current.

North of Medora the river flows through a comparatively wide flood plain dotted with groves of cottonwood, box elder, and ash trees, with high, many-colored buttes rising on both sides to form the deep valley.

At about 1 *m.* (R) is SHEEP CREEK, an intermittent tributary named for the bighorn mountain sheep that were found in the Badlands when white men first visited them. Along Sheep Creek are a few bull pines, *Pinus ponderosa scopulorum,* probably the northern limit of the species in the State.

At about 1.5 *m.* (L) is ANDREWS CREEK, and at about 1.8 *m.* downstream from Medora the river crosses the southern boundary of the Theodore Roosevelt National Memorial Park (*see* THEODORE ROOSE-VELT NATIONAL MEMORIAL PARK). At 2.8 *m.* the park highway fords the Little Missouri, and at times of low water caution is necessary here in navigating the ford. To the R. after passing the highway is one of the park picnic areas, and just below these grounds is the mouth of KNUT-SON CREEK (L), at about 4.3 *m.*

Below the buildings (R) of the PEACEFUL VALLEY RANCH (*see* THEODORE ROOSEVELT NATIONAL MEMORIAL PARK, SOUTH TOUR) is the mouth of PADDOCK CREEK (R), 5.8 *m.*, and at about 8.8 *m.* the route passes JUEL CREEK (R). At about 11.5 *m.* is GOVERNMENT CREEK (R), and at about 17 *m.* WANNAGAN CREEK (L), the northern boundary of the park.

A few miles below the boundary is the PARKER RANCH (L), formerly the Wadsworth, said to be the first cattle ranch in the Bad-lands. Downstream from these buildings is ASH COULEE CREEK (R), named for the many ash trees that line its broad valley. It should be reached in a day of ordinary drifting. (*Good camping place for first night is opposite the mouth of this little stream.*)

During the entire first day's journey the unusual beauty of the Badlands formations is revealed, but even more detail is evident as the setting sun lengthens the shadows cast by the hills and intensifies the reds, ochers, grays, greens, and taupes that form the weird color combinations of the region.

At 40 *m.* is the SITE OF THE CABIN OF THEODORE ROOSE-VELT'S ELKHORN RANCH (L). Only a few foundation stones and a depression in the flat river flood plain show where the cabin stood. The Rough Rider President, who ran cattle on two ranches in the Badlands in the 1880's (*see Tour* 8), spent the greater share of his time at the Elkhorn, using it as headquarters for hunting expeditions into the surrounding country.

Nearest neighbor of the future President was Howard Eaton, whose VI Ranch at 48 *m.* was near the mouth of BEAVER RIVER, the Little Missouri's largest tributary. (*Opposite confluence here is good camping place.*) Beaver River was first called Big Beaver Creek to distinguish it from Little Beaver (*see Tour 9*).

North of Beaver River the stream pursues its way in a meandering course, winding 14 miles to cross a single township, and passing MAGPIE and BEICEGEL (Bicycle) CREEKS. Magpie receives its name from the long-tailed black-and-white bird that is found in the area, while Beicegel (despite the spelling) is named for the Beisigl brothers, who were early ranchers along its banks. They later established a large ranch in North Dakota near Lemmon, South Dakota. (*Bet. Beicegel Creek and a point 2 m. farther down river are many places suitable for camp.*)

Thus far the river current has been anything but swift, and the stream has been flowing between banks quite widely separated. As the trip is resumed on the fourth day the river soon narrows and becomes a swiftly rushing stream. Snags and submerged tree trunks that heretofore were easily avoided now become a danger to the unwary voyager. The added speed makes navigation more difficult, and a snag through the bottom of the boat at this point would precipitate disaster, the probable loss of equipment adding to the hardships of getting out of the rough country on foot.

In the vicinity of REDWING CREEK are some of the finest views of the entire journey. Grotesque formations carved in the wind-blown, rain-washed buttes are set off by cedar-dotted slopes and river flats covered with sage.

In the Redwing Creek area the river enters the Theodore Roosevelt National Memorial Park (*see* THEODORE ROOSEVELT NATIONAL MEMORIAL PARK, NORTH TOUR), and a short hike left of the Little Missouri leads to one of the largest areas of PETRIFIED FOREST in the Badlands. Great silicified stumps, weighing many tons, are found perched atop slender pillars of gray, yellow, and ocher sandstone, and logs, sometimes several feet long and 12 to 14 inches in diameter, are found here.

Downstream from the Redwing, in a sharp bend of the river, SPERATI POINT rises to the L. The point is named for Dr. Carlo A. Sperati, director of the Luther College (Decorah, Iowa) Band at the time it visited here in 1927. From the summit is an exceptional view of the GRAND CANYON OF THE LITTLE MISSOURI. The river makes an almost right-angle turn to the E. here toward its confluence with the Missouri, and its flood plain again widens and the current is less swift.

The SQUAW CREEK PICNIC AREA (*see* THEODORE ROOSEVELT NATIONAL MEMORIAL PARK, NORTH TOUR) is the only man-made camping place on the entire trip. It was at a sheep ranch on Squaw Creek that the 'vigilantes' of 1884 dropped in for one of their raids, and burned

500 tons of hay, the barn, harnesses, and all machinery, and set fire to the prairie, burning a large area.

The glistening silver steel of the ROOSEVELT BRIDGE spans the Little Missouri, over which US 85 passes, and just E. of which is an entrance to the Theodore Roosevelt National Memorial Park (*see Tour 4*). US 85 is the eastern boundary of the northern park.

CHARLIE BOB CREEK (R) drains the area N. and W. of the Killdeer Mountains (*see Tour 8D*). Here the buttes R. of the river rise 500 to 600 feet above the stream bed; the noonday shadows cast by the scattered groves of cedar on the northern slopes are cool and inviting. A climb to the butte tops reveals their precipitous, barren southern slopes.

The wide valley (L) of CHERRY CREEK (*good overnight camping place opposite mouth*), together with Tobacco Garden Creek (*see Tour 6*), which drains N. into the Missouri, in pre-glacial times was probably the bed of the Little Missouri, the present valley of which was formed when the glacier blocked the former course and diverted the waters in an easterly direction.

At about a half-day's journey below Cherry Creek a climb to the high river bluffs, through thickets of red birch, aspen, and oak trees, leads to a superb view. Southward from the butte tops a blue haze outlines the Killdeer Mountains, from which the Sioux fled after the Battle of Killdeer Mountains (*see Tour 8D*) to take refuge in this very section of the Badlands, the rough terrain of which prevented the army from pursuing. It was in this vicinity in 1886 that young Theodore Roosevelt and two of his ranch hands captured three thieves who had stolen a boat from his Elkhorn Ranch and had plundered almost every ranch house along the river. Roosevelt and his men pursued the three for several days before surrounding their camp and taking them completely by surprise. He then sent his men home and took the culprits overland to Dickinson, where he preferred charges against the two leaders, who were tried and subsequently served their sentences; one was later hanged for horse stealing in Montana. The third marauder, an elderly man, Roosevelt said was the 'kind of person who was not capable of doing either much good or harm.' When the old man thanked him profusely for thus befriending him, the future President remarked that it was the first time he had been thanked for calling a man a fool.

Between ELK and JIM'S CREEKS (R) the Fort Berthold Indian Reservation lies to the L. (*Good camping places bet. Elk and Jim's Creeks.*)

Below Jim's Creek the river widens, its flood plain covers a large area on either side of the stream, broadening the valley along which the hills begin to be more grassy and less rugged and colorful. At the confluence with HANS CREEK (R) the river makes an abrupt right-angle turn L., and while the valley still remains wide, the stream itself narrows and runs more swiftly. (*Good overnight camp sites in the Indian reservation.*)

Below the northern half of the Theodore Roosevelt Park ranches are fewer, and people are seldom seen from the river.

The wider, majestic Missouri is soon reached, and forms the route for the remainder of the voyage. Up this avenue of exploration came Lewis and Clark, Maximilian, Catlin, Ashley, Lisa, and other adventurous explorers and traders; first in the round, unwieldy, skin bullboats of the Indians, and later in the chugging steamboats, plying the river in search of trade between the tribes and forts established along its course.

The seasonal rising and lowering of the Missouri's water level continually changes the channel, leaving shoals, sand bars, and snags, and these offered a problem to river pilots as long as steamboat traffic flourished on the river. When a flat-bottomed steamer ran aground it took hours, and sometimes days, to release it. It was from the odd device used to work the boats off sand bars that the term 'grasshoppering' came into use. Each steamer carried two long, heavy spars, similar to telephone poles, near the bow ready for use. Captain Grant Marsh, an old river pilot, describes the operation of these spars in Joseph Mills Hanson's *Conquest of the Missouri:*

When she became lodged on a bar, the spars were raised and set in the river bottom, like posts, their tops inclined somewhat toward the bow. Above the line of the deck each was rigged with a tackle-block over which a manila cable was passed, one end being fastened to the gunwale of the boat and the other end wound around the capstan. As the capstan was turned and the paddlewheel revolved, the boat was thus lifted and pushed forward. Then the spars were re-set farther ahead and the process repeated until the boat was at last literally lifted over the bar. From the grotesque resemblance to a grasshopper which the craft bore when her spars were set, and from the fact that she might be said to move forward in a series of hops, the practice came to be called 'grasshoppering.'

From the beginning river steamers were dependent on wood for fuel, and as traffic increased woodyards became more numerous along the stream. At first they were operated only by the hardiest of white frontiersmen, but as the agency Indians absorbed the white man's civilization they too began to cut wood to sell. Steamers usually burned either cedar or cottonwood, although the latter was suitable for fuel only when fully dried, while cedar burned readily either green or cured. Boat captains took all the cedar the Indians could stack, but would not stop their boats when they saw only green cottonwood corded. The Indians soon learned a subterfuge to surmount the difficulty of having only cottonwood on hand. They smeared the freshly hewn ends of cottonwood cuttings with vermilion so that it resembled cedar, stacked the wood with the painted ends toward the river, and trusted that when a boat stopped she would take the camouflaged cottonwood rather than waste more time.

The Missouri passes beneath the black steel span of FOUR BEARS BRIDGE, the bridge with 19 Indian names (*see Tour 3A*). Approximately 2 miles below the bridge the river passes within 2 miles of ELBOWOODS (*see Tour 3A*), inland to the L., the first town neared in the more than 200 miles of drifting since Medora was left behind. (*Good camp site on the Elbowoods side of the Missouri.*)

On the bluffs opposite Elbowoods is the SITE OF A HIDATSA INDIAN VILLAGE, which according to tradition was once besieged by the Sioux, who expected to win an easy victory by curtailing the village water supply. Hidatsa scouts, however, had learned of the planned attack, and the people in the village made rock-filled reservoirs and carried water from the river to fill them. Repulsing the first attack of the Sioux, the besieged rolled a skin of water down the hill toward their enemy, which, the legend says, so discouraged the besiegers that they abandoned their efforts to capture the village and withdrew.

The reservation borders both sides of the river from here to a point a short distance downstream from Ree.

Below Elbowoods the river passes the sites of GRANDMOTHER'S LODGE, FORT BERTHOLD, REE, and NISHU (*see Tour 3A*). EXPANSION (R) consists of a post office and store marking the site of a formerly active river town. (*Good camp site bet. Ree and Expansion.*)

Just upstream W. of Expansion is a large, easily detected sandstone promontory known as MANUEL ROCK (R), used as a landmark by old river pilots, and named for the fur trader Manuel Lisa.

Below Expansion are (L) the mouth of GARRISON CREEK and the SITE OF FORT STEVENSON. The site was selected by General Alfred H. Sully in 1864 on his trip down the Missouri during his second campaign, but the fort was not established until 1867. A two-company post named for Brigadier General Thomas G. Stevenson, the fort was abandoned in 1883 and the military reservation turned over to the Interior Department. For a short time the buildings were used as a school for Indian children from the Fort Berthold Agency. Garrison Creek was originally called Douglas Creek, but the name was changed when the Stevenson garrison began using it for bathing purposes.

A few miles below Garrison Creek is SNAKE CREEK (L), called *Ma po ksa a ti a zi* (Hidatsa, *snake house river*), where a cave along the banks of the Missouri near the mouth of the creek, according to legend, swarmed with snakes at certain seasons.

A short distance downstream from the Fort Stevenson site the course of the Missouri turns S. and passes MANNHAVEN (R), remnant of a once thriving river town. Near the present village in 1809 the Missouri Fur Company, directed by Manuel Lisa, erected a trading post known variously as Fort Manuel Lisa and Fort Lewis, the latter for Reuben Lewis—brother of Meriwether Lewis, co-leader of the Lewis and Clark expedition—who operated it until its abandonment in 1812. Under the name of Fort Vanderburgh, the site was later occupied briefly in 1822 or 1823. Lisa, born in New Orleans of Spanish parents, is said to have had more influence over the Indians with whom he dealt than any other trader to enter the Missouri area, although his activities in the Missouri basin were of only 13 years' duration. He died in St. Louis at the age of 48.

The mouth of the KNIFE RIVER is just upstream from STANTON (*see Tour 8D*). (*Camp can be made on R. river bank.*)

In the vicinity of the confluence of the Knife and Missouri are the sites of many Indian villages, Hidatsa, Mandan, and Arikara, the locations of which are easily traceable by the many round, dish-like depressions marking the sites of earth lodges in the villages. The Hidatsa had three villages here until 1837, when the smallpox epidemic reduced their population to only one village. Prior to their occupation of the Knife River vicinity the tribe lived near the mouth of the Heart River (*see Tour 8*), and in 1845, for protection from the Sioux, they moved to Fort Berthold. The Mandans, whose two villages some miles below the Knife were reduced to little more than 100 persons by the smallpox epidemic of 1837, moved to a small village near the Hidatsa and followed that tribe to Fort Berthold in 1845. Migrating up the Missouri at a later date, the Arikara built villages near the Knife as late as 1851, but they too, because of continued Sioux raids, moved to Fort Berthold.

It was at one of the Knife River villages that Charbonneau and his Shoshone Indian wife, Sakakawea, lived in 1804 when Lewis and Clark employed Charbonneau as interpreter of the expedition to the Pacific (*see* BISMARCK).

Below Stanton is DEAPOLIS (R), marked by a single grain elevator, all that remains of another of the towns that sprang up along the Missouri, flourished, and declined with the steamboat trade. The place was named by its founder, who replaced the first letter in the name of the ancient city Neapolis with the first letter of his own surname, Danielson.

Old residents tell the story that in the summer of 1894 the river at Deapolis was extremely low, exposing a huge boulder in the center of the stream. An interested group made their way to the stone and found it carved with peculiar markings they were unable to decipher. Before leaving they added the date of their visit to the inscription. Forty years later the river stage again was low enough to bring the stone above water, and a second party visited it, and found the same undecipherable markings as well as the carving of the 1894 party.

Near the Deapolis elevator is the SITE OF BIG WHITE'S MANDAN INDIAN VILLAGE. Big White was the Mandan chief taken to Washington by Lewis and Clark on their return from the Pacific, and his village was one of two Mandan towns visited by the expedition on the journey up the Missouri in 1804–5. The other, Black Cat's Village, was on the L. bank of the river farther upstream. Lewis and Clark's Fort Mandan was built on the L. bank downstream from the Deapolis site, but the changing river channel has removed all trace of the fort, and Black Cat's Village has never been definitely located (*see Tour 3*).

South of Deapolis is the SITE OF FORT CLARK TRADING POST (R), for which the present village of FORT CLARK (1,726 alt., 30 pop.), downstream 1.5 *m.*, is named. The post, a well stockaded fort

132 by 147 feet, was built in 1829 by James Kipp for the American Fur Company and named for William Clark of the Lewis and Clark expedition. Because of its flourishing trade with the Mandans it was for several years second only to Fort Union in Missouri importance, but it was closed during the smallpox epidemic of 1837, and a few years later was abandoned by the company. The Arikara Indians reoccupied the site in the 1850's in their migration up the Missouri. Today there are slight excavations and scars marking the outline of the fort stockade walls, and traces of the Indian habitation.

Scorched Village, according to Hidatsa legend, had its locale near the present city of WASHBURN (L) (*see Tour 3*), but the Indians say that the site of the legendary village has been swallowed by the ever-shifting channel of the river.

The river passes WILDWOOD LAKE and the PAINTED WOODS (L) (*see Tour 3B*), and the town (R) of SANGER (1,712 alt., 75 pop.), named for its first settlers, C. H. and George Sanger. (*Camp can be made in vicinity of town; L. bank more accessible.*)

The route passes (R) the post office of PRICE (1700 alt.), named for William Price, the first homesteader in the vicinity. Price is on the northern slopes of the flat-topped formations known as SQUARE BUTTES (*see Tour 3B*). Below these bold buttes is (L) DOUBLE DITCH INDIAN VILLAGE STATE PARK (*see Tour 3B*), and a short distance below that the route passes (R) the mouth of SQUARE BUTTE CREEK (*see Tour 8D*).

The resting place of the last physical traces of steamboating on the upper Missouri, ROCK HAVEN (R), is passed almost in sight of the black steel link of railroad bridge spanning the river near Bismarck. The advent of the railroad spelled the decline of river traffic, but before its coming Rock Haven was a river drydock and boat yard.

On the high bluffs across the river below Rock Haven are the reconstructed earth lodges of the LOOKING VILLAGE (L) of the Mandans, below which is the mouth (L) of BURNT CREEK (*see Tour 3B*).

Termination of the 350 *m.* voyage is made at Bismarck at a boat landing (L) reached just after passing under the N. P. Ry. Bridge. Downstream from the landing is the LIBERTY MEMORIAL BRIDGE over which passes US 10 (*see Tour 8*).

PART V
Appendices

Chronology

1682   La Salle, French explorer, by his *Procès Verbal* claims part of North Dakota drained by Missouri River for France.

1738   Pierre de la Verendrye, first white man to enter North Dakota, visits Mandan Indians on Missouri.

1742   Verendrye's sons return to North Dakota while searching for a western sea near high mountains.

1762   France transfers land claimed by La Salle to Spain.

1763   By Treaty of Paris England obtains title to part of State drained by Mouse and Red Rivers.

1768   Jonathan Carver explores Northwest through the Red River Valley for Provincial Government.

1797   David Thompson, English geographer, explores and maps Mouse and Missouri River basins.

Charles Chaboillez of the North West Company establishes first trading post in State at Pembina.

1800   Spain cedes American possessions back to France after adjustment of territorial holdings.

Alexander Henry, Jr., opens fur-trading post at Park River.

1801   Alexander Henry, Jr., moves post to Pembina.

1802   March 12, first non-Indian child in State, a girl, born to Pierre Bonza and wife, Negroes, at Henry's post at Pembina.

Charles le Raye explores western North Dakota while captive of Brulé Sioux.

1803   Louisiana Purchase makes southwestern North Dakota part of United States.

1804–5   Lewis and Clark, accompanied by Sakakawea, cross North Dakota on journey to Pacific.

1807   In May, Manuel Lisa sets out from St. Louis in search of suitable sites for trading posts along the Missouri River.

December 29, first white child in State born at Pembina.

1811   John Bradbury and Thomas Nuttall, English botanists, join Astoria Overland Expedition up Missouri and Yellowstone Rivers to Oregon.

1812   Selkirk colonists come to Pembina to make first attempt at permanent white settlement in State.

1818   Father Dumoulin and Father Provencher open first church in State, a Roman Catholic mission at Pembina.

First school, taught by William Edge, begun in connection with this mission.

United States acquires eastern North Dakota by treaty with England.

1820   Grasshopper plague destroys Red River Valley crops.

1822   General W. H. Ashley and other explorers establish fur-trading posts in Missouri Valley.

1823   General Stephen H. Long survey expedition designates official boundary between United States and Canada at point north of Pembina.

Selkirk colonists evacuate Pembina and move to Canadian soil.

1825   General Henry Atkinson and General Henry Leavenworth come up Missouri to make treaties with Arikara and other Indians.

1828   American Fur Company builds Fort Union at mouth of Yellowstone.

1831   Fort Clark built on Missouri by American Fur Company.

1832   *Yellowstone,* first steamboat to navigate Missouri in North Dakota, makes voyage to Fort Union.

George Catlin, artist and explorer, visits Mandan Indians.

1833   Maximilian, Prince of Wied, conducts scientific expedition up Missouri River.

1837   Smallpox epidemic nearly annihilates Mandan Indian tribe.

1839   John C. Frémont and Jean N. Nicollet lead first exploration through central North Dakota.

Father Pierre Jean De Smet begins missionary work among North Dakota Indians, and persuades Sioux, particularly Hunkpapas, to participate in peace councils.

1842   Joseph Rolette opens American Fur Company post at Pembina.

1843   Rival post built at Pembina by Norman Kittson.

John James Audubon, naturalist, studies animal life in present North Dakota.

1845   Bartholomew Berthold, representing American Fur Company, founds post named for himself on Missouri River.

1848   Father George Belcourt opens mission fields in Pembina, Walhalla, and Turtle Mountains.

Reverend Alonzo Barnard and James Tanner conduct first Protestant church service in State at Pembina.

First printing press brought into North Dakota by Barnard.

1851   First North Dakota post office established at Pembina with Norman Kittson postmaster.

Charles Cavileer brings settlers to Pembina from Minnesota to form first permanent white agricultural colony in State.

First flour mill in State constructed at Walhalla by Father Belcourt.

1853   Stevens survey sponsored by Federal Government to find most advantageous route for railway to Pacific.

1857   Fort Abercrombie, first military post in North Dakota, established on Red River.

1859   January 5, *Anson Northrup*, first steamboat on Red River, starts trip from Fort Abercrombie to Winnipeg.

1860   Regular steamboat transportation on upper Missouri begins.

1861   Dakota Territory is officially organized.

        President Lincoln appoints William Jayne first Governor of Dakota Territory.

1862   First Territorial legislature meets in Yankton.

        Refugees from Minnesota Massacre flee to Fort Abercrombie.

        Little Crow and followers seek refuge with Sioux near Devils Lake.

        Captain James L. Fisk guides parties across North Dakota to Montana gold fields.

1863   January 1, Dakota Territory opened for homesteading.

        General Henry H. Sibley and General Alfred H. Sully, sent out to punish Sioux who participated in Minnesota Massacre, conduct extensive campaign through North Dakota.

1864   In July, first North Dakota newspaper, the *Frontier Scout*, issued at Fort Union.

        General Sully supervises building of Fort Rice.

        Immigrant party under Captain James L. Fisk, besieged by Sioux, builds Fort Dilts.

1866   Fort Buford established opposite mouth of Yellowstone.

1867   Fort Ransom, second of chain of forts for protection of immigrants crossing the prairies, established on Sheyenne River by General A. H. Terry.

        Forts Stevenson and Totten, and Fort Totten Reservation established.

        Treaty with Sisseton and Wahpeton Sioux cedes United States rights to build roads and railroads across Indian lands.

1868   Sioux, influenced by Father De Smet, join peace council at Fort Rice.

        Laramie treaty defines reservation boundaries for Sioux, including Standing Rock Reservation.

        Joseph Rolette makes first North Dakota homestead entry, filing on land in northwest part of Red River Valley.

1870   Fort Berthold Indian Reservation boundaries defined.

        Treaty between Chippewa, Sioux, and whites at Fort Abercrombie brings about permanent peace in eastern area.

1871   Northern Pacific Railway reaches Fargo.

        First North Dakota telegraph line put in operation between Fort Abercrombie and Winnipeg.

        Whistler expedition begins survey of railway lines westward through North Dakota.

1872   Fort Seward replaces Fort Ransom.

        Fort McKeen, later named Fort Abraham Lincoln, built on Missouri.

1873   Fort Abraham Lincoln built.
        Bismarck becomes western terminus of Northern Pacific.
        July 11, Colonel C. A. Lounsberry publishes first issue of Bismarck *Tribune,* State's oldest newspaper.

1874   United States Weather Bureau established as part of Camp Hancock at Bismarck.
        First newspaper in Red River Valley, the *Express,* printed at Fargo.
        Custer brings back report of gold in Black Hills.

1875   Era of bonanza farming is begun.
        War Department permits white settlement on reservations in violation of Laramie treaty, precipitating uprisings among Sioux.

1876   May 17, Custer leaves Fort Abraham Lincoln for campaign of the Little Big Horn.
        June 25, Custer's immediate command annihilated by Sioux at Battle of Little Big Horn.

1878   Fort Yates completed to succeed Fort Rice.
        Ranching introduced in western North Dakota.

1880   James J. Hill begins building Great Northern Railway through State.
        Lignite mining opened in western North Dakota.
        Military reserves in eastern and central parts of State thrown open to homestead entry.

1881   Northern Pacific reaches Montana border.

1882   Great Northern completed through Red River Valley to Canada.
        Turtle Mountain Reservation established for Chippewa.

1883   Territorial capital moved from Yankton to Bismarck.
        Jamestown Presbyterian College established.
        University of North Dakota opens at Grand Forks.
        Marquis de Mores opens packing plant at Medora.
        Theodore Roosevelt comes to North Dakota for his health and begins ranching near Medora.
        First labor union in State formed at Bismarck.

1885   State hospital for insane opens at Jamestown.
        Territorial prison, later State penitentiary, opens at Bismarck.

1886   Bank of Hamilton founded: later becomes first State bank.

1887   Treaty with Sioux allows white settlement on Standing Rock Indian Agency.

1889   February 22, Congress passes Enabling Act.
        July 4, State constitutional convention held at Bismarck.
        October 1, State constitution adopted.
        November 2, President Harrison admits North Dakota to statehood. John Miller takes office as first Governor.
        November 19, first legislature meets at Bismarck.

1890   State Normal School opens at Valley City.
        State Agricultural College opens at Fargo.
        State Normal School opens at Mayville.
        Andrew Burke elected Governor.
        School for the Deaf opens at Devils Lake.
1891   Severe drought throughout State.
1892   Eli Shortridge, Democrat, elected Governor on fusion ticket
        in reaction against railway interference in State politics.
1893   Industrial School at Ellendale (later State Normal and In-
        dustrial School) established.
1894   Roger Allin, Republican, elected Governor.
1896   Frank Briggs, Republican, elected Governor.
1897   First free public library in State opens at Grafton.
        Red River Valley flood causes severe damage.
1898   Governor Briggs dies. Lieutenant Governor Joseph M. Devine
        completes term.
        Fred B. Fancher, Republican, elected to succeed Devine.
1900   Frank White, Republican, elected Governor.
1902   Governor White re-elected.
1903   New Fort Lincoln built and garrisoned.
1904   State School of Science opens at Wahpeton.
        School for the Feeble-minded (later Grafton State School)
        opens at Grafton.
        E. Y. Sarles, Republican, elected Governor.
1905   State Historical Society of North Dakota designated as State
        agency by the North Dakota Legislature.
1906   John Burke, first Governor of State to serve three terms,
        elected on Democratic ticket.
1907   State School of Forestry opens at Bottineau.
1909   First State child labor law enacted.
        State Library Commission created.
1912   L. B. Hanna, Republican, elected Governor.
1913   State Normal School opens at Minot.
1915   In February, Nonpartisan League organized.
1916   Lynn J. Frazier, first Nonpartisan Governor, elected.
1918   State Normal School opens at Dickinson.
        Seven initiated amendments, basis of league platform, ap-
        proved by electorate.
1919   Bank of North Dakota organized.
        Industrial Commission created.
1920   Recall measure passed.
        April 29, contract awarded for building State mill and ele-
        vator at Grand Forks.
1921   Governor Frazier recalled; succeeded by R. A. Nestos, I.V.A.
        Republican.
1922   Former Governor Frazier elected United States Senator.
        WDAY, first North Dakota radio station, opens at Fargo.

1924   Arthur G. Sorlie, Nonpartisan, elected Governor.

Gerald P. Nye appointed to fill United States Senate vacancy caused by death of Senator E. F. Ladd.

1927   Governor Sorlie dies in office; succeeded by Lieutenant Governor Walter Maddock.

1928   George F. Shafer, I.V.A. Republican, elected Governor.

Air mail service between Twin Cities and Winnipeg through North Dakota inaugurated.

1929   Prolonged drought throughout Northwest begins.

1930   December 28, Capitol destroyed by fire.

1932   October 8, Vice-President Charles M. Curtis dedicates cornerstone of new $2,000,000 capitol building.

William Langer, Nonpartisan, elected Governor.

Prohibition clause of State constitution repealed.

1934   July 18, North Dakota Supreme Court holds Governor Langer disqualified for office; Lieutenant Governor Ole Olson becomes Acting Governor.

1935   January 7, Thomas H. Moodie, Democrat, inaugurated Governor.

February 2, State Supreme Court declares Governor Moodie ineligible; Walter Welford, Nonpartisan Lieutenant Governor, becomes Acting Governor.

State Welfare and Planning Boards created.

1936   Langer defeats Welford for governorship, first Governor of any State elected in the individual column of ballot.

Referendum legalizes sale of liquor in State.

1937   North Dakota State Water Conservation organized.

1939   January 1, John Moses, Democrat, inaugurated Governor.

1945   January 1, Fred G. Aandahl, Republican, inaugurated Governor.

1948   The voters of North Dakota approved a state bonus for North Dakota veterans of World War II.

1949   Construction on Garrison Dam commenced.

June 4, Theodore Roosevelt National Memorial Park, the only National Memorial Park in the United States, dedicated at Medora, North Dakota.

Bibliography

il. = illustrated   B. = bibliography
o.p. = out of print

THE NATURAL SETTING

GEOGRAPHY

Wemett, William Marks. *Geography of North Dakota.* Fargo, Northern School Supply, 1929. 230 p. il. A travel sketch of North Dakota in textbook form.

GEOLOGY

Campbell, Marius R. *Guidebook to the Western United States.* Washington, Government Printing Office, 1915. 212 p. (U. S. Geological Survey, Bull. 611.) Part A, Northern Pacific Railway route, with a side trip to the Yellowstone Park.

Hard, Herbert A. *Soil and Geological Survey of North Dakota;* with a history of Barnes County by Katherine Hard, and a chapter on flora of North Dakota by Herbert F. Bergman. Bismarck, Tribune Publishing Company, 1912. o.p. 372 p. il. Sixth biennial report of the State agricultural college geologic survey.

Leonard, A. G. *North Dakota Geological Survey.* Bismarck, Tribune Publishing Company, 1906–27. o.p. V. 2, 3, 4, 5. Reports written and edited by the late Dr. Leonard while he was State geologist.

—— *Bismarck Folio.* Washington, Government Printing Office, 1912. 8 p. il. (U.S. Geological Survey, Geologic Atlas of the U.S., Folio 181.)

Simpson, Howard E. *Geology and Ground Water Resources of North Dakota.* Washington, Government Printing Office, 1929. 312 p. (U.S. Geological Survey.) Contains, besides a general summary survey, a detailed description of each county.

Upham, Warren. *Glacial Lake Agassiz.* Washington, Government Printing Office, 1895. 658 p. il. (U.S. Geological Survey, v. 25.) A description of the glacier that once covered North Dakota, and the results it had upon the surface of the State; also tells of plant and animal life in the Red River Valley.

Willard, Daniel Everett. *Jamestown-Tower Folio, Jamestown, Eckelson and Tower Quadrangles.* Washington, Government Printing Office, 1909. 10 p. il. (U.S. Geological Survey, Geologic Atlas of the U.S., Folio 168.)

—— *Story of the Prairies.* St. Paul, Webb Publishing Company, 1909. 265 p. il. Study of geology and physical characteristics of the State by a former professor of geology at the agricultural college.

—— and Hall, Charles M. *Casselton-Fargo Folio.* Washington, Government Printing Office, 1905. 9 p. il. (Geologic Atlas of the U.S., Folio 117.)

PALEONTOLOGY

Hornaday, W. T. *Tales from Nature's Wonderland.* New York, Charles Scribner's Sons, 1924. o.p. 235 p. il. Paleontology written for children. Also contains stories of strange animals on earth today.

Lucas, Frederic A. *Animals of the Past.* New York, printed for the American Museum of Natural History, 1916. 266 p. il. 4th edit. (Handbook Series No. 4.) An account in story form of some of the creatures of the ancient world.

Williams, Henry Smith. *Survival of the Fittest*. New York, Robert M. McBride and Company, 1932. 231 p. il. Vivid descriptions of some of the animals that once roamed the plains of North Dakota.

NATURAL RESOURCES

Burns and McDonnell Engineering Company. *Report of Missouri Dam and Diversion Project in North and South Dakota*. Minneapolis, 1933. For a discussion of the means of conservation of the water and soil resources of the State, see pp. 23–5.

North Dakota. State Geological Survey. *Report on Clay Resources in North Dakota*. Grand Forks, 1906. 324 p. il. (Fourth Biennial Report.)

—— *Report on Lignite Resources in North Dakota*. Grand Forks, 1902. 262 p. il. (Second Biennial Report.)

North Dakota. State Planning Board. *Second Progress Report to National Resources Committee*. Bismarck, June 1935. 3 v. in ms.

——*The Mineral Resources of North Dakota;* bentonite. University of North Dakota, Grand Forks, July 1935. (Circular Report No. 6.) Dr. Irvin Lavine, Consultant.

—— *The Mineral Resources of North Dakota;* gold. University of North Dakota, Grand Forks, July 1935. (Circular Report No. 7.) Dr. Irvin Lavine, Consultant.

—— *The Mineral Resources of North Dakota;* activated carbon. University of North Dakota, Grand Forks, July 1935. (Circular Report No. 9.) Dr. Irvin Lavine, Consultant.

North Dakota. University. Division of Mines and Mining Experiments. *Geology and Natural Resources of North Dakota*. Grand Forks, University Press, Jan. 1930. 79 p. (Departmental Bull. 11.) A brief description of the State, with special references to the lignite and clay deposits.

FLORA

Bergman, Herbert Floyd. *Flora of North Dakota*. Bismarck, Tribune Publishing Company, 1917. o.p. 372 p. A technical study of plant life in North Dakota.

Clements, Frederic Edward and Clements, Edith Schwartz. *Rocky Mountain Flowers*. New York, H. W. Wilson Company, 1920. 392 p. il. Field edit. A guide for plant-lovers and plant-users, with black-and-white and color plates.

Schmidt, C. C. *Nature Study and Agriculture*. Chicago, D. C. Heath, 1933. 508 p. il. Discussion by a University of North Dakota professor of education, based on appreciation of nature.

Stevens, O. A. *Wild Flowers of North Dakota*. North Dakota Agricultural College, Fargo, May 1933. 51 p. il. (Bull. 269.)

FAUNA

Audubon, Maria R. and Coues, E. *Audubon and His Journals*. New York, Charles Scribner's Sons, 1897. o.p. 1086 p. 2 v. A. description of Audubon's trip along the Missouri River, with zoological notes by Elliott Coues.

Bailey, Vernon. *Biological Survey of North Dakota*. Washington, Government Printing Office, 1926. o.p. 226 p. (U.S. Department of Agriculture, Bull. 49 in *North American Fauna*.) A study of North Dakota fauna.

Job, Herbert K. *Among the Water-Fowl*. New York, Doubleday, Page and Company, 1903. o.p. 224 p. il. A popular narrative account of waterfowl in the northern and middle States and lower Canada, east of the Rockies.

Judd, Elmer T. *List of North Dakota Birds*. Cando, N. Dak., published by author, 1917. 29 p. Birds in the Big Coulee, Turtle Mountain, and Devils Lake regions, as noted during the years 1890 to 1896 and verified in subsesequent years.

Larson, Adrian. *Birds of Eastern McKenzie County, North Dakota*. Wilson Ornithological Club, Sioux City, Iowa, 1928. 19 p. Reprinted from the *Wilson Bulletin*, March 1928, June 1928.

Reid, Russell and Gannon, Clell. *Birds and Mammals Observed by Lewis and Clark in North Dakota.* Bismarck, 1927. 24 p.
────── *Natural History Notes on the Journal of Alexander Henry.* Bismarck, 1928. 168 p. Reprinted from *North Dakota Historical Quarterly.*
Stevens, O. A. *Making Use of Our Birds.* Fargo, Dec. 1930. 30 p. (North Dakota Agricultural College, Bull. 241.)
Taylor, Joseph Henry. *Beavers and Their Ways. Twenty Years on the Trap Line.* Privately printed, n.d. o.p. 178 p. il. Animal studies by an old-time trapper and student of natural history.
Williams, H. V. *Birds of the Red River Valley of Northeast North Dakota.* Wilson Ornithological Club, Sioux City, Iowa, 1926. 37 p. Reprinted from the *Wilson Bulletin,* March-June 1926.
Wood, Norman A. *A Preliminary Survey of the Bird Life of North Dakota.* Ann Arbor, University of Michigan, 1923. 96 p. il. Discussion of North Dakota birds, with illustrations by Russell Reid.

INDIANS AND THEIR PREDECESSORS

Beede, Aaron McGaffey. *Toward the Sun.* Bismarck, Tribune Publishing Company, 1916. o.p. 199 p. Written by a pioneer missionary among the Indians of North Dakota, with commentary notes by Melvin R. Gilmore.
Byrne, Patrick E. *Soldiers of the Plain.* New York, Minton, Balch and Company, 1928. o.p. 260 p. Sympathetic account of red man's side in treaty negotiations, touches remarkable military work of Indians, presents 'high qualities' of the Indian 'as a factor in civilized life.'
Catlin, George. *Boys' Catlin. My Life among the Indians.* New York, Charles Scribner's Sons, 1909. 380 p. il. An abridged book for school use, telling of the manners, customs, and conditions of the North American Indians in the early 1800's.
────── *North American Indians.* Edinburgh, John Grant, 1926. o.p. 701 p. 2 v. il. Letters and notes on manners, customs, and conditions of North American Indians written during his travels in 1832–9.
Chandler, Katherine. *The Bird Woman of the Lewis and Clark Expedition.* New York, Boston, Silver, Burdett and Company, 1905. o.p. 109 p. il. A supplementary reader for first- and second-grade children.
Crawford, Helen. 'Sakakawea, the Bird Woman.' *North Dakota Historical Quarterly,* Apr. 1927, v. 1: pp. 6–15. The story of the Bird Woman in reference to the statue erected on the grounds of the State capitol, Bismarck.
Defenbach, Byron. *Red Heroines of the Northwest.* Caldwell, Idaho, The Caxton Printers, Ltd., 1930. 296 p. il. Stories of several Indian women, including Sakakawea.
Denig, Edward Thompson. *Indian Tribes on the Upper Missouri.* Washington, Government Printing Office, 1930. Pp. 375–628 il. (Smithsonian Institution, U.S. Bureau of American Ethnology, 46th annual report.)
Densmore, Frances. *Chippewa Customs.* Washington, Government Printing Office, 1929. 204 p. il. B. (Smithsonian Institution, U.S. Bureau of American Ethnology, Bull. 86.)
────── *Chippewa Music.* Washington, Government Printing Office, 1910–13. 541 p. 2 v. il. (Smithsonian Institution, U.S. Bureau of American Ethnology, Bull. 45.) Contains the music of Chippewa songs.
────── *Mandan and Hidatsa Music.* Washington, Government Printing Office, 1923. 192 p. il. (Smithsonian Institution, U.S. Bureau of American Ethnology, Bull. 80.) Indian music from both tribes.
────── *The American Indians and Their Music.* New York, The Women's Press, 1926. o.p. 143 p. il. B. Includes music for Indian songs and material on social life and customs among the Indians.
Dixon, Joseph K. *The Vanishing Race.* Garden City, New York, Doubleday, Page and Company, 1913. o.p. 231 p. il. A record of the last great Indian council participated in by Indian chiefs from nearly every reservation in the United

States, with the stories of their lives as told by themselves. Part 4 describes the Battle of the Little Big Horn.

Eastman, Charles A. *Indian Boyhood.* New York, Little, Brown and Company, 1902. 289 p. il. Tales of Dakota Indian children.

———*Smoky Day's Wigwam Evenings.* Boston, Little, Brown and Company, 1910. o.p. 148 p. il. B. Indian legends written for children.

Fiske, Frank B. *The Taming of the Sioux.* Bismarck, Tribune Publishing Company, 1917. o.p. 186 p. il. An account of the Custer massacre, with descriptive material on Indian life, dress, and customs.

Garland, Hamlin. *Book of the American Indian.* New York, Harpers, 1923. 274 p. il. Fifteen true Indian stories, including one of Sitting Bull.

Gilmore, Melvin R. *Ethnobotany of the Great Plains Area; Uses of Plants by the Indians of the Missouri River Region.* Reprinted. Washington, Government Printing Office, 1919. 154 p. il. (Smithsonian Institution, U.S. Bureau of American Ethnology, 33d annual report.)

———*Prairie Smoke.* New York, Columbia University, 1929. 208 p. Appreciatively written collection of Indian lore by former curator of State historical society.

Godfrey, Captain E. S. 'Custer's Last Battle.' *Century Magazine,* Jan. 1892. 29 p. il. One of Custer's troop commanders gives an authentic account of the campaign that culminated in this battle.

Graham, W. A. *Story of the Little Bighorn.* New York, Century Company, 1926. o.p. 174 p. il. A historical narrative describing the Custer massacre.

Hans, Frederic M., *The Great Sioux Nation.* Chicago, M. A. Donahue and Company, 1907. o.p. 575 p. il. A history of Indian life and warfare.

Hebard, Grace R. *Sacajawea.* Glendale, California, A. H. Clark Company, 1933. 341 p. il. A story of the life of the Bird Woman and her family.

Hodge, Frederick Webb. *Handbook of American Indians.* Washington, Government Printing Office, 1912. 1992 p. 2 v. il. (Smithsonian Institution, U.S. Bureau of American Ethnology.)

Hoffman, W. J. *The Mide'wimin or Grand Medicine Society of the Ojibwa.* Washington, Government Printing Office, 1891. Pp. 143–300 il. (Smithsonian Institution, U.S. Bureau of American Ethnology, 7th annual report.) An accurate account of Indian customs.

Holley, Frances C. *Once Their Home.* Chicago, Donahue and Henneberry, 1890. o.p. 405 p. il. Interesting account of early Dakota, stressing relations between white and red men.

Kelly, Mrs. Fannie. *Narrative of My Captivity among the Sioux Indians.* Chicago, Donnelley Gassette and Loyd, 1880. o.p. 285 p. il. Personal experiences of the author among the Indians, and an account of the Sully expedition.

McLaughlin, Major James. *My Friend the Indian.* Chicago, Houghton Mifflin Company, 1910. o.p. 404 p. A sympathetic account of Indian life.

McLaughlin, Mrs. Marie L. *Myths of the Sioux.* Bismarck, Tribune Publishing Company, 1916. o.p. 200 p. il. Thirty-eight myths related by the wife of Major McLaughlin, herself one-fourth Sioux.

Missionary Register, *Northwest American Indians.* London, L. B. Seeley & Son, 1826. o.p. 637 p. A report of missionary work among the Indians of the Red River Valley.

Radin, Paul. *Story of the American Indian.* New York, Boni and Liveright, 1927. 372 p. il. Contains an interesting description of the Mandan Indian villages.

Riggs, Rev. S. R. *Grammar and Dictionary of the Dakota Language.* Washington, Government Printing Office, 1893. 239 p. (Smithsonian Institution, U.S. Bureau of American Ethnology.)

Sarett, Lew. *Many, Many Moons: Indians of North America: Slow Smoke.* New York, Henry Holt and Company, 1925. 104 p. Poems of Indians and prairie life.

Schultz, J. W. *The Bird Woman, the Guide of Lewis and Clark.* Chicago, Houghton Mifflin Company, 1918. o.p. 235 p. il. The story of Sakakawea as told to the author by the daughter of a Mandan chief.

Seymour, Flora W. *The Indians Today*. Chicago, Benj. H. Sanborn Company, 1927. o.p. 235 p. il. Well-written, intended for boys and girls.

Standing Bear, Luther. *My People, the Sioux*. New York and Boston, Houghton Mifflin Company, 1928. 288 p. il. The social life and customs of his people described by a Sioux chief.

Vestal, Stanley. *Happy Hunting Grounds*. Chicago, Lyons and Carnahan, 1928. 220 p. il. Story of warfare between Mandan and Cheyenne Indians.

—— *New Sources of Indian History*. Norman, University of Oklahoma Press, 1934. 351 p. il. Description of the Dakota Indians, especially of their Ghost Dance, and a biography of Sitting Bull.

—— *Sitting Bull*. Boston and New York, Houghton Mifflin Company, 1932. 350 p. il. B. An interesting biography of this famous Sioux chief.

—— *Warpath*. Boston and New York, Houghton Mifflin Company, 1934. 291 p. il. B. A true story of Chief White Bull and his connection with Dakota Indian wars.

Walker, J. E. *Campaigns of General Custer in the Northwest, and Final Surrender of Sitting Bull*. London, Jenkins, 1881. o.p. 139 p. il. The story of the Custer massacre, prefaced with a history of the military life of General Custer.

Wall, Oscar G. *Diary*. Published by the author, 1909. o.p. 282 p. Recollections of the Sioux massacre, Yellow Medicine incident with its important battles, and the Sibley expedition.

Warren, William A. *Minnesota Historical Society Collections*. St. Paul, 1885. V. 5. pp. 21–394. A history of the Ojibway Indians.

Wemett, William Marks. *The Indians of North Dakota*. Fargo, Northern School Supply, 1927. 256 p. il. A history of Indian life written especially for school children.

Will, George Francis. *Archaeology of the Missouri Valley*. Anthropological Papers of American Museum of Natural History, v. 22: pp. 291–341. New York, 1924. A scientific discussion of the Missouri Valley.

—— 'Arikara Ceremonials.' *North Dakota Historical Quarterly*, July 1930, v. 4: pp. 247–63. An interesting paper on Arikara life.

—— 'The Mandans.' *North Dakota Historical Quarterly*, Oct. 1930, v. 5: pp. 38–48. A revision and condensation of an article on the life and language of these agricultural Indians, originally written for the Peabody Museum of American Archaeology and Ethnology. Also includes the story of the Mandan earth lodge on the grounds of the State capitol, Bismarck.

—— and Hyde, George E. *Corn among the Indians of the Upper Missouri*. St. Louis, Missouri, William Henry Miner Company, Incorporated, 1917. o.p. 323 p. il. A description of agriculture among the Indians.

Will, George Francis. 'Magical and Sleight of Hand Performances by the Arikara.' *North Dakota Historical Quarterly*, Oct. 1928, v. 3, pp. 50–65. Unusual description of Indian 'magic.'

—— and Spinden, H. J. *The Mandans*. Cambridge, Massachusetts, Peabody Museum, 1906. o.p. 219 p. il. A study of the culture, archeology, and language of the tribe.

Wilson, Gilbert L. *Indian Hero Tales*. Chicago, American Book Company, 1916. o.p. 203 p. il. Tales of the Abnaki, Micmacs, and Algonquins retold, with a section on Indian folklore in general.

—— *Myths of the Red Children*. Chicago, Ginn, 1907. o.p. 154 p. il. A collection of Indian legends.

—— *Waheenee; An Indian Girl's Story*. St. Paul, Webb Publishing Company, 1921. o.p. 189 p. il. Story of an Arikara woman, wife of the tribal chieftain Son-of-the-Star, as told by herself to the author.

Wilson, Thomas. *The Antiquity of the Red Race in America*. Washington, Government Printing Office, 1897. See pp. 1039–45. (Smithsonian Institution, U.S. Bureau of American Ethnology.) Deals with the origin and history of North American Indians.

Wissler, Clark. *Costumes of the Plains Indians*. Anthropological Papers of the American Museum of Natural History, v. 17: pp. 39–91. 1915. Part II describes the costumes and adornments of various North American tribes.

——— *North American Indians of the Plains*. New York, The American Museum of Natural History, 1927. 172 p. Authoritative discussion of society and culture of North American Indians.

HISTORY

Armstrong, Moses K. *The Early Empire Builders of the Great West*. St. Paul, E. W. Porter, 1901. o.p. 456 p. il. Early history of Dakota Territory by a pioneer surveyor of Yankton, Dakota Territory.

Arnold, Henry V. *Early History of Ransom County* (with references to Sargent County). Larimore, H. V. Arnold, 1918. o.p. 105 p. Historical sketches based on newspaper articles.

——— *Forty Years in North Dakota*. Larimore, H. V. Arnold, 1921. o.p. 96 p. A short history of the State in relation to Grand Forks County.

——— *History of Old Pembina*. Larimore, H. V. Arnold, 1917. o.p. 82 p. An entertaining sketch of the first settlement in the State from the coming of the Hudson's Bay Company to 1872.

Band, John Wesley. *Minnesota and Its Resources*. New York, Redfield, 1854. o.p. 412 p. il. Appendix includes notes on a trip from St. Paul to Pembina and the Selkirk settlement on the Red River of the North.

Black, Norman Fergus. *A History of Saskatchewan and the Old Northwest*. Regina, Saskatchewan, North West Historical Company, 1913. 605 p. il. A history of the settlement of Canada, with references to boundary-line settlements with the United States, and the story of the fur trade between the two countries.

Black, R. M. *A History of Dickey County*. Ellendale, Dickey County Historical Society, 1930. o.p. 331 p. il. Characteristic stories of early times in the county, with a chapter on each town and township.

Brady, Cyrus Townsend. *American Fights and Fighters*. New York, Doubleday, Doran and Company, 1928. o.p. 326 p. il. Includes vivid description of Northwest Indian wars, especially those engaged in by the Sioux.

Brininstool, E. A. *A Trooper with Custer*. Columbus, The Hunter-Trader-Trapper Company, 1925. o.p. 214 p. il. (Frontier Series, v. 1.) The story of a soldier in the Little Big Horn campaign.

Buffalo Bill (William Cody). *The Adventures of Buffalo Bill*. New York, Harpers, 1927. o.p. 35 p. il. An authentic history of many events in the exploration, settlement, and development of the western plains.

Burdick, Usher L. *Last Battle of the Sioux Nation*. Stevens Point, Wisconsin, Worzalla Publishing Company, 1929. 164 p. il. A story of Indian wars written by a North Dakota congressman.

——— *Marquis De Mores at War in the Badlands*. Fargo, privately printed, 1929. 24 p. il. Explains the enmity between the young nobleman and his western neighbors, and gives an account of his trial for the murder of a cowboy.

Burgum, Jessamine Slaughter. *Zezula, or Pioneer Days in the Smoky Water Country*. Valley City, Gettchell and Nielsen, 1937. 195 p. il. B. Early history of Dakota Territory along the Missouri River.

Chardon, Francis A. *Chardon's Journal at Fort Clark*. Pierre, South Dakota, privately printed, 1932. 458 p. il. Description of life on the Upper Missouri 1834–9. A fur-trader's experience with Mandans, Gros Ventres, and their neighbors, especially describing the smallpox epidemic of 1837.

Chittenden, Captain Hiram Martin. *History of the Fur Trade in the Far West*. New York, Harpers, n.d. o.p. 1003 p. 3 v. il. Carefully written history of fur trade in the territory west of the Missouri River, with North Dakota forming the background for much of the material.

——— and Richardson, A. T. *Life, Letters and Travels of Father Pierre Jean DeSmet, S. J. 1801–75*. New York, Harpers, n.d. o.p. 1600 p. 4 v. il. Edited from the original unpublished manuscript journals of a pioneer missionary. Volume III contains a description of his travels through the Northwest.

Cochrane, C. N. *David Thompson*. Toronto, Macmillan, 1924. 173 p. il. B. A biography of Thompson, explorer and geographer who visited North Dakota in 1797.

Coues, Dr. Elliot. *History of the Lewis and Clark Expedition*. New York, Harpers, 1893. o.p. 1364 p. 4 v. il. B. A detailed history of the expedition, with an essay on Indian policy.

————— *New Light on the Early History of the Great Northwest*. New York, Harpers, 1897. o.p. 1027 p. 3 v. Manuscript journals of Alexander Henry and David Thompson. Volume I tells of their experiences in the country around the Red River of the North.

Cowie, Isaac. *The Company of Adventurers*. Toronto, W. Briggs, 1913. o.p. 515 p. il. Interesting narrative of the author's experiences with Hudson's Bay Company in the Northwest during 1867–74.

Crawford, Lewis F. *History of North Dakota*. New York and Chicago, American Historical Society, 1931. o.p. 1911 p. 3 v. il. B. One volume by Crawford on the history of the State, and two volumes of biography by various authors.

————— *Rekindling Camp Fires*. Bismarck, Capital Book Company, n.d. o.p. 324 p. il. B. A narrative of 60 years in the West as an Indian fighter, cowboy, and hunter.

Curtis, Carrie. *History of Ransom County*. Manuscript, privately owned. Written for Federated Women's Club in 1923.

Custer, Mrs. Elizabeth B. *Boots and Saddles*. New York, Harpers, 1885. 312 p. The story of Custer's life in the Dakotas and his Indian wars.

————— *Following the Guidon*. New York, Harpers, 1890. o.p. 341 p. il. Story of Kansas frontier days, including the battle of Washita in which Custer defeated the Cheyennes by tactics similar to those used in the Battle of the Little Big Horn.

Cyclorama of General Custer's Last Fight. Boston Cyclorama Company, 1889. o.p. 30 p. il. An account of the Battle of the Little Big Horn with biographies of Custer and Chief Gall, and an interview with Sitting Bull.

Fish, Herbert C. and Black, R. M. *A Brief History of North Dakota*. Chicago, American Book Company, 1925. 244 p. Good reference text written by former curator of the State historical society and former president of the State Normal and Industrial School at Ellendale.

Gass, Patrick. *Gass Journal of the Lewis and Clark Expedition*. Chicago, A. C. McClurg Company, 1904. o.p. 298 p. Gass was a carpenter on the expedition and kept a journal. He later participated in the War of 1812.

Hagedorn, Hermann. *Roosevelt in the Bad Lands*. Chicago, Houghton Mifflin Company, 1930. 475 p. Interesting story of early North Dakota days woven about the life of Roosevelt in the Badlands.

Hennessey, William B. *History of North Dakota*. Bismarck, Tribune Publishing Company, 1910. o.p. 633 p. il. A history of the State from earliest times, including biographies of the builders of the commonwealth.

History of the Northwest and Its Men of Progress. Minneapolis, The Minneapolis Journal, 1901. o.p. 592 p. il. Part V contains a historical sketch of North Dakota written by C. A. Lounsberry.

History of the Red River Valley. Grand Forks, Herald Publishing Company, C. F. Cooper and Company, Chicago, 1909. o.p. 645 p. 2 v. il. Includes many amusing sketches of pioneer life in the valley.

Hughes, Katherine. *Father Lacombe, The Black-robed Voyageur*. New York, Moffat, Yard and Company, 1911. 467 p. il. A well-written biographical sketch.

Illustrated Album of Biography of the Famous Red River Valley of the North. Chicago, Alden, Ogle and Company, 1889. o.p. 845 p. il. Contains biographical sketches of early settlers and residents of eastern North Dakota and western Minnesota.

Jarrell, Myrtris and Hewitt, J. N. B. *Journals of Rudolph Frederich Kurz.* Washington, Government Printing Office, 1937. 382 p. il. (Smithsonian Institution, U.S. Bureau of American Ethnology, Bull. 115.) Experiences among fur traders and American Indians on the Mississippi and Upper Missouri Rivers during the years 1846–52.

Kelly, Luther S. *Yellowstone Kelly.* New Haven, Yale University Press, 1926. o.p. 268 p. il. Personal recollections of a famous scout and plainsman told in entertaining style.

Kimball, Maria B. *A Soldier-Doctor of Our Army: James B. Kimball.* New York, Houghton Mifflin Company, 1917. o.p. 192 p. Biography of an Army surgeon who spent ten years in Dakota Army posts, coming to Fort Buford in 1867.

Larpenteur, Charles. *Forty Years a Fur Trader on the Upper Missouri.* New York, 1898. o.p. 430 p. 2 v. Autobiography of a pioneer hunter and fur trader stationed at Fort Union during the 1830's. Edited by Dr. Elliot Coues.

Laut, Agnes C. *The Blazed Trail of the Old Frontier.* New York, R. M. McBride and Company, 1926. 271 p. il. The log of the Upper Missouri Historical Expedition of 1925.

―――― *The Conquest of the Great Northwest.* New York, Moffat, Yard and Company, 1911. 413 p. 2 v. il. History of the Hudson's Bay Company in Canada and the Northwest.

―――― *The Fur Trade of America.* New York, Macmillan, 1921. 341 p. A history of the fur trade, with a descriptive section on fur-bearing animals.

―――― *Pathfinders of the West.* Chicago, Macmillan, 1923. 380 p. il. Account of the explorations of Lewis and Clark.

Lewis and Clark. *Original Journals of the Lewis and Clark Expedition 1804–1806.* New York, Dodd, Mead and Company, 1904. o.p. 2758 p. il. 7 v. and atlas. The journals of the famous expedition exactly as written during the journey to the Pacific, with introduction, notes, and index by Reuben Gold Thwaites.

Lounsberry, Clement A. *Early History of North Dakota.* Washington, Liberty Press, 1919. o.p. 247 p. il. Detailed history of State from fur-trading days to twentieth century by a pioneer newspaperman of Bismarck.

Maximilian, Prince of Wied. *Travels in the Interior of North America.* Cleveland, Arthur H. Clark Company, 1905. o.p. 1134 p. 3 v. Translated from the German's original entries, relating his adventures in the Missouri River Valley. Edited with introduction, notes, and index by Reuben Gold Thwaites.

Meinzer, Edgar G. *Brief History of North Dakota.* Fargo, E. S. Elliot, 1915. o.p. 24 p.

Miles, General Nelson A. *Personal Recollections of General Nelson A. Miles.* Chicago, Warner, 1897. o.p. 590 p. il. The author's own experiences in the Northwest.

North Dakota Biography. Chicago, George Ogle and Company, 1900. o.p. 1410 p. il. A compendium of biographical sketches of prominent old settlers, and accounts of early settlement, Indian occupancy, Indian history and traditions, and Territorial and State organization.

Ordway, Sergeant John. *The Journals of Captain Meriwether Lewis and Sergeant John Ordway.* Madison, State Historical Society, 1916. 44 p. il. A first-hand account of travel in the Northwest.

'The People of the Red River Valley.' *Harpers,* Jan. 1859, pp. 169–76. il. An early magazine article on life at old Fort Pembina.

Reid, Russell and Gannon, Clell G. *Historical and Pictorial Map of North Dakota.* Bismarck, Capital Publishing Company, 1930. Historical items by Reid and illustrations by Gannon.

Scott, Hugh L. *Memories of a Soldier.* New York, Century Company. n.d. o.p. 673 p. il. Memoirs of an officer in the campaigns and investigations from 1876–91.

Slaughter, Linda. *Fortress to Farm.* Published as serial in Bismarck *Daily Tribune,* beginning Sept. 30, 1893. o.p. Reminiscences of early days in Burleigh County, North Dakota.

Spokesfield, Walter Ernest. *History of Wells County.* Valley City, printed by the author, 1929. A sketch of North Dakota history, especially Wells County, and the origin of place names.

Stanton, Edward M. *Expedition from Fort Abercrombie to Fort Benton; a letter from the Secretary of War.* U.S. Congress, House, 1862. 37th Congress. Third Session House. (Executive Document No. 80.)

State Historical Society of North Dakota Collections. Bismarck, Tribune Publishing Company; Grand Forks, Normanden; 1906–24. 3596 p. 7 v. Edited by Dr. O. G. Libby, secretary of the society. Included in the various volumes are histories of many of the towns and counties in the State, biographies of pioneers, and interesting Indian legends.

Taylor, Joseph Henry. *Sketches of Frontier and Indian Lives on the Upper Missouri and Great Plains.* Bound with *Kaleidoscopic Lives.* Valley City, E. P. Getchell, 1932. Reprinted by Washburn's 50th Anniversary Committee. o.p. 200 p. il. The story of the author's life in the Dakotas from 1864–89.

Trinka, Zena Irma. *Out Where the West Begins.* St. Paul, The Pioneer Company, 1920. o.p. 432 p. il. Early romantic history of North Dakota.

Van de Water, Frederick F. *Glory-Hunter.* Indianapolis, New York, Bobbs-Merrill Company, 1934. 392 p. il. B. Critical biography of General George A. Custer.

Van Osdel, A. *Historic Landmarks.* Printed by the author, 1915. o.p. 400 p. il. A narrative of the adventures of early traders in the Northwest Territory.

Waldo, Edna LaMoore. *Dakota: an informal study of Territorial Days.* Caldwell, Idaho, The Caxton Printers, Ltd., 1936. 297 p. B. The story of pioneer life in Dakota, written from articles in contemporary newspapers.

———— *Yet She Follows: The Story of Betty Freeman Dearborn.* Bismarck, Capital Publishing Company, 1931. 205 p. A pioneer story centering about events in the life of the author's mother.

Walsh, Richard J. *The Making of Buffalo Bill.* Indianapolis, The Bobbs-Merrill Company, 1928. 391 p. A character study.

Wellman, Paul I. *Death on the Prairie.* New York, Macmillan, 1934. 298 p. il. B. A story of life on the plains of the Northwest from 1862–92.

Wemett, William Marks. *The Story of the Flickertail State.* Valley City, printed by the author, 1923. o.p. 315 p. il. Simple, entertainingly written history of the State by the head of the history department of the Valley City Teachers College.

Wetmore, Mrs. Helen. *Buffalo Bill.* Duluth, The Duluth Press Printing Company, 1900. o.p. 267 p. il. The story of Buffalo Bill told by his sister.

Wheeler, Olin D. *The Trail of Lewis and Clark,* 1804–1904. New York and London, G. P. Putnam's Sons, 1904. o.p. 2 v. il. Includes a description of the old trail based upon actual travel over it, and the changes found a century later.

Williams, Mary A. *Fifty Pioneer Mothers of McLean County, North Dakota.* Washburn, The Leader, 1932. 200 p. il. Historical sketches of the State from the women's point of view.

GOVERNMENT

Boyle, James E. *The Government of North Dakota.* New York, American Book Company, 1922. o.p. 320 p. il. A discussion of politics and government in the State.

Brigham, Albert Perry. *Our Home State and Continent.* New York, American Book Company, 1934. 178 p. il. A chapter by Arthur C. Selke and Charles T. McFarlane deals specifically with North Dakota.

Brinton, J. W. *Wheat and Politics.* Minneapolis, Rand Tower, 1931. 270 p. il. A treatise on agricultural credit, wheat trade, and politics, with a chapter on the birth of the Nonpartisan League.

Bruce, Andrew A. *The Non-Partisan League.* New York, Macmillan, 1921. o.p. 284 p. A study of the politics and government of North Dakota and the National Nonpartisan League.

———— *Property and Society.* Chicago, A. C. McClurg Company, 1916. o.p. 150 p. National Social Science serial, edited by F. L. McVey, North Dakota educator.

Gaston, H. E. *The Non-Partisan League*. New York, Harcourt and Co., 1920. o.p. 325 p. The story of the league, with a biography of A. C. Townley, its founder.

North Dakota Blue Book. 1889–1919 (no books published 1915–17). o.p. Official publication of the Secretary of State of North Dakota.

Woods, Almond L. *Civil Government for North Dakota*. Grand Forks, published by the author, 1910. o.p. 278 p. il. A text on North Dakota government.

Young, Clyde L. *Civil Government for North Dakota and the Nation*. Chicago, American Book Company, 1932. 289 p. il. B. Comprehensive discussion by former chairman of Children's Civil Code Commission.

AGRICULTURE AND FARM LIFE

Coulter, John Lee. *Cooperation among Farmers*. New York, Sturgis and Walton Company, 1911. o.p. 281 p. il. A discussion of rural life by a former president of the State agricultural college.

Fossum, Paul Robert. *The Agrarian Movement in North Dakota*. Baltimore, Johns Hopkins Press, 1925. o.p. 183 p. il. A thesis on the economic aspects of North Dakota agriculture.

Gillette, John M. *Constructive Rural Sociology*. Chicago, Macmillan, 1928. 165 p. il. B. A study of rural conditions by an internationally recognized authority, a faculty member of the University of North Dakota.

Thayer, William M. *Marvels of the New West*. Norwich, Connecticut, Henry Bill Publishing Company, 1888. o.p. 715 p. il. A history of progress in the West, with an especially good chapter on bonanza farms.

INDUSTRY AND LABOR

Cable, Margaret. *Pottery from North Dakota Clay*. Grand Forks, University of North Dakota, Division of Mines, 1926. il. A discussion of the experiments made by the ceramics department of the university with plastic clays found within the State.

Harrower, Henry Draper. *The New States*. New York and Chicago, Ivison Blakeman and Company, 1889. o.p. 72 p. il. Included in Part 1 is a sketch of the history and economic development of North Dakota.

RACIAL GROUPS AND FOLKWAYS

Beck, Richard. 'Founding of the Icelandic Settlement in Pembina County.' *North Dakota Historical Quarterly*, Jan. 1932, v. 6: pp. 150–64.

――――'Icelandic Settlement in Pembina County, Largest in United States.' *The Northwest Pioneer*, Aug. 1936, v. 6: pp. 13–15.

Bercovici, Konrad. *On New Shores*. New York and London, Century Company, 1925. 302 p. il. Contains chapters on French settlement at Wild Rice, North Dakota, and on the Russo-Germans of North Dakota.

Hofstead, John A. *American Educators of Norwegian Origin*. Minneapolis, Augsburg Publishing House, 1931. 316 p. A 'Who's Who' of Norwegian educators in the United States, in which several prominent North Dakotans are included.

Qualey, Carlton C. 'Pioneer Norwegian Settlement in North Dakota.' *North Dakota Historical Quarterly*, Oct. 1930, v. 5: pp. 14–37.

SCHOOLS, CHURCHES, AND SOCIAL CURRENTS

Arvold, A. G. *Little Country Theater*. Chicago, Macmillan, 1922. o.p. 220 p. il. B. Author is professor of dramatics at State agricultural college and has been recognized as a leader in the promotion of community drama in the United States. Book tells of the origin of the Little Theater in Fargo and of the movement in general.

Beck, Richard. 'Continent's Oldest Icelandic Church.' *The Northwest Pioneer*, Feb. 1936, v. 4: pp. 5–7.

Gillette, John M. *Current Social Problems*. New York, Cincinnati, American Book Company, 1933. 819 p. il. B. A textbook on social problems.

——*Family and Society*. Chicago, American Book Company, 1914. o.p. 164 p. B. An interesting sociological study.

Grassick, Dr. J. *North Dakota Medicine Sketches and Abstracts*. Grand Forks, North Dakota Medical Association, 1926. 378 p. Contains a roster of members of the association, with biographies of pioneer doctors, and unusual incidents encountered in their practices.

McFarland, George A. 'Educational Administration in North Dakota.' *Quarterly Journal of the University of North Dakota*, Jan. 1923, v. 13: pp. 186–207.

Norton, Sister Mary Aquinas. 'Catholic Missions and Missionaries among the Indians of Dakota.' *North Dakota Historical Quarterly*, Apr. 1931, v. 5: pp. 149–65.

Robertson, Edward P. 'Retrospect after Twenty Years.' *Quarterly Journal of the University of North Dakota*, Apr. 1925, v. 15: pp. 277–9. The story of the founding of Wesley College and its affiliation with the State university, written by the president emeritus of the college.

Sullivan, Helen J. *Know Your North Dakota*. Bismarck, Department of Public Instruction, 1931. 96 p. il. B. An interesting and authentic handbook of information about the State.

Trinka, Zena Irma. *North Dakota of Today*. Bismarck, Tribune Publishing Company, 1919. o.p. 259 p. il. A brief study of North Dakota, with descriptions of its larger cities and towns.

TRANSPORTATION

Briggs, Harold E. 'Early Freight and Stage Lines in Dakota.' *North Dakota Historical Quarterly*, July 1929, v. 3: pp. 229–61.

——'Pioneer River Transportation in Dakota.' *North Dakota Historical Quarterly*, Apr. 1929, v. 3: pp. 159–81.

Chittenden, Captain Hiram Martin. *History of Early Steamboat Navigation on the Missouri River*. New York, Harpers, n.d. o.p. 461 p. 2 v. An accurate account of early navigation on the Missouri.

Hanson, Joseph M. *The Conquest of the Missouri*. Chicago, A. C. McClurg Company, 1909. o.p. 436 p. il. Navigation on the Missouri River as Captain Grant Marsh lived it.

Stevens, I. I. *Narrative and Final Report of Explorations for a Route for a Pacific Railroad from St. Paul to Puget Sound*. Government report on survey of 1885. Contains much interesting information on early North Dakota.

ARCHITECTURE

Ellis, Charles L. 'Foundation Problems in the Red River Valley.' *Quarterly Journal of the University of North Dakota*, Jan. 1929, v. 19: pp. 132–47.

Simons, Kenneth W. *North Dakota State Capitol*. Bismarck, Tribune Publishing Company, 1934. il.

CITIES

Arnold, Henry V. *Early History of Grand Forks*. Larimore, H. V. Arnold, 1918. o.p. 92 p. B. Some interesting sketches of the early settlement of Grand Forks, and the relation of the city to the development of the State.

——*History of Grand Forks County*. Larimore, H. V. Arnold, 1900. o.p. 147 p. A historical outline of the Red River Valley, with emphasis on the first ten years in the history of the city of Grand Forks.

LITERATURE

Beach, Rex. *The Spoilers.* New York and London, A. M. Burt and Company, 1930. 315 p. il. A popular novel of Alexander McKenzie, North Dakota politician, and the Klondike Gold Rush.

Beede, Aaron McGaffey. *Heart in the Lodge.* Bismarck, Tribune Publishing Company, 1915. o.p. 61 p. A three-act play based on Whitestone Battle, which took place near Ellendale, North Dakota.

────── *Sitting Bull-Custer.* Bismarck, Tribune Publishing Company, 1913. o.p. 50 p. il. B. A picture of the Custer massacre in dramatized form, written from the Indian point of view.

Bliss, Paul Southworth. *Cirrus from the West.* Bismarck, The Cirrus Company, 51 p. il. Poems inspired by scenes in North Dakota.

────── *Spin Dance.* Chicago, Lakeside Press, 1934. 98 p. il. Nature poems of North Dakota.

────── *The Rye Is the Sea.* Bismarck, The Cirrus Company, 1936. il. A collection of nature poems about North Dakota and an account of hunting and fishing experiences of the author.

Bojer, John. *Emigrants.* New York, Century, 1925. o.p. 134 p. A vivid story of pioneer Dakota life, translated from the Norse.

Borner, Florence. *Modern Poems for Modern People.* Bismarck, Tribune Publishing Company, 1919. o.p. 158 p. A collection of poems by a North Dakota poetess.

Brady, Cyrus Townsend. *Britton of the Seventh.* Chicago, A. C. McClurg Company, 1914. o.p. 319 p. il. A romance of the Northwest, dealing especially with General George A. Custer.

Clark, Badger. *Sun and Saddle Leather.* Boston, Gorham, n.d. 56 p. il. Poems by a South Dakota poet who writes spiritedly of cowboy and frontier days.

Collins, Hubert Edwin. *Warpath and Cattle Trail.* New York, W. Morrow and Company, 1928. 296 p. il. A story of ranch life, with preface by Hamlin Garland.

Cowdrey, Mary Boynton. *The Checkered Years.* Caldwell, Idaho, Caxton Printers, Ltd., 1937. 265 p. il. The diary of the author's grandmother, presenting an interesting account of life in eastern North Dakota during bonanza farm days.

Crawford, Lewis F. *Badlands and Bronco Trails.* Bismarck, Capital Book Company, 1926. o.p. 114 p. il. The adventures of Ben Arnold Conner, an Indian fighter, gold miner, cowboy, hunter, and Army scout who came up the Missouri with his regiment after the Civil War, told in an entertaining manner.

Dye, Eva. *The Conquest.* Chicago, A. C. McClurg Company, 1902. o.p. 443 p. Historical novel of Lewis and Clark expedition.

Foley, James W. *Boys and Girls.* New York, E. P. Dutton and Company, 1913. o.p. 239 p. il. Verses of a North Dakota poet, reprinted from periodicals.

────── *Friendly Rhymes.* New York, E. P. Dutton and Company, 1918. o.p. A book of light verses.

────── *Prairie Breezes.* Boston, R. B. Badger, 1905. o.p. 103 p. A book of verses that appeared originally in the Bismarck *Tribune, The New York Times,* and *Century Magazine,* mostly about Dakota.

────── *Tales of the Trail.* New York, E. P. Dutton and Company, 1914. o.p. 170 p. il. Sketches of the West done in verse.

────── *The Verses of J. W. Foley.* Bismarck, R. D. Hoskins, 1914. o.p. 239 p. 3 v. A collection of poems by the North Dakota poet.

Gannon, Clell G. *Songs of the Bunch Grass Acres.* Boston, Badger, 1924. o.p. 96 p. il. Thirty-eight poems of prairie life.

Garland, Hamlin. *The Moccasin Ranch.* New York and London, Harpers, 1909. o.p. 136 p. il. A historical novel of North Dakota.

────── *Prairie Song and Western Story.* Boston, New York, Allyn and Bacon, 1928. 268 p. il. Shows the march of settlement in the Middle West.

Gates, Eleanor. *The Plow Woman.* New York, Grosset and Dunlap, 1906. o.p. 364 p. Novel of pioneering days in southwest North Dakota.

Gordon, Hanford L. *Indian Legends*. Salem, Massachusetts, The Salem Press Company, 1910. o.p. 405 p. Poems of the Dakota Indians.

Hanson, Joseph M. *Frontier Ballads*. Chicago, A. C. McClurg Company, 1910. o.p. 92 p. il. Western ballads of Army, prairie, and river life.

Hough, Emerson. *Story of the Cowboy*. New York, Grosset and Dunlap, 1897. o.p. 349 p. il. A vivid description of ranch life in western Dakota.

Hueston, Ethel. *Star of the West*. Indianapolis, Bobbs-Merrill Company, 1935. 372 p. Historical novel in which is retold the story of the Lewis and Clark expedition.

Hughes, Mrs. Edith Wakeman. *Motoring in White*. New York, Knickerbocker Press, 1917. o.p. 97 p. il. A story of a trip from Dakota to Cape Cod.

Johnson, Clifton. *Highways and Byways of the Rocky Mountains*. New York, London, Macmillan, 1910. o.p. 279 p. il. A travelogue, one chapter of which deals with 'A Dakota Paradise.'

Koch, Frederick H. *A Pageant of the Northwest*. Grand Forks, University of North Dakota, 1914. o.p. A communal drama depicting the history of North Dakota, written by students for presentation at the opening of the Bankside Theater.

Laut, Agnes C. *The Story of the Trapper*. New York, D. Appleton and Company, 1902. o.p. 284 p. il. Narrative of the Northwest States and Canada.

Lillibridge, Will. *Where the Trail Divides*. New York, Burt, 1907.

Mackin, Marie. *The Sylvan Portal*. Bismarck, Bismarck Book Company, 1925. 247 p. il. A novel of life in North Dakota.

Meigs, Cornelia L. *Railroad West*. Boston, Little, Brown and Company, 1937. 326 p. il. The building of the Northern Pacific from Minnesota to the Yellowstone forms the background of this romance.

Modern Masters of Etching No. 24. Levon West. New York, William Edwin Rudge, 1930. 22 p. il. Biography and etchings of the third American artist to be included in this series. Levon West spent much of his boyhood in North Dakota.

Neal, Bigelow. *The Last of the Thundering Herd*. New York, Sears Publishing Company, Inc., 1933. 287 p. il. A narrative of the life of a bison near the close of the era when those animals roamed the Plains States.

Neihart, John G. *Song of Hugh Glass*. Chicago, Macmillan, 1915. o.p. 126 p. A narrative poem based on an episode taken from the era of the American fur trade.

—— *Song of Indian Wars*. Chicago, Macmillan, 1925. 231 p. il. Narrative poems of early days in the Northwest.

—— *The River and I*. New York and London, G. P. Putnam's Sons, 1910. o.p. 325 p. il. A beautifully illustrated book telling of the author's trip on the Missouri and Yellowstone Rivers.

Palliser, John. *The Solitary Hunter; or Sporting Adventures on the Prairies*. London, Routledge, Warne, and Routledge, 1859. o.p. 234 p. il. Author's hunting experiences on the western plains, told in the profuse style of the day.

Palmer, Bertha Rachel. *Beauty Spots of North Dakota*. Boston, Richard G. Badger, 1928. o.p. 266 p. il. History and description of interesting points in the State.

Putnam, Grace Brown and Ackermann, Anna. *North Dakota Singing*. New York, Paebar Company, 1936. 252 p. An anthology of poems by North Dakota authors, compiled by two residents of the State.

Rickaby, Franz. *Ballads and Songs of the Shantyboy*. Cambridge, Harvard University Press, 1926. o.p. 244 p. il. Lumbermen's songs, many learned by the editor from North Dakota men who had worked in the north woods. Includes music.

Rollins, Philip A. *The Cowboy*. New York, Charles Scribner's Sons, 1926. o.p. 363 p. il. The part played by the cowboy in the development of the West.

Rolvaag, O. E. *Giants in the Earth*. New York, Harpers, 1927. 465 p. A story of Norse immigrants to Dakota, based on true incidents.

—— *Peder Victorious*. New York, Harpers, 1929. 350 p. A sequel to *Giants in the*

Earth, this novel tells the story of the second generation in the Norwegian colony.

Roosevelt, Theodore. *Hunting Adventures in the West.* New York, G. P. Putnam's Sons, 1927. o.p. 372 p. Contains descriptions of hunting expeditions at his Badlands ranch.

——— *Hunting in Many Lands.* New York, Forest and Stream Publishing Company, 1895. o.p. 447 p. il. The book of the Boone and Crockett Club, edited by Roosevelt and George Bird Grinnell, in which Roosevelt includes a chapter entitled 'Hunting in the Cattle Country.'

——— *Hunting Trips of a Ranchman.* New York and London, G. P. Putnam's Sons, 1885. o.p. 318 p. il. Roosevelt's own story of his life in North Dakota.

——— *The Wilderness Hunter.* New York and London, G. P. Putnam's Sons, 1922. o.p. 296 p. 2 v. Sketches of sport on the northern cattle plains.

Rowbotham, Frances Jameson. *A Trip to Prairie-Land.* London, S. Low, Marston, Searle, and Rivington, 1885. o.p. 243 p. An interesting story of social life and customs of pioneer Dakota.

Stefansson, Vilhjalmur. *My Life with the Eskimo.* New York, Macmillan, 1913. o.p. 539 p. il. A fascinating autobiography of the North Dakota explorer's experiences during the expedition in which he discovered the white Eskimo colony.

Tooker, Richard. *The Day of the Brown Horde.* New York, Payson and Clarke, Ltd., 1929. 309 p. A story of prehistoric days.

Wilkins, Sir Hubert. *Flying the Arctic.* New York, G. P. Putnam's Sons, 1928. 336 p. il. Describes the expedition from Fairbanks to Point Barrow, Spitzbergen, claimed by Stefansson and Amundsen to be the greatest flight in history. Carl Ben Eielson, North Dakota aviator, was pilot for the flight.

Winsted, Huldah Lucille. *North Dakota, Land of the Sky and other poems.* Minot, North Dakota, 1927. A collection of North Dakota verses.

Index

Aandahl, Fred G., 63
Abercrombie (Lt. Col. John J. Abercrombie), 192–3
Abercrombie, Fort, 44, 45, 192–3; State Park, 193
Abraham Lincoln, Fort, 45; *see also* Fort Abraham Lincoln State Park
Ackley, P. P., 213
Agassiz, Lake, 11–12, 183, 192, 267
Agricultural Experimental Station, 227
Agriculture, 64–75
Airplane transportation, 107–8, 185, 191
Akra, 226
Alexander, 215
Alfalfa Day, Fessenden, 77
Allen, J. D., 277
Allin, Roger, 56
Altamont Moraine, 7, 245–6, 274
Ambrose, 234
American Fur Company, 258, 259–60
Amidon (Charles F. Amidon), 216–17
Amlie, Thomas R., 293
Amphion Male Chorus, 136
Anamoose, 261
Anderson, Maxwell, 157, 270
Andrew's Creek, 312
Animal life, 16–17
Ansonia Kennels, 294–5
Antelope, 279
Apple Creek, 275
Architecture, 112–15
Ardoch, 187
Argus, Fargo, 190, 293
Argusville, 190
Arikara Indians, 20, 24–5, 33, 207–8, 317, 318
Arlington House, Grand Forks, 154
Armour & Co., 265–6
Armstrong, Moses, 50, 51, 53
Arnegard (Evan Arnegard), 215
Arnold, Camp (Historic Site), 267
Arrowood Lake, 200–201
Arrowood Migratory Refuge, 201
Artesian wells, 12
Arvilla, 239
Arvold, Prof. A. G., 144
Ash Coulee Creek, 312

Ashley, Gen. William, 42
Ashley, 273
Ashtabula, 268
Assiniboin Indians, 21, 30, 34
Atcheson, Camp (Historic Site), 294
Athenais Chapel, 285
Atkins, C. J., 44
Atkinson, Gen. Henry, 42
Auburn, 186
Audubon, John James, 42

Babcock, E. J., 83
Back, Henry S., 137, 139
Bacon, J. D., 152
Badlands, the, 7, 10, 116, 174–80, 215, 282; battle of, 46
Baer, John M., 287
Bagg, F. A., 193
Balfour, 262
Bank of North Dakota, 60, 132–3
Barlow (F. G. Barlow), 200
Barnard, Rev. Alonzo, 100, 109
Barnum, I. W., 269
Bartholomew, Joseph M., 54
Bartlett (Frank Bartlett), 241
Bathgate, 226
Baukol-Noonan Coal Mine, 234
Beach, Rex, 122
Beach (Capt. Warren Beach), 287
Beadle, W. H. H., 98
Bear Den Hillock, 289
Beardsley, Maj. G. G., 137
Beaver Lake State Park, 273
Beekeeping, 74
Beets, sugar, 72–3
Beicegel Creek (Beisigl brothers), 313
Belcourt, Rev. George Antoine, 80–81, 96, 100, 229, 236
Belcourt, 229
Belden, 209
Belding, John P., 52
Belfield, 282
Belknap, William W., 124–5
Belle of Richmond, 270
Belmont, 189
Bentonite, 83
Berthold, Bartholomew, 207
Berthold, 245

341

Berthold, Fort, 35–6, 207; Indian reservation, 206–9
Berwick, 243
Beulah, 303
Bicknell, Thomas W., 221–2
Bierens, Rev. G. C., 195
Big Butte, 233
Big Mound, 45
Big White's Mandan Indian Village, site of, 317
Binford (Ray Binford), 294
Birch Creek Historic Site, 288
Birdzell, L. E., 59
Birkbough, Konrad Elias, 87
Bismarck, 18, 45, 52–3, 61, 121, 204–5, 275
    general information, 121
    history, 121–7
    points of interest, 127–33
Bismarck Junior College, 99
Black, Mustache Maude, 300
Black, Ott, 301
Black Building, Fargo, 144
Black Butte, 7, 217–18
Black-earth belt, 66–70
Blaine, James G., 190
Blaisdell (Alfred Blaisdell), 246
Bliss, Col. Paul S., 307
Bodmer, Carl, 42
Bonanza farms, 64, 68–9, 139–40, 266, 292
Boney, Seth, 141
Bonza, Pierre, 41, 184
Borland, Earl, 198
Bottineau (Pierre Bottineau), 230–31
Bottineau Junior College, 99
Bowbells, 264
Bowen, A. C., 58
Bowesmont (William Bowes), 185
Bowman (E. W. Bowman), 218, 308
Braithwaite, Capt. William, 125
Breien, 297
Briggs, Frank, 56
Brinsmade (Rev. S. Brinsmade), 200
Broken Bones Lake, 243
Brown, Sadie P., 239
Brown, William H., 225
Bruce, Andrew, 57
Bruflat Academy, 197
Brushy Banks, 306
Buchanan (James Buchanan), 201
Bucyrus, 308
Buffalo, 267
Buffalo Creek Historic Site, 267
Buffalo Springs, 308
Buford, 257
Buford, Fort (Gen. John Buford), 258
Buildings, 112–15, 127–32, 144–8, 154, 194, 204, 262
Bull Owl, 278

Burke, Andrew, 55, 56
Burke, John, 57, 228
Burke, R. T., 228
Burleigh, Dr. Walter, 50
Burleigh County Courthouse, 131
Burleightown, 123
Burlington, 162, 262–3
Burman Historic Site, 272
Burning Coal Mine, 180, 217, 222
Burnstad (C. P. Burnstad), 273
Burt (A. M. Burt), 222
Bus lines, 107, 163
Butte de Morale, 261
Butte St. Paul Park, 230
Buxton (Thomas Buxton), 188

Cameron, John, 150
Campbell, Robert, 259
Campbell, Gen. T. C., 50
Canadian population, 89
Cando, 199
Canfield, Thomas H., 137
Cannon Butte, 10
Cannonball, 298; River, 10, 22, 297
Capitol, State, 112, 127–9
Carleton City, 123
Carpio, 263
Carrington (M. D. Carrington), 200, 260
Carson (Frank Carter and Simon Pederson), 224
Cartwright (Samuel George Cartwright), 214
Casey, Lyman, 34
Cass, G. W., 68, 266
Casselton, 266
Catfish Joe, 151
Catlin, George, 22, 23, 27, 29, 42, 105, 209
Cavileer, Charles, 43, 67, 79, 184, 187, 226, 235–6
Cavalier, 226
Cedar Canyon Horse Trail, 178; Lookout, 178
Center, 301–2
Central High School, Grand Forks, 154
Central Park, Grand Forks, 155
Centralia, 138
Cesky Zakopnik, 296
Chaboillez, Charles, 40–41, 183
Chahinkapa Park, Wahpeton, 194–5
Chalky Butte, 216
Chaloner Creek Horse Trail, 178
Chandler, Elwin, 158
Charbonneau, Baptiste, 130
Charbonneau, Toussaint, 42, 130, 317
Charlie Bob Creek, 314
Chaska Historic Site, 274
Chautauqua Park, 277
Cheney, B. P., 68

Cherry Creek, 314
Cheyenne Indians, 20, 33, 290
Chippewa Indians, 21, 25, 34, 229
Chisholm Trail, 213
Christine, 192
Churches, 100–101, 145–6, 148, 204, 257, 285
Churchs Ferry, 242
Clark, William, 318; see also Lewis and Clark expedition
Clay deposits, 83
Cleveland, 272
Climate, 8
Clyde, 228
Coleharbor, 203
Colleges, 97–9, 143–5, 155–9, 164, 196–7, 202, 227, 228, 231
Columbus (Columbus Larson), 233
Columnar Cedars, 217
Comfort, Camp, 226
Concrete, 227
Conservation, 12–13, 64–5
Consumers United Stores Company, 60
Cooke, Jay, 47, 268
Cooperatives, 4, 82, 163, 251
Cooperstown (T. J. and Rollin C. Cooper), 293
Corliss, Guy C. H., 54
Corn, 73
Coteau des Prairies, 7
Coteau du Missouri, 7
Council Fires, 33
Courier, Cooperstown, 293
Court Lake, 257
Crawford, Lewis F., 43, 57
Crazy Man's Coulee, 251
Creel, Brevet Gen. H. M., 290
Crosby, 234
Crowley Flint Quarry State Park, 279
Crystal Springs, 272; Lake, 272; Stock Farm, 239–40
Cummings (Henry Cummings), 189
Custer, Gen. George A., 33, 48, 106, 124, 171
Custer, Tom, 299
Custer Trail Ranch, 285

Daily Alert, Jamestown, 201
Daily News, Minot, 164
Dakota State Journal, 164
Dakota Territory, 38–9, 50–53, 68
Dalrymple, Oliver, 68
Danzig, 273
Davis, Hannah E., 156
Dawson (Dawson Thompson), 272
Dazey (Charles T. Dazey), 292
Dead Buffalo Lake, 45
Dead Man's Gulch, 304
Deapolis, 317
Deffenbach brothers, 71

De Long, Harry, 52
Denbigh Reforestation Project Headquarters, 244
Densmore, Frances, 25
DeRemer, Joseph Bell, 127
Des Lacs, 245, 263
De Smet, Father Pierre Jean, 278
Devil's Ears, 256
Devil's Heart, 254
Devils Lake, 7, 241–2, 252–4
Devils Lake Junior College, 99
Devil's Tooth, 256–7
Devine, Joseph M., 56
Diamond C. Ranch, 304
Dickinson (H. L. Dickinson), 280–81
Dill, Col. Daniel J., 309
Dilts, Jefferson, 309
Dmitri, Ivan, 197
Dodge, 303
Dog Tooth Buttes, 224
Donnybrook, 263
Double Ditch Indian Village State Park, 211
Dove, Dr. L. P., 83
Dovre Moraine, 294
Doyle, Jack, 161
Doyle Memorial Park, 273
Doyon (Charles H. Doyon), 241
Drake (Herman Drake), 261
Drayton, 185
Drift Prairie, 6–7, 12
Driscoll, 274
Dumoulin, Father Joseph, 96
Dun, Finlay, 140–41
Dunkers, 89, 199
Dunn Center, 304
Dunseith, 229
Dwight (Jeremiah W. Dwight), 193

Eastman, George, 266
Eaton, Howard, Willis, and Alden, 285, 313
Eckelson (A. O. Eckelson), 269
Eclipse, 125
Edgeley, 201
Edmunds, Newton, 51
Edmunds, 200
Education, 96–100
Edwinton, 45, 123
Eielson, Carl Ben, 87, 197–8
El Zagal Park, Fargo, 147
Elbowoods, 315
Eldridge, 271–2
Elephant's Pass, 305
Elgin, 223
Elk Creek, 314
Elk River Valley Farm, 240
Ellendale (Ellen Dale Merrill), 202
Elmer, Rev. Oscar H., 100, 139
Emigrant's Guide, 69

Emmons, James A., 124
Emmons County Breeders Association
    Stock Show, 78
Emmons County Courthouse, 205
Episcopal Church, 101
Epping, 248-9
Equity Exchange, 58
Erickson, Edward, 203
Euren, William, 145
Explorers, 39-42
Express, Fargo, 141

Fairmount, 195
Fairs, 77-8, 118
Fancher, Frederick B., 56
Far West, 49, 124, 172
Fargo, William G., 137, 141
Fargo, 265-6
    general information, 134
    history, 134-43
    points of interest, 143-8
Faribault, Alexander, 193-4
Farm life, 75-8
Farmers Educational and Cooperative
    Union of America, 4, 56, 82, 163, 251
Farming-grazing belt, 70
Fauna, 16-17
Federal aid to schools, 99
Federal Building, Bismarck, 132; Grand
    Forks, 154
Ferris, Joe, 284
Fertile Valley Lake No. 2, 219
Fessenden (Cortez Fessenden), 261
Finnish population, 91, 209, 223
First Lutheran Church, Fargo, 145-6
First Presbyterian Church, Fargo, 146
Fisher, Asa, 131
Fishes, 17, 116
Fisk, Capt. James L., 46, 261, 294, 309
Fitch, George, 105
Fjelde, Jacob, 194
Fjelde, Paul, 87, 268
Flasher (Mabel Flasher), 224-5
Flat Top Butte, 286-7
Flax, 72
Flaxton, 264
Flood control, 65-6
Flora, 14-16
Flour mills, 81
Flowers, 15-16
Flumerfelt, William, 161
Foley, James W., 126, 173
Folkways, 92-5
Fort Abraham Lincoln State Park,
    169-73
    Fort Abraham Lincoln site, 171-3
    Fort McKeen, 170-71
    Slant Village, 169-70
Fort Buford State Park, 259-60

Fort Clark, 317
    State Park, 302
    Trading Post, site of, 317-18
Fort Dilts State Park, 309
Fort Mandan State Park, 204
Fort Rice State Park, 278
Fort Union formation, 10
Forts, 44-7
Fortuna, 213-14
Forum, Fargo, 141
Four Bears Bridge, 209, 315
Foxholm, 263
Frazier, Lynn J., 59, 60, 186
French, H. E., 102
French-Canadian population, 90, 236,
    237-8
Frog Point, Belmont, 189
Frontier Scout, 109
Fur companies, 43
Fur trade, 79, 82, 113, 183-4

Gall, Chief, 45, 257, 258, 278
Game, wild, 16-17, 117
Gannon, Mr. and Mrs. Clell G., 115, 131
Gardner, 190
Garrison, 206-7; Creek, 316; Dam, 65,
    310
Gascoyne, 308
Gaston, Herbert, 58
Gazette, Richland County, 194
Genin, Father J. B., 193
    Mission House, 140
Geographic Center of North America,
    243
Gerard, F. F., 212
German population, 87-9
Gilbertson, Gilbert, 294
Glasston (Archibald Glass), 186
Glen Ullin, 279
Godfrey, Gen. E. S., 49
Goiffon, Rev. Joseph, 185
Gold, 44, 125
Golden Valley, 303
Good Furred Robe, Chief, 278
Good Samaritan School for Crippled
    Children, 147-8
Goose Rapids, 151
Government, 54-63
Governors, 51-2
Governor's Mansion, 131
Grace, Dick, 232
Grace, R. H., 59
Grafton, 186
Grafton, Camp (Lt. Col. Gilbert C.
    Grafton), 254
Grain elevators, 114
Grand Canyon of the Little Missouri,
    178

Grand Forks, 188
  general information, 149
  history, 149–53
  points of interest, 154–9, 239
Grand Rapids, 290–91
Grandin (J. L. Grandin), 190
Grant, Ewen, 261
Grant, Ulysses S., 52, 126
Granville (Granville M. Dodge), 244–5
Grassick, Camp (Dr. J. Grassick), 273
Grassy Butte, 216
Gray, Mrs. W. H., 204
Grazing-forage belt, 70–71
Great Northern Railroad, 48, 153, 161
Greeley, Camp, 23
Green Lake, 273
Grenora, 219
Griggs, Capt. Alexander, 44, 150–52
Gringas, Anton, 100
Grinnell, George, 249–50
Gronna, Sen. A. J., 59–60, 189

Hagan, John, 60
Half Moon Mandan Indian Village site,
  211
Halliday, 304
Halling Dance, 86
Hallson (Johan Hallson), 226
Hamilton, 186, 226
Hancock, John M., 159
Hancock, Camp, 123
Haney, Bert, 151
Hankinson (R. H. Hankinson), 195
Hanks (W. F. Hanks), 219
Hanna, Louis B., 57
Hannaford (J. M. Hannaford), 292
Hans Creek, 314
Hansboro, 199
Hansbrough, Henry Clay, 54, 199
Hanson, Joseph Mills, 315
Harrison, Benjamin, 39
Harvest festivals, 77
Harvey (Col. James S. Harvey), 261
Harwood (A. J. Harwood), 190
Hastings (Gen. Henry Hastings Sibley),
  288
Hatton (Frank Hatton), 197–8
Haupt, Gen., 52
Havelock, 222
Hawksnest, 260
Hayes, Camp (site of), 289–90
Haymow Theater, Langdon, 228
Haynes (George B. Haynes), 307
Hazelton (Hazel Roop), 205
Hazen, Gen. William H., 257
Hazen (A. D. Hazen), 302
Headquarters Hotel, Fargo, 148
Heart River, 20–21, 32
Hebron, 279

Hector, Mr. and Mrs. Henry, 146
Hector Airport (Martin Hector), 191
Heerman, Capt. Edward, 241
Height of Land, 7, 203
Hell's Hole, 179
Henry, Alexander, Jr., 41, 66–7, 150,
  184
  Trading Post, 236
Herald, Grand Forks, 110, 152
Hersey, H. T., 239–40
Hettinger (Mathias Hettinger), 307–8
Hickson (Ole Hicks), 191
Hidatsa Indians, 20, 23, 33, 207, 209,
  316, 317
Hidden Wood Creek, 306
Highways, 183–310
  ND 1, 288–91, 292–3; ND 3, 229–30;
    ND 5, 225–34; ND 6, 296–7; ND
    7, 196–7, 293–5; ND 8, 208–9,
    304; ND 13, 193, 290–91; ND 14,
    244; ND 15, 188–9; ND 17, 186–7;
    ND 18, 197–8, 240; ND 20, 252–4;
    ND 21, 221–5, 297; ND 22, 222,
    304–5; ND 23, 214; ND 24, 297–
    301; ND 25, 301–5; ND 27, 289–
    90; ND 30, 228, 272; ND 31, 224;
    ND 32, 226–7, 235–7, 267; ND 37,
    206–8; ND 40, 247; ND 44, 185–6;
    ND 46, 191–2, 288–9; ND 49, 223–
    4; ND 55, 237–8; ND 57, 254–7;
    US 2, 238–52; US 10, 210, 265–87;
    US 12, 305–10; US 52, 260–64; US
    81, 183–98; US 83, 202–6, 210;
    US 85, 213–18; US 281, 198–202
Hill, James J., 47, 48, 106, 150, 153,
  189, 240
Hillsboro, 189–90
Historic sites, 267, 272, 274, 288, 289,
  294
Historical Society Museum, 129
History, 38–9
  early explorers, 39–42
  frontier days, 42–9
  politics since statehood, 53–63
  territorial government, 50–53
Hoffman, Nicholas, 150
Holes, Andrew, 137
Holidays, 92–3
Holmes, D. M., 153
Holy Cross Cemetery, 191
Holy Hill of the Mandans, 297–8
Hoople, 186
Hoskins, Lake, 273
Houston, D. H., 266
Hudson's Bay Company, 152, 189
Huff, 21; Indian Village State Park, 278
Hughes, Alexander, 52
Hull, 206
Hungry Gulch, 248

Hunt, Father Jerome, 254
Hunt, Wilson P., 42
Hunting, 116–17

Ibsen, Henrik, 194, 242
Ibsen, Lake, 242
Icelanders, 227
Iktomi, 31
Imperial Ward County, 162–3
Independent, Ward County, 164
Independent Voters Association, 60
Indians, 48–9, 91–2, 99, 206–9, 211
  coming of tribes, 19–22
  decline of tribes, 32–3
  early life, 22–32
  prehistoric, 18–19
  present-day tribes, 34–7
Industry, 79–84
Ingomar, 308
International, 189
International Peace Garden, Inc., Rolla, 228, 230
Inyan Bosdata, 288–9
Irrigation, 64–5
Isabel, Lake, 273
Island Park, Fargo, 147
Ivers, Dr. M. U., 192

James Memorial Library, Williston, 249
James River, 7
Jamestown, 201, 269–71
Jamestown College, 97, 270–71
Jayne, Dr. William, 50
Jefferson, Thomas, 41
Jessie, Lake (Jessie Benton), 252, 294
Jim's Creek, 314
Johnson, G. A., 224
Johnson, Sveinbjorn, 227
Joliette, 185
Jones, Hell-Roaring Bill, 282
Joseph, Chief, 45, 257, 258
Junior colleges, 98–9

Keeney, G. J., 138
Kellogg, Mark, 124
Kenmare, 263
Keogh, Capt. Myles, 172
KFJM, 11, 154
KFYR, 126, 275
KGCU, 277
Killdeer, 304
Killdeer Mountains, 46, 304; battle of, 304
Kimball, Camp (Historic Site), 261
Kincaid, 233
Kindred (F. E. and W. A. Kindred), 191
Kingsbury, George, 50
Kipp, James, 318
Kittson, Norman, 43, 100, 184, 236

Kittson Line, 140
Klaus Park (Anton Klaus), 271
KLPM, 164
Knife River, 18, 302, 317; Coal Mining Co., 302–3
Knox, 242
Knutson, Col. Andrew, 154
Knutson Creek, 312
Koch, Prof. Frederick, 158
KOVC, 268
Kramer Equity Cooperative Elevator, 232
KRMC, 271
Kurke, William F., 127

LaBarge, Joseph, 44, 248
Labor, 84
Lac aux Mortes, 199
Ladd, Dr. Edwin F., 59–60, 103
Lagweise, Joe, 220
Lake Metigoshe State Park, 231
Lake Road, 231
Lake Superior and Puget Sound Company, 135, 139
Lakewood Park, 253
Lakota, 240–41
Lamb, James, 240
LaMoure, Judson, 55–6, 290
LaMoure, 290; County Memorial Park, 291
Lance formation, 10
Land grants, 67–8
Land surface, 6–7
  formation, 8–12
Langdon, 227–8
Langer, William, 60, 61–3, 266
Larimore (N. D. Larimore), 240
Larpenteur, Charles, 259
Larson (Columbus Larson), 233
LaSalle, Sieur Robert de, 38
Leach, Mr. and Mrs. O. A., 194
Leader, 62
Leavenworth, Col. Henry, 42
Leeds, 242
Legislature, 54–63
Lehigh, 280
Leith, 224
Lemke, William, 60
Leonard, Dr. A. G., 83
Leonardite, 83
LePage, Baptiste, 311–12
LeRaye, Charles, Camp (site of), 303
Leroy, 237
Levingston, Dr. William, 186–7
Lewis, Reuben, 316
Lewis and Clark expedition, 32–3, 41–2, 210, 249, 311–12
Liberty Memorial Bridge, 318

Liberty Memorial Building, Bismarck, 129
Libraries, 100, 132, 146–7, 165, 194, 249
Lien, O. W., 147
Lignite, 233
Lignite (mineral), 82–3, 164, 176, 280, 302–3
Lincoln, Fort, 275
Lincoln Park, Grand Forks, 155
Linton, 205
Lisa, Manuel, 42
Lisbon, 289
Little Beaver Creek, 9
Little Beaver Dome, 310
Little Big Horn, battle of, 33, 49, 172–3
Little Country Theater, Fargo, 137, 144
Little Eagle, 37
Little Heart Butte, 297
Little Missouri, site of, 286
Little Missouri River, 176, 179, 215, 286
Little Muddy Creek, 214, 249
Lonetree, 162, 245
Long, Stephen H., 195
Looking Village, 211
Loon, August, 150
Louisiana Lottery, 55, 122
Louisiana Purchase, 38, 41
Lounsberry, Col. Clement A., 49, 109, 124, 173, 273
Lowell, Jacob, Jr., 137
Ludden (Mr. and Mrs. J. D. Ludden), 291
Luella, 44
Lynn, George W., 205

McCanna (S. A. McCanna), 240
McClure, Marshall, 162
McCumber, Sen. Porter J., 58, 195
McHench, Andrew, 137
McHugh, *see* Langdon
McKeen, Fort (Col. Henry Boyd McKeen), 45, 170–71
McKenzie, Alexander, 52, 56, 122, 131, 215, 274
McKenzie, 274
McLaughlin, Major James, 306
McPhail, Col. Samuel, 272
McPhail's Butte Historic Site, 272
Maddock, Walter, 61
Magpie Creek, 313
Mandan, 276–7; Fort, 42
Mandan Indians, 19–20, 22–4, 25, 26, 27–8, 32, 39–41, 104, 112, 122, 169–70, 207–9, 210–11, 297–8, 317
Manitou, 247
Mannhaven, 316
Manuri, Josephine, 250
Manvel (Gen. A. A. Manvel), 187
Mapes (Emery Mapes), 240

Mapleton, 266
Marie, 277
Marmarth, 309–10
Marsh, Capt. Grant, 44, 124, 172, 315
Martin, 261
Masonic Library, Fargo, 146–7; Museum, 146
Mathews, George, 52
Matthews, Robert, 249, 251
Max, 203
Maximilian, Prince, 42
Mayville (May Arnold), 196
Mayville State Teachers College, 196–7
Maza, 199
Medicine Butte, 223
Medicine Hole, 305
Medicine Lodge Spring, 251–2
Medina, 272
Medora, 8, 282–5, 312
Melville, 200
Menoken, 39; Indian Village Site, 274
Mercer, John, 258
Merrifield, Webster, 156, 157, 227
Mesozoic era, 9–10
Metigoshe, Lake, 231
Mexican workers, 73, 91
Michigan City, 240
Miles, Gen. Nelson A., 298
Military posts, 44–7
Miller, John, 193
Mills, Walter Thomas, 58
Miner Memorial (Hazel Miner), 302
Minnekosh, Lake, 249
Minnesota Massacre, 33, 201–2
Minnewaukan, 200
Minnie H., 241
Minot, Henry D., 160
Minot, 203, 245, 262
   general information, 150
   history, 160–64
   points of interest, 164–5
Minot State Teachers College, 164
Minto, 187
Missouri Coteau, 70
Missouri Plateau, 7
Missouri River, 43–4, 105, 125, 214, 252, 276, 298, 302, 315
Missouri Slope, 7, 70, 221
Mix, Tom, 285
Moffit, 205
Mohall (M. O. Hall), 232
Montrose, Archibald, 191
Monuments, 147, 154, 195, 247, 254, 262, 302
Moodie, Thomas H., 62
Moore, A. H., 141
Mooreton, 193
Moorman, James, 248
Moravians, 89

Mores, Marquis de, 126, 283-6; chateau of, 286
Mores, de, Storage Plant, 132, 283, 285
Morrow, Ashley, 273
Mortimer, Fort, 259
Moses, John, 63
Moslem families, 246-7
Mott, 222
Mountain, 227
Mouse River Park, 232
Murphy, Josh, 255
Museums, 129-31, 146-7, 157, 173, 191, 192, 195, 197, 198, 231, 241, 247
Myers, Charles, 52

Napoleon (Napoleon Goodsill), 273
Natural resources, 12-14
Nelson, F. P., 195
Nelson, Mercy, 140
Nestos, R. A., 60-61, 87, 189
Nettie Baldwin, 290
New England, 221-2
New Leipzig, 223
New Rockford, 200
New Salem, 279
Newspapers, 109-10, 126, 141, 142, 152, 162, 164, 201
Newton, George, 250
Niagara, 240
Nickeus Park (Fannie B. Nickeus), 271
Nicollet-Frémont Expedition, 292, 294
Nilsson, Christine, 192
Nishu, 208
Njaa, Torkel, 295
Nonpartisan League, 4, 57-60, 81
Noonan, 234
North Dakota Agricultural College, 100, 143-5
North Dakota Agricultural Experiment Station, 281
North Dakota Home Builders' Association, 60
North Dakota State Mill and Elevator Association, 59
North Dakota Winter Show, 78
North West Fur Company, 40-41
Northern Lights, 32
Northern Pacific Railway, 47-8, 68, 79, 106, 122, 123-4, 137
Northern Packing Company, 153
Northland Greyhound Line, 107
Norwegian population, 84-7
Norwich, 245
Nye, Gerald P., 61, 293

Oak Grove Park, Fargo, 147
Oak Lawn Historic Site, 227
Oak Park, Minot, 165
Oakdale, 304
Oakes (Thomas Fletcher Oakes), 291

Oakwood Cemetery, 289
Oasis Gardens, 249
O'Connor, J. F. T., 61
Ojibway, see Chippewa Indians
Okeepa, feast of, 27-8
Okiedan Butte, 290
Olson, Ole, 62, 87, 200
Ordway (Territorial Gov.), 53
Oriska, 267
Orkney Lad, 41, 184

Packing plants, 81
Paddock Creek, 179
Painted Canyon, 282
Painted Woods, 210-11
Painter, Capt. Sam, 189
Paleozoic era, 8-9
Palermo, 246
Palliser, John, 305
Park Hotel, Grand Forks, 154
Park River, 186-7; Fair, 77
Parker, P. P., 199
Parker Ranch, 312
Parks, 147, 155, 165, 185, 190, 194-5, 271, 277, 290, 291
    Beaver Lake State, 273
    Butte St. Paul, 230
    Crowley Flint Quarry State, 279
    Double Ditch Indian Village State, 211
    Fort Abercrombie State, 193
    Fort Abraham Lincoln State, 169-73
    Fort Buford State, 259-60
    Fort Clark State, 302
    Fort Dilts State, 309
    Fort Mandan State, 204
    Huff Indian Village State, 278
    Lake Metigoshe State, 231
    Mouse River, 232
    Pembina State, 185
    St. Claude State, 228
    Sheyenne River, 191-2
    Sully's Hill National Game Preserve, 256
    Theodore Roosevelt National, 116, 174-80, 282
    Turtle River State, 239
    Walhalla State, 236
    Whitestone Hill Battlefield State, 201-2
    Writing Rock State, 220
Parshall, 8
Paul Wilhelm, Prince, 42
Peaceful Valley Ranch, 179-80, 312
Pederson, Simon, 224
Pembina, 40-41, 67, 96, 183-5, 237-8
    Airport, 185
    County Fair, 77
Pembina, Fort, 45

Pembina Escarpment, 6
Pembina Mountains, 6, 235
Pembina River, 236
Pembina State Park, 185
Petersburg, 240
Petrified Forest, 179, 180
Pierce, Bob, 218
Pierce, Gilbert, 54
Pingree (Hazel Senter Pingree), 201
Pioneer Park, 211
Pioneer Scout, 109
Plaindealer, 152
Plant life, 14–16
Playgrounds, *see* Fort Abraham Lincoln
    State Park; Parks; Theodore
    Roosevelt National Memorial Park
Pleasant Lake, 242–3
Pleistocene era, 18
Plummer, Col. W. C., 190
Point Pleasant, 123
Political parties, 53–63
Pope, Camp, 292
Population, 61; foreign-born, 84–93
Portal, 264
Portland, 197
Potatoes, 72
Poultry-raising, 74
Powers, John J., 161–2
Prairie-Dog Towns, 179
Presbyterian Church, 100
Press, 109–10
Press, Dickinson, 281
Price (William Price), 318
Prohibition, 61
Public libraries, 100, 132, 165
Public Welfare Board, 103
Pursian Lake, 274

Rabbit's Ears, 217
Racial groups, 84–93
Radio, 110–11, 145, 154, 164, 268, 271,
    275, 277
Rae, John A., 281
Railroads, 47–8
Rain-in-the-Face, 171, 299
Rainy Buttes, 221
Raleigh, 224
Ramstad, Erik, 161
Randall, Frank, 291
Ransom, Fort, 289
Ray (Al G. Ray), 247
Raye, Charles le, 42
Record, Emmons County, 50–51
Record, Granville, 244–5
Recreation, 116–18
Red River, 44, 105, 140, 150–51
Red River Oxcart Trail, 187
Red River Valley, 6, 11–12, 68–70, 183
Red Willow Lake, 295

Redwing Creek, 313
Reeder (E. O. Reeder), 308
Reeves, Bud, 188, 196–7
Regent, 222
Religion, 100–101
Reno, Maj., 172
Reservations, Indian, 48–9, 206–9, 306
Resources, natural, 12–14
Reynolds, Charlie, 255
Reynolds (Dr. Henry Reynolds), 188
Rhame (M. D. Rhame), 308–9
Rice, Fort, 44–5
Richardton (C. B. Richardton), 280
Richland County Courthouse, 194
River Road, 210–12
Roads, *see* Highways
Robert Campbell, 248
Robertson, Dr. E. P., 290
Robinson, James E., 59
Rock Haven, 318
Rock Lake, 199
Rockefeller, William Avery, 186–7
Rodeos, 118
Rolette, Joseph, 43, 68, 100
Rolf, Gange, 147
Rolla, 228
Rolla University, 228
Roosevelt, Theodore, 3, 281, 282–3,
    284–5, 309–10, 312, 314
Roosevelt Bridge, Watford City, 215–16
Roosevelt Cabin, 130–31
Roosevelt Park, Minot, 165
Rosehill Cemetery, Minot, 165
Ross, 246–7
Rosser, Gen. Thomas L., 138
Rugby, 243
Rural Electrical Administration, 75
Russell, Charles Edward, 58
Russian Orthodox Greek Catholic
    Church, 204
Russo-German population, 87–9
Rustad, Hjalmer, Museum, 191
Rustler-Tribune, Minot, 162

Sackville-West, Hon., 52
St. Anthony, 297
St. Claude State Park, 228
St. John, 228
St. Joseph's Mission, Walhalla, 236
St. Mary's Cathedral, 148
St. Mary's Cemetery, Bismarck, 133
St. Michael's Mission, 257
St. Thomas, 186
SS. Peter and Paul Greek Catholic
    Church, Wilton, 204
Sakakawea, 42, 129–30, 204, 317
Salt Lake, 272
Sanborn (J. N. Sanborn), 269

Sanborn, Cooperstown & Turtle Mountain R. R., 293
Sand Slides, 236
Sanish, 247
Sarles, E. Y., 57
Sawyer, 262
Scart, John, 41
Scattered Village, site of, 302
Schafer (Charles Schafer), 215
Schmidt, 277
School lands, 98
Schools, 96–100, 113, 147–8, 154, 194, 197, 226, 277
Scoria Lily Ranch, 307
Scott, Gen. Hugh E., 257
Scott, Milo, 52
Scranton, 308
Seed production, 81
Seeman, L. D., 205
Selkirk, Earl of, 42–3, 96, 183–4
Selkirk, 44, 189
Sentinel Butte, 287
Sermon in Stone, 195
Seton, Ernest Thompson, 285
Seven Mile Hill, 248
Seward, William H., Fort, 45, 271
Shafer, George, 61
Sheardown, Camp (Historic Site), 267
Sheep Creek, 312
Shell Butte, 180
Shell Creek, 209
Sheridan, Gen. Philip H., 250
Sheyenne, 200
Sheyenne, 140
Sheyenne River, 7, 200, 295; Park, 191–2, 200
Shortridge, Eli C. D., 56, 131
Sibley, Gen. Henry H., 33–4, 45–6, 191, 193, 201–2, 261, 275, 289–90
Sibley expedition, 292–3
Sibley Island Park, 275
Sibley Lake, 294
Signal Rock, 305
Silver Fox Farm, Grand Forks, 187
Simpson, William, 247
Sinclair, James H., 293
Sioux County Fairgrounds, 298
Sioux Indians, 21, 25–7, 30, 33–4, 37, 45–6, 48, 212, 248, 253, 260, 286–7, 298, 309
Sitting Bull, Chief, 45, 49, 257, 258, 278
grave, 298–9
Slade, G. L., 273
Slant Village, 169–70
Slaughter, Linda, 44–5, 123
Smith, John, 100
Snake Creek, 316
Snyder Lake, 199

Social conditions, 101–3
Sodium sulphate, 83, 219
Soldier's Monument, Grand Forks, 154
Solen, 297
Sommers, Jim, 50
Son-of-the-Star, 207
Sorlie, Arthur G., 61, 87, 189
Sorlie Memorial Bridge, Grand Forks, 154
Souris River, 160–61, 163, 243; Valley, 7, 12
South Branch Park River Project, 186
South Heart, 281
Spalding, Burleigh, 52
Spencer, David, 100
Sperati Point (Dr. Carlo A. Sperati), 178, 313
Spicer, Mr. and Mrs. Thomas, 301
Spiritwood, 269; Lake, 269
Sports, spectator, 118; winter, 117
Square Butte Creek, 301
Square Buttes, 211
Squaw Creek, 313–14; Picnic Area, 178
Stair, Edward D., 293
Standing Rock, 34, 35–7, 299–300; Reservation, 306
Stanley, 246
Stanton, 41, 302, 317
State Agricultural College, Fargo, 227
State Durum Wheat Show, 78
State highways, *see* Highways
State Historical Society Museum, Bismarck, 198
State Mine, 307
State Normal and Industrial School, Ellendale, 202
State Penitentiary, 275
State Regulatory Department Laboratory, 132–3
State School for Blind, Bathgate, 226
State School for Deaf, Devils Lake, 241
State School of Forestry, Bottineau, 231
State School of Science, 98, 194
State Training School, 102, 277
Stavens, Thorval, Museum, 197
Steele (Col. W. P. Steele), 273–4
Stefansson, Vilhjalmur, 157, 227
Stephenson, Stephen G., 227
Stevens, J. J., 261
Stevens Survey, 47, 292
Stevenson, Fort (Brig. Gen. Thomas G. Stevenson), 45
site of, 316
Stickney (Ojata), 239
Stokes, Olive M., 285
Stony Point, 190
Strasburg, 205–6
Streeter, James, 240
Strommen, John, 162

Strong Memorial Park, 290
Stroud, Joseph, 250
Stump Lake, 7, 295
Sublette, William, 259
Sugar beets, 72–3
Sullers, Col., 218
Sully, Gen. Alfred H., 33–4, 44, 46, 175, 201–2, 256, 278, 280, 286–7, 304
Sully's Hill National Game Preserve, 256
Sun, Bismarck, 124
Sun Haven, 229
Superstitions, 95
Surrey, 245
Swift Runner, 203
Sykes, Richard, 201, 261
Sykeston, 261

Tabashaw, 191
Tagus (Taguson), 246
Tanner, James, 100
Tappen, 272
Tawiyaka, 220
Taylor, Joseph Henry, 203–4, 212
Taylor, 280
Telegraph lines, 106
Teller, Henry M., 52
Tepee Buttes, 222
Territorial government, 50–53
Terry, Gen. A. H., 255
Terry, Elijah, 100
Teton Sioux, 34
Thaw, William K., 289
Thayer, James Bradley, 54
Theodore Roosevelt National Memorial Park, 116, 174–80, 216, 282
  general information, 174–5
  history, 175–7
  North Tour, 178–9
  South Tour, 179–80
Thirty Mile Creek, 223
Thompson, David, 40; Memorial, 262
Thompson, Dawson, 272
Thompson, M. B., 52
Thompson, 188
Thunderbirds, 31–2
Tobacco Garden Creek, 247–8
Tofthagen, A. M., 241
Tokio, 254
Totten, Fort (Gen. Gilbert Totten), 34, 37, 45, 241, 255
Tours, 183–318
  1, Pembina—Wahpeton (*US 81*), 183–98
  1A, Mayville—Hatton (*ND 7 and 18*), 196–8
  2, Hansboro—Ellendale (*US 281*), 198–202

Tours (Cont.)
  3, Westhope—Linton (*US 83*), 202–6
  3A, Garrison—Stanley (*ND 37 and 8*), 206–9
  3B, 'River Road,' 210–12
  4, Ambrose—Bowman (*US 85*), 213–18
  4A, Hanks—Writing Rock (*ND 50*), 218–20
  4B, New England—Flasher (*ND 21*), 221–5
  5, Cavalier—Crosby (*ND 5*), 225–34
  5A, Walhalla—Leroy (*ND 32 and 35*), 235–8
  6, Grand Forks—Williston (*US 2*), 238–52
  6A, Devils Lake—Devils Lake (*ND 20 and 57*), 252–7
  6B, Buford—Fort Buford State Park, 257–60
  7, Carrington—Portal (*US 52*), 260–64
  8, Fargo—Dickinson (*US 10*), 265–87
  8A, Valley City—Oakes (*ND 1*), 288–91
  8B, *US 10—US 2* (*ND 1* and *7*), 292–5
  8C, Mandan—Fort Yates (*ND 6, 21, 24*), 296–301
  8D, Center—Killdeer (*ND 25*), 301–5
  9, Hettinger—Marmarth (*US 12*), 305–10
  10, Medora—Bismarck (Water Route), 310–18
Tower City (Charlemagne Tower), 267
Towle, George W., 186–7
Towner (Col. O. M. Towner), 243–4
Townley, A. C., 58
Traill Center, 196
Transportation, 104–8
Tree claims, 67
Trees, 14–15
Triangle Apartments, Grand Forks, 154
Tribune, Bismarck, 109–10, 124, 125
Truax-Traer Company, Minot, 164
Truax-Traer Lignite Strip Mine, 233
Tunbridge, 243
Turner, Father, 50
Turtle effigies, 19
Turtle Mountain Reservation, 34, 35–7
Turtle Mountains, 116, 228
Turtle River, 239; State Park, 239

Underwood, 203
Union, Fort, 258
Unions, 84
United Farmers and Workers League, 209

US Highways, *see* Highways
U.S. Indian School, 194
United States Post Office and Court-
    house, Fargo, 146
United States Weather Bureau, 123, 132
University of North Dakota, 97, 155–9;
    museum, 157
University Park, Grand Forks, 155
Upham, 232
Upper Des Lacs Lake, 264
Upper Souris Migratory Waterfowl
    Project, 263

Valley City, 267–9, 288
Van Hook, 209
Vanderburgh, Fort, 316
Velva, 262
Verendrye, Pierre de la, 39–40, 104, 112,
    262
Verendrye, 262
Verendrye National Monument, 247
Verona, 291
Veterans' Hospital, Fargo, 145
Viets, Frank, 152
Villard, Henry, 52, 126
Voltaire, 262
Von Hoffman, Medora, 283

Wahpeton, 193–5
Wainwright, Rev. Robert, 101
Wakantanka, 32
Walhalla, 236; State Park, 236
Wallin, Alfred, 54
Walsh, George, 152
Walsh County Agricultural and
    Training School, 186
Walstrom, Alex, 152
Walters, Emil, 227
Walum, 292
Wamduska Hotel, 295
Ward County Courthouse, Minot, 164–5
Washburn (Gen. W. D. Washburn),
    203–4, 318
Wasiya, 32
Water conservation, 12–13, 64–5
Water Route, 310–18
Watford City, 215
WDAY, 111, 145
Weiser, Dr. J. S., 272, 289
Weiser, Camp (Historic Site), 289
Welford, Walter, 62

Wells Fargo Express Company, 110
Wesley College, 97, 159
West, Rev. and Mrs. A. M., 197
Westhope, 203
Wheat, 69, 71–2
Wheatland, 267
Wheelock (Ralph W. Wheelock), 248
Whetstone Buttes, 308
Whiskey Point, 123
White, Maj. Frank, 56–7
White Earth, 247
White River formation, 11
White Shield, 207
Whitestone Hill, battle of, 46
Whitestone Hill Battlefield State Park,
    201–2
Wilbur, Curtis D., 270
Wild life, 16–17
Wild Rice, 191; River, 191
Wildwood Lake, 210
Wilkins, Sir Hubert, 198
Will, Oscar H., Co., 126–7
William, Fort, 259
Williston (S. Willis James), 249
Williston Basin, 84
Wilton, 204
Wind Canyon, 179
Winship, George, 150–51, 152
Winter rye, 72
Winter sports, 117
Wisconsin glacier, 11–12
Wishek (J. H. Wishek), 273
Wood, Fred, 58
Wood Lake, 254
Woodland Park, Hillsboro, 190
World War Memorial Building,
    Bismarck, 132
Worthington (Valley City), 267
Writing Rock State Park, 220
Writing rocks, 19
Wrong Side Up Mountain, 278–9
Wyoming Territory, 39

Yankton, 50, 52
Yates, Fort (Capt. George Yates), 45,
    299–301
Yellowstone, 27, 43, 105, 249
Yellowstone River, 214
Yerxa Hose Team, 135
York, 242
Young Men's Butte, 279–80